D1365249

JOHN CHRISTIAN BACH

JOHN CHRISTIAN BACH

JOHN CHRISTIAN BACH

by

CHARLES SANFORD
TERRY

Second Edition
with a Foreword
by
H. C. Robbins Landon

LONDON
OXFORD UNIVERSITY PRESS
NEW YORK TORONTO
1967

Oxford University Press, Ely House, London W.1

GLASGOW NEW YORK TORONTO MELBOURNE WELLINGTON
CAPE TOWN SALISBURY IBADAN NAIROBI LUSAKA ADDIS ABABA
BOMBAY CALCUTTA MADRAS KARACHI LAHORE DACCA
KUALA LUMPUR HONG KONG

First published 1929
Second edition 1967

new material
© Oxford University Press 1967

Printed in Great Britain

PREFACE

OF all Bach's sons, his youngest, the Benjamin of his old age, lived the most adventurous, in some respects the most successful, career. His activities were cosmopolitan: he frequented the Court of Frederick the Great, briefly occupied the Cathedral organ-loft at Milan, won his spurs on the stages of Italy, the Mother of Opera, filled the position at the English Court recently held by Handel, and, shortly before his death, exhibited his genius in the capital of France. The careers of his brothers, by comparison, were commonplace, his father's reputation provincial. A prolific composer, his music was as familiar to Vienna, Stockholm, Naples, as to London, Amsterdam, and Berlin. Yet, the first 'Life' of him appears almost two centuries after his birth! He lived nearly half his years in England, but no English pen has been drawn to delineate him. His own countrymen at the outset were estranged from him: for he followed Handel out of Germany, but lacked Handel's genius to condone his desertion. Hence, while the personality of his brothers has invited investigation and applause, John Christian has slumbered in a neglected grave.

A glance at Gainsborough's portrait suffices to indicate that Bach moved with easy grace in a society to which his profession was ordinarily admitted on another footing. The elegant distinction of his dress, his confident pose, betoken a man accustomed to the drawing-rooms of the 'Nobility and Gentry', the patrons of his enterprises. None of his brothers approached him in this: Carl Philipp Emanuel was the servant of a commercial republic; Johann Christoph Friedrich submitted to the humdrum ritual of a petty German Court; Wilhelm Friedemann drifted haphazard on a rudderless course. So, the earliest recorded impressions of Bach picture a dilettante rather than an artist, a man of the world rather than a musician, acquisitive of money, a renegade from the long tradition of artistic concentration inherited from generations of professional ancestors. 'Ein Mann von Weltkenntniss' is Forkel's summary of him in his *Musicalischer Almanach für Deutschland* (1782), a deserter from the standards of his father and brothers, one who had sold himself for the flesh-pots of England. Forkel added an innuendo which furnished others with material for more definite accusation; in an article, otherwise almost devoid of biographic detail, he hinted at feminine attachments as the magnet that drew Bach into Italy on the threshold of

his adult career. Cramer gave Forkel's summary wider currency
in his *Magazin der Musik* (1783). So, at the outset of its voyage to
posterity, Bach's reputation started under the implication of
gallantry, worldliness, and the sordid prostitution of high talents,
of a great name.

In Gerber's *Lexicon der Tonkünstler* (1790), a concise, but kindly,
notice complimented the qualities in Bach's music which won it
popularity 'in den Conzerten jeder Nation', and afforded a more
complete catalogue of it than so far was available. But Reichardt,
who called Bach 'ein sehr leichtgesinnter jovialischer Mensch' in
his *Musikalischer Almanach* (1796), set in circulation another
canard to establish the portrait. Like Burney, he had toured the
Continent in search of material for musical criticism, and from some
informant received the story that Bach was once reproved for his
'Sorglosigkeit als Künstler und Mensch' by a friend, who contrasted the rectitude and artistic conscience of his Hamburg brother.
Bach declared the criticism just; 'My brother lives to write music',
he admitted, 'I write for a livelihood' ('Ey was, mein Bruder lebt
um zu komponiren, und ich komponire um zu leben.') Rochlitz,
early in the nineteenth century, added another stroke of colour to
the canvas. In his *Allgemeine musicalische Zeitung* he declared
that Bach frequently received his brother's admonition to follow
worthier ideals; 'Put off childish things' ('Werde kein Kind'), was
his constant burden, which received the invariable reply, 'I write
for children and must speak in syllables' ('Ich muss stammeln,
damit mich die Kinder verstehen'). Perhaps the story reached
Rochlitz through Schubart, who recorded it in his *Ideen zu einer
Ästhetik der Tonkunst*, published posthumously in 1806. Both
likened Bach to the Proteus of fable, now babbling like water, now
glowing like fire, a man on whom some of the giant spirit of his
father had descended, fluent, brilliant, even profound at will, but
content to sink his genius to the standards of the public whose
'Liebling' he was.

Carl Hermann Bitter gathered up these scanty fragments in a
brief chapter in his *Carl Philipp Emanuel und Wilhelm Friedemann
Bach und deren Brüder* (1868), a memoir of little value; its information is not materially in advance of Gerber, while its appreciation
is expressed in a lengthy quotation from Rochlitz, with Bitter's own
conclusion—that Bach's name alone availed to rescue his personality
from oblivion ('Nur dass er der Sohn des grossen Sebastian war,
rettet den Namen des einst Vielbewunderten vor Vergessenheit').
Seven years later (1875), Carl Ferdinand Pohl contributed the
article 'Johann Christian Bach' to the *Allgemeine deutsche Bio-*

graphie, chiefly noteworthy for its inclusion of a few details of Bach's London career, unearthed by the author in the course of his investigation of Mozart's visit (1764). Thus, at the beginning of the present century little more of Bach's life had been unravelled than the bare facts of his Berlin apprenticeship, his migration to Italy, and meagre details of his twenty years' residence in England. This moderate store of material was somewhat enlarged in 1901 by Max Schwarz, in a contribution to the *Sammelbände der Internationalen Musik-Gesellschaft*, chiefly valuable for its revelation of Bach's association with Martini, and for a table of his compositions more adequate than the brief catalogues of Cramer and Forkel.

I have exposed the foundations, fragmentary and indistinct, of the biographic fabric constructed in these pages. For, though Schwarz's article roused dormant interest in a neglected son of the great Sebastian, it manifested itself, in the past quarter-century, in studies of his accessible compositions, not in investigation of his career. Landshoff, Schökel, and Tutenberg have made important contributions towards a juster appreciation of Bach's genius, while Abert and Wyzewa and Saint-Foix have disclosed the youthful Mozart's obligation to him. But the obscurity which veiled the circumstances of his life has not been penetrated, nor have the aspersions upon his character been probed. The neglected task is the major purpose of this book, and its materials are set out on pages xiii–xvi. I need only remark, that while they leave Bach's career in Leipzig and Berlin still in shadow, the Martini letters, all but one of which are now published for the first time, and the discovery of some of Bach's larger works of that period in the Royal Collection in the British Museum, have contributed to furnish a clear picture of his Italian sojourn; while his English career, which coincided with the quarter-century that followed Handel's death in 1759, unfolds itself with a fullness I hardly anticipated till I assembled the contents of my note-books.

I express my particular thanks to Professor Francesco Vatielli, Bologna, for a transcript of the Martini letters, and for other assistance in exploring Bach's unlighted Italian paths. Also to Miss L. M. Middleton, who has aided me conspicuously in regard to his London haunts. I am indebted to the librarians of the many institutions whose contents have been explored to construct the Thematic Catalogue which forms the second part of this volume. But I especially acknowledge the help of Dr. Charles van den Borren, Brussels; Dr. Johannes Wolf and Fräulein Ellinor Dohrn, Berlin; Dr. Gustav Binz, Basel; Dr. Arno Reichert, Dresden; Dr. L. Voltz, Darmstadt; Fr. Canisius Zuend and Dr. Ignatius

Staub, Einsiedeln; Signore Fausto Torrefranca, Milan; Professor Guido Gasperini, Naples; Mr. C. F. Hennerberg, Stockholm; Dr. Robert Haas, Dr. Eusebius Mandyczewski, and Dr. Leopold Nowak, Vienna.

I am indebted to Lord Hillingdon and the authorities of the Liceo Musicale, Bologna, for permission to publish the Gainsborough portraits of Bach in their possession. To the latter institution also I owe the striking portrait of Padre Martini, which hangs there. Some years ago the late Mr. Barclay Squire drew my attention to a portrait of 'Johann Sebastian Bach' exhibited at the Crystal Palace. A letter to *The Times* put me in touch with its owner, Mr. George v. Pirch, who kindly gave me facilities to satisfy myself that the portrait is actually of John Christian, by an unknown artist. It came into Mr. Pirch's possession from his uncle, the late C. B. Birch, A.R.A. Of the medallion composition by Bartolozzi after Cipriani there exists a German version ('Leipzig bei Breitkopf & Härtel. F. Bartolozzi fec. F. S. Schröter fecit 1789'), identical with the Bartolozzi-Cipriani engraving, except that the medallion and surrounding design are inverted. The Mathieu portrait at Berlin is marked 'Matthieu pinxt. 1774,' an impossible date. The note, Dr. Johannes Wolf informs me, is not contemporary. The portrait must have been painted shortly before Bach left Berlin for Italy. For photographs of old Carlisle House, Soho, I am indebted to Messrs. Keeble, Limited, its present owners.

C. S. T.

King's College,
   Old Aberdeen,
      August 1929.

CONTENTS

Preface . . . v

List of Illustrations . . x

Authorities and Abbreviations . xiii

Foreword to the Second Edition
   by H. C. Robbins Landon . xvii

Corrigenda . . . xxiv

   I. Leipzig and Berlin . . 1

   II. Milan . . . 14

   III. The King's Theatre . . 59

   IV. Soho and Haymarket . . 88

   V. Mannheim and Paris . . 125

   VI. The Last Years . . 138

   VII. Bach's Instrumental Compositions . 170

Thematic Catalogue of Bach's Works,
   vocal and instrumental . . 193

Index . . . 363

ILLUSTRATIONS

John Christian Bach . . . . . . *Frontispiece*
(From the portrait by Gainsborough in the Liceo Musicale, Bologna.)

Preceding the Thematic Catalogue

1. Carl Philipp Emanuel Bach
(From the silhouette in possession of Messrs Breitkopf and Härtel, Leipzig.)

2. The Opera House, Berlin, 1750

3. John Christian Bach *circa* 1754
(From the portrait by Georg Mathieu, in the Preussische Staatsbibliothek, Berlin.)

4. Giovanni Battista Martini
(From the portrait in the Liceo Musicale, Bologna.)

5. Chiesa di San Francesco, Bologna, 1760
(From an engraving.)

6. John Christian Bach
(From the portrait, by an unknown artist, in possession of George v. Pirch, Esq.)

7. Chiesa di San Fedele, Milan
(From an engraving.)

8. Bach's musical autograph, 1758
(From the *Magnificat* in C. By permission of H.M. The King. Copyright reserved.)

9. The King's Theatre, Haymarket, 1783
(From the print by William Capon.)

10. The King's Theatre, Haymarket, interior, 1783
(From a woodcut in *The European Magazine*.)

11. The King's Theatre, Haymarket, interior
(From prints in possession of the Royal College of Music.)

12. Carl Friedrich Abel
(From the portrait by Gainsborough.)

13. Soho Square and its environs, 1763
(From Roque's map.)

14. Soho or King's Square, looking north
(From the Grace Collection, British Museum.)

15. Soho or King's Square, looking south
(From the Grace Collection, British Museum.)

16. The new Carlisle House, 1764
    (From the Grace Collection, British Museum.)

17. Teresa Cornelys
    (From the Fillingham Collection, British Museum.)

18. Old Carlisle House, Main Staircase

19. Old Carlisle House, the Conversazione Room

20. Domenico Angelo
    (From the Print Room, British Museum.)

21. Mrs. Angelo, by Sir Joshua Reynolds
    (From the Print Room, British Museum.)

22. Old Vauxhall Gardens
    (From a woodcut in the Royal College of Music.)

23. Mrs. Weichsell singing at Vauxhall, by Rowlandson
    (From the Grace Collection, British Museum.)

24. Almack's, 1767
    (From the Grace Collection, British Museum.)

25. Ferdinando Tenducci
    (From his *Instruction of Mr. Tenducci to his Scholars*.)

26. Hanover Square Rooms, by T. A. Shepherd
    (From the Grace Collection, British Museum.)

27. Hanover Square Rooms, 1843
    (From Charles Knight's *London*.)

28a. A Bach-Abel Concert Ticket, engraved by Bartolozzi after Cipriani
     (British Museum, Portfolio VI., Wrapper 15.)

28b. Title-page of Bach's Op. 5
     (Engraved by Bartolozzi after Cipriani.)

29. M. Vestris junior, in *Les Amants surpris*, 1781
    (From the Gabrielle Enthoven Collection, Victoria and Albert Museum.)

30. Signora Bacelli, in *Les Amants surpris*, 1781
    (From the Gabrielle Enthoven Collection, Victoria and Albert Museum.)

31. John Christian Bach, by Gainsborough
    (From the portrait in possession of Lord Hillingdon.)

32. John Christian Bach, medallion, engraved by Bartolozzi after Carlini
    (From the Print Room, British Museum.)

AUTHORITIES AND ABBREVIATIONS

A B C D ='ABCDario Musico.' Bath: 1780.

Abert='Joh. Christian Bachs italienische Opern und ihr Einfluss auf Mozart.' By Hermann Abert, in 'Zeit. für Musikwissenschaft,' Jhrg. 1, Heft 6, 1919.

A.D.B.='Allgemeine deutsche Biographie.' 1875–1912.

Adler='Handbuch der Musikgeschichte unter Mitwirkung von Fachgenossen.' Ed. Guido Adler. Frankfurt am Main: 1924.

Angelo='Reminiscences of Henry Angelo, with memoirs of his late father and friends.' 2 vols. London: 1828–30.

Armstrong='Gainsborough and his place in English art.' By Sir Walter Armstrong. London: 1904.

Bach (E)='Karl Philipp Emanuel Bach. Versuch über die wahre Art das Klavier zu spielen.' New edn. Ed. Walter Niemann. Leipzig: 1925.

Bach (J.)=Méthode où Recueil de connoissances élémentaires pour le Forte-Piano où Clavecin. Œuvre mêlé de Théorie et de Pratique. Divisé en deux Parties. Composé pour le Conservatoire de Naple.' By Joh. Christian Bach and F. P. Ricci. Paris: n.d.

B.-J.='Bach-Jahrbuch: Herausgegeben von der Neuen Bachgesellschaft.' Leipzig: 1904—.

Baretti='An account of the manners and customs of Italy.' By Joseph Baretti. 2 vols. London: 1769.

Bitter='Carl Philipp Emanuel und Wilhelm Friedemann Bach und deren Brüder.' By Carl Hermann Bitter. 2 vols. Berlin: 1868.

Bott.=Opera programme-books. By G. G. Bottarelli and others. They contain the words of the operas, cast, &c., and, for convenience, their press-marks in the British Museum are stated.

Breggi='Serie degli spettacoli rappresentati al teatro regio di Torino dal 1688 al presente.' By Paolo Breggi. Turin: 1872.

Bur.='A general history of music, from the earliest ages to the present period.' By Charles Burney. 4 vols. London: 1776–89.

Burney='Dr. Charles Burney's Continental travels 1770–1772.' Ed. Cedric Howard Glover. London: 1927.

Burney (F.)='The early diary of Frances Burney 1768–1778.' Ed. Anne Raine Ellis. 2 vols. London: 1889.

Busby (1)='A general history of music from the earliest times to the present.' By Thomas Busby. 2 vols. London: 1819.

Busby (2)='Concert-room and Orchestra anecdotes.' By Thomas Busby. 3 vols. London: 1825.

Cardwell='Men and women of Soho.' By Rev. John Henry Cardwell and others. London: 1904.

Cocks='Notes, historical and miscellaneous, concerning the Queen's Concert Rooms, Hanover Square.' Robt. Cocks and Co. London: 1862.

Court='Court and City Register.' London: 1775.

Cramer='Magazin der Musik.' Ed. Carl Friedrich Cramer. Hamburg: 1783-86.

D.J.F.L.='Das jetzt lebende und jetzt florirende Leipzig.' Leipzig: 1736.

Dent='Foundations of English Opera.' By Edward J. Dent. Cambridge: 1928.

Dittersdorf='The autobiography of Karl von Dittersdorf.' Trans. by A. D. Coleridge. London: 1896.

Edwards = 'Musical haunts in London.' By F. G. Edwards. London: 1895.

Eitner = 'Biographisch-Bibliographisches Quellen-Lexikon der Musiker und Musikgelehrten.' Ed. Robert Eitner. 10 vols. 1898–1904.'

Florimo = 'La scuola musicale di Napoli.' By Francesco Florimo. 4 vols. Naples: 1880–81.

For. = 'Musikalischer Almanach für Deutschland auf das Jahr 1782.' Ed. Johann Nikolaus Forkel. Leipzig.

Forkel = 'Johann Sebastian Bach, his life, art, and work.' Tr. Charles Sanford Terry. London: 1920.

Galiani = 'Correspondance inédite de l'Abbé Ferdinando Galiani.' 2 vols. Paris: 1818.

Gent. Mag. = 'The Gentleman's Magazine.' London.

Gerber = 'Historisch-Biographisches Lexicon der Tonkünstler.' By Ernst Ludwig Gerber. 2 vols. Leipzig: 1790–92.

Grimm = 'Correspondance littéraire, philosophique et critique par le Baron de Grimm' (1760–82.) 17 vols. Paris: 1812–14.

Grove = 'Grove's Dictionary of music and musicians'. 3rd edn. Ed. Henry Cope Colles. London: 1927–28 (reprinted and revised 1928).

Haböck = 'Die Kastraten und ihre Gesangskunst.' By Franz Haböck. Berlin: 1927.

Harris = 'A series of letters of the first Earl of Malmesbury, his family and friends, from 1745 to 1820.' 2 vols. London: 1870.

Heinse = 'Hildegarde von Hohenthal.' By Wilhelm Heinse. 3 vols. Berlin: 1804.

Hilgenfeldt = 'Johann Sebastian Bach's Leben, Wirken und Werke.' By C. L. Hilgenfeldt. Leipzig: 1850.

Hohenzollern = 'Hohenzollern-Jahrbuch.' Ed. Paul Seidel. Jhrg. 1 (1897). Berlin.

Jahn = 'W. A. Mozart. Von Hermann Abert. Neubearbeitete und erweiterte Ausgabe von Otto Jahns Mozart.' 2 vols. Leipzig: 1923–24.

Jesse = 'Memoirs of the life and reign of King George the Third.' By John Heneage Jesse. 3 vols. London: 1867.

Junker = 'Zwanzig Componisten, eine Skizze.' By Carl Ludwig Junker. Bern: 1776.

Kingsford = 'The early history of Piccadilly, Leicester Square, Soho, and their neighbourhood.' By Charles Lethbridge Kingsford. Cambridge: 1925.

La Mara = 'Musikerbriefe aus fünf Jahrhunderten.' Ed. La Mara. 2 vols. Leipzig: 1886.

Mac Kinlay = 'Mrs. Cornely's entertainments at Carlisle House, Soho Square.' By (?) T. Mac Kinlay. London: 1840 (?).

Marpurg = 'Historisch-kritische Beyträge zur Aufnahme der Musik.' By Friedrich Wilhelm Marpurg. Vol. 1. Berlin:1754.

Martini = Letters to Padre Martini, from John Christian Bach and others, in the Liceo Musicale, Bologna.

Mount Edgcumbe = 'Musical reminiscences of an old amateur, chiefly respecting the Italian Opera in England' (1773–1823). By Richard Earl of Mount Edgcumbe. 2nd edn. London: 1827.

Musik. R.-Z. = 'Musikalische Real-Zeitung. Numero 8. Mittwoch, den 25. Hornung 1789.'

Northcott='Covent Garden and the Royal Opera.' By Richard Northcott. London: 1924.

Nugent='The history of Vandalia.' By Thomas Nugent. 3 vols. London: 1766–73.

Papendiek='Court and private life in the time of Queen Charlotte, being the journals of Mrs. Papendiek.' 2 vols. London: 1887.

Parke='Musical memoirs' (1784–1830). By William Thomas Parke. 2 vols. London: 1830.

Pohl='Mozart in London.' By Carl Ferdinand Pohl. Vienna: 1867.

Polko='Der englische Bach.' By Elise Polko, in 'Die deutsche Musikzeitung' (Bagge). Vol. 1. 1860.

Prod'homme='L'Opéra (1669–1925).' By J.-G. Prod'homme. Paris: 1925.

P.A.='The Public Advertiser.' London.

Reichardt='Musikalischer Almanach.' Ed. Johann Friedrich Reichardt. Berlin: 1796.

Riemann='Opern-Handbuch.' By Hugo Riemann. Leipzig: 1887.

Rimbault='Soho and its associations, historical, literary, and artistic.' By E. F. Rimbault, ed. George Clinch. London: 1895.

Rolland='Voyage musical au pays du passé.' By Romain Rolland. 4th edn. Paris: 1920.

Sacerdote='Il teatro regio di Torino.' By G. Sacerdote. Turin: 1892.

Sachs='Musik und Oper am kurbrandenburgischen Hof.' By Curt Sachs. Berlin: 1910.

Salvioli='Bibliografia universale del teatro drammatico italiano.' By Giovanni Salvioli. Venice: 1903.

Schiedermair='Die Briefe W. A. Mozarts.' Ed. Ludwig Schiedermair. 5 vols. Leipzig: 1914.

Schneider='Geschichte der Oper und des königlichen Opernhauses in Berlin.' By L. Schneider. Berlin: 1852.

Schökel='Johann Christian Bach und die Instrumentalmusik seiner Zeit.' By Heinrich Peter Schökel. Wolfenbüttel: 1926.

Schubart='Christ. Fried. Dan. Schubarts Ideen zu einer Ästhetik der Tonkunst.' Vienna: 1806.

Schwarz='Johann Christian Bach.' By Max Schwarz, in 'Sammelbände der internationalen Musikgesellschaft,' Jhrg. II, Heft 3. 1901.

Sharp='Letters from Italy in the years 1765 and 1766.' By Samuel Sharp. 2nd edn. London: 1767.

Spitta='Joh. Seb. Bach.' By Philipp Spitta. 2 vols. Leipzig: 1921.

St.-F.='A propos de Jean-Crétien Bach.' By Georges de Saint-Foix, in 'Revue de Musicologie'. 1926.

T. B.='Bach: a biography.' By Charles Sanford Terry. London: 1928.

Tutenberg='Die Sinfonik Johann Christian Bachs.' By Fritz Tutenberg. Wolfenbüttel: 1928.

U.='The Origin of the Family of Bach Musicians (Ursprung der Musicalisch-Bachischen Familie). Edited, with Pedigree Tables and a Facsimile of Bach's Manuscript, by Charles Sanford Terry.' London: 1929.

Vogler='Betrachtungen der Mannheimer Tonschule.' Ed. Georg Joseph Vogler. Speier: 1778–80.

Walpole='The letters of Horace Walpole, fourth Earl of Orford.' Ed. Mrs. Paget Toynbee. 19 vols. London: 1903–25.

Walter = 'Geschichte des Theaters und der Musik am kurpfälzischen Hofe.' By Friedrich Walter. Leipzig: 1898.

Wheatley = 'London past and present.' By Henry B. Wheatley and Peter Cunningham. 3 vols. London: 1891.

Wotquenne = 'Alphabetisches Verzeichnis der Stücke in Versen aus den dramatischen Werken von Zeno, Metastasio und Goldoni.' By Alfred Wotquenne. Leipzig: 1905.

Wyndham = 'The annals of Covent Garden Theatre from 1732 to 1897.' By H. Saxe Wyndham. 2 vols. London: 1906.

Wyzewa = 'W.-A. Mozart, sa vie musicale et son œuvre, de l'enfance à la pleine maturité (1756-1777).' By T. de Wyzewa and G. de Saint-Foix. 2 vols. Paris: 1912.

FOREWORD TO
THE SECOND EDITION

A generation has gone by since Terry published the first full-length and scholarly biography of Johann Christian Bach. During these years, our knowledge of and interest in the 'English' Bach's music has increased greatly. There has been a dissertation on the operas (Edward O. D. Downes, for Harvard University—to be published shortly by the Harvard University Press), and *Temistocle*, in a new edition (Universal Edition) by Dr. Downes and the present writer, is about to be launched in Germany. The late Dr. Fritz Stein, with whom this writer had a pleasant and instructive exchange of correspondence, published a number of instrumental works by J. C. Bach, including the now very popular Overture to *Lucio Silla* (Edition Peters) and the important volume of Bach's instrumental pieces in the *Erbe Deutscher Musik* (Breitkopf & Härtel). Dr. Alfred Einstein published several symphonies with Edition Eulenburg, and Eulenburg is gradually continuing the tradition. It is interesting that the gramophone, which has done so much to bring little-known music of the eighteenth century to a wider public, has also materially helped in the gradual recognition of Bach's manifold talents: recently a major composition, the *Dies Irae* for double choir and orchestra, has received its first publication, not on the printed page but on the long-playing record; and this work was soon followed by the gramophonic first publication of the *Confitebor* (1759), also a large (fifty-minute) work which was unknown except in Terry's thematic catalogue (p. 202, top entry). Similarly, many of the symphonies, *sinfonie concertanti*, concertos, and chamber music have reached the general public not so much by the printed score as by their 'publication' —for that is essentially what the process is—on gramophone records.

Thus it was obvious that a new edition of Terry's standard biography, which has been out of print for many years, was urgently required. It was at first planned to rewrite the section of Terry's book devoted to the music and to make a kind of symposium of that section; but after five years it became clear that our contributors, who shall out of kindness remain anonymous, were not going to deliver their promised manuscripts; and it was decided to proceed with a new edition of Terry unaltered except for this foreword and the *corrigenda* attached to it. The strong point of

Terry's book is, of course, the biographical section, with its hitherto unpublished letters of Bach's Italian period and its exhaustive
documentation of Italian opera in London in the 1760s and 1770s.
There is practically nothing about the music of the operas and
very little about the church music of the Milan period; but we
may expect Dr. Downes's new book to provide us with detailed
musical analyses of Bach's fascinating operas, as well as a revised
thematic catalogue of their contents, so that the lack of comment
about them in Terry is not so grave as it otherwise would be. For
those who would like to know more about Bach's symphonies
there is an excellent German book by Fritz Tutenberg, *Die
Sinfonik Johann Christian Bachs* (Wolfenbüttel, 1928) which in
many ways is more important than the slightly earlier book by
H. P. Schökel (see Terry's bibliography). We need a comprehensive
article on the early church music, but the sources are listed in
Terry's catalogue and we may hope that their partial resuscitation
on gramophone records will incite someone to do the necessary
research. Messrs. Schott and Co. are about to publish a critical
edition, by the Abbé Carl de Nys (who was responsible for the
Dies Irae recording), of the *Messa de' Morti* from which the *Dies
Irae* comes; and this publication will undoubtedly go a long way
to further our knowledge of Bach's church music.

Despite these gaps, then, Terry's biography is still essential and
remains the standard work on the subject. It is, of course, clear that
a pioneer effort such as Terry's was bound to go out of date more
quickly than, say, Abert's *Mozart* or, indeed, Terry on J. S. Bach.
We must consider that Terry, in preparing the J. C. Bach material,
was in most cases working from scratch; no one had investigated
the Padre Martini correspondence or the church music of that
period (Terry gives enough musical examples to whet the appetite);
no one had made a proper thematic catalogue except for the symphonies (and even in that sector, Terry found new sources); no
one had collated the material in British newspapers, diaries, and
so forth. Books of this kind, to quote a witty phrase of Professor
Otto Erich Deutsch, ought to appear only in the second edition;
unfortunately, this is not possible; and it is a compliment to Terry
that after nearly forty years, his work is still indispensable to the
scholar and highly interesting to the general reader.

In preparing the *corrigenda*, I have been greatly assisted by the
notes of my friend, Dr. Edward O. D. Downes of New York City,
with whom I have worked on Johann Christian Bach for several
years; Dr. Downes also kindly lent me his annotated copy of Terry;
without his aid and encouragement, I would not have attempted

to provide a list of *corrigenda* at all. Actually, many of the *corrigenda* will perhaps strike the reader as unimportant minutiae; and so they are; but since Terry's book is primarily a reference tool, it is important that such matters as catalogue numbers for sources are absolutely correct. Many of the Continental sources Terry lists were sent to him by libraries and he had no way to check their information at first hand. A valuable aid in preparing these *corrigenda* was also the review of Terry's book by Heinrich Miesner in the *Zeitschrift für Musikwissenschaft* xvi (1934), pp. 182–8, of which Dr. Downes owns a copy with further corrections by Dr. Miesner. Apparently Dr. Miesner was planning a German translation of Terry's book before the Second World War; we have not been able to ascertain Dr. Miesner's present whereabouts, or even whether he is still living.

As to the authenticity of the many instrumental compositions listed in the thematic catalogue, it is clear that some are doubtful. Terry simply lists the works at their face value. There is, for example, a series of symphonies attributed in a single set of manuscripts in the Gesellschaft der Musikfreunde, Vienna, to 'Giuseppe Bach' or 'Baach' or even 'Pach' (Terry, pp. 278ff., Nos. 9, 10, 14, 17): one of these, the F major No. 14, is probably by J. J. Lang. Terry's No. 2, as the *corrigenda* show, is a highly disputed work which is hardly by J. C. Bach. The 'English' Bach was sufficiently fashionable, and his family name so well known, that mis-attributions were bound to occur. I have tried to cast the shadow of doubt over those works which I have been able to examine personally and which seem to me, from the stylistic point of view, and because of the paucity of good sources, to be of doubtful authenticity.

A few words on the subject of Christian Bach's music may not be amiss here, especially since our awareness of its special qualities has, as we have suggested above, grown considerably in the past thirty years.

Terry, like most scholars and musicians a generation ago, approached the music of J. C. Bach with two rather natural prejudices: first, J. C. Bach obviously stood in the shadow of his father; and secondly, Christian's music was compared to Haydn's and Mozart's and found wanting. Thus the average music lover chalked up two bad marks against Christian before, as it were, he was given a chance. The basic prejudice against this music may be condensed to one word: *galant*. All the supposed faults of the *galant* style—and this could equally well apply to other arts as well as music—were found to be typical of J. C. Bach's music:

courtly, superficial, gay, facile, cold, etc. etc., *ad nauseam*. Even now, in fact, we have not recovered from the nineteenth-century swing of the pendulum away from rococo art—or at least we have not entirely recovered. It is hard for us to realize that the nineteenth century often lumped Mozart in this category, but a curious story that my beloved old teacher, Alfred J. Swan, related to me may perhaps put the matter in its proper perspective. Professor Swan recalls a concert at St. Petersburg where the 'Haffner' Symphony was 'revived' as a historical curiosity; he was sitting in a box behind a famous music critic, who listened, repelled and fascinated, to the Mozart symphony, shaking his head and murmuring, 'What incredibly *childish* music' over and over again. It was, quite literally, beyond his comprehension and appreciation. Nowadays the 'Haffner' Symphony is part of our musical life's blood, and such an attitude is as incomprehensible to us as was the symphony to the nineteenth-century Russian critic. I do not think, however, that the whole problem can be explained away by saying *tempora mutantur, nos et mutamur in illis*.

It is clear that works of art go out of fashion. The most famous case in point is J. S. Bach's music, which hardly existed at all—except in obscure manuscript copies—when his youngest son's music was in vogue. It is safe to predict that the *St Matthew Passion* will not easily again disappear from the consciousness of Western man. But the very fact that it could is a warning to all of us. A somewhat similar case is Haydn, whose music was very out of fashion a hundred years ago, though it never entirely disappeared from the general repertoire, as J. S. Bach's did. It seems to me that the disappearance and subsequent reappearance of Christian Bach's music does not mean much except as a footnote of historical interest—it certainly does not tell us whether his music is good, bad, or indifferent. No doubt part of the reason for his reappearance is due to our renewed interest in eighteenth-century music altogether. But it is something of a mystery that Antonio Vivaldi should be vastly more popular than J. C. Bach nowadays; it cannot be because Vivaldi is more profound, or even that people think he is more profound. I am convinced that a great deal of Vivaldi's present popularity is because you can listen through his music. You cannot really talk against the *St Matthew Passion* or Beethoven's Ninth unless you are completely unmusical, whereas Vivaldi's *The Seasons* seems to be the perfect background music to the cocktail party in Rome, Vienna, London, or New York. It is also no good saying that the people who use Vivaldi for such purposes are cultural idiots, because it is just those people who have made Vivaldi the popular composer he now is, not the musicians and not, perish the thought, the musicologists who rarely make any music popular even among themselves.

It would be nice to think that we could make J. C. Bach as popular as Vivaldi, because Bach's music is on the whole much superior; but I sense, in many people, that old prejudice against the rococo which allows them to enjoy immensely Vivaldi (which is 'baroque') but makes them suspicious of J. C. Bach. And here we have, I think, the crux of the situation.

Some scholars have recently put forward the 'true' Christian Bach as the composer of the Symphony in G minor (Terry, p. 265, No. 6), which is an interesting and rather angry *Sturm und Drang* work with distinct parallels in Haydn (Symphony No. 39), Johann Baptist Vanhal (Symphony in G minor, new edition by Doblinger Verlag), and even Mozart (the 'Little' G minor Symphony, K. 183). They quote the famous—and not wholly authenticated— remark of J. C. about his brother Carl Philipp Emanuel to the effect that C. P. E. 'lives to compose whereas I [J. C.] compose to live', whereupon J. C. played some stormy music with the remark, 'This is what I could do', or words to that effect. Like many such apocryphal stories, this one has the ring of half truth about it. The Symphony in G minor is *not*, when all is examined, character- istic of J. C.'s style; but on the other hand, he obviously thought it popular enough to publish it (or, if the Hummel edition is not authentic, then Hummel thought it was popular enough to pirate). *Sturm und Drang* composers such as Franz Beck did exist and published scores of most eccentric and fascinating symphonies. If J. C. Bach is, as many of his most recent admirers would seem to believe, a *Sturm und Drang* composer *manqué*, it is the greatest cover-up in music history. The early church music, too, is not really 'Storm and Stress' music even if it is in C minor, such as the *Dies Irae* which we have mentioned earlier. It is very unlikely that ninety-five per cent of J. C.'s music was composed in a style in which he did not believe; I am sure that these recent admirers are, in some oblique way, trying to apologize for Christian Bach's essentially *galant* style. In my opinion they make a grave error.

We do not need to apologize for the *galant*, or the rococo, or whatever word one uses to describe the essence of J. C. Bach's style. Why is it necessary for all music to drip with blood? (Romain Rolland in *Beethoven the Creator* talks about a high A, in the Sonata Op. 31, No. 2, as a 'distracted cry being repeated three times' and later, of a chord of F sharp minor in triplet arpeggio, 'A torrent of blood follows in their wake'.) There was a time when only Michelangelo would do in the visual arts, but nowadays many of us are equally, if not more, at home with Masaccio. Does everything have to be measured from the Beethovenian standpoint? Surely we stand to lose a great deal of delightful music, and music was usually, prior to Beethoven (but also including a great deal of Beethoven), meant to entertain and not necessarily to edify or uplift (in the Victorian moral sense). We must, if we are to enjoy Christian Bach's music, break away from the idea that to attend a concert is to purify the soul; it *may* do that but it *need* not. In Vienna, going to a Bruckner symphony is the equivalent for many people of going to St. Stephan's Cathedral to hear Mass. One does not wish to deny people this experience, but there are surely times in our lives when a good, rattling D major symphony by J. C. Bach can be a heart-warming experience. There is another point, too: Christian Bach's music is impeccably put together and orchestrated with the utmost taste and sense of colour. If Mozart could learn so much from his music—and Terry's biography furnishes clear documentary proof of the fact, as do Mozart's letters—there is no reason for us to be more snobbish than Mozart. (I can see, with a sinking heart, that this point will weigh more than actually hearing a J. C. Bach opera or symphony. . . .)

With the exception of the early church music, which is now emerging from its long sleep, most of our knowledge of Christian Bach's style is from his instrumental music. This does not give us a wrong picture but there is no doubt that it is an incomplete one; for his operas are filled with marvellous things. Nowadays it is unlikely that any *opera seria*, even Mozart's *La clemenza di Tito*, will ever again become part of the general operatic repertoire; and Christian wrote only serious operas. But if we examine these stage works, we can see at once some of the things that so attracted Mozart: J. C.'s speciality is the long, languid vocal line, often in a key with flats (E flat is a favourite), and with a wonderful sense of melodic warmth and breadth. Such a melody as that quoted on page 147 of Terry's book is typical: it sings itself, as do many of Mozart's arias. And as with Mozart, J. C. Bach appropriated this 'singing line' for his instrumental works: you will find it not only in the slow movements—there is a pretty Andante from a three-movement *sinfonia* quoted on page 53—but also in many of the second subjects of the quick movements, such as in the first movement of the E flat Symphony, Op. 9, No. 2 (Terry, p. 268, No. 2: miniature score, ed. Einstein, published by Eulenburg). In some respects, Bach's vocal style was more influential than his instrumental style: in it, he artfully combined, as Mozart was to do, Italian *bel canto* with the thorough contrapuntal and instrumental knowledge of his own country. J. C. Bach's operas are on the whole more profound, and certainly more beautifully orchestrated, than those of his Italian contemporaries before Paisiello and Cimarosa, most of whose best works were composed after Christian's death on New Year's Day, 1782.

It is generally the fashion to place Christian's music not only below that of his father, and Haydn, and Mozart—which is of course obvious—but also below that of his brothers, particularly Wilhelm Friedemann and C. P. E. While there is no doubt that they occasionally had bursts of fantasy, even genius, that reach higher than did J. C., on the whole it is Johann Christian who is the better balanced composer. Much of Friedemann's music has something four-square and wooden about it, and a great deal of C. P. E.'s is wildly experimental, almost to the extent of a Gesualdo; both men are to some extent ends of the road, or if you will, side roads, which do not lead anywhere. Christian is far more in the main stream, and his influence more direct on his followers. It has often been asserted, even by Haydn himself, that C. P. E. had a lasting influence on Haydn; but if we examine Haydn's early style, we will see little that can be traced to C. P. E., except in some of the piano sonatas. On the other hand, the influence of Christian on Mozart's early years (up to his return to Salzburg after the Paris journey) is obvious in dozens of smaller and larger works; J. C. Bach's is basically a much more fundamental influence on the Mozartian style than was that of the intellectual Haydn.

It is not Christian's historical importance that needs to be stressed at this late date; many Mozart scholars have shown us this aspect of the 'English' Bach. What we tend to forget is the quality of the music itself. It is as warm-hearted and affectionate as the man himself. So for days when we wish to come down from the Olympian heights, what better composer to choose than Johann Christian Bach? If Terry's book continues to whet the appetites of music students, scholars, and conductors—as it obviously has done for a good generation—for J. C. Bach's music, then that is the book's principal *raison d'être*.

Myrifield, Heath, Massachusetts.

September 1965.   H. C. R. L.

CORRIGENDA

p. x Illustration No. 6, the portrait of J. C. Bach (which is in my opinion very dubious), was sold at Sotheby's in July 1965.

p. xi Illustration No. 27, for 'T. A. Shepherd', read 'T. H.'

pp. xiii–xvi Bibliography. The following titles may prove useful to students seeking further information: Daffner, Hugo: *Die Entwicklung des Klavierkonzertes bis Mozart*, Publ. der I. M. G. (Leipzig, 1906). Brenet, Michel: *Les concerts en France sous l'ancien régime* (Paris, 1900). Brozzi, A. P.: *Il Regio Ducal Teatro di Milano nel Secolo XVII* (Milan (Ricordi), 1894). Brenet, Michel: 'Un fils du grand Bach à Paris 1778–1779' in *Guide Musical* (1902), pp. 551 ff. Bladon (editor): *The Diaries of Col. the Hon. Robert Fulke Greville* (London, 1930). Ellis, S. M.: *The Life of Michael Kelly, musician, actor and bon viveur* (London, 1930). Kretzschmar, 'Mozart in der Geschichte der Oper', *Peters-Jahrbuch 1905*, pp. 56 ff. L. Landshoff, 'Die weltliche Vokalmusik Johann Christian Bachs' in *Zeitschrift für Musikwissenschaft* iv (1921/2), pp. 121 ff. Mannlich, C. von: *Lebenserinnerungen* (Berlin (Mittler), 1913). Miesner, Heinrich: Review of Terry in *Zeitschrift für Musikwissenschaft* xvi (1934), pp. 182 ff. Wirth, Helmut: Article on J. C. B. in *Musik in Geschichte und Gegenwart*. The forthcoming book by Dr. Downes has been mentioned in the Foreword to the Second Edition. Some of the above additions to the bibliography were made by Terry himself (in a letter to Dr. Miesner quoted in the review listed above). Additional articles, mostly of a specialized nature, will be listed in the course of the *corrigenda*.

p. xiv Under 'For.' read 1783 for 1782.

p. 5 Three lines from top, for '1767' read '1768' (H. Miesner, 'Eine Anmerkung zu Ch. S. Terrys "John Christian Bach"' in *Zeitschrift für Musikwissenschaft* xiv (1931/2), 226f.).

p. 13 Miesner, in the same article, thinks that 1754 as the date of departure is probably right: C. P. E.'s records are unusually accurate and Marburg (see footnote 4) says of J. C. Bach, 'Ist vor kurzem nach Italien gereist'. In fact two female singers did leave Berlin for Italy in 1754 according to the *Rechnungen von Einnahmen und Ausgaben bei der Königlichen Kapelle von*

Trinitas 1753 bis Trinitas 1754 formerly in the Brandenburg–
Preussisches Hausarchiv in Charlottenburg and probably destroyed in the Second World War. The names are Anna Lorio
Campolungo who left on 1 April 1754 and one Delbine, who
left on 1 May at the same time as Carestini. Both names have
after them 'cessat, hat ihren Abschied erhalten'. So perhaps the
story (p. 11 *passim*), that 'er mit vielen italienischen Sängerinnen
bekannt wurde, deren eine ihn beredete mit ihr nach Italien zu
gehen', has some truth in it after all. Miesner later seemed to
think Campolungo (or Campo Lungo) was the girl in question
(see his article, 'Bach-Gräber im Ausland', *Bach-Jahrbuch 1936*,
pp. 109–14).

p. 14, n. 1   Miesner established that four Italian language
teachers lived near C. P. E. Bach's Berlin address.

p. 18   The Italian text of the letter of 21 May 1757 is in an article
by M. Schwarz (see Terry bibliography), p. 440.

p. 22   In Perti example, bar 2, last note of alto should read G,
not B.

p. 26   Italian original of the letter at bottom in Schwarz, *op. cit.*,
440f. Schwarz dates the letter December. Bach abbreviated
'10bre' for December and Terry no doubt misread the old
method for our modern, where '10' would mean October.
Similarly the date of the letter at the top of page 28 should read
'Leinate in Camp[agna] li 16 di 9bre 1757', *i.e.* November.
Leinate is an old-fashioned (and perhaps Bachian) spelling for
Lainate, seventeen kilometres north of Milan. These corrections
from Dr. Miesner's review.

p. 32   Concerning the letter of 8 October 1758, Dr. Downes
mentions that the *Aria cantabile* can only have been a concert
aria, since Brozzi (see *corrigenda* to bibliography) lists no opera
in the Royal Ducal Theatre between May and 26 December
of 1758.

p. 33   Dr. Downes doubts that the Aria 'Principe, non temer' (see
line one) can be as early as 1758 if it is by Bach. Concerning
the Aria, 'Misero pargoletto' mentioned in the letter of January
1759, Dr. Downes has established that it is from *Demofoonte*,
which was performed at the Royal Ducal Theatre at Milan on
26 December 1758, as the first opera of the carnival season. The
libretto in the Library of Congress lists Elisi for the rôle of
Timante, to whom Metastasio gives this aria.

p. 51 Cast of *Artaserse*. Read Pietro de Mezzo (not di Mezzo) and Antonio Goti (not Gotti).

p. 52 Cast of *Catone in Utica*, read Nicolò (not Nicola) Coppola. Bach's sojourn in Naples is documented in B. Croce, *Teatri di Napoli* (Naples, 1891), pp. 495 ff. Most of the material in question is cut in the editions of 1915 and 1926. Croce says that Bach arrived at Naples in September 1761; he gives no source for his statement but there is a letter from Count Karl Joseph Firmian (1718–82) to the Marchese Tanucci, the Neapolitan Minister in charge of the theatres, introducing Bach and dated 15 September 1761:

Eccellenza
Portandosi costà il signor Bach, celebre maestro di cappella a comporre per codesto Regio Teatro, ha desiderato di essere da raccomandato a V. E.; Essendo egli un uomo di molto merito, tanto più discendo a compiarcerlo, quanto che ho tante riprove dell'uminità di V. E. e posso con fondamento lusingarmi, che gli accorderà quella protezione che desidera, e per cui le ne porto le mie preghiere; si accresceranno con ciò ecc. ecc.
Milano 15 sett. 1761

Dev.^{mo} obblig.^{mo} serv. vero
Conte C. di Firmian.

I quote these and the following documents in the original, because the archives in Naples from which they were copied were destroyed in the Second World War and the original edition of Croce's book is very difficult to find. *Catone* was first performed early in November (in one place Croce says the 4th, but on p. 494 he says the first performance of the season was put forward a day). The opera was such a success that Tanucci could write to Firmian, 'L'applauso, che ha qui meritato la musica del Catone, fatto dal maestro di cappella Bach, che da V. E. con suo gentilissimo foglio mi viene raccomandato, fa sempre più ammirare il buon gusto e la giudiziosa maniera di pensare della E. V.^a . . .' (24 Nov. 1761); and Firmian answered (Mantua, 7 Dec. 1761) 'Mi piace sommamente d'intendere . . . che il maestro di cappella Bach, siasi attirato l'applauso di una città, che in matiera di musica prevale a tutte le altre . . .'.

Croce discovered in the archives an amusing incident concerning the young Bach and a *prima ballerina*, Colomba Beccari, whom Bach had possibly known from Turin (where she was permanently engaged), and with whom he had an affair in Naples ('ha dato motivo ai sfacendati di parlare del suo amore per la ballante Beccari' says the document). The *uditore* called Bach to him and gave him a lecture on the subject. But one evening in January, when the ballets were being given, Bach was seen 'assistere nel palchetto dei cantanti e ballerini dentro delle scene'; the *uditore* sent the theatre copyist behind stage 'che senza far rumore, l'avesse detto che quel sito non era per lui'. The next day Bach was not in his place behind the harpsichord, but had given his post to a substitute. They found him back with the singers and ballet girls. The *uditore* sent for him at once 'e buonamente gli disse che S. M. aveva reitertamente proibito a tutti, e finanche agli ufficili delle sue reali guardie, di entrare nelle scene e di trattare colle donne del teatro, in tempo che si rappresentava l'opera.' Bach was very annoyed but had to leave; he said, however, that in all other theatres the *maestri* could go behind the scenes. The *uditore*, who was 'assediato dall'impegno dei sui protettori', said he would try to get permission for another time, 'sul motivo di togliere un'idea di mormorazione nata per la probizione', but despite Bach's annoyance, the rule could not be altered and the flirtation with *la Beccari* had to take place elsewhere. Dr. Downes kindly gave me his notes from Croce for this amusing episode. On page 54, Terry says that Bach provided a new overture to *Catone* when it was repeated at Naples in 1764; but Dr. Downes has located the score for this 1764 performance and the overture is the same one as the 1761 version (see also *corrigenda* to *incipit* for *Catone*, p. 222, *infra*). It was repeated at Brunswick not only in 1766 but also in 1768 (Terry, p. 54, line two after first music example).

p. 59   Concerning Bach's departure for London, a new document was discovered by Claudio Sartori ('A Milano J. C. Bach in disaccordo con il tesoriere' in *La Scala*, 15 Nov. 1950, pp. 29–31). It reads: 'Giov. Bach, Organista della V.a Fabrica del Duomo, e servitore umil.mo delle Sig.rie Loro Ill.me e Rev.me; essendoglisi presentata l'occasione d'andare in Inghilterra per ivi conporre due Opera con stipendeo assai bono e di sommo suo vantaggio Umilmente ricorre supplicando le Sig.rie Loro Ill.me e Rev.me graziarlo della Licenza per un anno, principiando dal mese di Luglio venturo mentre il medesimo sostituisce Persona abile, già provata, benevisa al Coro, a giudicata capace del Sig.r M.o di Cappella di detta V.a Fabbrica del Duomo, che della Grazia V.

Giov. Bach.'

Sartori dates this document 17 maggio 1761, but since Bach was still in Milan in April 1762 (see letter quoted by Terry on p. 58), Dr. Downes thinks that '17 maggio 1762' is more likely.

pp. 59f. It has now been established, by Dr. Miesner, that the receipt is in C. P. E. Bach's hand, not in Christian's; thus the whole Strelitz episode has nothing to do with Christian at all. Ludwig Landshoff had an ingenious theory for Bach's invitation to England: Landshoff thinks it must have been the singer Filippo Elisi, for whom Bach had composed an aria in 1759 (see Terry, p. 33), who brought Bach's name to the attention of the London musical world. Elisi was in correspondence with Padre Martini (Bach's teacher) and wrote ('Londra, 14 maggio 1761') to him, they will not allow him (Elisi) to leave London and he must stay on another year.

p. 62 Line 5, 'But it can be', etc. must be changed in accordance with the information listed above for pp. 59f.

p. 66 Penultimate line. The text actually reads 'Pupille vezzose' but in the original printed libretto this aria is not marked by an asterisk, as are the other insertions by Bach.

p. 67 In fact, Bach did write an aria with the text 'Pupilla vezzosa' (Terry, p. 228) for the pasticcio *La calamità de' cuori*, and possibly the music for the other aria in *Astarto* is identical (there is no known copy of the aria in question from *Astarto*, but Dr. Downes owns a copy of the original libretto).

p. 69 2nd paragraph. 'Burney especially remarked his disuse of the *da capo* aria . . .'. There are, however, several *da capo* arias in *Orione* and Terry, thinks Dr. Downes, has simply misread Dr. Burney, who was referring in general to Bach's gradual abandonment of the *da capo* aria.

p. 83 First line, last paragraph. The subject of *Adriano in Siria* is not Hadrian's suppression of the Jewish revolt.

p. 103 2nd paragraph. Dittersdorf (*Lebensbeschreibung*, p. 108) heard the 17-year-old Cecilia Grassi in Gluck's *Trionfo di Clelia*: 'sie hatte eine reine und angenehme Stimme, aber war noch Anfängerin'. See also Corrado Ricci, *I Teatri di Bologna* xvii, xviii. (From Miesner's review.)

p. 106 Cast of *Carattaco*, under 'Brigantians' the second name on the left should read 'Pratusago' (Dr. Downes).

p. 113 Line 7, 'But Opus V, published in 1768 . . .'. In the catalogue, p. 338, ?1770. Dr. Miesner, using Wyzewa–St. Foix i,

160 as the authority, suggested 1765, because the young Mozart arranged three of the sonatas as clavier concertos; but Mozart can have used manuscript copies.

p. 116 2nd paragraph, line 11, 'his voice changed to a soprano...'. Dr. Miesner points out that this is not true. In 1761 he sang the low alto part of Bach's *Artaserse* (p. 51), in 1770 he sang Orfeo in Gluck's opera (p. 118) and Gioas, an alto part, in Bach's oratorio of that name (p. 120).

p. 123 *Endimione*. Dr. Miesner points out that there exists a textbook in the Mannheim theatrical archives wherein there is a MS. note saying that the opera had been performed in 1770 at the Castle Theatre in Oggersheim ('vorher Oggersheim 1770'). But Dr. Downes notes that the textbook in question has been greatly altered by MS. additions: pages torn out and replaced in MS., the Finale much shortened, and these changes do not correspond to Bach's score. Possibly another *Endimione* was given at Oggersheim in 1770.

p. 130 Line 3, 'For Dorothea Wendling...'. Bach's Cantata is not for solo voice (see next sentence). In note 3 there is an error: the Cantata Vogler describes is not 'Amor Vincitore': in the volume of musical examples, Vogler prints this other Cantata complete, a pastoral dialogue between Nice and her lover, beginning with the Recitative, 'No, non turbarti, O Nice'. There is a MS. copy of this Cantata in the Gesellschaft der Musikfreunde, Vienna. (Dr. Miesner.) There is an account of the first performance of 'Amor Vincitore', which was in honour of Gluck (who was present), in the *Lebenserinnerungen* of Christian von Mannlich (see bibliography, *supra*). (Terry's correction.)

p. 131 2nd paragraph, line 5, for 'June 1778' read 13 April 1778 (Terry's correction). 2nd paragraph, penultimate line, 'Baron Bach'. Dr. Miesner thinks Baron Kurt-Ernst Bagge is meant, for Mozart speaks of 'Capellmeister Bach' in his letter of 9 July 1778.

p. 133 2nd paragraph. For further information on *Amadis de Gaule*, see Brenet's article, 'Un fils du grand Bach à Paris 1778–1779' (additions to bibliography, *supra*). *Amadis de Gaule* was performed on 14, 17, 21 December 1779 and 14, 16, 23 January and 1 February 1780 (Miesner). In the orchestration there are four, not two horns.

p. 145 Line one, 'his opera *Tigrane*'. *Tigrane* was, however, a pasticcio containing only one aria by Sacchini (Terry, p. 110).

p. 147 Three lines above music example, for 'Pasini' read Rauzzini (correction by Terry).

p. 150 2nd paragraph, line one: Dr. Downes questions the date 29 December 1776. Should 1776 read 1775?

p. 155 2nd paragraph, line 6, for date of *Lucio Silla* read 1774.

p. 156 Line 8 from bottom, 'For he searches . . .'. Terry is quite wrong about this. There were often lengthy criticisms of opera and concerts (Dr. Downes).

p. 158 Note 2. Dr. Downes considers this unlikely. 'Dal dolor' is no bravura piece. Probably the aria in question was 'Confusa abbondonata', an allegro with much coloratura (printed score, p. 21).

p. 166 2nd paragraph, line five, for 'Miss Greenland, or Greenlands' read 'the Misses Greenland' (correction by Terry).

p. 168 Note 3, bottom line, fourth word should read *Cefalo* (correction by Terry).

p. 172 Opus 16 is dedicated to the Misses Greenland (*vide supra*).

p. 175 The third symphony quoted is a highly doubtful work—see *infra*, p. 276; and in any case the Basel MS. specifies *clarini* (trumpets) and not *clarinetti* (clarinets). Following the *incipit*, 'also in a set of Symphonies in MS. at Bückeburg . . .' refers to works which are, according to Tutenberg, not symphonies at all but cassations, typical open-air music, for wind band. As such they are listed in Terry's catalogue, p. 285, after the Longman and Broderip print.

p. 181 For the vexed question of the Symphony in D of which the *incipit* is given, and which Terry later ascribes to Galuppi (p. 274), see p. 274, *infra*. In the next paragraph, the last four lines, beginning with 'of the two *Catone* overtures' should be cancelled. It will be seen that the Overture to *Alessandro nell'Indie* (p. 277, No. 3) exists and was later used as the Overture to *Astarto* and, in one manuscript (Hausbibliothek, Berlin) as the 'Sinfonia nell'opera Catone' (of which the original Overture is p. 277, No. 6).

p. 198   under WOLF. The library is now in the Landeshauptarchiv. Under these abbreviations add 'WASH. Library of Congress, Washington', which contains important libretti and manuscript copies of J. C. Bach operas.

p. 211   There is an unpublished dissertation by Alexander Wenk, 'Beiträge zur Kenntnis des Opernschaffens von Johann Christian Bach', wherein a number of errors in Terry's catalogue is listed. Wenk seems not to have studied the non-German sources, however. The corrections to the operatic entries have been taken from the forthcoming book by Dr. Downes.

pp. 211 f.   *Adriano in Siria*
Overture: Terry p. 181 thinks No. 6 of the Walsh print of 'Six Favourite Overtures set for the Harpsichord or Organ' (p. 274) is the Overture to *Adriano*, but on p. 274 the author is, probably correctly, given as B. Galuppi. It is very unlikely that this *sinfonia* is by J. C. Bach. The only known source for the opera is the skeleton score. Text by Metastasio. The order in the print is not correct. The following table will show the chronological order as found in the original libretto:

Terry	'The Favourite Songs'	Number in opera itself
1		4
2		8
3		6
4		5
5		2
6		20
7		23
8		11
9		14
10		1
11		10
12		12

No. 6 (Terry) as 'Oh turn, behold my streaming eyes' in 'The Favourite Songs in the Opera of Athridates. Perf. in Dublin. A Pasticcio compiled by Tenducci. London, John Johnston'. WASH, M 1508 A 2 T 29.

pp. 212 f.   *Alessandro nell'Indie*

Text by Metastasio. Add to complete MS. scores, Milan Conservatorio 112 (copy of that MS. in WASH. M 1500 B 14 A 5).
MS. scores of arias, duet, two *accompagnati* and the Overture
in Naples Conservatorio 24–5–19. The Overture is missing in
Terry: it is the three-movement work listed *inter alia* as No. 9
on p. 273 and No. 3 on p. 277. No. 1 'Andante maestoso', No.
2 'Allegro', No. 3 'Allegro', No. 4 (Poro) 'Andante', No. 5
'Allegro', No. 6 (Poro), not Gandarte, 'Andantino con espressione', No. 7 (Erissena) 'Allegretto', between Nos. 7 and 8 there
is a *Marcia*

No. 8 'Andantino affettuoso', No. 9 bar 23rd to 5th notes a third
lower, No. 10 'Andante'. Act II, No. 11 'Allegro'. There follow,
between Nos. 11 and 12, three missing numbers,

No. 12 'Largo, ma non tanto', No. 13 'Andante', No. 14 'Allegro',
No. 15 'Andante' (also used in *Sifari*, see p. 238 No. 2), No. 16
'Allegretto', No. 17 (Erissena), 'Allegro'. Act III, No. 18 'Allegretto', No. 19 'Andante assai' and text from Metastasio's
Olimpiade, No. 20 (Poro), 'Allegro assai', No. 21 'Andante', No.
22 'Allegretto', No. 23 'Larghetto' (marked 'Cavatina' in sources),
followed by a *Coro*:

pp. 215 ff. *Amadis de Gaule*

The printed score has 'Amadis des Gaules' but the other sources
have 'Amadis de Gaule'. The three-movement Overture is
listed completely on p. 278 (2nd movt. in Paris sources 'Un peu
lent', 3rd '1ᵉʳ Mouvement'). The situation of the sources is
considerably more complicated than can be seen in Terry (where
the source at DARM. should be placed among the manuscripts
and not with the copies of the printed score), and in this case
the *incipits* in Terry are particularly incomplete. We therefore
extract the following complete set of *incipits*—including those
of the revised versions and the ballet numbers, all of which are
completely lacking in Terry—from Dr. Downes' forthcoming
book.

OVERTURE

ACT I

¹ The page numbers refer to the printed score.
² This air, which appears in the printed score, was originally included in the
Paris Opéra manuscript, but subsequently deleted from it; it is not included in
the Darmstadt manuscript.

11 Pantomime, Entrée de la fausse Oriane[1] (p. 149)

12 Gavotte (p. 151)

ACT II

13 Chorus (p. 156)

De___ l'A-mour   goû-tez___ tous les char-mes

14 Ensemble (p. 161)

Ciel! ___   fin-is-sez nos pei-nes

15 Air (p. 176)

Bien-tôt   l'en-ne-mi   qui m'ou-tra-ge

16 Pantomime[2] (p. 182)

17 Air (p. 189)

Mâ-nes plain-tifs   mâ-nes plain-tifs

18 Chorus (p. 193)

Tout fré-mit   et tout trem-ble

[1] The printed score gives no title or other designation for this selection. However the MS. *Partie des Ballets* (Library of the Paris Opéra, call number A-274) gives the title.
[2] This item is designated 'Cérémonies funèbres' in the MS. *Partie des Ballets*.

19 Air (p. 203) — *Larghetto (Amadis)*

Ah, si— vo-tre âme— est at-ten-dri-e

20 Pantomine (p. 207) — *Larghetto*

21 Ballet (p. 207) — *Allegretto*

22 Air (p. 212) — *Allegretto (Coriphée)*

Ve-nez dans de plus doux— a-zil-es

23 Ensemble[1] (p. 218) — *Andante (Coriphée & Chorus)*

Ve-nez dans de plus doux— a-zil-es

Substitute for No. 23[2] Ballet, 'Gavotte'

24 Ballet (p. 225)[3] — *Gigue*

25 Chorus (p. 229) — *Allegro*

Sor-tons d'es-cla-va-ge,

26 Ballet, 'Tambourin' (p. 238) — *Allegro*

[1] This ensemble, which forms part of the printed score, was originally part of the Paris MS. but was deleted from it, the following Gavotte being substituted. The Darmstadt MS. agrees with the final state of the Paris MS.

[2] In both the Paris and Darmstadt MSS. this Gavotte appears in place of No. 23 above. The Gavotte does not appear in the printed score.

[3] This Gigue was used as the final movement of J. C. Bach's Symphony Op. 18 No. 6 where it appears in D major.

ACT III

27 Air (p. 255) — *Larghetto* (Oriane) — A qui pour-rai-je a-voir ___ re - - cours?

28 Air (p. 267) — *Allegro assai* (Oriane) — Cru-el re-mord qui me tour-men-te

29 Duo (p. 274)[1] — [*No tempo indication*] (Arcalaus & Arcabonne) — Ah! quel plai-sir

30 Chorus (p. 276) — *Andante* — Trem-blés, trem-blés

31 Air (p. 281)[2] — *Allegro assai* (Arcalaus) — Dis-si-pons ces vai-nes al-lar-mes

32 Ensemble[3] (p. 300) — *Andante* (Chorus, Amadis & Oriane) — Jeu-nes A-mans, re-voy-és la Lu-mi-ère

33 Trio (p. 306) — *Andantino* (Oriane, Urgande & Amadis) — Ai-més vous, ai-més vous

34 Chorus (p. 313) — *Allegro* — Ur-gan-de ne de-scend des cieux

[1] This duet, which appears in the printed score, is not included in the Darmstadt MS.

[2] In the Darmstadt MS. the text of this air begins with the words 'Que l'horreur qui vient me surprendre,' and is changed throughout. The music remains the same.

[3] In the Darmstadt MS. the choral beginning of this ensemble is omitted: the duet section, which remains, begins with Amadis' words, 'Que vois-je, o ciel,' pp. 302-3 of the printed score.

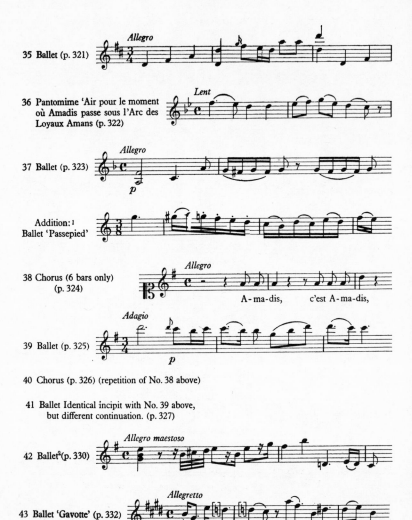

35 Ballet (p. 321)

36 Pantomime 'Air pour le moment où Amadis passe sous l'Arc des Loyaux Amans (p. 322)

37 Ballet (p. 323)

Addition: [1]
Ballet 'Passepied'

38 Chorus (6 bars only) (p. 324)

A-ma-dis,   c'est A-ma-dis,

39 Ballet (p. 325)

40 Chorus (p. 326) (repetition of No. 38 above)

41 Ballet Identical incipit with No. 39 above, but different continuation. (p. 327)

42 Ballet[2] (p. 330)

43 Ballet 'Gavotte' (p. 332)

[1] This Passepied is added in the Darmstadt MS. between Nos. 37 and 38. It does not occur in the printed score.
[2] This ballet, which appears in the printed score, is omitted from the Darmstadt MS.

44 Ensemble ('Ariette et Choeur') (p. 336)[1]

Andante (Amadis & Chorus)

Jeu - nes coeurs que l'a-mour en - ga - ge

45 Ballet 'Chaconne'

46 Ballet 'Passecaille'

Très lent

47 Ballet 'Chaconne' Identical incipit with No. 45 above, but different continuation.

48 Ballet 'Marche'

Marche

SOURCES:

1. Printed full score of the opera (see p. 215). Copies in the Berlin Oeffentliche Wissenschaftliche Bibliothek (former Preussische Staatsbibliothek), call number 9460; British Museum, H. 740 a.; British Museum (Paul Hirsch collection); Brussels Conservatory, 1359; Paris Conservatory; Paris, Bibliothèque Nationale, Vm.2 478; Vienna, National Bibliothek, SA. 83 B. 37; Library of Congress, M 1500. B14 A6; E. Downes's collection.

Another copy (presumably of the printed score, although the source does not specify) was in the library of Count Nicholas Petrovich Cheremetief at Kouskovo when the catalogue of his library was compiled in 1915.[2]

2. *Amadis de Gaule.* Eighteenth-century manuscript full score of Acts I and II only. Two volumes. Library of the Paris Opéra, call number A 274 a. This manuscript, which appears to have been used as the conductor's score, contains numerous alterations, substitutions, and additions. It differs substantially from the printed score. The earliest state of this manuscript precedes the version of the printed score and it also contains many changes which were made after the publication of the printed score.

3. *Amadis de Gaule, Opéra de Mr Bach, representée le 10 [sic] Décembre 1779.* Eighteenth-century manuscript full score of the entire opera. Three

[1] The printed score ends with No. 44. The following ballet numbers are included in the Darmstadt MS. and in the MS. *Partie des Ballets* in the Library of the Paris Opéra.

[2] R. A. Moser, *Annales de la Musique et des Musiciens en Russie au 18e Siècle* (Geneva, 1948–52) iii, 855.

acts in 3 volumes, formerly in the Hessische Landes- und Hochschul-
bibliothek, call number 134. Destroyed in Second World War.

This manuscript, which differed substantially from the printed score,
reproduced in detail the final version of the Paris Opéra manuscript listed
above. The correspondence between these two manuscripts in the first
two acts was so exact that one may probably assume that the third act of
the Darmstadt manuscript represented the final version of Act III, which
is missing from Paris Opéra manuscript.

pp. 217 ff.   *Artaserse*

Text by Metastasio. The only score is the autograph (listed by
Terry under BM.) and several numbers are now missing. We
list the words here. After Overture (complete *incipit*, p. 272,
No. 3, at bottom going over to top of p. 273) there is an Aria of
Mandane, 'Conservati fedele'. After No. 2 there is an Aria of
Artabano, 'Sulle sponde' which Bach later used in his additions
to *Orfeo* (see Terry, p. 234, No. 5). After No. 4 there is an Aria
of Artabano, 'Non ti son padre'. After No. 7 there is an
accompagnato (which the manuscript has) followed by a missing
Aria, of Arbace, 'Vo solcando un mar' crudele'. At the beginning
of Act II there is a missing Aria (Artaserse), 'Rendimi il caro
amico', and after No. 10 a missing Aria (Megabise), 'Non temer
ch'io mai'. After No. 12 there is a *Marcia*

In No. 15, the words have later been changed to 'Nacqui agli
affanni in seno' (see *Catone* No. 10). No. 17 see *Orione* p. 237,
No. 7. At the beginning of Act III there are two missing arias,
Arbace's 'Perchè tarda è mai la morte' and Arbace's 'Vivrò se
vuoi così', of which latter Aria the late Ludwig Landshoff owned
a copy which disappeared in the German invasion of France in
1940. After No. 21 there is an Aria (Semira), 'Non è ver che sia
contento' which may be identical except for the altered text with
No. 1 of the added songs in *Orfeo*, p. 234, No. 1. After No. 23
there is a *Marcia*

There are then two *accompagnati* followed by a (lost) chorus,
'Giusto Rè, la Persia adora'. There is another MS. of No. 13 in
PAR(C), Mss. 17.

p. 219 The Aria from *Berenice* was taken from *Catone* (No. 17).

pp. 219–22 *Carattaco*

The Overture is listed at the bottom of p. 275, but the second movement is wrong for the *Carattaco* Overture. It is

mezza voce

The movement Terry lists is the one Bach substituted when using this symphony as the Overture to *Temistocle* (it also exists in still another version: see p. 270, No. 4, 2nd movement). Terry for some reason does not give the numbers of the opera in chronological order, but separates the opera into two groups: (1) 'The Favourite Songs' and (2) those numbers—two marches are omitted—from the Brussels MS. missing in the 'Favourite Songs'. The order is as follows:

No. of complete opera	Favourite Songs	Manuscript (pp. 221 f.)
1 (Coro)	—	13
'Allegro moderato' and words are 'Odio, giuriamo'		
2 (Cartismandua)	—	14
3 (Teomanzio)		15
4 (Guideria)		16
5 (Pratusago)	4	
6 (Publio Ostorio) Text is 'Vanne'		17
7 (Carattaco)	2	
8 (Trinobanta)	3	
9 (Cassibelane)	1	
10 (Coro)		18
	Act II	
11 (Carattaco)		19
12 (Teomanzio)		20
13 (Giuderia)	5	
14 (Carattaco)	6	
15 (Publio Ostorio)		21
First word of the text is 'È' and not 'Lo'.		
16 (Cassibelane)	missing in signature	22
17 (Cartismandua)	8	
18a Marcia (not listed in Terry)		

18b (Carattaco) 12
19 (Coro) 'Padre, addio' from printed libretto; missing in only extant copy of score (BRUSS 2039).

Act III

20 (Marco Osterio) with faulty *incipit*   23

Se   la   pie - tà   co -

21 (Carattaco & Cassibelane)   9
22 (Trinobanta)   7 for other settings see p. 254 last *incipit*, p.
  255 ditto, p. 258.
23 (Pratusago)   11
24a Marcia (not listed in Terry)

pp. 222–5   *Catone in Utica*

Text by Metastasio. Produced at Teatro San Carlo, Naples, on
4 (5?) November 1761. The original and authentic version of
the Overture may be found on pp. 277 (No. 6) and 278. The
second version of the Overture, which Terry prints, is that of
p. 273, No. 6 (*Alessandro*, also *Astarto*), again on p. 277, No. 3.
Dr. Downes thinks that the second version may be connected
with the performance at Braunschweig (Brunswick) in 1768.
Terry has listed the 1761 version, minus the final 'Marchia'.
For the other versions, *vide infra*. No 2 'Andante maestoso', No.
3 'Allegro', No. 4 'Andantino', No. 6 'Largo', No. 7 'Andante',
No. 8 'Allegro', No. 9 read all the notes a note higher, No. 10
'Allegretto', No. 11 'Larghetto', No. 12 'Allegro', No. 13
'Allegro assai', No. 14 'Andante', No. 15 'Allegro maestoso',
No. 16 'Allegro' and 2nd note a third lower (g' for b'), No. 17
no tempo but 'Andante espressivo' in *Berenice* (see p. 219), No.
18 'Allegretto', No. 19 'Allegro', No. 20 is a recitative, No. 21
'Larghetto'. The March is:

Libretto: WASH Schatz 526 for Pavia performance 1763, Schatz
527 for Brunswick 1768. The sources for the 1761 version are
Naples Conservatorio 6505, 6506 (minus *secco* recit.); another
MS., same library, 6504 (no recits.). A third source for the 1761
version is WOLF 13a, 13b, 13c, with changes for a performance

at Brunswick in 1768 (but the original can be clearly seen
beneath the later changes), with all the *secco* recits. and the
concluding March.

The second version was for Naples in 1764; a MS. score of
Acts I and II is in the Naples Conservatorio, 6505 and 6506,
with the *secco* recits.; Act III is missing. Three new arias were
substituted, as follows:

for No. 3

for No. 8

for No. 14

It is possible that Bach made the changes indicated since we
know that he kept in close touch with Naples after he had settled
in London. See also *infra*, 234 f. in connection with *Orfeo*. On
the other hand, it is doubtful if he made the changes in the version of which only one MS. score exists, in the Paris Conservatoire D 622, 623, 624, although one of the substitutions is from
Artaserse. When the opera was given at Brunswick in 1768,
several changes were made, including heavy cuts in the *secco*
recitatives and four substitutions (one keeping the middle section
as Bach wrote it); it is doubtful if Bach was responsible for this
score. The source has been listed above, under the 1761 version
for reasons there explained. Add to the sources: No. 19 in BM.
Add 31717 (different characters and slightly changed text), add
to No. 14 NAP. 33–38, to No. 17 STOCK. Nos. 20–21 in NAP.
57–2–3, Nos. 7, 11, 14, 17, 19, 20, 21 in NAP. 33–5–1.

p. 225   *Ezio*
Libretto in WASH. ML 48 M 2 N. No. 1 is from *Alessandro*,
No. 19, with a new middle section; No. 2 from *Alessandro*, No.

16. *Gioas* is, of course, an oratorio and not an opera. As usual, Terry lists the work twice, once with 'The Favourite Songs' and once from the manuscript sources. It will be noted that no choruses are listed or seem to be included in the MSS. Possibly the chorus in D—an eighteenth-century MS. with British watermarks, apparently a unique copy, is owned by this writer— has some connection with *Gioas*. The *incipit* may be examined in the new edition of *Temistocle* (Universal Edition, Vienna), where we have used this chorus as the Finale of Act I; the original words were 'Ad te, gloria'.

p. 226 First *incipit* of *Gioas Sinfonia*; the tempo must of course be *Largo*, as the third *incipit* of the work shows.

pp. 229–31   *La clemenza di Scipione*

Between Nos. 2 and 3 there is an *accompagnato*—the *secco* recits. are all missing in the only known source, which is the printed score—followed by a chorus:

S'o - da il ,suon del - la trom - ba guer - rie - ra

No. 3 Arsinda, No. 4 Idalba, after No. 4 a March is mentioned in the libretto but is missing in the score (perhaps No. 2 was repeated), No. 5 Luceio, No. 6 Scipione, No. 7 Marzio, No. 8 Arsinda, No. 9 Luceio & Arsinda, No. 10 Idalba, after No. 10 there is a chorus:

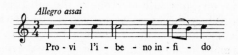

Pro - vi l'i - be - no in - fi - do

In the libretto there follows another chorus which is missing in the score, 'L'orror della catene'. No. 11 Scipione, No. 12 Luceio, No. 13 Marzio, No. 14 Arsinda, No. 15 Arsinda, Luceio & Scipione, No. 16 Luceio, No. 17 Luceio, No. 18 Arsinda, after No. 19 there are the following three numbers:

No. 20 Coro

I suòi stra - li, ter - ror

No. 21 Quintetto — *Andante* — Se me - sti e — do - len - ti voi

No. 22 Coro — *Allegro* — Tri - on - fi l'o - no - re

p. 231 Sources for *La clemenza*, under 'In Manuscript', the first item, BRUN. No. 218 has now been transferred to the Landeshauptarchiv (Niedersächsisches Staatsarchiv) at Wolfenbüttel and is not the score and parts of the whole opera but only the Aria No. 14 with the preceding *accompagnato*. Libretto: WASH. Schatz 628.

p. 232   *Lucio Silla*

No. 2 'Allegro', No. 3 'Andantino di molto', No. 4 'Andante', No. 5 'Largo assai', No. 6 'Allegro assai'. After No. 6 there follow:

Ensemble (Giunia & Chorus) — *Larghetto con moto* — Fuor di quest' ur - ne do - len - ti

Duetti (Cecilio & Giunia) — *Larghetto con moto* — D'E - li - so in sen m'at - ten - di

No. 7 'Allegro maestoso', No. 8 'Larghetto con moto', No. 9 'Andante', No. 10 'Allegro non tanto presto', No. 11 'Allegro', No. 12 'Largo ma non tanto', No. 13 'Andante'. After No. 13 there are:

Coro — *Allegro* — Se glo - ria il crin ti cin - se

Terzetto (Silla, Celia, Giunia) — *Allegro* — Quel or - go-glio - so

No. 14 'Allegro moderato', No. 15 'Allegro moderato', No. 16 'Andantino', No. 17 'Allegro di molto', No. 18 'Andante'.

Coro ultimo:

Il gran Sil - la, a Ro-ma in se - no

Libretti (Metastasio): WASH Schatz 529 (Italian libretto for first perf.), Schatz 530 is contemporary German translation for Mannheim perf. *Lucio Silla* was performed at the Kiel opera house in the 1930s.

p. 234 Possibly in connection with the success of the Bachian *Orfeo*, there seems to have been an attempt to get Bach to return to the San Carlo Theatre for the season 1774–5; and it seems that Bach actually intended to go. They staged the new pasticcio *Orfeo* with the Bach inserts, and Bach was expected from London to conduct it (Croce, *Teatri, op. cit.* 553): a letter from Bach to the theatre was formerly in the archives there (20 Feb. 1774), in which he excused himself for not being able to come. On 2 April 1774 someone wrote about Bach, 'le sue opere erano stato molto applaudite . . . le arie del Alessandro girano tuttavia pei cembalo di tutti i dilettanti della nostra capitale'. King Ferdinand IV was evidently expecting Bach in the early Summer of 1774, for the following document shows that Bach was supposed to reorganize the violin section of the S. Carlo orchestra:

'E venuta S. M. in risolvere che l'orchestra si abassi e mantagna nell'antico sito, che li Bassi siano situati come anticamente, che il cembalo sia qual dev'essere di mole e di sito. Finalmente è venuta la M.S. in risolvere che il nuovo Maestro di Cappella Bach scelga li migliori violini della città, sapendo che non son tali quelli che ora servano. Palazzo, 2 maggio 1774—Bernardo Tenducci.' In the archives there is, moreover, the following document: 'Il maestro di Capella Bach approvato da S. M. per scrivere in musica le due opere del prossimo Novembre e nel venturo Carnevale, he con lettera partecipato all'Impresario del R. Teatro, che per inopinata novità, gli è stata sospesa la licenza di poter qui venire da Londra come aveva promesso' (6 September 1774). From Prota-Giurleo, 'La grande orchestra del R. Teatro San Carlo nel '700', p. 36.

As to the 'Favourite Songs in the Opera Orfeo', Dr. Downes suggests that this print may have been later than 1770, since only five of the arias (Nos. 1–4 and 7) are included in the original libretto of 1770; the others may have been added for the revivals of 1771 or 1773, for which copies of the libretti have not yet been located.

p. 235 Sources for *Orfeo*. No. 2 also NAP. 57–2–8; BRUSS. 12834 in 19th cent. MS. of Gluck opera. No. 7 also NAP. 57–2–8.

pp. 235 ff.   *Orione*

All that has survived of *Orione* is in fragments, and neither the 'Favourite Songs' nor the manuscripts in the British Museum and St. Michael's College Tenbury are in the proper order. As will be seen, Terry has simply copied out both sources, so that the themes are in many cases duplicated. By using the original libretto (BER. Mus. Tb. 51), Dr. Downes was able to establish the original order, in so far as the music has been preserved at all.

Act I

Overture
Coro (repeated after *accompagnato*)

Aria (Enopione) p. 237, No. 2
Aria (Retrea) 'Per questa volta almeno' no copy survives
Aria (Argia) 'Della misera germana' no copy survives
Aria (Orione) 'Nel' trionfare il fato' no copy survives
Aria (Candiope) p. 236, No. 6
Duetto (Nice & Tirsi) 'Fonti amiche, ombroso rio' no copy survives
Aria (Nice) p. 236, No. 8 marked *Cavatina*
Marcia no copy survives
Coro 'Ecco d'Arcadia e Tebe' copy supposedly in Tenbury MS.

Act II

Aria (Mercurio) 'Bella diva, colma omai' no copy extant
Aria (Diana) 'Se de' miei strali' no copy extant
Aria (Orione) p. 236, No. 4, p. 237, No. 5—tie missing 2nd to third notes and text in second *incipit* should be adjusted. In the printed score, the Aria is in full *da capo* form, in the MS., the Aria is cut somewhat.
Aria (Argia) p. 237, No. 4 (add three dots after 'tuo').
Aria (Retrea), p. 236, No. 7, p. 237, No. 6 (in BM. with preceding *accompagnato*, 'Misera! che ascoltai?'), in both *incipits* read 'perso' for 'Perso'. Again, the Aria is shortened in BM.

Aria (Nice) p. 236, No. 5
Aria (Tirsi) 'Nocchier che si abbandona' no copy survives

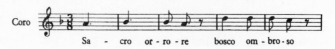

Coro   Sa - cro or - ro - re   bosco om - bro - so

Aria (Candiope) p. 236, No. 3 and quite wrongly in A flat on
p. 237, No. 3 (the BM. copy is in E flat, too). In BM. preceded
by *accompagnato* 'Eterni Dei ! che vedo?'.

Act III

Aria (Orione) p. 235, No. 1
Aria (Candiope) p. 236, No. 2 (last two notes of bars 1 and 3
should have rhythm of example on p. 245, *incipit* three)
Aria (Enopione) 'Del fato il giusto sdegno' no copy survives
Aria (Tirsi) 'Cara Nice, io ti parli' no copy survives
Aria (Retrea) 'Alfin, tra tanti affanni' no copy survives
Coro 'Della fama all'aurea tromba' no copy survives
Coro ultimo 'Al Nocchier in preda a' venti' no copy survives

p. 238   Pasticcio *Sifari*: the first Aria is from *Catone* (No. 4, p.
223), the second from *Alessandro* (No. 15, p. 214—notice added
grace note and *tr*). Another copy of print in WASH. M 1500.
B 14 S 4.

pp. 238–41   *Temistocle*
Libretto: Verazi's adaptation of the Metastasio text.
Overture: some confusion with regard to the *incipits* arises. On
pp. 275 f. Terry lists, as *Carattaco* Overture, the three movements
of the *Temistocle* (this has been corrected *supra*). On p. 278 2nd
group, Terry lists *Temistocle* but for the first movement he has
taken the bass line and put it in the G clef, whereas the correct
beginning is on p. 275 (bottom) and, without the bottom part
of the chords, on p. 238. The Overture, which has three clarinetti d'amore obbligati, is printed in the J. C. Bach volume of
the *Erbe Deutscher Musik*, edited by the late Fritz Stein (Breitkopf & Härtel). Yale University School of Music Library owns
a complete manuscript copy of the opera, Ma 31 B 117t., including the *secco* recitatives. On p. 241, 2nd *incipit*, add two
sharps to signature. The text of Aria No. 5 is identical with that
of Aria No. 3 in *Adriano in Siria* (p. 211).

pp. 241f.   *Zanaida*

The only musical source for this opera is 'The Favourite Songs', which is, of course, very incomplete (another copy in WASH. M 1500. B 14 Z 3). Dr. Downes has established the correct order of the individual numbers.

Overture: Terry identifies the B flat *sinfonia* listed at the top of page 269 as the Overture, probably on the basis of the 'Six Favourite Opera Overtures . . .' (Walsh, ?1770) catalogued on p. 274.

Act I

Aria (Osira) 'Allo splendor del trono' no copy survives
Aria (Roselane) 'Lieta parto, e della sorte' no copy survives
'Symphony' no copy survives
Coro 'Ecce a noi dal ciel sen viene' no copy survives
Aria (Tamasse) p. 242, No. 8
Aria (Mustafà 'Almen la parca irata' no copy survives
Aria (Zanaida) p. 241, No. 4 (add tie first to 2nd notes)
Aria (Cisseo) 'La speme mi dice' no copy survives
Quartetto (Mustafà, Tamasse, Zanaida, Roselane) 'Empio, paventa omai, barbaro traditor' no copy survives

Act II

Aria (Roselane) 'Ogni ragion mi chiama' no copy survives
Aria (Osira) 'Fra le tue ritorte' no copy survives
Aria (Cisseo) 'Nel tuo poter sovrano' no copy survives
Aria (Tamasse) p. 214, No. 1
Aria (Zanaida) p. 241, No. 3
Aria (Mustafà) 'Ah, l'impresa scellerata' no copy survives
Aria (Aglatida) 'Compagni d'amore son speme e timore' no copy survives
Aria (Silvera) 'Se potessi ognun' per giuoco' no copy survives
Aria (Zanaida) p. 241, No. 2
Coro 'Voi del cielo, eterni Dei' no copy survives

Act III

Aria (Ganguir) 'A un cor forte, a un alma grande' no copy survives
Aria (Silvera) p. 241, No. 5
Aria (Zanaida) p. 242, No. 7
Aria (Mustafà) 'Pensa che sei mia figlia' no copy survives
Aria (Tamasse) p. 242, No. 6

Aria (Roselane) 'Chiudo in petto un cor altero' no copy survives
Coro ultimo 'Ecco al fine' no copy survives.

In his list of the operas, Terry has for some reason omitted the
following:

Astarto, Rè di Tiro (Pasticcio)
Produced at the King's Theatre, London, 4 December 1762

'The Music of the Airs is selected from various celebrated
authors, excepting what are marked with an asterisk, which are
Mr. John Bach's, a Saxon master of music, under whose direction
the whole is performed' (Terry, 66). The following numbers
were by Bach:

Overture (taken from his *Alessandro nell'Indie*, p. 273, No. 6)
Quartetto 'Deh, torna in te stesso'. We now return, for a
moment, to *Orione*. The BM. manuscript, which is not bound
in any particular order, contains several bits of music not from
Orione: p. 237, No. 7 is from *Artaserse*, No. 17 (where it is in
the bass clef), and No. 8 is also not from *Orione*, while No. 9 is
the middle section of the Aria p. 236, No. 3. The Quartetto
from *Astarto* is bound in the MS. after p. 237, No. 6, and the
music turns out to be from *Catone in Utica*, where it is also a
quartet (p. 224, No. 19). Duetto 'Io so ben' no copy survives
Aria 'Per quel primero affetto' is a reworking of the Aria 'Per
quel paterno amplesso' in *Artaserse* (p. 218, No. 13)
Duetto 'Deh, seconda' no copy survives
Aria 'Pupille vezzose'—Terry thinks this Aria is identical
with 'Pupilla vezzosa' in the pasticcio, *La Calamità de Cuori*.
Curiously, the Aria is not printed in the original libretto of
Calamità though it was included in the 'Favourite Songs' (Terry,
p. 228).

Issiple

Performed at the Teatro San Carlo, Naples, 26 December
1763.

The libretto for this production (Biblioteca Angelica, Rome,
E. I. 12. 7) designates 'Sig. Bach' as the composer of one Aria,
'Per il bosco, con torpido ciglio', of which no copy has been
located (Dr. Downes).

p. 245 Penultimate *incipit*: see *Orione*, No. 2, p. 236. Another
copy of the print in WASH. M 1503, A 77 M 2 & M 22 case.

pp. 245 f. 'Amelia, a musical entertainment of two acts', London, T. Becket, 1771, 32 pp., mostly taken from 'The Summer's Tale' and not to be confused with another *Amelia* performed on 12 April 1768 in London. Libretto: WASH. Longe 105. First performance Drury Lane, 14 December 1771. Music by Dibdin, Piccinni, Potenza, Cocchi, Bach, Stanley, Arnold, Richter. (From Dr. Miesner.)
The following are also missing in Terry:

'Tom Jones. A comic opera: as it is performed at the Royal Theatre in Covent Garden. By Joseph Reed. London 1769, Becket and De Houdt', first performance on 14 January 1769. From the novel by Fielding. There were three arias by Bach, six by Arnold, eleven by Arne and one each by many other composers. Libretto: WASH. Also: 2nd edition.
'Zophilette. Conte de Mr. Marmontel mis en scènes et en ariettes et représenté le 17 mail 1765' (published 1768), from Marmontel's 'Lausette', with arias by Bach and many others. Libretto: WASH.

p. 247 Cantata 'Amor Vincitore', to sources add WIEN(M). The DARM. score contains, apart from *secco* recitatives, ten numbers, including three big choral scenes; the textbook is different from the Darmstadt score. *Vide supra*, 130.
Aurora. The print may be dated *c.* 1825 (according to the late Otto Haas). The work is part of a larger Cantata entitled 'Cefalo e Procuri. Cantata a tre voci del Sigr. G. C. Bach, Londra 1776', Autograph score in WASH. ML 96 B 185.

p. 248 Libretto of *Endimione* in Mannheim Theaterarchiv No. 222.

p. 251 No. 5, bar 2 the notes should read instead of e flat-d

p. 252 No. 10 also NAP. 33–5–1 as 'Parto se vuoi così'.
No. 12 from *Endimione* (p. 249, No. 9).

p. 253 1758 for first *incipit* is an impossible date if the aria is by Bach, says Dr. Downes; the text is from *Catone* (p. 222, No. 2).

There is an *Accompagnato* ('A si barbaro colpo cede la mia costanza') and Aria ('Morte vieni') not in Terry: copies in WIEN(M). and another formerly owned by Ludwig Landshoff. Text from Metastasio's *Eroe Cinese*.

p. 254 First set of songs, under sources cancel BRUN., read WOLF. Bündel xl, No. 224. For 'A Second Collection of Favourite Songs' add under sources: No. 1 in: 'The Musical journal for the piano-forte' arr. by Benjamin Carr. Baltimore (1803–4?), Vol. 5, No. 99, pp. 9–11. WASH. M 1 A 1 M 98 case & M 1 A 1 M 982 case.

p. 255 top *incipit*, add broad-sheet 'In this shady blest retreat, sung by Mrs. Weichsell compos'd by Mr. Bach' for voice and continuo, Yale Univ. Lib. Vj 8 05/37. 'A Third Collection' was announced in London newspaper in July 1771 (Dr. Miesner).

p. 256 top *incipit* published in Philadelphia 179– by G. Willig. WASH. M 1 A 1 B as 'A favourite rondo by Sr. Bach'.

p. 257 top *incipit* also published in Philadelphia by G. Willig. Another edition in Philadelphia published by John Aiken (1820?) as 'A favorit song by Mr. Bach', WASH. M 1 A 1 B case. A duet, missing in Terry, 'My life, my joy, my blessing' as insertion on Samuel Arnold's 'The Maid of the Mill'—see also p. 254, *supra*.

p. 260 Opus IV: another copy in WASH. M 1552 B. case. No. 5 in NAP. 33–5–1, No. 8 (MS. copy).

p. 261 Opus VI: add to MS. sources—No. 1, NAP. 33–5–1 No. 10, No. 4–9, No. 5–7.

p. 263 Sources: No. 1 in MS., STOCK. On the whole, the many secondary MSS. of doubtful textual value in the Austrian monasteries (*e.g.* Göttweig, Lambach) and Czech libraries (Prague, Brno, etc.) have not been listed: the principal sources for Bach's symphonies are the English prints done presumably under his supervision, the Hummel editions, and so on.

p. 265 No. 6 in Thurn und Taxis Archives Regensburg as Mitscha—but it is clearly by Bach.

p. 268 No. 2: in the Sieber edition there is a Finale. For details, see the Eulenburg score.

p. 271 No. 6: middle movement (between I and II) omitted: the *incipit* is identical with that of p. 278, No. 8 'Andante': the final two movements are taken from music to *Amadis de Gaule*. Under sources, add 'Two grand overtures . . .' William Forster, London—copy in STOCK. Under printed editions, note that the BM. copy lacks the clarinets. 'Another edition (London: Walsh)' is a mistake: the BRUSS. signature contains the Overtures for Harpsichord, p. 274. Similarly on p. 274 at the very top, the BRUSS. entry also contains the same Walsh Overtures.

p. 275 After 2nd *incipit*, for Bremner addition, add call no. RM 17 b 1. 'An Overture in Eight Parts . . .': another copy as 'The Periodical Overture' in STOCK.

p. 276 Symphonies in manuscript. No. 1, if genuine, must be an Italian product, since no English source exists. No. 2 is very dubious: as *Haydn* in a late copy in Brussels; as Leopold *Hofmann* in Göttweig as early as 1762, Lambach 1768, Kremsmünster and Copenhagen; as Ignaz *Holzbauer* in Berlin (Hausbibliothek), Breitkopf Catalogue 1766, and Berlin Staatsbib. (now Marburg–Lahn); as *anonymous* in Oettingen–Wallerstein Library in Harburg Castle.

p. 277 No. 4, if genuine, must also be an Italian product (EIN owns, by the way, several of Bach's religious works and seems to have had great affection for the music of the young composer). No. 5 is not by Bach (note that 'Beck' is similar to 'Back').

pp. 279ff. Nos. 9, 10, 14, 17 very dubious and No. 14 probably J. J. Lang: in any case Giuseppe Pach or Baach does not necessarily mean Johann Christian at all. Nos. 11, 12, 21, and 22 may be Italian works. No. 13 is not, according to Tutenberg, a symphony at all but a divertimento or trio sonata. No. 15: unlikely that this is J. C. B. (only one source and very remote). No. 16, on the other hand, seems to be a genuine work. The works only preserved in STOCK.—Nos. 18, 19—are dubious. Nos. 23 and 24, though from the standpoint of the sources rather dubious, have certain very Christian Bach-ish elements, but this is not enough to consider them genuine works. The last work on p. 283 is, on the other hand, a beautiful and apparently late-period symphony which is undoubtedly genuine.

pp. 286, 288 No. 4 is not a concerted symphony but a real concerto: it is published by the Universal Edition, Vienna. Similarly the work listed as No. 9 on p. 288 is a real bassoon concerto and not a *sinfonia concertante*. No. 11 on p. 288 is a *Notturno* and not a concerted symphony.

This is perhaps the place to say that on the Continent there exists a score of dubious works attributed to 'Bach'. The further away these sources are from Italy or England, the more dubious they are (we refer, of course, to works which are not in Terry). To give one instance, there is a Symphony in E flat

which is attributed to Bach in the Kremsmünster Monastery Library; but we find the work also as Haydn in Munich, as Anton Filtz in an early print by Huberty (Op. 1, No. 4) and in the Breitkopf Catalogue of 1766, as Ignaz Fränzl in the Monastery of Stams in Tyrol, and as Wenzel Pichl in the Thurn und Taxis Archives, Regensburg. It was not thought necessary to include these works, which are certainly not by Bach, and which would only serve to make the thematic index still longer, without any real practical—as opposed to musicological—purpose.

pp. 298 ff. There is considerable doubt about the authenticity of these many clavier concertos: recently there has been some attempt to attribute some to Friedemann Bach; in any case, it is highly unlikely that all these works are really by Johann Christian, particularly in view of the 'severe style' in which many of them are written.

pp. 317 ff. Similarly, it is doubtful if all these string and other trios are authentic. Some no doubt were written 'Del Sig^re Bach in Milano', as the sources indicate; but such remote sources as those for the last two works on p. 319 and the whole of those on p. 320 do not suggest Christian as the composer: we must not forget that there were several other Bachs composing at this time, including the 'Bückeburg' Bach (Johann Christoph Friedrich, Christian's elder brother), about whose exact *oeuvre* we know relatively little (for a good beginning, see the article in *MGG*), and that the name 'Bach' on a manuscript was almost as good as putting 'Haydn' on a French print to sell the unknown work in question more easily.

p. 337   These sonatas also have *basso continuo* (Dr. Miesner) and are dubious, as Terry himself suggests.

p. 346   No. 5 for 'Catone' read 'Alessandro'.

H. C. R. L.

CHAPTER I

LEIPZIG AND BERLIN

AMONG the lesser luminaries of the eighteenth century the sons of Sebastian Bach form a constellation brilliant and particular. Their colossal father passed from view in 1750, Handel followed in 1759, and though Gluck survived in creative activity, Haydn, who composed his first Mass a year or two after Bach's death, did not enter Prince Esterhazy's service till 1761, while Mozart first amazed the continent in 1763, when Beethoven's birth was seven years distant. In this interregnum the sons of Bach prolonged the already unique record of their name, giving it a European currency the profounder genius of their father had not been able to achieve. The eldest, Wilhelm Friedemann, talented, but incorrigibly indolent, died at Berlin in 1784, reputed the one of Bach's sons who, as an organist, most nearly approached his incomparable sire.[1] At Hamburg Carl Philipp Emanuel held a situation his father had filled at Leipzig, but with an admission of his talents and authority Sebastian never equally enjoyed: Mozart and Haydn owned his mastership and used his example to perfect the musical forms in which, before his death in 1788, they were pre-eminent. At Bückeburg a third brother, Johann Christoph Friedrich, the son of Bach's second marriage, was in honourable service as Concertmeister to Count Wilhelm of Schaumburg-Lippe. Like his brothers a prolific composer, and like his father comparatively unknown to his generation, he died in 1795, the last survivor of Sebastian's sons. All three brothers, constant to the traditions of their ancestry, gave exclusive service to their fatherland and its Lutheran Confession. Their youngest brother was not similarly controlled: cosmopolitan and Catholic, he belongs to Italy and France as much as to Germany, but to England most of all.

Johann Christian Bach[2] was born at Leipzig on Monday, 5 September 1735,[3] the youngest son of Sebastian Bach's marriage to Anna Magdalena Wilcken. Ten children of that union preceded and two daughters followed him, most of them short-lived and one of them imbecile, a sorry record which impeaches

[1] Cf. Forkel, p. 61.
[2] In Italy he was known as Giovanni Cristiano, in France as Jean-Crétien, and in England as John Christian.
[3] The date is recorded by his father in the family Genealogy. Cf. T.B., p. 3.

an unhealthy nursery rather than the stamina of their parents. Christian and his Bückeburg brother probably owed their survival to the reconstruction of the Cantor's lodging within the Thomas-schule in 1731–2; of the children born there before that event only one had normal health, and, of the rest, but one outlived extreme infancy. Christian himself did not attain his fiftieth year, though his portraits do not indicate the fragile physique of his elder brothers and sisters. Two days after his birth he was carried to church for his christening,[1] to receive his first name from his godfathers, Johann August Ernesti, Rector of the Thomasschule, with whom his father was on the eve of acrimonious controversy,[2] and Johann Florens Rivinus, a Professor in the University, in whose honour Sebastian had lately (1733) performed the cantata 'Die Freude reget sich'. The Cantor's relations with these academic dignitaries accorded with his office. But, for his son's godmother Bach entered another circle and found Christiane Sibylla, daughter of Georg Heinrich Bose, a prosperous Leipzig merchant recently deceased, Bach's neighbour on the Thomas-kirchhof, whose father and uncle had increased the amenities of their city by laying out the large and small gardens called after them.[3] She gave her godson her name and, possibly, more material proof of her regard.

Christian entered a household strangely composed. His father was in his fifty-first year, his mother within a few days of her thirty-fourth. Of Sebastian's children by his first wife, the eldest, Catharina Dorothea, alone remained under the paternal roof, a spinster approaching her twenty-seventh year. Of Anna Magdalena's own children only three survived to greet the new-comer—Gottfried Heinrich, a half-witted lad in his twelfth year, Johann Christoph Friedrich, later of Bückeburg, nearly four, and their sister Elisabeth Juliane Friederica, a girl of nine summers. She would fall to her mother's care. But the boys needed sterner control, which their father was too occupied to exert. In 1738, therefore, he admitted his cousin Johann Elias Bach of Schwein-furt to his house, charging him with their education during hours spared from his attendance at the University. Elias acted also as Bach's amanuensis; his letters are among the few documents which illuminate the interior of the Cantor's home.[4] Before

---

[1] Sp. ii. 955; U. p. 17.   [2] Cf. T.B., pp. 223f.
[3] I am obliged to Dr. Friedrich Schulze, Director of the Stadtgeschichtliches Museum, Leipzig, for information regarding the Bose family. D.J.F.L., pp. 76 and 90, names other members of the family holding prominent positions in Leipzig in 1736. Cf. *ibid.*, p. 137, for the two gardens.
[4] Cf. T.B., p. 243.

Christian was eight Elias left Leipzig and surrendered his charges to other hands. But for the unhappy controversy with Ernesti, Christian, like his half-brothers, would probably have attended the lower classes of the Thomasschule. Unfortunately the school register is lacking after 1739,[1] nor does the other Stadtschule, the Nikolaischule, reveal the boy's attendance. There were also available various private schools (Winkelschulen), supervised by the junior clergy, in which juveniles were instructed 'im Christenthum und andern benöthigten Stücken'.[2] Christian may have frequented one or other of them. But, wherever he found instruction, he signally failed to absorb the sturdy Lutheranism his father received from his own school-days.

Bach's pupils were brought up on a plan so closely modelled on his own experience, that Christian's earliest clavier lessons can be supposed to have been received in 1744, his ninth year. His father first took instruction from his Ohrdruf brother at that age, and Wilhelm Friedemann began to play at the same stage of his career. Friedemann's well-thumbed 'Clavier-Büchlein' (1720) and the first part of 'Das wohltemperirte Clavier' (1722) served again for Christian's information. But it cannot be a mere coincidence that in 1744 Bach completed the second part of the latter work, a fact which may indicate Christian's precocious ability or his father's partiality. Bach, however, was so occupied in engraving his organ music, and in answering calls upon his talent from outside, that Christian's systematic instruction must have been given by another competent hand. Perhaps Bach entrusted the task to his former pupil Johann Schneider, organist of the Nikolaikirche, or to Johann Christoph Altnikol, who early in 1749 became his son-in-law.[3] He superintended, corrected, even punished his young genius, however. Christian recalled in after life an occasion on which he received castigation for a too adventurous harmonic exercise.[4]

His father's death, when he was barely fifteen, launched Christian upon the first stage of his cosmopolitan course. Bach died intestate; the division of his estate between his widow and surviving children was completed on 11 November 1750, when the beneficiaries signed the deed of distribution. Christian, his Bückeburg brother, and two younger sisters, being under age, their mother invited Johann Gottlieb Görner, the University's 'Director Musices', to act in their behalf. Through him Christian

---

[1] So I am informed by Dr. Tittel, the present Rector.   [2] D.J.F.L., p. 88.
[3] Altnikol married Elisabeth Juliane Friederica Bach on 20 Jan. 1749.
[4] Schökel, p. 23.

claimed three pedalled claviers, which, he declared, his father had given him before his death. His mother and Altnikol confirmed the statement, and the elder children, though grudgingly, admitted it. Thus Christian faced the world with three claviers, each valued at about fifty thalers, a third of his father's stock of linen shirts, magnanimously surrendered by the elders, a sum of thirty-eight thalers, after contributing to discharge his father's inconsiderable debts, and the prospect of more from the sale of his instruments and valuable souvenirs.[1]

Bach's death broke up his household and scattered its members. His widow and two youngest daughters lived on precariously at Leipzig till her death in 1760. Her eldest daughter, recently (1749) married to Altnikol, took the half-witted Gottfried Heinrich under her roof at Naumburg; while Johann Christoph Friedrich was already in service at Bückeburg. Christian alone was a problem to his relatives. Of his two half-brothers, Wilhelm Friedemann, now at Halle, was the one to whom he naturally looked: for neither Halle nor Dresden, where Friedemann was first employed, were too distant to prevent his frequent visits to Leipzig.[2] But he was on the eve of matrimony,[3] nor disposed by circumstances and temperament to take his young brother's upbringing on his shoulders. Carl Philipp Emanuel, though more remote at Berlin and a less familiar figure in the Leipzig household, could offer not only a home but also a specialist's instruction upon the instrument on which Christian already showed promise of excelling. To their grave reproach, Bach's eldest sons permitted his widow to suffer the cruel hardships of her last years. But the fact that Carl Philipp took Christian's upbringing on his shoulders is creditable to him, even if he found the compulsion irksome. For Christian, certainly, the association was advantageous.

Carl Philipp Emanuel Bach,[4] now in his thirty-seventh year, had served since 1740 as cembalist in the royal Capelle at Berlin and Potsdam. Already restive under the martinet discipline of his master, Frederick II, his duty bound him to attend the royal concerts in the palace every evening except Mondays and Fridays, when opera was performed. Frederick's taste was conservative; his preferences selected a repertory of some three hundred concertos for flute and orchestra, through which he manœuvred in orderly rotation. Nor was he agreeable to accompany; he took liberties with his text, exacting deference from his musicians which

---

[1] Cf. Sp. ii. 956–76. [2] T.B., *passim*.
[3] He married Dorothea Elisabeth Georgi at Halle on 25 Feb. 1751.
[4] Illustration No .2.

Emanuel found it irksome to concede. He had hoped to succeed his father at Leipzig in 1750, and, as his migration to Hamburg did not take place until 1767, the irritations of his Berlin post were sweetened by the friendship of Princess Anna Amalia, Frederick's sister, and the society of the distinguished musicians who served the Prussian court. At Berlin and elsewhere Emanuel was a recognized master of his instrument. Five years before his father's death, Balthasar Schmidt of Nürnberg had engraved his Concerto in D major for clavier and strings.[1] In 1752 another, in B flat major, came from the same press.[2] Ten years earlier (1742) Schmidt published six clavier sonatas dedicated to Frederick II,'[3] while in 1744 six more made their appearance, with a dedication to Emanuel's pupil, the Duke of Württemberg.[4] His reputation, already high, was confirmed by a work which appeared shortly after Christian became his pupil, 'Versuch über die wahre Art das Clavier zu spielen', the first part of which he published at Berlin in 1753.[5] The treatise developed the principles Emanuel received from his father, and, expanded by Muzio Clementi (d. 1832), Johann Baptist Cramer (d. 1858), and Johann Nepomuk Hummel (d. 1837), founded modern pianoforte technique. Christian was no stranger to his father's method; like Emanuel himself, he could declare that he 'laboured for the first years of his life, without intermission', at the 'extremely difficult' exercises of 'Das wohltemperirte Clavier'.[6] Under his brother's tuition he acquired the technical facility which impressed his English patrons in later years, moving a writer shortly before his death to applaud him as 'the most capital harpsichord player of his time'.[7] Burney, also,[8] eulogized his 'expressive and masterly performance on the piano forte,' attributing his excellence to his brother's example and instruction; the more confidently, seeing that he had it from Christian himself, that in Italy 'he made little use of a harpsichord or piano forte but to compose for or accompany a voice', his chief occupation in that period having been the production of vocal music.

In his brother's household Christian's studious and receptive mind had ample opportunity to receive abiding impressions from musicians of high eminence, whose genius invited him into paths his father's older traditions had not allowed him to explore. Among Emanuel's associates were the two Grauns—Johann

[1] Wotquenne, p. 2, No. 11.
[2] *Ibid.*, p. 4, No. 25.   [3] *Ibid.*, p. 8. No. 48.   [4] *Ibid.*, p. 9, No. 49.
[5] An edition (Walter Niemann) is published by Kahnt, Leipzig. The first part was republished in 1759; the second part followed in 1762. The latter deals particularly with the art of accompaniment.
[6] Burney, p. 240.   [7] ABCD, p. 8.   [8] Bur., p. 482.

Gottlieb (*d.* 1771), who once had Friedemann Bach as his pupil at
Merseburg and now directed the royal Capelle, an eminent
violinist and prolific composer; and Carl Heinrich (*d.* 1759),
Frederick's Capellmeister and chief composer of opera. Others
were František Benda (*d.* 1786), who succeeded J. G. Graun in
1771; Johann Friedrich Agricola (*d.* 1774), a pupil of Sebastian
Bach, Court composer and eventually (1759) Capellmeister to
Frederick; Johann Philipp Kirnberger (*d.* 1783), another of Sebastian's pupils, composer, theorist and, later, Capellmeister to
Princess Amalia; Christoph Nichelmann (*d.* 1762), second cembalist in the Prussian Capelle; Christoph Schaffrath (*d.* 1763), a
voluminous composer of chamber music and member of the royal
Capelle; and Johann Joachim Quantz (*d.* 1773), Frederick's tutor
for the flute. Some of these masters had strong ties with Italy,
and in their company Christian entered a new world. His father,
the friend of Hasse and his brilliant wife, and an admirer of Graun
and Caldara,[1] had shown himself unresponsive to the idiom in
which they excelled. Opera had precarious vogue in Leipzig, and
though it flourished at Dresden, Bach was infrequently drawn to
what he good-humouredly called its 'Liederchen'. Christian may
have accompanied him on these rare excursions, but was not permitted to wander from the routine his father imposed. Perhaps
Emanuel was as severe in repressing his brother's curiosity and
enthusiasm. Yet restriction was futile: at his door Christian found
Italianized opera in full vigour, surrendered himself to its glamour,
and at an early opportunity exiled himself to Italy to become
perfect in its technique.

On his succession Frederick the Great had set himself to restore
the Opera in his capital, in precarious state since the accession of
his parsimonious father in 1713. The best German actors,
foreign singers, and French dancers were engaged at handsome
salaries; an imposing Opera-house was erected,[2] in which serious
or classical opera was performed on Mondays and Fridays, while
the other evenings were devoted to lighter entertainments.[3] The
foundation-stone of the new building was laid by Frederick on
5 September 1741, and a year later, on 7 December 1742, Graun
conducted the first performance in it, his *Cleopatra e Cesare*,
seated at the clavier, wearing a full wig and red mantle.[4] Until the
outbreak of the Seven Years War, in 1756, Frederick interested
himself closely in the Opera, attended rehearsals, and imposed
upon its company regimental discipline. 'In the Opera-house,

---

[1] Forkel, p. 109. [2] Illustration No. 3.
[3] Marpurg, p. 75f. [4] Schneider, pp. 67, 86.

as in the field', Burney remarked,[1] 'his majesty is such a rigid disciplinarian, that, if a mistake is made in a single movement or evolution, he immediately marks and rebukes the offender; and if any of his Italian troops dare to deviate from strict discipline by adding, altering, or diminishing a single passage in the parts they have to perform, an order is sent *de par le Roi* for them to adhere strictly to the notes written by the composer, at their peril'. The royal martinet, however, was not debarred from interpolating airs of his own composition: as in 1749, when he introduced into Graun's *Coriolano* a tune so popular that it was whistled all over Berlin.[2] Even at the public performances, which began at six o'clock, Frederick stood behind the *maestro di cappella*, in sight of the score, which he frequently looked at, acting as if he were *generalissimo* in the field.[3]

Though Frederick's prejudices would not admit that a German could sing—he declared he would as readily expect pleasure from a neighing horse![4]—the Opera was closed against any but native composers. During his seasons in Berlin Christian heard none but Graun, Hasse, and Agricola. For the Carnival in 1750–51 Graun's *Mitridate* and *Fetonte* were staged, and in March his *Armide*, with ballets by Denis and scenery by Joseph Galli Bibiena, of Parma. In 1752 Graun's *Britannico* was given during Carnival, and in March his *Orfeo*, with ballets and scenery by the same artists. The Carnival of 1753 was marked by the production of Hasse's *Didone abbandonata*, with Pasqualino Bruscolini, the altist, in the principal part, while, in March, Angelo Maria Monticelli came from Dresden to sing in Graun's *Silla*. Agricola's *Cleofide* was given in 1754, and in March Graun produced his *Semiramide*. His *Montezuma* and *Ezio* were staged in 1755, and in 1756 he directed his *I Fratelli nemici* and *Merope*, the last opera given before the outbreak of the Seven Years War smothered the artistic life of Frederick's capital.[5] There was no bar to Christian's fullest enjoyment of these opportunities: the King was at the whole expense of the Opera, and entrance was free. Strangers of distinction were allotted seats according to their degree upon application to the Chamberlain; while any person 'decently dressed' was admitted to the 'vast pit', where thirteen boxes, each seating thirty persons, along with the second and third tiers above, were reserved for ministers, the diplomatic corps, and persons of rank, while the first tier accommodated the court and nobility.[6]

Christian was his brother's pupil in composition as well as for

[1] Burney, p. 212. [2] H.J., p. 58. [3] Burney, p. 216.
[4] *Ibid.*, p. 213. [5] Schneider, pp. 134f. [6] Burney, p. 216.

the clavier, and, according to Gerber, won the applause of Berlin at public performances of his own music.[1] Emanuel preserved a few of Christian's earliest essays—two polonaises, six minuets, and an aria.[2] His Berlin pieces are maturer and already exhibit qualities which distinguished him throughout his career. That he should first select the Concerto in which to express himself was natural: it was popular, while its scheme and content were still sufficiently irregular to add the spice of adventure to his manuscript. Emanuel himself was prolific in this form while Christian was under his roof—concertos for violoncello, flute, oboe, and particularly for clavier.[3] Christian displayed a similar preference, natural in a composer who desired to exhibit himself as a performer; his Berlin compositions, such as survive, are therefore chiefly concerti for clavier and orchestra. Among them are five, the autograph of which is in the Preussische Staatsbibliothek[4]; preserved by Emanuel, they are definitely assigned to the years preceding Christian's departure for Italy. Scored for strings, they are all in three movements, the first *Allegro* or *Allegro assai* or *Allegretto*, the second *Andante* or *Adagio*, and the last *Allegro* or *Presto*. The scheme of the first movements follows the example of Vivaldi, introduced to Germany by Sebastian Bach—the theme is stated (*tutti* and solo) in the tonic, modulates to the dominant, returns to the tonic, and concludes with a reprise of the first *tutti*. The middle movements do not display similar uniformity, while the last are built like the first, but more concisely.[5] We remark the ear for melody which was one of Christian's characteristics, and not infrequently are reminded that he was the son of his mighty parent: for instance, in the first movement of the Concerto in F minor:

---

[1] Gerber, i. 83.
[2] They are named in the Catalogue (1790) of his library. Schwarz (p. 406) describes them as 'kleine, unbedeutende Stückchen aus zwei Perioden zu 8 Takten bestehend'. I have failed to find them in the Preuss. Staatsbibliothek.
[3] Cf. Wotquenne, pp. 1, 59, 60.
[4] Cf. *infra*, p. 298.
[5] Cf. Schökel, p. 27 ; Schwarz, p. 433.

Again, the last movement of the Concerto in D minor:

The Italian influence of the Opera-house is also apparent; for instance, the middle movement of the Concerto in F minor:

The autograph improbably represents the total of Christian's Berlin essays in the Concerto form. Indeed, the Preussische Bibliothek possesses the manuscript of another, in F minor, for clavier and strings, labelled 'riveduto dal Sigr. C. P. E. Bach'.[1] Another, in A major,[2] also appears to date from this period, though its technique is more brilliant and its material more mature:

[1] *Infra*, p. 301.   [2] *Infra*, p. 300, No. 12.

Christian apparently did not compose a clavier sonata under his
brother's eye—a neglect due, perhaps, to the fact that the sonata
form was still in the stage of experiment at Emanuel's hands.[1] But
a Sonata in F major 'a Flauto traverso e Cembalo concertato' may
date from this period.[2] To it would also appear to belong a choral
ode, *L'Olimpe*, composed 'pour l'anniversaire du jour de naissance
du Roi',[3] three choruses with an accompaniment of strings, horns,
and clarinets, a vigorous and tuneful paean which Frederick may
have accepted from the son of a father whom he held in high esteem.
If so, we have in it one of the earliest examples of music for the
clarinet, an instrument in whose use Christian was a pioneer.[4]

It is improbable that Christian's position in his brother's household was merely that of pupil; his host could not afford to keep
him in idleness. Emanuel's post in the Capelle did not require an
assistant, but Christian probably found occupation in that organization and also gave his brother assistance with his pupils. So
precarious a livelihood could not satisfy a young man approaching

[1] Cf. Schökel, p. 39.   [2] *Infra*, p. 332.   [3] *Infra*, p. 249.
[4] Marpurg does not name a clarinettist among the members of Frederick's
Capelle.

his twentieth year, while Christian's eagerness to enlarge his knowledge and experience added another cause of restlessness. But the circumstances that attended his departure from Berlin are obscure. Writing twenty years later, Emanuel annotated his brother's name in the Genealogy with the remark: 'reiste ao. 1754 nach Italien'. Gerber, still later, discovered a motive:[1] 'in ihm [Christian] die Bekanntschaften verschiedener ital. Sängerinnen die Lust erwecken Italien zu sehen'. Forkel, at about the same period (1782), told the same story:[2] 'er mit vielen italienischen Sängerinnen bekannt wurde, deren eine ihn beredete mit ihr nach Italien zu gehen'. The implication of gallantry invited romantic elaboration, and Elise Polko provided it in a composition (1860) unsurpassed for audacious invention. According to her narrative, bored by the lessons he was obliged to give, out of humour with dull pupils whose stiff fingers he was goaded to rap, and repelled by the prospect of passing his life as an organist in some obscure German community, Christian found relaxation under the *beaux yeux* of Benedetta Emilia Molteni, *prima donna* of the Berlin Opera, on whose arias he preferred to write fugues rather than apply himself to serious duty. The lady married Agricola, Frederick's Hofcomponist, and the pair were hindered by their coachman's death from starting for a honeymoon in Italy. Christian snatched his opportunity, concealed his round and boyish face under a false beard, secured the place of the dead Jehu, and drove his Emilia and her husband to Milan, only removing his disguise on Italian soil.[3]

In this farrago of fiction is concealed a substratum of fact. Emanuel was not disposed to extend his generosity for an indefinite period, and perhaps showed himself alert rather than discriminating in his quest of an organ-loft. The Molteni's marriage to Agricola is certainly a historical fact, though it took place in 1751, some years before Christian's alleged exploit. Nor, in face of more contemporary references, can the implication of impetuous gallantry be evaded. Christian was an engaging fellow, good-looking, eager, with a gift for making friendships which captivated both sexes equally and, in after life, made him 'der Liebling der Engländer'.[4] But that his life was immoral at any period of its duration is an innuendo no evidence supports.[5] At the moment,

---

[1] Gerber, i. 83.
[2] For., p. 150. So also Bitter, ii. 142 ; A.D.B., i. 747.
[3] Polko, p. 194.   [4] For., p. 150. See Illustrations Nos. 4 and 7.
[5] In the *Imperial Dictionary of Universal Biography* G. A. Macfarren did not scruple to speak of the 'sensuality' of Christian's disposition. Mendel's *Conversations-Lexikon* declares him a drunkard as well.

undoubtedly, his altar fed a purer flame, and his association with the foreign singers of the Berlin Opera-house is an accurate indicator of the serious purposes that swayed him. Whether the prospect of tuition at Padre Martini's hands already lured him cannot be decided. But for Italy he longed with passionate ardour, proposing to drink deep of her wells of wisdom and experience. If he entered Italy with Molteni, or another, the association was due to her art rather than the enthralment of her graces.

It is altogether unlikely that Christian made the long and costly journey without the prospect of welcome or employment at the end of it. One or other of the many Italians in Frederick's service may have been his introducer to the Milanese Maecenas in whose employ we find him bound in 1757. If Martini at Bologna was his goal, his father's name, his brother's repute, even Frederick's intervention, may have afforded the passport. The need for migration at least is clear: the storm-clouds were gathering and the ample revenues of the Berlin Opera-house were marked for pruning. On 1 January 1754, Baron von Schwertz, one of the directors, writes to his sovereign:

> 'Sire, j'ai communiqué au Maître de Ballets les ordres de V. M., qu'Elle ne veut absolument rien payer pour les répétitions, et voici la lettre qu'il m'écrit: Les Choristes et les Comparses ne viennent jamais au Théatre qu'on ne les paye. Il m'est impossible de rien rabatre sur les dépenses des représentations que j'ai déjà réduites par mon économie de 700 écus, où elles étoient, à 400 écus. Je me mets aux pieds de V. M. pour lui représenter que le bien de la chose exige qu'Elle paye les répétitions générales et particulières à part, sans lesquelles nous ne pouvons ni devons risquer de donner un Opéra.'[1]

Another theory presents itself: in the following April (1754) Frederick instructed his agent in Paris to recruit the Berlin Ballet with 'ein Freudentöchterchen mit schelmischen Augen, einem artigen Gesichtchen und einem feinen Wuchse, die wohl Lust hätte, auf unserm Theater in Berlin Cabriolen zu machen'.[2] At the moment, Frederick was superintending the production of Graun's *Montezuma*,[3] for which he had written the libretto, and Christian may have been dispatched, like the recruiting sergeants of an earlier reign, to procure the materials Berlin required.

These speculations, however, though they may suggest the public circumstances of his departure, fail to reveal the compulsion of Christian's own character. His letters patently declare that,

---

[1] Schneider, Beilage XXII.   [2] Ibid., p. 144.
[3] Frederick proposed to make Cortez the villain of the plot, and thereby to afford Graun opportunity 'lâcher en musique même quelques lardons contre la barbarie de la religion catholique' (Schneider, p. 145).

like his father, he was swayed by an imperative inclination to perfect himself in his art. His eye may or may not have been fixed on Bologna and the great teacher under whose charge we find him almost immediately placed. But, like his father's career, his own displays such clear and confident progress along a self-mapped course, that we cannot hesitate to conclude that Christian left Berlin at his own time and for a purpose clearly formed.

Emanuel's note in the Genealogy gives 1754 as the year of Christian's exodus. But there are considerations which point rather to 1756, a date which provides a practical reason for Christian's departure, and incidentally furnishes the feminine companionship that is alleged. Graun's *Merope*, produced on 27 March 1756, was the last opera given before Frederick took the field in the Seven Years War[1] and concluded the great days of the Berlin Opera. After the war an impoverished exchequer forbade the extravagances of a former time. Frederick came rarely to Berlin and showed little of his former interest. 'For seven years', he wrote in 1770, 'the Russians, Austrians, and French led me such a dance that I have lost my taste for the ballet and theatre.'[2] The cessation of the Opera would turn Christian's face to other skies, while, as a Saxon subject, residence in Berlin threatened complications he would desire to avoid. Nor need he undertake an unguided journey to an unknown goal. Giovanna Astrua, a native of Turin, one of the stars of the Berlin stage since 1747, fell ill early in 1756, and, after the production of Graun's *Merope*, lost her voice so completely that Frederick awarded her a pension of 1,000 Rth., permitting her to recuperate in her native Italy, where she died in 1758.[3] If Christian accompanied her, a love-intrigue becomes a companionship of mutual accommodation. He was recently turned twenty and not indifferent to feminine charm. But, for the moment, art was his only loadstone, Italy his single mistress.[4]

[1] Schneider, p. 147.   [2] H.J., p. 59.   [3] Schneider, pp. 119, 147.
[4] The evidence for 1754 as the year of Christian's journey is, at first sight and perhaps definitely, conclusive. Emanuel Bach and Gerber both give it, and Marpurg records the event in a section of his first volume (p. 505) bearing the imprint 1755. But Emanuel's note was written long after the event, Gerber's statement has no independent authority, and the date of imprint on Marpurg's title-page does not necessarily indicate the actual year of publication. The matter is not of great importance, except in so far as it elucidates the circumstances of Christian's departure.

CHAPTER II

MILAN

BACH announces himself from Italy, early in 1757, in a letter to Padre Martini at Bologna:[1]

Most reverend Father and honoured master,
Now that I am in Naples, I must fulfil at least a part of my duty by giving your Reverence news of my arrival, with a letter from a friend in Bologna, who complains that he has had no communication from me. So, I am afraid your Reverence may be displeased with me, supposing me remiss in my duty and neglectful of my professions of service; for in the letter I wrote to my friend, which he says he has not received, were others addressed to yourself acknowledging my obligations to you, which are considerable. I intended to visit Bologna last month to kiss your hand, but Chevalier Litta's particular favour granted me another month's stay here, owing to the inclement weather. However, in the middle of February I hope to find myself at Bologna.

I was astonished to see the Roman[2] in the street here dressed in the habit of the Conservatorio.[3] The reason for the change I do not understand, nor did the Roman vouchsafe one. If your Reverence has any commands for me I await them anxiously; you know with what consideration I shall receive them. So, kissing your hand obediently, I remain always

Your Reverence's most humble and devoted servant,
Naples, 18 January 1757. G. C. Bach.

The letter reveals Bach's situation. He was dependent on a patron's approval of his movements, and contemplated a course of instruction at Martini's hands at Bologna, apparently in continuation of a curriculum already begun. Chevalier Count Agostino Litta, a Milanese noble of wealth, maintained a private Cappella, and had both inclination and means to further the musical education of a young genius who roused his interest, and for whom his letters reveal genuine regard. By what avenues Bach had been led to him is not apparent. But, until he secured an independent income in 1761, the Count maintained and treated him with brotherly affection. He was, in fact, little more than seven years Bach's senior.[4] His father, Count Antonio, was a noble of high military

---

[1] Bach's letters to Martini, and others relating to him, are preserved in the Liceo Musicale at Bologna. They are in Italian, a language in which Bach must be supposed to have acquired proficiency in Berlin.
[2] 'il Romano', presumably a common acquaintance at Bologna.
[3] 'in abito di Conservatorista', i.e. of one of the Naples institutions.
[4] He was born on 13 March 1728. I am indebted to Signore Villani, Superintendent of the Archivio di Stato, Milan, for information regarding the Litta family.

rank; his mother, Donna Paola Visconti Borromeo Arese, the daughter of Count Giulio Visconti Borromeo Arese, a prominent public man. Count Agostino was the younger of their two sons, himself a Knight of Jerusalem and the Golden Key, and a Magnate of the Kingdom of Hungary and Transylvania. Forty years earlier, under different circumstances, Bach's father had formed as helpful a friendship with the young Prince Leopold of Anhalt-Cöthen.[1]

Giovanni Battista Martini,[2] now past his fiftieth year, was universally recognized as one of the most informed and scientific musicians of his generation. After a novitiate spent in the Franciscan convent at Lago, he was ordained in 1722, and three years later returned to his native Bologna as *maestro di cappella* of the Franciscan church.[3] Here he acquired a library of unusual completeness, and from it a mass of knowledge which gave him primacy among his contemporaries. His reputation extended over Europe and brought him into touch with its prominent personalities, Frederick the Great among them. Scholars sought him from all parts, whom he instructed in the traditions of the Roman school his own compositions illustrate, a characteristic of which, as of Sebastian Bach's, was the melodious movement of their separate parts.[4] His generous, eclectic outlook was evidenced in 1770 by his warm reception of Mozart, whose 'premature and almost supernatural talents' Burney, then in Bologna, also admired, remarking at the same time the infirm constitution, swollen legs, hacking cough, and sickly countenance of the veteran,[5] who, none the less, outlived Bach and survived till 1784, having triumphantly conducted three volumes of his *Storia della musica* to the threshold of the Middle Ages.

Bach's sojourn at Naples indicates that the interests which drew him to Italy were still active, and that the exigencies of a livelihood, or the discipline of Martini, had not wholly diverted him to music of another kind. Naples boasted San Carlo, one of the largest and most famous Opera-houses in Italy. Her three music schools[6] were the models of similar institutions in Italy and elsewhere: Santa Maria di Loreto, San Onofrio a Capuana, and the Conservatorio della Pietà de' Turchini. They received boys between the ages of eight and twenty, who, excepting such as paid fees, were bound for a period of eight years. San Onofrio maintained about 100 scholars, La Pietà 120, Santa Maria 200, distinguished respectively by uniforms of white, blue, and white with

[1] Cf. T.B., p. 116.   [2] Illus. No. 5.   [3] Illus. No. 6.   [4] Cf. Grove, iii. 333.
[5] Burney, p. 42.   [6] A fourth was converted to other uses in 1744.

a black sash. Especially frequented as nurseries for young composers, they also imparted instruction in singing and playing. On
his visit to San Onofrio, Burney found on the first flight of stairs
a trumpeter 'screaming upon his instrument till he was ready to
burst'; on the second flight, a French horn 'bellowing in the same
manner'; and, in the common practice-room, a 'Dutch concert'
of seven or eight harpsichords, a larger number of violins, and
several vocalists, all performing different pieces and in different
keys, while others were working exercises in harmony, a jumble of
activities which Burney supposed convenient to the house, and to
the scholars, in so far as it taught them to concentrate, but otherwise productive of the 'slovenly coarseness' he remarked in their
public performances. Even the beds in the dormitories served as
seats for harpsichords; but the flutes, oboes, and other wind
instruments had a room to themselves, while the trumpets and
horns were exiled to the stairs or the top of the house. Burney also
noticed sixteen youthful *castrati* housed in warmer apartments,
for fear of colds, which might render their delicate voices unfit for
exercise, or even endanger them.[1]

Italy's musical primacy in the eighteenth century was due as
much to the excellence of her schools as to the natural disposition
of her people.[2] In both characteristics Naples was pre-eminent.
She had nurtured the Scarlattis, Pergolesi, Porpora, Cimarosa,
Durante, Leo, Traetta, Feo, Paisiello, and Sacchini. She claimed
also the two most famous names of the mid-eighteenth century—
Jommelli and Piccinni. The latter, Gluck's rival, quitted San
Onofrio only three years before Bach's visit; his *Zenobia*, produced
at San Carlo in 1756, followed by as signal successes at Rome,
announced a new star in the operatic firmament. Burney met both
composers in the autumn of 1770; Piccinni gave him information
regarding the Neapolitan schools, while he assisted at the *première*
of Jommelli's *Armida* in San Carlo. He was impressed by the
brilliant auditorium, the spacious stage, the magnificence of the
scenery, dresses, and decorations, embellishments in which he preferred Naples to Paris. But he was dismayed by the noisy inattention of the audience, so excessive that 'neither the voices nor
instruments' could be heard distinctly. He was told that 'on
account of the King and Queen being present, the people were
much less noisy than on common nights. There was not a hand
moved by way of applause during the whole representation,
though the audience in general seemed pleased with the music.'[3]
Samuel Sharp, visiting Naples five years before (1765), also drew

Burney, p. 63.   [2] Cf. Rolland, p. 176.   [3] Burney, p. 69.

attention to the ill-behaviour of the audience,[1] but received a rebuke from Joseph Baretti for his 'solemnity of scolding, as if we were committing murder when we are talkative in the pit, or form ourselves into card parties in our boxes'. Caffarello, who showed displeasure at the audience's chattering, Baretti remarked with satisfaction, 'was soon taught better manners. . . . He was taken to jail in his Macedonian accoutrements for several nights as soon as the opera was over, and brought from the jail to the stage every evening, until by repeated efforts he deserved universal acclamation'.[2]

It cannot be accidental that Bach's letters to Martini infrequently refer to his operatic interests. His reticence leaves the impression that Martini, like Litta, preferred him to train his talents for a career less dazzling, but more assured. He was, in fact, assiduous in the composition of liturgical pieces, and in 1760 briefly bound himself to the service of the church. Meanwhile, he was at Naples, studying the technique of Opera in its principal seat. Burney, who heard Bach's first English operas a few years later, while he remarked 'the science of his father and brother in his harmony', found 'the Neapolitan school . . . manifest in his cantilena'.[3] Its characteristics were homophonic writing, melodic charm, and the prominence of the Aria, standing out brilliantly from the *recitativo secco*,[4] qualities conspicuous in Bach's scores, supplemented by a peculiarly rich and facile orchestral technique.

Bach's promise to revisit Bologna was fulfilled. He spent March and the Easter festival with Martini, and announced his return to Milan in the last days of April:

Most reverend Father, *maestro*, and revered patron,
    That I may not neglect my duty (or fail to acknowledge)[5] my obligations to your Reverence, I send news of my safe arrival, by the grace of God, in Milan, where I am treated with consideration and much kindness by my patrons.[6] They are highly pleased with my studies under you and look for great results from them. Chevalier Agostino Litta is anxious to do some service agreeable to you, as an expression of his gratitude for the trouble your Reverence has taken on my behalf. May I beg you to honour me with a letter, and to give me permission to take advantage of the valuable counsel you have imparted to me?[7] Wishing you complete health,
    I am your Reverence's most humble and obedient servant,
                                    Giov. Christiano Bach.
Milan, 30 April 1757.

---

[1] Sharp, pp. 77 f. [2] Baretti, i. 303. [3] Bur. iv. 483.
[4] Cf. Adler, *Handbuch der Musikgeschichte* (1924), p. 645.
[5] The MS. is illegible here.
[6] 'quei Signr. Cavagliere.' In his letter of 21 May 1757 Bach calls them 'questi Eccellent^mi Signori', and clearly indicates the musical amateurs of Litta's circle.
[7] *i.e.* by submitting his compositions to Martini's correction.

By the same post Litta directed a letter to Martini exhibiting the warmest concern for the welfare of his *protégé*:

Most reverend Father and *maestro*,

Our Bach has come back in good health, and everlastingly indebted to you for the knowledge you have imparted to him. From the continual protestations he makes to me daily, he will never cease to be grateful to you; his only grief is that he is so far from his revered master. I hope he will be the better pleased with us here in the future;[1] for we are seriously considering how to settle him suitably in his profession. Meanwhile, I am under a heavy obligation for the inconvenience you have suffered through your care for him, for which I am, and shall always remain, with all consideration and respect,

Your Reverence's most devoted and obliged servant,

Milan, 30 April 1757.   Conte Cav. Agostino Litta.

Litta's intentions for his *protégé* were not immediately fulfilled. That the organistship of Milan's Duomo was in contemplation is evident, and Bach assiduously equipped himself for its duties. A month after his return to Milan he writes again to Martini:

Most reverend Father, and revered patron,

I received your esteemed letter with much regard, and read in it the kindness with which you still favour me. You wish to know how I have been received in Milan. I can assure you I have been welcomed by my patrons here with consideration quite beyond my deserts. They continue their favours, especially the Chevalier, whose kindness is always on the alert for my advancement and happiness. He is now trying to obtain for me a secure and permanent situation in Milan, and I hope he will soon succeed. I am on the best of terms with Signore Balbi.[2] The letter you received from him had reference to a musical passage on which you had given your opinion. I maintained that it was a licence and irregular, as your esteemed letter declared, while Signore Balbi held the opposite opinion. I was not inclined to prolong the argument, especially because Signore Balbi did not appear altogether pleased to discuss musical problems with me. It will be a lesson to me for the future not to engage in similar contentions, nor should I have done so in the present case with any but a friend, such as Signore Balbi. I thought I ought to send you an account of what took place, so that you may know the actual facts, and not suppose I was trying to play the doctor without ground to stand on. Of your generous offer to help me I shall make full use, and should I need advice, or, more accurately, correction, I shall not fail to trouble you with my compositions for improvement.[3] At the moment I am working at the *Officio*, having finished the *Invitatorio* and *Dies irae*. So, begging your Reverence to convey my compliments to my patrons the other reverend Fathers, and to all the school, I subscribe myself always and unchangeably

Your Reverence's and my revered patron's most humble and obedient servant,

Milan, 21 May 1757.   Giov. Christiano Bach.

[1] 'Spero sarà contento di nostra casa molto piu in avvenire'.
[2] Probably Ignazio Balbi, a composer and singer, who about this time left Italy for Lisbon. Cf. Gerber, i, p. 101.
[3] 'con qualche composizione per essere purificata'.

Bach's *Invitatorio* and the three 'Lezioni' of the *Officio per gli morti*, composed in 1757, exist in his autograph, with thirteen other works of similar character, in four volumes now in the Hamburg Staats- und Universitätsbibliothek.[1] They were brought from England by Friedrich Chrysander, having previously belonged to Vincent Novello,[2] and, before him, to Miss Emma Jane Greenland, to whom Bach dedicated his Six Sonatas for the Harpsichord (Op. 16); she probably acquired Bach's MS. at the sale of his effects in 1782.[3] The *Invitatorio* (*Regem cui omnia vivunt*),[4] modal in character, is scored for four voices, strings, oboes, and horns; while the three 'Lezioni' (*Parce mihi, Domine*; *Taedet animam meam*; and *Manus tuae*) are written for Bass or Soprano Solo, with similar accompaniment. The *Dies irae*, of which several manuscripts exist,[5] is a considerable work scored for double chorus, strings, oboes, and corni da caccia, and exhibits the composer's dramatic vein. It opens with a short orchestral prelude:

which leads to a declamatory *Adagio* for the two choirs (see p. 20).

A significant fact emerges from the manuscript of these composi-

[1] Sig. Ms. ND. VI. 540.
[2] The cover of vols. 1 and 2 is inscribed: 'Vincent Novello, 69 Dean St., Soho Square. This book contains some curious and rare scores by C. Bach in his own handwriting.'
[3] Copies of the Hamburg pieces, and a great number of others of similar character, are at Einsiedeln. Augur Greenland witnessed Bach's signature to his Will.
[4] *Infra*, p. 208.   [5] *Infra*, p. 202.

tions: the scores of the *Invitatorio* and *Officio*, both of them dated 1757 in Bach's hand, conclude with the ascription 'LD ac BMV'

(Laus Deo ac Beatae Mariae Virgini). Bach therefore had been already received into the Roman Church. It would be agreeable to suppose his conversion an act of conviction. Indeed, his brother's comment in the Genealogy, '*inter nos* machte es anders als der ehrliche Veit', may be interpreted to imply, that whereas the worthy Veit, ancestor of their lineage, *came back* to Germany to preserve his religion, Christian *left* his native land to find it. On the other hand, he does not reveal himself as a man swayed by religious impulses, though, in the altered circumstances of his later career, he remained loyal to the Church of his adoption. His letters to Martini so clearly imply his acceptance of Martini's creed, that his conversion must have followed quickly upon his arrival in Italy.[1] Meanwhile, another letter to his mentor reveals him indefatigably attacking the problems of a not yet familiar technique:

Most reverend Father and revered patron,

I cannot think that a letter written some time ago to your Reverence has been lost, and so conclude that your many occupations have delayed your esteemed reply, which I look forward to receiving with much anticipation. When you write, will you tell me whether in *a cappella* music consecutive fourths are allowed between the parts, though the Bass

[1] Inquiries at Bologna and Milan have failed to elicit any facts bearing on the matter.

moves in contrary motion?[1] I found a not disagreeable instance in a score
of Signore Perti,[2] and have followed his example, but feel that I am being
strongly criticized for doing so. In the second place, please tell me whether
one may proceed from the third to the fifth by direct motion, or use consecutive fourths, in 8-part *a cappella* music. Lastly, why must one end
a minor[3] composition on a major chord? Pardon, your Reverence, the
trouble I give you. I should not dare to inconvenience you, did I not
remember your generous promise to assist me in any difficulties I may
meet with. I beg you to continue your favour to me, and declare myself
your Reverence's, my most revered patron's,

most humble and devoted servant,

G. C. Bach.

Milan, 24 June 1757.

Consecutive Fourths.

Signore Perti's passage *a 3 a cappella.*

From Third to Fifth *a 8 Reali a cappella.*

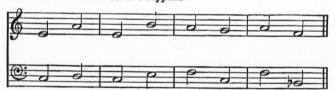

A *Tantum ergo* for Tenor and orchestra is also among Bach's
ecclesiastical exercises in 1757,[4] and in the hot July of that year he
was occupied with the rehearsal of a *Messa* (*Requiem aeternam*),

---

[1] 'se sia permesso di fare a cappella due Quarte fra le parti, con tutto che il Basso
non abbia l'accompagnamento di sorte.'

[2] Giacomo Antonio Perti (1661–1756), one of the most distinguished church
composers of the seventeenth century.

[3] 'in 3♭.'   [4] *Infra*, p. 210.

for eight voices, strings, horns, oboes, and organ, which he had begun at Bologna under Martini's supervision.[1] It had a full rehearsal on Friday 29 July; on the following day Bach sent Martini news of it:[2]

Most reverend Father, and revered patron,
The delay in the arrival of a letter from you is due, no doubt, to your many occupations. But I must not fail to tell you that in Count Litta's house here yesterday a rehearsal took place of the *Messa* I began under your auspices. The success of the performance and the universal applause the work received make me realize my indebtedness to your Reverence; for this satisfactory result is wholly due to your encouragement and instruction. I cannot sufficiently tell you how impressed are Count Litta's household, and the entire musical circle here, by your Reverence's learning. His Excellency has just received a letter from you. He begs me send you his greeting, and to assure you there was no need to thank him. By the next post you will receive another letter from him and the rest of the chocolate. He hopes you will continue to give me your invaluable advice and experience. May I, too, beg permission occasionally to send you my work for correction and criticism? There is no one in Milan to compare with your Reverence; all who have looked at the eight-part work I did under your instruction are amazed at the remarkable and exact training I received from you. Your Reverence, I hope, is assured of my veneration, and of my earnest desire to profit by your counsel; for, as I have already written, and as I have repeatedly declared in Milan, the success of my *Messa* is entirely due to the help you gave me. I beseech you, therefore, not to stint me with your letters. You may be sure neither his Excellency nor I will be backward in expressing to your Reverence the gratitude we feel. The kindness and affection I receive from the quality here prevents me from coming to Bologna to consult you in person. But the recollection of your generous promise to help me in any musical matter assures me that your assistance, of which I stand so much in need, will be available; its value can never be approached by anyone else. Pray command me in anything in which I can be serviceable to your Reverence, continue your goodness to me, and favour me with a letter to tell me you are willing to correct my work. Relying on your Reverence's continuing good-will,
I am your Reverence's most grateful servant and pupil,
G. C Bach.
Milan, 30 July 1757.

A letter from Litta to Martini, revealing affectionate concern in their young *protégé*, explains Bach's reference to the gift of chocolate:

Most reverend Father, *maestro*, and honoured sir,
Neither words nor deeds can adequately thank your Reverence, or requite the kind unwearying help you offered our young Giovannino Bach

[1] MSS. of it are at Einsiedeln and Munich. Cf. *infra*, p. 208.
[2] The original is in the National-Bibliothek, Vienna. A German text of it is in La Mara, i. 256.

while he was with you at Bologna, where your incomparable knowledge instructed him in the advanced stages of musical science. May his recognition of what he owes to you, and mine too—(for I consider myself equally favoured in him)—measure our inexpressible gratitude. To mark the disinterested kindness of your Reverence, I beg you to accept a small present of home-made chocolate. Half a *rubbio*[1] goes meanwhile by post, on which I have fully paid duty and carriage; as much more will follow later. If it has your approval, I will give myself the pleasure of renewing the small tribute annually, as an affectionate acknowledgement of your great kindness to Giovannino in response to my particular request. On the morning of the 29th inst. a rehearsal of his solemn Requiem Mass is to take place in my house; you know it well. I hope it will extort praise even from the most pedantic and grudging Aristarci. You shall have speedy and accurate news of it. Pray continue to accord me your valued regard, and be no less liberal in commanding me than you have been in giving me pleasure. I remain always, and with genuine regard and friendship sign myself,

> Your Reverence's most obedient and obliged servant,
> Conte Cav. Agostino Litta.

Milan, 20 July 1757.

Martini replied, that 'his highest reward was Bach himself',[2] and received the remaining half *rubbio* of chocolate, with a more detailed account of the rehearsal than Bach had offered:

Most reverend Father, *maestro*, and honoured sir,
    I send you franked the second half *rubbio* of chocolate, and with the greater pleasure on learning your approval of the first half, which I sent you as a slight token of the obligation which, no less than our beloved Giovannino Bach, I take pleasure in acknowledging for having trained and perfected him in the style and taste of *perfetta musica*. The pupil's glory is reflected on his teacher, for you have made a *maestro* of him. So your Reverence will be gratified to learn that universal applause attended the rehearsal of his *Officio* and *Messa di Requiem* here on the 29th of last month by sixty-four singers and players. The leading music critics and connoisseurs were present, who all combined to praise the composition, declaring it correct, impressive, clear, eloquent, and deliciously harmonious. From their faces it was evident that their praise was sincere, and the unanimous good reports they have circulated afford further proof. Bach admits that he owes his success to your profound teaching, and I repeat the acknowledgement, with my own heartfelt thanks. When there is occasion and need I therefore beg you to give him the safe guidance of your counsel, retaining for me a friendship which, on my side, will impel me to fulfil your esteemed commands, and deepen the unwavering esteem with which I sign myself,

> Your Reverence's most devoted and obedient servant,
> Conte Cav. Agostino Litta.

Milan, 13 August 1757.

---

[1] A *rubbio*=28 lbs.　　　　　　[2] Schwarz, p. 409.

Bach's was now a name of credit in Milan, resounding in circles where his father's was barely known. Late in August a performance of his much-praised *Messa* was given in the sumptuous interior of Tibaldi's San Fedele.[1] Again his success was conspicuous, as he informed Martini a week later:

Most reverend Father, *maestro*, and revered patron,

It distresses me not to have been favoured with a letter from your Reverence, on account of the deep respect and regard I bear you, and still more because of my anxiety to avail myself of your valuable advice. I know my defects, but am consoled when I recall your gracious promise to Chevalier Litta and myself, at all times to afford me the help I so much need. On the 23rd of this month I performed my music in San Fedele, and, thanks to God and your teaching, won much applause. I had no doubt that the composition would be successful, for it was written under your direction, and the wish grows stronger in me to continue to profit by your authoritative teaching. I propose therefore shortly to send you a piece in eight parts on which I am now engaged; after it has your correction I can venture to submit it here without fear of criticism in the slightest detail. His Excellency the Chevalier bids me send you his respects, and, hopeful of enjoying your favours, I declare myself unchangeably

Your Reverence's most humble and obedient servant,

Giov. Christiano Bach.

Milan, 30 August 1757.

The *Pater noster* on which Bach desired his master's opinion has not survived. Martini declared his readiness to receive it, and on September 6, almost on its composer's twenty-second birthday, it was dispatched to Bologna:

Most reverend Father and honoured patron,

I give you infinite thanks for your kindness in sending me so generous a letter, and am much beholden to you for the instruction it conveys. With this I am making bold to send you a composition in eight parts, in which, I admit, my zeal has outrun my ability. But I have learnt that a man who does not courageously adventure never makes progress, and, moreover, have so long experienced your Reverence's indulgence to your pupils, that I have no fear. I should like to have sent you at the same time a *Kyrie* in eight parts, but have not time to finish it, and so must keep it for another occasion.[2] For the present, therefore, I beg you to look over the *Pater noster*; it will be seen by many of our professors here, and I would rather not bring it forward until your Reverence has done me the honour to correct it. Thereafter I dare show it to anybody. I beg you to pardon the liberty I take, and to believe that I am ready to execute your gracious commands in any way in which I can be of service. The Chevalier, who desires me to convey his respects, will not fail to protect one who has your recommendation. Many professors here

---

[1] Illustration No. 8.   [2] *Infra*, p. 208.

charge me with their compliments to you, and I do myself honour in
subscribing myself

Your Reverence's most humble and obedient servant,

Giov. C. Bach.

Milan, 6 September 1757.

P.S. Please remove a difficulty which has presented itself. In *a cappella*
music may one resolve a discord on the second quarter of the beat? e.g.

Would it therefore be permissible to write the following in eight parts
a cappella?

Martini solved these problems, and Bach wrote again:

Most reverend Father, *maestro*, and honoured patron,

Another of your esteemed letters has reached me, and, with it, the
Pater noster. I am more than ever in your debt for the assistance I so
much require. I shall not fail to apply your corrections and wise counsels,
and, as I readily admit my sore need of it, shall always receive even your
severest treatment of my music with satisfaction. I say this in earnest
and not lightly. To tell you the truth about the situation here: Chevalier
Litta, my patron, has a habit of making me do things I have never attempted. Some time ago he bade me write a *Pater noster* in eight parts,
and, when I told him I had done nothing of the kind without assistance,
he answered, 'You must try'. I told him I could not pass it without your
correction, and, whenever he asked for it, told him you still have it. He
is at present out of town hunting and will be away all next week. So,
would your Reverence be good enough to favour me with a couple of
lines to say that I can show the *Pater noster* to the Chevalier after I have
made the corrections you have marked? Would to heaven I could return
to Bologna for the benefit of your valuable teaching! But I am dependent
on those above me, and cannot act as I would choose. So, I beg once
more that you will continue to assist me and point out my mistakes; for

I assure you, without your help I should not dare to put myself forward as a composer.

I take the liberty to burden you with an *Introito a* 7 with *canto fermo*, the latter *scartato e mutato*, the form they use here, as I am told by Signore Balbi and several others. I have also been working at a *Magnificat* in eight parts,[1] and have nearly finished it. I shall make bold to send it by Signore Pietro Tibaldi, who will shortly finish his engagement here. I am trying to do a good deal of writing, partly for my own improvement and profit, partly to please my patron, who takes the utmost pleasure in what I do and never fails to encourage me. Please let me receive the two lines I asked for before my patron returns, and also give me news of your health, which, for my own sake, I hope is fully restored by God's favour. May He repay you for all your goodness to me! Chevalier Litta will not fail to thank you too, or to write to you upon any matter you may command. Forgive me the trouble I give you. Kissing your hands, I declare myself

Ever your Reverence's most humble and devoted servant,

G. C. Bach.

Milan, 22 October 1757.

P.S. Signore Balbi bids me send you his compliments.

Bach's assiduity is patent; his concentration and resolve to get to the root of his art indicate a legacy from his father more precious than his three claviers. If it appears strange that he should still be dependent on a master for instruction, it must be remembered that he was navigating waters for which his previous experience as a Lutheran provided no chart. At no far distance he turned to channels more familiar, but for the moment his proposed career called him to submit to discipline which alone could qualify him for the duties that awaited him. Thus, in answer to Martini's advice, he writes on December 16:

Most reverend Father, *maestro*, and honoured patron,

I have received your highly esteemed letter, and with it the *Requiem* in seven parts. Thank you warmly for the kindness you so consistently show me; your letter has given me the utmost pleasure, containing, as it does, so much to instruct me. As to your advice, that I should study Palestrina, I must tell you that there are few, if any, of his scores here in Milan. I have asked his Excellency Chevalier Litta to have several of them copied. He knows your Reverence has a large number of them, and as you understand better than I do which will be serviceable to me, I doubt not your Reverence will let me have those which will be most helpful, and that herein I can rely on your invariable kindness. The Chevalier begs you to note the cost of copying them; he will unfailingly and at once meet the expense. Pray retain your goodwill for me; I profit much by it, and more than anything it is the object of my desires. May I also receive news of your health? I send you the Chevalier's compliments. He apologizes for not writing to you himself; with his household he is in the country hunting, or waiting on the Duke of Modena, and so cannot

[1] *Infra*, p. 207.

write to you. Signore Balbi sends his compliments, and I declare myself
Ever your Reverence's most humble and devoted servant,
Leinate, in the country,   G. C. Bach.
    16 December 1757.

Litta's musicians evidently accompanied him to entertain his
ducal companion, Francesco III, who through his mother claimed
kinship with the English Guelphs, and now had opportunity to
applaud his host's German *maestro*, their future servant. Bach's
letters to Martini give infrequent indications that his pen was
active in other music than that his master supervised. He was,
however, not idle in other forms, and his chamber music for
Litta's Cappella betrays none of the immaturity he deprecated in
his compositions for the Church. Six string trios and seven sonatas
for violin and clavier date from this period;[1] some, perhaps, were
written for Duke Francesco's entertainment. But Bach's relaxation
was brief: a letter from Milan three months later reveals him
again immersed in his ecclesiastical discipline, and even appointed
to play a conspicuous part in the approaching festival of St. John
Nepomuk, recently (1729) canonized:

Most reverend Father and honoured patron,
    The debt and obligations I owe to your Reverence impel me to tell
you that my patrons have called on me to play a prominent role on the
feast of St. John Nepomuk, to be celebrated here in the great church of
the Minori conventuali di San Francesco. My duty to my protector, my
maestro, and myself compels me to turn to you again, begging your kind
help for the occasion. You already have received, I hope, the *Magnificat*
I sent by the regular post a short time ago. Thanks to the two *Bassi*
supplied by your Reverence's kindness, it is, I think, of some merit, and
I should be grateful if you would look at it, for I really think it will
bring me considerable credit. May I also beg you to examine the eight-
part *Kyrie*,[2] and return both as soon as may be convenient to you?
I have already received the *Credo*[3] and *Dixit Dominus*[4], composed under
your eye, and I shall make bold to send another piece for your judicious
supervision, after which I shall have the greater courage to bring it
forward. I sincerely regret to trouble you so often, but I count on your
indulgence as you increasingly realize the profound respect and regard
I bear you as my honoured teacher. The applause my *Officio per gli morti*
won me here leads me to hope for equal success under similar guidance on
this new occasion. The Chevalier bids me convey his compliments to you
and again recommends me to your goodness. I hope, too, your Reverence
will favour me with the first volume of your great work[5] as soon as it is
published. And so, commending myself once more to your consideration,
I subscribe myself
    Your Reverence's most humble, devoted, and obliged servant,
Milan, 22 March 1758.   Giov. Christiano Bach.

[1] See Them. Catalogue.   [2] *Infra*, p. 208.   [3] *Infra*, p. 202.   [4] *Infra*, p. 202.
[5] The first volume of Martini's *Storia della musica* was published in 1757.

The *Magnificat*, to whose performance Bach refers in a later letter, is scored for two choirs, strings, trumpets, and organ.[1] Motet-like in construction, like the contemporary *Te Deum*, it gives the impression of an intention to modernize old forms. The 'Gloria' concludes with a brilliant 'Amen', but the character of the composition as a whole is indicated by its opening bars:

[1] The autograph, dated 1758, is among the King's Music in the British Museum. The excerpts here and elsewhere in the text are printed by permission of H. M. The King. Copyright is reserved. See Illustration No. 9.

a - ni - ma me - a   Do - mi - num.

me - a,   a - ni - ma me - a   Do - mi - num.

Martini received, approved, and corrected the *Magnificat*, and returned it with suggestions for the improvement of the 'Amen'. Bach acknowledged his advice in a short letter:

Most reverend Father and honoured patron,
    The *Magnificat* has arrived, and I thank you for the trouble you have taken over it. As soon as I have a little time to myself I shall not fail to alter the 'Amen' of the canticle in the manner you suggest, and when it is in order I will return it to you. Do be so kind as to send me the first volume of your great work directly it is published; my anxiety to read it is very great. His Excellency the Chevalier bids me send you his compliments, and once more I subscribe myself
                Your Reverence's most humble, obliged, and devoted servant,
Milan, 28 April 1758.   Giov. Christ. Bach.

A week later Bach writes again, offering a contribution to Martini's well-stocked bookshelves, and propounding new problems:

Most reverend Father, *maestro* and honoured patron,
    I hope you are enjoying unbroken good health. I trouble you with this letter to ask whether I can be of service to you in regard to an old book on the theory of music, entitled *Toscanello in Musica di Messer Piero Aron fiorentino, dell' Ordine Gierosolimitano et Canonico in Rimini, novamente stampato con l'aggiunta da lui fatta e con diligentia corretto.* The year of imprint is not stated.[1] The book was given to me, but I have no use for it. Please tell me if I may send it to you, and at the same time give me good news of yourself. Herewith I humbly subscribe myself
                Your Reverence's most humble and obedient servant,
Milan, 5 May 1758.   Giov. Chr. Bach.

    P.S. In connection with a fugue I wrote under your direction the

    [1] Five editions of Aaron's treatise are noted between 1523 and 1562.

criticism was lately offered, that the answer must enter on the down beat
if the original subject does so: e.g.

I could think of no better answer than to take up my pen and divide the
tempo C into 2/4: e.g.

remarking that I had often seen fugues so written in *a cappella* music, and
that, even if subject and answer both entered on the down beat, the eye
might find the same difficulty. I beg your Reverence to instruct me on
this point. The Chevalier bids me convey his greetings.

Bach's questions reveal his associates' interest in his work and
the growing esteem in which he was held. The performance in the
Franciscan Church, to which he had already referred, enhanced
it. He writes again to Martini in an undated letter:

Most reverend Father and honoured patron,
    For some time past I have been hoping to receive a letter from you,
and I must reassure myself by assuming that your arduous labours, and
they alone, prevent you from favouring me. Still, I must not fail to let
you know that yesterday I rehearsed my *Messa* and Vespers,[1] which are
to be performed on June 22 in the great church of the Minori conventuali
di San Francesco. My music won general applause at the rehearsal, to
the honour of God and of yourself, whose teaching has brought me some
small distinction. The Chevalier passed through Bologna a short time
ago and, I hope, visited you, unless in his urgency he posted on to Rome.
I commend myself eternally to your goodness, for I am deeply conscious
of the benefits I reap from your help. And now, begging you not to forget me when your book is published, I humbly subscribe myself
    Your Reverence's most humble, obliged, and devoted servant,
                                        Giov. Christ. Bach.

        [1] Cf. *infra*, p. 202, '*Domine ad adiuvandum.*'

The public performance of the *Messa* confirmed the success of the rehearsal. With evident pride Bach informed Martini of his triumph:

Most reverend Father and honoured patron,

On Thursday last, June 22, my music was performed in the Franciscan church, and, thanks to God, was most successful. My duty, and the fact that to you I owe my musical being, require me to tell you this. I hope you will experience the pleasure a master must feel when his pupil wins distinction. I am, and for some time have been, longing for one of your esteemed letters. Now that I have a little time to myself I will not fail to write out the compositions you ask for. Some time ago I began to copy the *Dies irae* I wrote last year under your direction, but this year's work intervened and I could not finish it. You must therefore be indulgent with me. Begging with increasing earnestness for your valuable guidance, and hoping for an esteemed letter at your convenience, I sign myself unchangeably

Your Reverence's most humble, devoted, and obliged servant,
Giov. Christ. Bach.

Milan, 1 July 1758.

But Bach's allegiance was already veering to another altar. That his residence at Milan brought him from the outset into touch with its Opera-house may be supposed; but his direct association with it is first revealed in the autumn of 1758, in a letter to Martini:

Most reverend Father and honoured patron,

I am much concerned to hear from Signore Valentini[1] that you have been again troubled with the old flux in your leg. I should have expressed my concern ere this had I not been expecting a letter from you, and had I heard of it sooner. I hope you have by now received a letter from me with my *Pater noster* in eight parts. Your Reverence must take your own time to return it; it will be quite soon enough if you send it back at your own convenience. Signore Pietro Tibaldi, whom you recommended, has done you credit. Cicognani[2] has made himself an immortal name here, and is obliged every evening to repeat my *Aria cantabile*, which he sings very well; the Milan *impresarii* will certainly engage him for the Carnival. Chevalier Litta charges me with his compliments to you, and I commend myself to your kindness. Wishing you a speedy and complete cure of your complaint, I declare myself ever

Your Reverence's most humble and devoted servant,
Giov. Chr. Bach.

Milan, 8 October 1758.

The *Aria cantabile* which procured Bach his earliest success in Opera cannot be identified. Gerber asserts that his *Catone in Utica* was performed at Milan in 1758, and Salvioli[3] repeats the statement, placing the event in the Carnival season. There survives, in fact, in the autograph of the celebrated singer Ludwig Fischer,

[1] Michel Angelo Valentini.
[2] Giuseppe Cicognani, an altist, from Bologna. Cf. Gerber, i. 282.
[3] Salvioli, i. 690.

a Recit. and Aria (Principe, non temer) which bears the date 1758,[1] of which the Aria's words are those of the opening song of *Catone in Utica* (Con sì bel nome in fronte). Bach's excursion into Opera, however, was brief. The next letter to Martini finds him again in his ecclesiastical groove:

Most reverend Father and honoured patron,
I am sending you the book[2] by the hand of Signore Barbieri, professor of music, together with the eight-part *Dies irae* which I composed under your Reverence's supervision. I am sorry not to have done so earlier, but lacked a messenger, the parcel being too large to send by post. I had no time to make a copy of the *Dies irae* myself, so I employed a copyist. If you find slight mistakes in it, therefore, please excuse them. The Chevalier particularly sends you his compliments, and, commending myself to your kindness, I subscribe myself
Your Reverence's most humble, devoted, and obliged servant,
Milan, 29 October 1758.   G. C. Bach.

To the year 1758, besides the *Domine ad adiuvandum*, belong a *Gloria*, *Beatus vir*, and *Laudate pueri* for soprano 'con Sinfonia', dated 12 August 1758.[3] Apparently Bach did not submit them to Martini, or his letters relating to them are lost. He already felt himself on his feet in his chamber music and operatic essays, and his earliest letter in 1759 gives his mentor another instance of his success in the latter *genre*:

Most reverend Father and honoured patron,
Signore Tibaldi has handed me the Palestrina scores you so kindly had copied for me; please let me know the cost, that I may at once repay you. Chevalier Litta sends his compliments and begs to be forgiven for not writing to you; he is extremely occupied, but very willing to assist Signore Filippo Elisi,[4] whom you recommended to him, as circumstances may suggest. Signore Elisi was not well treated by the composer of the first opera presented here, and consequently did not make an appearance. After three or four performances the Chevalier commissioned me to write an Aria for him on the words 'Misero pargoletto',[5] which had the good fortune to meet with approval, as did he, so that he is now much applauded, and has to repeat the Aria every evening. The two books of Ambrosian plain-song have been obtained with difficulty, and almost by accident; had the bookseller been visited a quarter of an hour later they might never have been found anywhere. I will send them by Signore Tibaldi, who returns to Bologna after the Carnival. I looked into them on one point to make sure I had been serviceable to your Reverence and your *protégé*.[6] In conclusion I beg you to retain your goodwill towards me, and to believe me always
Your Reverence's most humble, devoted, and obliged servant,
Milan, January 1759.   Giov. Christ. Bach.

[1] *Infra*, p. 252.   [2] *Supra*, p. 30.   [3] *Infra*, pp. 200, 203, 204, 206.
[4] Elisi later sang in London under Bach. Cf. *infra*, p. 98.
[5] *Infra*, p. 252.   [6] Cf. Bach's letter of 4 May 1759 *infra*.

Returning to Bologna after Easter, Tibaldi carried with him the Ambrosian volumes and a short letter from their donor:

Most reverend Father and honoured patron.

As Signore Tibaldi is willing to convey them, I send you by him the two volumes of Ambrosian plain-song, hoping it will please you to have them. May I beg for an answer to the letter[1] I sent by the young Milanese who so desired to place himself under your direction? I have no time to add more than that I am at your esteemed commands, and that the Chevalier sends you his compliments. And so I subscribe myself

Your Reverence's most humble and obliged servant,

G. C. Bach.

Milan, 4 May 1759.

Three months passed before Bach again reported his activities to Martini:

Most reverend Father and honoured patron,

I hardly dare write to you, remembering my remissness in sending you respectful greeting. But I am not altogether to blame, for until now I have been extremely occupied, to the neglect of my duty. However, you already know that I value your friendship above everything. I am hard at work, but my understanding is slow and does not carry me through my difficulties. Still, I have written an 8-part Te Deum and some Fughette in three or four parts, and as soon as I am at leisure I will give them the advantage of being submitted to your correction. I beg you not to put me in your bad books, for the Chevalier can bear witness that I have been very busy at my composition. So please favour me with your honoured handwriting, or, should your occupations not permit, at least send me a message through Father Cascani, who occasionally writes to me, so that my apprehensions, which are becoming more than I can bear, may be relieved. Your Reverence, I hope, will also favour me with the first volume of your book. I have just begun to study geometrical proportion, the better to understand the contents of so perfect a treatise.[2] The Chevalier bids me convey his respects, and, kissing your hands, I subscribe myself unchangeably

Your Reverence's most humble, devoted, and obliged servant,

Giov. Christ. Bach.

Milan, 7 August 1759.

The autograph of Bach's Te Deum is among the Royal Music in the British Museum. Bearing the date '1758' and scored for double chorus, strings, oboes, horns, trumpets, and timpani, it opens with a short and spirited instrumental prelude of 15 bars:

[1] Apparently lost.
[2] 'a studiare le proporzionali geometriche per poter meglio intendere le belle lezioni che contiene un libro così perfetto.'

The opening clauses of the canticle are declaimed antiphonally by the two choirs and orchestra.

At the words 'Te gloriosus apostolorum chorus' the antiphony
is maintained by solo voices:

The music proceeds to an arresting pause after the words
'Iudex credimus esse venturus', followed by a change of key
and *tempo*:

quos pre - ti - o - so san-gui-ne re - di -

quos pre - ti - o - so san-gui-ne re - di -

quos pre - ti - o - so san-gui-ne re -

quos pre - ti - o - so san-gui-ne re - di -

ni, quos pre - ti - o - so san-gui-ne

ni, quos pre - ti - o - so san-gui-ne

ni, quos pre - ti - o - so san-gui-ne

ni, quos pre - ti - o - so san-gui-ne

an impressive and effective movement written above a pulsing
quaver Continuo. It is followed by a jubilant *Allegro*, in which the
Basses give out a masterful and soaring subject:

The section, one of great animation, is succeeded by a prayerful
movement for *soli*:

From this point the instrumental parts are not inserted in the score. But, about forty bars from the end, Bach adds a new stave marked 'Organo', and brings the work to an end on a prayerful close:

The *Te Deum* is a fine work, restrained, sincere, and charged
with religious feeling; Schubart praised it as 'one of the most
beautiful in Europe'.[1] Meanwhile, it failed to reach Bologna, for
reasons Bach declares in his next letter:

Most reverend Father and honoured patron,
    You must surely think me one who professes much and performs
little, for I have so often said I was sending music to you which you have
not received. It is not for want of intention, I assure you, but of time.
The music is ready, but I have no leisure to copy it, and I want to copy it
myself; for from a copyist a correct text is not to be looked for. The
Chevalier, who charges me with his compliments to you, will bear out my
statement that at the moment I am particularly hard at work. I am busy

---

[1] Schubart, p. 203: 'eines der schönsten, dass wir in Europa besitzen'.

writing a new *Messa* and Vespers[1] for St. Joseph's festival, and have only just begun the *Gloria*. So you will realize that between now and then I have my work before me. This very morning I have set the 'Suscipe deprecationem nostram' as a four-part fugue, and shall make bold to send it to you, along with the 8-part *Te Deum*, that both may receive your correction.

Father Lampugnani,[2] who communicated your favours to me, assured me that I retain your goodwill, which affords me much relief; for the Chevalier gives me hope that I may return to Bologna to resume my studies under your Reverence's expert direction. I hope to find my good *maestro* as ready as of old to bring out his manuscripts for my instruction. I trust the young student the Chevalier commended to you is doing well. He has been in Milan, but I was unable to see him, being then in the country. I beg you to hold me in your regard, and in that hope have the honour to subscribe myself

Your Reverence's most humble, devoted, and obliged servant,
Giov. C. Bach.

Milan, 18 December 1759.

P.S. My best wishes for Christmas and the New Year.

After an unusually brief interval, the Chevalier's behests sent another letter to Bologna. On December 27 Bach writes again:

Most reverend Father and honoured patron,
The Chevalier makes his excuses for not writing in person; he is immersed in the Carnival's amusements and stands on no ceremony with you, whom he believes to be assured of his zeal in your service, and of his readiness to fufil your commands. Your Reverence will remark the interest and celerity he has shown in finding the books you desired. He wishes you to know that he has been approached by a lady who has in her house a youth whom she wishes to study counterpoint with you at Bologna; she has asked for an introduction to you, hoping you will be willing to assist the youth in his studies. The lad is well behaved and not a beginner in music; the Chevalier therefore desires to know whether you can receive him. The lady would like him to come to you this Lent. At the first opportunity I will send the books, and I hope you will keep me in your favour. With the Chevalier's particular compliments, I subscribe myself

Your Reverence's most humble, obliged, and devoted servant,
G. C. Bach.

Milan, 27 December 1759.

Amid these absorbing occupations did Bach keep in touch with his kindred in Germany? The times were not propitious; Europe was in the throes of the Seven Years War, and communications were neither regular nor secure. But it would be agreeable to believe that her children did something to lighten with their love the declining years of their mother, the devoted helpmeet of their

---

[1] *Infra*, p. 203. A *Tantum ergo* and *Confitebor* also belong to 1759. Cf. *infra* pp. 202, 209.   [2] Giovanni Battista Lampugnani.

mighty sire. She died on 27 February 1760, an almswoman in receipt of public charity, and was carried to her grave in the churchyard which had received her husband ten years before. Christian, like his brothers, viewed his mother's circumstances from the standpoint of their generation, for which the term 'Almosenfrau' perhaps carried no stigma. Anna Magdalena's liberty, at least, was not restricted; she was not confined to an almshouse, but resided till her death in the Hainstrasse, probably in the house of her husband's old friend, Dr. Friedrich Heinrich Graf. Still, the pittance she received from the city's treasury was a dole to which poverty entitled her rather than a pension to the widow of a public official. Her youngest son at least was not in a position to alleviate her circumstances, and probably was not yet aware of his loss, when, after a long interval, he again addressed to Martini a letter which reveals his increasing association with the Opera in Milan and elsewhere:

> Most reverend Father and honoured patron,
> I deserve—and I acknowledge it—every kind of reproach, and yet I hope my neglect will not put me in disgrace with your Reverence, partly because I rely on your goodness, partly because I can offer good excuses. It is not merely that I have been very busy. I hoped from week to week to visit Bologna, but was disappointed. True, I was a week at Reggio, but so pressed that I only heard the last performance of Opera. Thence I went to Parma, where I stayed but two nights, and from there returned to Milan after only six days' journeying. I was obliged to travel post, as I had so little time for my business. My purpose was to hear two singers who are to appear at Turin next Carnival; for, being engaged to compose for that theatre, I was anxious to learn something of their qualities. I have not yet seen Signore Fioroni[1] to be your ambassador to him, but when I do I will at once fulfil your Reverence's commands. When I have time I will copy my compositions and submit them to your correction. Next spring shall not go like the last; I am determined at all costs to visit Bologna for some months' stay, and to make use of your manuscripts, if, as before, you will give me that privilege. The Chevalier bids me send you his respects, and with all humility I subscribe myself
> Your Reverence's most humble, devoted, and obliged servant,
> Giov. Christ. Bach.
> Milan, 17 June, 1760.

Bach was now approaching his twenty-fifth year. Four years, perhaps more, had passed since he left Germany, and for that period, as his letters disclose, he was dependent upon Litta, who controlled his actions. The Chevalier for some time past[2] had concerned himself to secure a livelihood for his *protégé*, and

---

[1] Giovanni Andrea Fioroni, since 1747 *maestro di cappella* of the Duomo, Milan.
[2] Cf. Bach's letter of 21 May 1757 *supra*, p. 18.

shortly after his journey to Reggio Bach was able to announce
laconically that an appointment had been obtained:

> Most reverend Father and honoured patron,
>
> I received your most welcome letter and at once fulfilled the mission
> you charged me with to Signore Fioroni, who sends you his compliments,
> and says that he has received five compositions, but has not yet had time to
> examine them; he promises to tell me next week which of them he con-
> siders the best. And now I can give you the news that I have been
> appointed organist of the Duomo here, a post which will give me 800
> *lire* and not much to do. I hope you received the letter in which I told
> you I had been in the neighbourhood of Bologna, but, owing to lack of
> time, only for a single day. The Chevalier bids me give you his compli-
> ments, and, kissing your hand humbly, I remain
>
> Your Reverence's most humble, devoted, and obliged servant,
>
> Giov. Bach.
>
> Milan, 28 June 1760.

The distinguished position to which Bach was now promoted
was vacant through the resignation of Michele Angelo Caselli, who,
a few days before Bach's letter to Martini was written, had executed
the following document:[1]

> Michele Angelo Caselli, organist of the metropolitan Church, the
> humble servant of the reverend and illustrious Signoria, owing to his
> advancing age and its attendant infirmities, desires to surrender his
> situation to Signore Giovanni Bach, provided the illustrious and reverend
> Signoria approves, and upon the understanding that the said Giovanni
> Bach surrenders to him the whole income and salary of the organistship,
> observing all other conditions and agreements as in such compacts are
> usual. The income shall continue to be paid to the said Caselli by the
> Veneranda Fabbrica, as in the past, during his natural life. But if—which
> God forbid!—the said Bach shall predecease the said Caselli, or shall
> suffer some unforeseeable accident, then the said Caselli shall be restored
> to the full enjoyment of the appointment as before his resignation. As-
> suring the reverend and illustrious Signoria that the church will be
> competently served by the person proposed, Michele Angelo Caselli
> humbly approaches the reverend and illustrious Signoria and begs for
> its approval.

On 25 June 1760 Caselli's proposal was approved by the Signoria,
and Bach entered upon a brief tenure of the organ-loft. His
letter to Martini states the income at 800 *lire*, but he could claim
only the reversion of it until Caselli's death, which did not take
place till seven months later.[2] The transaction, in fact, was

---

[1] I am obliged to Signore Vatielli for procuring a copy of this document from
the Cathedral archives.

[2] It was registered in the *registro dei morti* on 15 January 1761. Caselli was then
seventy-one years old. Signore Villani, Superintendent of the *Archivio di stato*,
Milan, kindly interested himself in the matter on my behalf.

analogous to the practice current in Germany, under which an elderly organist accomplished his retirement by marrying a daughter to his successor, in whose household he passed his declining years.[1] Bach was loaded neither with a wife[2] nor heavy duties. He was not required to compose, a task which rested upon Fioroni, the *maestro di cappella*; the Hamburg autograph contains only two minor compositions completed in 1760[3] and none at all subsequent to that year.[4] Bach, in fact, was irrevocably set upon a secular course at the actual moment when his patron's interest procured him an ecclesiastical sinecure, being on the point of producing his first opera at Turin, and otherwise so tied to Litta's service that his visit to Bologna was abandoned. Early in 1761 Martini received his excuses:

Most reverend Father and honoured patron,
　　I have been too busy to answer your esteemed letter, and beg your kind indulgence for my neglect. It was my firm intention to visit Bologna, and all would have fallen out as I planned; indeed, I commissioned Signore Francesco Carnaccia to engage a lodging. But now I find myself unable to fulfil my plans, as more than one reason forbids me to travel. To mention only one: his Excellency the Chevalier will not consent, for he gives weekly performances of music throughout Lent, and as I am his Director he thinks it inconvenient for me to be absent. This, you admit, is an objection I cannot contest; I must submit to my bread-giver. Still, I am, I assure you, heartily sorry for this mischance; I could almost find it in my heart to be angry with the Chevalier, and to demand permission to visit Bologna; for it really is very advisable for me to do so, seeing that for some time past I have almost had to put my studies aside, being every day called on to write something for concerts—a Symphony, Concerto, Cantata, and so forth—for Germania or Parigi.[5] As you can imagine, when one is working like that there is not much time for study. I hope, however, my plans will not be completely frustrated, and, as you have so often and kindly declared, I know that my hopes are shared by you. The Chevalier sends you his compliments, and I kiss your hand humbly, subscribing myself
　　　　　Your Reverence's most humble, devoted, and obliged servant,
　　　　　　　　　　　　　　　　　　　　　　　　Giov. Bach.
Milan, 14 February 1761.

---

[1] Cf. T.B., p. 68.
[2] Polko weaves romantic fiction round Bach's relations at Milan with his future wife, Cecilia Grassi, and the famous singer, La Bastardella.
[3] A *Domine ad adiuvandum* (*supra*, p. 47) and *Laudate pueri*.
[4] His second *Te Deum* is dated 1762, however (cf. *infra*, p. 210). Less elaborate than the 1758 setting, it supports Schubart's (p. 203) criticism, that in his treatment of the canticles Bach affected 'the ancient style'.
[5] 'tanto per Germania come anche per Parigi.' Bach refers to the singer Maddalena Parigi. 'Germania' may represent another; it is difficult to suppose that at this stage of his career his music was in demand in Germany. On the other hand, he appears to have been in touch with his Berlin brother.

A week later Bach writes again:

Most reverend Father and honoured patron,
No doubt you received my last letter by the ordinary post, telling
you the reasons which keep me here in Milan and prevent me from visiting
Bologna, as I proposed. So I need say no more on that matter. This
letter will reach you after Dom. Carlo Dassio has delivered the book you
asked for. He is a great friend of mine, a priest, distinguished, and
worthy of regard for his virtues and uprightness, and a great lover of
music. I take pleasure in promoting his desire to be introduced to one so
famed throughout Europe as is your Reverence. He is travelling to Rome
on business, and, as he expects to stop at Bologna, I beg that he may
receive your protection, a favour for which I shall ever be grateful.
The Chevalier charges me with his particular compliments to you, and,
eager to fulfil any commands of yours, I have the honour to subscribe
myself, with much respect and esteem,
Your Reverence's most humble, devoted, and obliged servant,
Giov. Bach.
Milan, 22 February 1761.

For more than a year there is a gap in the correspondence
Martini preserved and evidently treasured. For the greater part
of the interval, we learn from Litta's letter of 7 April 1762, Bach
was an absentee from Milan, finding his duties no bar to activities
elsewhere, though he had invoked them to excuse his failure to
visit Bologna. These fourteen months, in fact, were decisive in his
career; they established his name as a lyric composer, carried his
reputation to London, conclusively separated him from the career
for which he had been so laboriously preparing, and formed the
bridge over which he passed to the English period of his adventurous life. In 1761 his earliest operas were heard in two of the most
famous theatres in Italy, a coincidence which indicates his rapid
and conclusive success in a form of composition upon which his
letters to Martini are almost silent.

In the Carnival season of 1761 Bach produced his first opera,
Artaserse, in the Teatro Regio, Turin. The autograph score,
somewhat incomplete, is among the Royal Music in the British
Museum, in three volumes, each of which bears the inscription
'This Volume belongs to the Queen, 1788', while the outer leaf of
the first exhibits the note in Bach's hand, 'Artaserse, Atto primo,
Di Giov. Bach. In Torino 1761', along with the cast:

Arbace	.	.	.	Gaetano Guadagni
Mandane	.	.	.	Maddalena Barigi [Parigi]
Artaserse	.	.	.	Carlo Nicolini
Artabano	.	.	.	Pietro di Mezzo
Semira	.	.	.	Teresa Mazzoli
Megabise	.	.	.	Antonio Gotti

Among the singers were those whom Bach had recently visited Reggio to hear, but the only one of superlative merit was Guadagni, one of the great male contralti of the century.[1] In London he had already attracted the notice of Handel, under whom he sang in the *Messiah* and *Samson*, and returned there in 1769 to be associated again with Bach. Nicolini was famed for the length and diversity of his cadenzas,[2] while, shortly after his appearance at Turin, Gotti secured an engagement at Stuttgart under Jommelli.[3] The qualities remarked later in *Catone* are as apparent in *Artaserse*, scored, as was Bach's usage at this period, for strings, oboes, corni da caccia, and trombe. There is no record of the Turin performance, save that it was lengthened by three Ballets by Antonio le Messier, *La morte e il rinascimento del pastore Adone*, *Ridotto di maschere di varie nazioni*, and *Persiani adoratori del Sole*.[4]

Bach's second opera, *Catone in Utica*, was produced at San Carlo, Naples, in 1761, and was revived there in an altered form in 1764.[5] The cast in 1761 is not recorded; in 1764 it was as follows:[6]

Catone	.	.	.	.	Anton Raaf
Cesare	.	.	.	.	Andrea Grassi
Arbace	.	.	.	.	Antonio Muzio
Fulvio	.	.	.	.	Nicola Coppola
Marzia	.	.	.	.	Catterina Gabrielli
Emilia	.	.	.	.	Anna Brogli

Anton Raaf, the most distinguished member of both casts, one of the first tenors of his generation, had returned to Naples in 1759 from Spain, where he had been idolized by the Court and public. Like Mozart at a later time, Bach had the highest regard for him, composed the Motets *Attendite mortales* and *Si nocte tenebrosa* for him, and in his third opera, *Alessandro nell' Indie*, gave him one of his most melodious and popular airs.[7] Grassi was surely related to Bach's future wife Cecilia, who was born at Milan in 1743, and grew to womanhood while he was in Litta's service. Withholding her authority for the statement, Polko asserts that Cecilia's father was a singing-master, her mother a German, her elder brother

---

[1] Cf. Haböck, p. 399.   [2] Gerber, ii. 29.   [3] *Ibid*, i. 526.
[4] Cf. Breggi, and G. Sacerdote, *Il Teatro Regio di Torino* (1892).
[5] On 26 December 1764. Florimo, iv. 237: 'Questo dramma fu rappresentato la prima volta nel 1761, ora con i recitativi abbreviati e qualche aria cambiata'. Salvioli (p. 690) asserts that the opera was first produced at Milan in 1758 and 'nel 1764 riformata in Londra'.
[6] Florimo, iv. 237.   [7] *Infra*, p. 55.

a singer, and the younger a violinist.[1] Andrea may have been her
uncle, even her father. Gerber mentions[2] Luigi Grassi,[3] a Roman
tenor who made his way to Berlin in 1768, where, more than one
hundred and fifty years earlier, Bernardo Pasquini Grassi, of
Mantua, another tenor, also found employment.[4] Catterina
Gabrielli, the daughter of Prince Gabrielli's cook, known as 'La
Cochetta' or 'Cochettina' from her origin, was one of the most
accomplished, as she was one of the most capricious, singers of
her generation. Her adorers were legion, and her retort to Catha-
rine of Russia is famous. The imperious and impressionable
Tsarina objected that the singer's fee exceeded the pay of a field-
marshal. 'Then let your field-marshals sing to you!' retorted La
Cochetta. She visited London in 1775–76, and exhibited there
'all the grace and dignity of a Roman matron', impressing Burney
as 'the most intelligent and best bred virtuosa' with whom he had
ever conversed.[5]

Bach's appearance as a composer of Opera found the school of
Hasse in full vigour in the achievements of Jommelli and Traetta,
the one in Stuttgart, the other in Parma, while Francesco di Majo
upheld its traditions in Naples. Bach's genius groups him with
Hasse's school, but his *Catone* charmed with qualities of its own:
its melodic fluency, deft and expressive instrumentation, bring him
into close touch with Mozart's finer genius. How delicate and
tuneful is the middle movement of the overture !

---

[1] P. 202.   [2] Vol. i. 533.
[3] Schneider, p. 159. Gerber erroneously names him Antonio. He died at Pisa
in 1789.
[4] Sachs, p. 48.   [5] Bur. iv. 502.

while the first movement, as Hermann Abert remarks,[1] suggests Mozart's *La Clemenza di Tito*:

Allegro assai.

The popularity of Bach's *Catone* is attested by its repetition at Naples in 1764, when it received a new overture, while in 1766 it was heard at Brunswick, with Antonio Muzio again in the cast. The work was never given in London, but Bach thought so highly of Marzia's song, 'Confusa, smarrita', that he introduced it into the pasticcio *Berenice* in 1765:

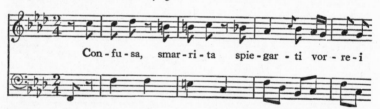

Con - fu - sa, smar - ri - ta spie - gar - ti vor - re - i

Burney praised it as 'the best song in the printed collection'.[2]

Evidently Naples greeted the new *maestro* with exceptional favour. On 20 January 1762 Bach's *Alessandro nell' Indie* was produced at San Carlo with the following cast:[3]

Alessandro	.	.	.	Anton Raaf
Poro	.	.	.	Tommaso Guarducci
Gandarte	.	.	.	Salvatore Consorti
Timagene	.	.	.	Luigi Costa
Cleofide	.	.	.	Clementina Spagnoli
Erissena	.	.	.	Catterina Flavis

[1] Abert, p. 317.　　　[2] Bur. iv. 486.　　　[3] Florimo, iv. 236.

Guarducci for the past fifteen years had been in high favour throughout Italy, and in 1766 visited England along with Cecilia Grassi, with whom he made his appearance in another of Bach's operas.[1] For Raaf in *Alessandro* Bach wrote his most beautiful and popular aria, the favourite of Mozart, who heard it in another setting in London some years later:[2]

Largo.

Non so . . d'on-de vie-ne quel

te-nero af-fet-to quel mo-to che ig-

-no-to mi na-sce nel pet-to

Cleofide's aria, 'Se il ciel mi divide', was also a favourite of its composer, who introduced it, along with 'Non so d'onde', into *Ezio* in 1764:[3]

[1] *Infra*, p. 106.   [2] *Infra*, p. 131.   [3] *Infra*, p. 225.

Se il ciel mi di - vi - de dal

ca - ro mio spo - so

The numerous manuscripts of it that exist declare the popularity also of the duet for Poro and Cleofide, 'Se mai turbo', with its preceding recitative, 'Lode a gli dei'.

Se . mai tur - - bo il tuo . . . . ri-

- po - so, se . . . . m'ac-cen - do ad

al - - tro lu - me

The three operas patently revealed Bach's genius as a lyric composer and placed him among the leaders of the Neo-Neapolitan school, whose influence was shortly to fall upon Mozart. Conscious of his powers, and infatuated once more by the glamour of the stage, Milan and his duties there were forgotten. Even Martini, whom Bach evidently managed to visit at this juncture,[1] appears to have recognized that the success of his pupil established his right to follow the new course. Litta, on the other hand, remained unreconciled to that opinion, and, three months after Bach's latest success at Naples, communicated his anxiety to Bologna:

Most reverend and honoured patron,
    I should like to do as you wish regarding *il mio Bach*, for I know you desire his advantage. But his various duties here compel me to advise him to come back at once to fulfil them. He has to serve our Cathedral as organist, but for almost the whole of last year was absent and unable to fulfil his duty. It would certainly not be to his advantage to sacrifice a nice little post which brings him 800 *lire* a year, and very likely may lead to something better. Such posts are excellent stays in old age. So it behoves him to be diligent in his duty, and not to act in such a way as to cause the one who helped him to obtain the appointment to regret having done so. Our people here are already murmuring, especially the Monsignori. I know what a deep interest your Reverence takes in him, and so am confident you will see your way to counsel him for his future welfare, and enable him to disarm those who, whether through jealousy or interested motives, complain of him as negligent and careless. Meanwhile, I thank you warmly for your kindness, and beg you to believe that I shall welcome every opportunity to be of service to you. With unchanging esteem I subscribe myself
                    Your Reverence's most devoted and obliged servant,
                            Conte Cav. Agostino Litta.
Milan, 7 April 1762.

Three days later Bach returned to Milan, and wrote his last letter from Italy to his revered *maestro*:

[1] See his letter of 10 April 1762, *infra*, p. 58.

Most reverend Father and honoured patron,

Thanks to heaven I have returned safe and sound to Milan and resumed my duties this morning. I thank you warmly for all the favours received during my sojourn with you.[1] Awaiting your honoured commands, and begging you to give my compliments to Signore Francesco de Majo, I remain, with all respect,

Your Reverence's most humble, devoted, and obliged servant,

Giov. Bach.

Milan, 10 April 1762.

Fourteen months elapsed before Bach again broke silence. In July 1763 he is discovered in London, already domiciled and in high favour there, after a series of happenings the next chapter must explore.

[1] 'nel mio soggiorno costi.'

CHAPTER III

THE KING'S THEATRE

BACH'S return to Milan in April 1762 indicated that, for the moment, his obligation to Litta prevailed over an impulse to break the ties that moored him there. Had events followed a normal course his decision might have been final, despite Martini's sympathy in his dilemma. But his horizon was surprisingly widened by invitations from abroad, flattering and agreeably indicative that his fame was no longer local. His summons to the London Opera he owed to his own conspicuous talent. But simultaneously, through Martini's intervention, we must suppose, another door opened to him in England, promising occupation more distinguished. Bach hesitated no longer, bade a last farewell to Milan and his patrons, and, three months after resuming his neglected duties, is discovered in Germany, at Strelitz, where on 8 July 1762 he received one hundred thalers from the ducal exchequer 'to defray the expenses of his journey'.[1] The honorarium admits of but one explanation. Ten months earlier, in September 1761, the youthful Princess Sophia Charlotte of Mecklenburg-Strelitz had become the wife of George III of Great Britain, whose musical tastes matched her own. That she should desire a compatriot as her music-master was as natural as that she should

[1] 'Aus der Herzoglichen Rentey sind mir Hundert Thaler in Sächsl. Dritteln richtig ausgezahlet worden.

Bach.

Strelitz, d. 8 Julius 1762.'
Bach's receipt was forwarded with the following instruction to the Landrentmeister:
'S. d. C.
Es haben Serenissimus gnädigst resolviret d. Hrn. Bach zu Bestreitung seiner Reise Kosten 100 Thlr. sächsische 1/3tel praesentiren zu lassen. Ew. Hochedelgebl. belieben also nebst einliegenden Billet solche an den Hrn. Conzertmeister Zeller so fort zu schicken, da denn, wenn er solche annimmt, das Belag dazu expediret werden soll. Der Quitung bedarf es vor der Hand nicht darüber. Ich bin Ew. Hochedelgebl. ergebener Diener
gez. v. d. Knesebeck.
d. 9ten Jul. 1762.
Dem Hrn. Landrentmeister Schütte, Hochedelgebl.'
I am obliged for the document to Herr Ober-Archivar Witte, who searched the Mecklenburg-Strelitz archives at my instigation. They contain no other reference to Bach.

invite her brother Duke Adolph Friedrich to provide one. He maintained a small, but competent, Capelle under Georg Bernhard Leopold Zeller,[1] to whom, it may be, he communicated his sister's requirement. For, at the English Court the position Bach was soon to fill was vacant since Handel's death in 1759, and among the small colony of German musicians in London none was of sufficient reputation and merit to be promoted to his place. The national bias of a German Queen rejected an Italian master;[2] and, moreover, Bach appears already to have attracted the notice of his future mistress. Among her music in the British Museum is John Lockman's *Ode on the auspicious Arrival and Nuptials of Her present most gracious Majesty Queen Charlotte* 'Set to Music by Mr. Bach'. Lockman's conventional sentiments are interpreted in music of corresponding banality, judiciously suited to the patriotic effusions of its libretto. Scored for Soprano or Tenor solo, three-part Chorus, harpsichord and violin obbligato, its merits may be judged by the following illustrations:

[1] Thomas Nugent, *Travels through Germany* (1768), i. 348. For Zeller see Gerber, ii. 847 and Eitner's *Quellen-Lexikon*.
[2] It is noteworthy that Forkel, Gerber, Bitter, and Polko all suppose that Bach came to England in 1759 as Handel's successor.

to Him whom the

winds o - bey.

CHORUS. (3 parts)

Allegro.

O see one u - ni - ver - sal Smile Re-

- ceive thee, Prin - cess, in our Isle.

When, and by what agency, Lockman's Ode reached Bach's
hands is obscure; nor is there any record of its public performance
during the royal wedding celebrations. After all, he may have put
it to music *after* his arrival in England, though the conjecture is
improbable. But it can be reasonably inferred that Bach came to
London with credentials from Strelitz to the English Court, and
that he amply supported them by his distinguished air, courtly
manners, ability as a harpsichordist, and the reputation his recent
achievements at Turin and Naples had won him as a *maestro* of the
Neapolitan school. His formal appointment to the Queen's
Household was not long delayed.

Arriving in London in the summer of 1762, Bach entered a
community which had not considerably expanded since the re-
building that repaired the ravages of the Great Fire. The King's
Theatre, with which Bach was henceforth intermittently associated,
standing at the foot of the Haymarket, was almost on the extreme
fringe of the town. Westward, the nobility frequented St. James's
Square and the locality of fashion between Piccadilly and Pall Mall.
Southward, St. James's Palace looked across its Park to the Abbey
and Palace of Westminster, and, to the west, over the Green Park
to open fields about Knightsbridge. Turnpikes at Hyde Park
Corner and King's Road, behind Buckingham House (the Queen's
Palace), opened to the coaches of the quality threading country
lanes to Kensington, Richmond, and Chelsea. On the north, from
the turnpike, where Marble Arch now stands, to Tottenham
Court Road the town had invaded the country between Oxford
Street and the New Road. But the newly instituted British
Museum, and its neighbour Bedford House, still faced open fields
northward to Tottenham turnpike, Paddington, and more distant
Highgate and Hampstead. Thus, Bach's London was bounded on
the west by Tyburn (Park) Lane, and, on the north, by the New
Road from Paddington to Islington, south of which wide spaces of
green country about Lambs Conduit Fields, the Foundling Hos-
pital, and Bagnigge Wells, still defied the builder.[1] Upon this
northern frontier Soho Square, with its surrounding streets, was
a fashionable residential quarter; in it, as bachelor and benedick,
Bach lived the greater part of his London life.

London in 1762 was well provided with musical entertainment,
concert halls, and musicians, chiefly foreigners, attracted to its
service by the generosity of its purse. Covent Garden Theatre,
now thirty years old, offered English Comedy and Opera under the

---

[1] I follow 'A New and Accurate Plan of the Cities of London' in *The Gentleman's
Magazine*, vol. 33 (1763).

management of John Beard, for whom Handel composed the great Tenor parts in *Israel in Egypt*, *Messiah*, *Samson*, *Judas Maccabaeus*, and *Jephthah*. Here, a few months before Bach's arrival, Dr. Thomas Arne, the most prominent English musician of his generation (*d.* 1778), had produced (1 February 1762) his *Artaxerxes* in English, choosing for his libretto the text Bach used at Turin a year before.[1] Drury Lane Theatre, in process of enlargement in 1762–3, was also associated with Arne, who performed there his *Comus*, and other works which contain his best songs, before, in 1760, he transferred his service to Covent Garden. Under Garrick's management its reputation was enhanced by his production of Shakespeare, until his retirement in 1776, six years before Bach's death. Opposite the Opera-house, adjoining the site of the present Haymarket Theatre, stood a small playhouse opened in 1720 by a company of French comedians, and therefore known as the French, or Little, Theatre,[2] in which Samuel Foote (*d.* 1777) provided satirical entertainments that drew the town. In another quarter, Sadler's Wells was much frequented for open-air concerts, and in 1765 received a concert-room, with which Charles Dibdin (*d.* 1814) and his sons were connected in the latter half of the century. Vauxhall and Ranelagh were other popular resorts; for the former Bach composed his most agreeable English songs.[3]

Of concert-giving societies there was no lack. St. Cecilia's Day was intermittently celebrated since 1703, but the Academy of Ancient Music, founded seven years later (1710), continued its activities till 1792, having Dr. Samuel Arnold as its conductor for the last years of its existence. Though it occasionally performed complete oratorios, its programmes were chiefly devoted to motets, madrigals, and anthems by Travers, Purcell, Morley, Byrd, and others of that school.[4] The Madrigal Society, which survives, was founded (1741) twenty years before Bach came to London, with a membership confined to singers in Cathedral choirs, and others vouched for as competent. Favourite taverns in the city were its resort, but it provided at least one annual concert for the entertainment of its friends. Among its members, Bach's contemporaries, were Sir John Hawkins (*d.* 1789), the musical historian; Thomas and Michael Arne; Joah Bates (*d.* 1799), conductor of the Concert of Ancient Musick; Benjamin Cooke (*d.* 1793), organist of Westminster Abbey; John Worgan (*d.* 1790), composer to Vauxhall Gardens; and Jonathan Battishill (*d.* 1801). The Noblemen and

---

[1] The performance was marked by the famous 'riot'. See a contemporary illustration in Wyndham, i. 154.
[2] Kingsford, p. 94.   [3] *Infra*, p. 254.   [4] Pohl, p. 18.

Gentlemen's Catch Club, formed in 1761 to encourage the composition of canons, catches, and glees, annually offered prizes with
that object, and held weekly dinners at the Thatched House
Tavern in St. James's Street. The Society of Musicians of Great
Britain, founded in 1738, pursued its benevolent work, and the
Corporation of the Sons of the Clergy annually held imposing
services. During Lent the theatres provided Oratorio; the youthful Mozart, visiting London in 1764, was able to hear in five weeks
as many of Handel's masterpieces.[1] Individual musicians, singers,
and instrumentalists, however, were the most active concert-givers,
and Bach soon made himself conspicuously prominent among
them.

The chief resort of the world of fashion, musical and unmusical,
was the King's Theatre, or Opera-house, on the site of the present
His Majesty's Theatre in the Haymarket.[2] Designed by Vanbrugh
and opened in 1705, Handel's early operas and oratorios were
produced in it before he engaged his genius to Covent Garden in
1734. Beneath the black glazed tiles of its roof a narrow, inconvenient entrance from the Haymarket admitted through a
vestibule to the large and imposing interior. The auditorium was
completely ringed by three tiers of Boxes looking down upon a
spacious Pit, whose seats rose from the orchestra level. Above the
top tier of Boxes the Crown Gallery filled the whole circle of the
house, except on either side of the proscenium, where six Boxes,
twelve in all, invited subscribers. Above the Crown Gallery another accommodated the footmen, lackeys, and chairmen of their
masters below. The Royal Box was upon the right-hand side of the
stage, beneath the deep arch of the proscenium. The one opposite
was allotted to the Prince of Wales. During the season, which
lasted from November to June or July, operas were performed on
Tuesdays and Saturdays by two casts of singers, engaged respectively for *opera buffa* and *opera seria*. Saturday was the more
fashionable, a preference which presented a serious problem to
'society' patrons when offered a tempting bill on an unfashionable
night.[3] The curtain rose at 6.15 p.m., and the duration of the performance permitted the audience to frequent the coffee-room, an
agreeable interlude which Horace Walpole recommended to
churches with inconstant congregations!

When Bach arrived in London, Colomba Mattei, with her husband Trombetta, ruled the Opera-house as *impresaria*. She had
taken over its precarious fortunes in 1759, coveting 'the sovereign

[1] Pohl, p. 37.   [2] See Illustrations Nos. 10, 11, 12.
[3] On the Tuesday-Saturday rivalry see *infra*, p. 85.

privilege of self-ruin',[1] and, assuming the position of 'first woman', inaugurated her reign with an innovation. Her predecessors, Regina Mingotti and Felice de' Giardini, leader of the orchestra, had not employed a regular composer, preferring to produce operas already popular elsewhere. Mattei, however, invited Gioacchino Cocchi to assist her,[2] a composer whose reputation was high in Rome, Naples, and Venice, though Burney, who methodically tested his ability, while admitting his 'good taste, and knowledge in counterpoint, and in all the mechanical parts of his profession', found 'his invention very inconsiderable', and that 'even what he used from others became languid in passing through his hands'.[3] Cocchi's invention, in fact, was exhausted by the end of the season 1759–60, when Burney remarked with astonishment that Giovanni Gallini, the principal dancer, was frequently encored in a *pas seul*, a circumstance outside Burney's experience and due, he supposed, to the dullness of the musical entertainment.[4] In *opera buffa* Cocchi was equally ineffective. 'Without humour, gaiety, or creative powers of any kind, his comic opera was the most melancholy performance I ever heard in an Italian theatre,' Burney noted.[5] Mattei apparently held the same opinion: at the close of the season in 1762 Cocchi's engagement ceased. Bach was invited to fill his place, and Mattei retired from the stage for the final year of her management.

Fresh from the standards of Italy, Bach was disappointed, even mortified, to find the singers engaged by Mattei of inferior quality, and that the best of the women was Clementina Cremonini, 'a good musician, with a modern style of singing, but almost without voice',[6] while Domenico Ciardini, a male Soprano, the 'serious first man', according to the same critic, 'disappointed every hope by turning out a singer who seemed to have been possessed of no very capital powers originally, but now wholly in decay'. Gaetano Quilici and Giuseppe Giustinelli were the other men, while the Cremonini was supported by Giovanna Carmignani, Livia Segantini, and Marianna Valsecchi.[7] Some months therefore elapsed before Bach consented to give the public a complete opera from his pen. Unwilling to trust his reputation to the singers at his disposal, he declined to compose an original score, and merely carried on Cocchi's work in the arrangement of pasticcios and direction of the productions.

Announced by Mattei on 24 October 1762,[8] with the usual

[1] Busby, ii. 446. [2] Bur. iv. 468. [3] *Ibid.* iv. 470.
[4] *Ibid.* iv. 473. [5] *Ibid.* iv. 478. [6] *Ibid.* iv. 485.
[7] *Ibid.* iv. 480. [8] P. A. 24 Oct. 1762.

request for subscriptions, the season opened, 'By Command of Their Majesties', on Saturday 13 November,[1] when Bach made his first appearance before an English audience with the comic opera *Il Tutore e la Pupilla*, or *Il Matrimonio alla moda*, a pasticcio, the programme announced, whose music, 'selected from various celebrated authors', was 'performed under the direction of Mr. John Bach, a Saxon Master of Music', while the libretto was by Giovan Gualberto Bottarelli, official librettist to the Opera.[2] Bach composed the overture,[3] distinguished by a characteristically melodious middle movement. But the plaudits of the house were chiefly won by Anna Lucia de' Amicis, whom Mattei had engaged, with her father and their manager, Giovan Battista Zingoni, for *opera buffa* (*burletta*), but whose immediate success won her promotion to *opera seria*, in which she soon became preeminent, captivating Bach as later she charmed Mozart.[4] Burney, who also acknowledged her fascination, found her figure and gestures elegant and graceful, her countenance high-bred and interesting, her voice and style polished and sweet. 'She had not a motion that did not charm the eye, or a tone but what delighted the ear', he recalled with pleasure, and she ascended to E flat *in altissimo* 'with true, clear, and powerful *real* voice'.[5] Three weeks later, Ciardini having arrived,[6] Mattei produced (December 4) the first 'serious' opera of the season, the pasticcio *Astarto, Re di Tiro*.[7] 'The Music of the Airs', the programme announced, 'is selected from various celebrated authors, excepting what are marked with an asterisk, which are Mr. John Bach's, a Saxon master of music, under whose direction the whole is performed'. Bach again provided the overture,[8] and also an aria for Ciardini, 'Pupilla vezzosa', which Burney, whom the production otherwise failed to entertain, found 'very pleasing'.[9]

---

[1] Bur. iv. 479 gives the inaccurate date 18 November.
[2] The cast was as follows: *Rosmira*, Giovanna Carmignani; *Lindoro*, Giuseppe Giustinelli; *Pascasio*, Giovan Battista Zingoni; *Timitilla*, Anna Lucia de' Amicis; *Don Sabbione*, Domenico de' Amicis; *Contrappunto*, Gaetano Quilici; *Serpilla*, Marianna Valsecchi; Principal Dancers, Giovanni Gallini, Mlle. Asselin, Signore and Signora Binetti (Bott. 907 i. 9/4).
[3] *Infra*, p. 273.
[4] Jahn, i. 208.
[5] Bur. iv. 479, 481.
[6] *Ibid*. iv. 480.
[7] Cast: *Elisa*, Livia Segantini; *Astarto*, or *Clearco*, Domenico Ciardini; *Fenicio*, Gaetano Quilici; *Sidonia*, Giovanna Carmignani; *Nino*, Giuseppe Giustinelli; *Agenore*, Giovan Battista Zingoni (Bott. 907, i. 9/6.).
[8] *Infra*, p. 273.
[9] Bur. iv. 480. The Aria was included among those published from *La Calamità de' Cuori*. (*Infra*, p. 228.)

So far the season had produced no important novelty, though Bach's gifts promised a more interesting continuation. Encouraged by his discovery of the de' Amicis' attractive talents, he was at work upon a libretto by Bottarelli, but meanwhile continued to arrange pasticcios. On 8 January 1763, 'by Command of Their Majesties',[1] a 'Drama Giocoso', entitled *La Cascina*, was produced 'under the direction of Mr. John Bach, a Saxon master of music', to music drawn from 'various celebrated Authors'.[2] 'The elegant and interesting De Amicis was the chief attraction of the burletta', Burney remarked;[3] 'but the rest of the singing was so despicable, that only her songs have been printed'. Bach composed the overture,[4] which passed unremarked by an audience for whom only the rise of the curtain signalled the beginning of the performance. A month later, on 3 February 1763, *La Calamità de' Cuori*[5] was produced 'under the Direction of Mr. Bach, a Saxon Master of Music', who contributed the overture,[6] but otherwise revived the music of Baldassare Galuppi's opera. Though its airs were more than ten years old, they were so deliciously sung by her in the character of Bellarosa that, in Burney's judgement, they seemed to have been 'originally intended for the display of all the enchanting powers of the young Anna De Amicis'.[7]

While *La Calamità* and the fascinating Anna Lucia continued to draw the town, Bach at length, on Saturday 19 February 1763, offered the public an opera entirely from his pen. In the legend of Orion his librettist Bottarelli found a subject comparatively neglected by composers for the stage,[8] whose novelty enhanced the interest of the occasion, the distinction of which was marked by the presence of the King and Queen in the Royal Box. The programme announced the cast:[9]

[1] P. A., 8 Jan. 1763.
[2] Cast: *Lavinia*, Giovanna Carmignani; *Costanzo*, Giuseppe Giustinelli; *Count Ripoli*, Gaetano Quilici; *Pippo*, Domenico de' Amicis; *Cecca*, Marianna Valsecchi; *Berto*, Giovan Battista Zingoni; *Lena*, Anna Lucia de' Amicis. Text by Goldoni, arranged by G. G. Bottarelli (Bott. 907, i. 9/8).
[3] Bur. iv. 480.
[4] *Infra*, p. 273.
[5] Cast: *Albina*, Giovanna Carmignani; *Armidorus*, Giuseppe Giustinelli; *Bellarosa*, Anna Lucia de' Amicis; *Jacinthus*, Domenico de' Amicis; *Saracca*, Gaetano Quilici; *Belinda*, Marianna Valsecchi; *Pignone*, Giovan Battista Zingoni (Bott. 907, i. 9/10).
[6] *Infra*, p. 272.
[7] Bur. iv. 480.
[8] Riemann, p. 388, records only two eighteenth-century operas on the subject other than Bach's, the more recent of which was produced at Paris in 1728.
[9] Bott. 907 i. 10/1.

ORIONE, o sia Diana Vendicata. Drama.

Orion, or Diana Reveng'd. A Tragic Opera.

By Mr. Bottarelli. As it is performed at the King's Theatre in the Hay-Market. The Music is a new Composition by Mr. Bach, a Saxon Professor.

Dramatis Personae

Enopione	Sig. Gaetano Quilici.
Retrea	Sig[a]. Livia Segantini.
Orione	Sig. Domenico Ciardini.
Nice	Sig[a]. Clementina Cremonini.
Candiope	Sig[a]. Anna Lucia de Amicis.
Argia	Sig[a]. Giovanna Carmignani.
Tirsi	Sig[r]. Giuseppe Giustinelli.
Diana, in the character of Calisto, a Theban Princess . .	Sig[a]. Marianna Valsecchi.
Mercurio, concealed under the person of Arcades	Sig[r]. Giovan Battista Zingoni.

Oracolo—Chorus of Priests, Warriors, and Shepherds.

Dancers

Signor Giovanni Gallini, Mlle. Asselin, Sig. and Sig[a]. Binetti.

Produced upon a scale of unusual lavishness, the advertisements in the *Public Advertiser* drew particular attention to the 'grand chorus's' and to the fact that 'several Vocal and Instrumental Performers' were engaged outside the normal establishment. The employment of clarinets was especially remarked in an orchestra otherwise consisting of strings, flutes, oboes, corni da caccia, and bassoons. Burney observed that this was 'the first time that clarinets had admission in our opera orchestra'.[1] Bach's employment of them, however, was neither adventurous nor remarkable: in the overture they are prominent in the first movement only in a single passage of four bars, which occurs twice:

Allegro con brio.

Otherwise the clarinets are grouped with the horns and third oboe ('Tallie'). In the middle movement (*Andante*) they are silent, and in the Finale (*Allegro*) are conspicuous only in a short passage:

---

[1] Bur. iv. 481. The instrument, whose invention is attributed to Joh. Christoph Denner, of Nürnberg, *c.* 1700, had hardly passed beyond the experimental stage; but Handel employed it in *Tamerlane* in 1724. Cf. Pohl, p. 72.

Allegro.

In the arias Bach's use of them is equally tentative: they are employed only in Enopione's 'Frema crudello sdegno' and Candiope's
'Di quest' alma desolata'.

Orione immediately captured public favour, and was 'extremely
applauded by a very numerous audience'.[1] 'Every judge of Music',
Burney adds, 'perceived the emanations of genius throughout the
whole performance'. The texture of its harmony, skill, fullness
of instrumentation, and, above all, the melodiousness of its arias,
were patent qualities which won the young composer instant approval. Burney especially remarked his disuse of the *da capo* aria
and the delicacy of his orchestral technique, which led him to
praise Bach as 'the first composer who observed the law of *contrast*
as a *principle*'. The richness of his accompaniments, the same
listener observed, was so unusual that, excepting those sung by
the de' Amicis, whose delightful art completely realized their
beauty, the arias in the opera, being indifferently rendered, were
'more admired as instrumental pieces than compositions for the
voice'.[2] Bach, in fact, pleased by his unusual combination of the
Italian and German idiom.

The success of *Orione* was so emphatic that no new 'serious'
opera was required till May, and in the interval it was frequently
repeated. The Court signified approval by also attending the
second performance, on the Tuesday (22 February) following its
production, an unusual and significant compliment. Public interest in the event is revealed by the fact that the occasion was
advertised in the *Gazetteer*, an irregularity rebuked by the management in the *Public Advertiser*:[3] 'Mr. Crawford [4] begs leave to inform the Nobility and Gentry, that the Advertisement of the last
new serious Opera of Orione being inserted in Yesterday's
Gazeteer to be performed the same Evening was advertised by the
Printer of the said Paper without any Authority whatever; and that
no Advertisements have ever been inserted for the Operas at The

[1] Bur. iv. 481.   [2] *Ibid*. iv. 482.   [3] P.A. 22 Feb. 1763.
[4] One of the managers of the Opera. He retired, temporarily, with Mattei in
June 1763 (P.A. 1 June 1763). The Opera account at Drummond's Bank names
him Peter (15 Jan. 1765.).

King's Theatre, but in the Public and Daily Advertisers'. An anonymous author, at the cost of one shilling, offered the public his *Critical Observations on the Tragic Opera of Orion, in a Course of Lectures to a Country Gentleman, in which the Poetry, Music, Translation, Performers, and Decorations of that Piece are impartially examined*,[1] a critical homily which, unfortunately, has not outlived its subject. Early in March 1763 a set of 'Favourite Songs' from the opera was published ; Bach's first essay on the London stage elicited patent signs of public interest and approval.

While *Orione* held the serious stage, a new 'drama comico', *La finta Sposa*, was produced on Thursday in Easter week (14 April 1763).[2] The programme announced the work as 'extracted from divers authors . . . under the direction of Mr. Bach, a Saxon Professor'. He probably contributed the overture, though none of those in print bears an indication of its association with the pasticcio, into which, 'by particular Desire', Bach introduced 'a Dance of last Year call'd The Industrious Farmer'.[3] Burney does not mention the production.

In the interval between the productions of *Orione* and its successor *Zanaida* the columns of the *Public Advertiser* reveal Bach active in other fields and displaying his fertility in other forms. On 17 March 1763 he published his first set of Harpsichord Concertos (Op. I)[4] and dedicated them to the Queen, an act that clearly indicates his privileged position at Buckingham House, though his appointment as Music Master was not yet gazetted. Graceful, melodious, and of elementary simplicity, the form of the first movements of the six concerti connects them with the Concerto in E major composed at Milan,[5] though the last movement of the sixth offers unsophisticated variations on 'God save the King'. The publication revealed the composer's facility as a harpsichordist, and also the deficiencies of his technique.   Burney's criticism is just:[6] 'When [Bach] arrived in England, his style of playing was so much admired, that he recovered many of the losses his hand had sustained by disuse, and by being constantly cramped and crippled with a pen; but he never was able to reinstate it with force and readiness sufficient for great difficulties; and in general his compositions for the piano forte are such as ladies can execute with

[1] P.A. 26 March 1763.
[2] Cast: *Eugenia*, Giovanna Carmignani; *Ismene*, Clementina Cremonini; *Leandro*, Giuseppe Giustinelli; *Lisetta*, Anna Lucia de' Amicis; *Piombon*, Domenico de' Amicis; *Camillo*, Gaetano Quilici; *Ottavia*, Marianna Valsecchi; *Ridolfo*, Giovan Battista Zingoni (Bott. 907 i. 9/11).
[3] P.A. 14 April 1763.   [4] *Ibid.* 17 March 1763.
[5] Published in Ed. Steingräber. *Infra*, p. 300.   [6] Bur. iv. 482.

little trouble; and the Allegros rather resemble bravura songs than
instrumental pieces for the display of great execution. On which
account they lose much of their effect when played without the
accompaniments, which are admirable, and so masterly and interesting to an audience, that want of hand, or complication in the
harpsichord part, is never discovered'.

Anna Lucia de' Amicis, who shared with Bach the plaudits of
the season, took her 'benefit' on 24 March 1763, when Bach
directed the second and third acts of *Il Tutore e la Pupilla* and
Pergolesi's *La Serva Padrona*, an 'Interlude', the advertisement
announced, which 'Signora de Amicis will present in its own
natural Beauty, such as it originally came from the Hands of the
ingenious Author Signor Pergolesi, and as it was first done at
Naples,[1] in order to give the Nobility and Gentry the most favourable Idea of so masterly a Piece'.[2] Giovanni Gallini, the principal
dancer, took his 'benefit' on April 21, when two Acts of *La
Calamità de' Cuori* were repeated, along with *La Serva Padrona*
'with new Dances', while 'by Desire' Gallini and the de' Amicis
danced the minuet in the former opera.[3]   Four days later Bach
was represented for the first time at a concert of the Society of
Musicians of Great Britain 'for the benefit of Decayed Musicians',
to whose programme he contributed an overture, probably one
of those already heard during the season.[4]

It is observable that Bach rejected an affectation of Italianism in
the style of his address, and, though he was described as 'a Saxon
Professor', preferred to be known as 'John Bach'.[5] His imminent
Court appointment perhaps governed his preference; for though
custom readily submitted to the foreigner's monopoly of the con-
cert-halls, public feeling was jealous to exclude him from the
favours of royalty. Nor, at this moment, did the name 'Bach'
necessarily suggest a German connexion: it was current in English
usage, and there attached to it none of the associations which make
it immortal to-day; Carl Philipp Emanuel had not begun his career
at Hamburg, and the greater genius of his father was still hidden
from the world. The London Bach owed nothing to his name, but
built his reputation upon his own merit and ability.   His second

---

[1] In 1731.
[2] P.A. 24 March 1763. Tickets were offered 'at her house in Great Suffolk-
street'.
[3] *Ibid.* 21 April 1763.
[4] *Ibid.* 25 April 1763.
[5] He seems for the time to have dropped his middle name altogether, for upon
the French title-page of his Op. I he calls himself 'Jean Bach'. His letter to
Martini of 1 July 1763 (*infra* p. 74) also is signed 'Giov. Bach'.

opera, produced on Saturday 7 May 1763, enhanced it. The programme unfolds the plot and exhibits the cast:[1]

ZANAIDA, drama per Musica.

Zanais, tragic opera, paraphrased in English Verse.
As it is represented at the King's Theatre in the Hay-Market.

The Argument

Soliman, Emperor of the Turks, and Tamasses, Sophi of Persia, after a long war, agreed to treat about a peace; and to this end they sent hostages to each other. Accordingly the preliminaries were signed, in which it was stipulated, in order to make the alliance more solid, that Tamasses should marry Zanais, Soliman's daughter. In the mean time the Sophi grew enamoured with Osira, hostage in Persia on the part of the Emperor. The intended Consort arrives in Ispahan with a magnificent retinue. Here the action of the drama commences, for the intrigue of which the infidelity of Tamasses, the magnanimity of Zanais, the ambition of Roselane and Osira, and the honesty of Mustapha, are managed in such a manner as to interest the passions.

N.B. The subject of this Opera was first handled by Signor Bulgherelli,[2] in a piece called Syphax, and afterwards by the famous Metastasio, in six characters only. It is now new-modelled, with nine persons, by Mr. Bottarelli, who has taken from Syphax no more than the fable, and Mustapha's fine air in the first Act; in the rest, he has varied entirely the plan, and the episodes.

With regard to the translation, a paraphrase or imitation, after the manner of our tragedy, has been aimed at, as well in the recitative as in the airs; but the public are desired to excuse any imperfections there may be found, since the whole was obliged to be done in a few days; and besides it is the first attempt of a youth. It is to be hoped that the English reader will not be displeased at meeting with parodies on some passages in our authors, or entire lines taken from them, where they are found to express the sense of the original in the best terms.

The Music is a new Composition by Mr. Bach, a Saxon Professor.

Dramatis Personae

Zanaida	Signora	A. L. de Amicis.
Roselane	„	Livia Segantini.
Osira	„	Carmignani.
Aglatida	„	Marianna Valsecchi.
Silvera	„	Cremonini.
Mustafà	Signor	Gaetano Quilici.
Tamasses	„	Domenico Ciardini.
Cisseo	„	Giustinelli.
Gianguir	„	Giovan Battista Zingoni.

Chorus of Persians and Turks.

Principal Dancers: Signor Gallini, Mlle. Asselin, Signor and Signora Binetti.

[1] Bott. 907 i. 9/9.
[2] The husband of Marianna Bulgarelli ('La Romanina'), the patroness of Metastasio.

As in *Orione*, the normal establishment was augmented by 'several Vocal and Instrumental Performers'[1] in order to meet the requirements of Bach's elaborate score. The opera was not less applauded than its predecessor; eight of its 'Favourite Songs' were published,[2] and, after as many performances, it brought the season to an end on June 11.

Bach's co-operation had given distinction to Mattei's last season as *impresaria*. On 1 June 1763 the *Public Advertiser* announced her intention to 'leave England soon after the Operas are over', adding, that 'as Mr. Crawford intends to have no farther Concern with the Management of Operas, all the Cloaths used in the Burlettas and Dances, with many other Articles, being his Property and that of Signora Mattei's, will be sold'.[3] Felice de' Giardini and Regina Mingotti resumed the responsibilities surrendered to Mattei in 1757, a change of management already decided before 3 March 1763, when Giardini, through the medium of the *Public Advertiser*, 'humbly requests the Nobility and Gentry who have done him the Honour to subscribe to his Operas for the ensuing Season, to pay in Half their Subscription to Mess. Drummond at Charing-Cross, to enable him to give Security for the Payment of several of the most eminent Singers from Italy and other Parts. Mr. Giardini would not have presumed to make this early Application to the Public, had he not already received the Sanction of a Licence from the Lord Chamberlain'. The announcement excited anticipations imperfectly realised, but enabled Giardini, on August 6, to allege 'the great Demand for Boxes for the ensuing Season' as 'a sufficient Apology' for reminding negligent patrons of their liabilities.

The change of management affected Bach's fortunes. Either Giardini did not appreciate his abilities or found it inconvenient to employ them. Certainly, Bach's name does not appear in the Opera programmes during the season 1763-4. But the omission left him other avenues to reputation and a livelihood. As a harpsichordist he was already established in the favour of the public, which conceded him pre-eminence unchallenged till Schroeter's advent.[4] His personal address and agreeable qualities admitted him to the withdrawing-rooms of Society, and obtained no lack of pupils. Above all, he enjoyed the patronage of the Court, whose favour had been conspicuously shown during the past season, and was soon to declare itself in more flattering form. Pondering his circumstances in the summer of 1763, when Mattei's departure

[1] P.A. 7 May 1763.
[2] On May 25. Cf. P.A. of that date.
[3] P.A. 1 June 1763.
[4] Cf. *infra* p. 124.

terminated his engagement in the Haymarket, it was the favour, indeed the command, of the sovereigns that determined him to stake his fortunes permanently in London. In a brief letter he intimated his resolve to Martini, to whom, apparently, he had not written since his departure from Milan:

Most reverend Father and honoured patron,

Long ago I ought to have fulfilled my duty to you, but many important occupations and ill-health have prevented me; so I beg, and hope to receive, your kind forgiveness.

With this letter your Reverence will receive two books, the Life of Handel[1] and Dr. Smith's *Harmonics*.[2] I have not been able to find 'La Poesie dell' Avaro'. What I have to send you you will receive through Signora Carmignani's father.

It was my intention to visit[3] Italy this year, but the infinite kindness of their Majesties the King and Queen obliges me to obey their request that I should remain here. I beg you to convey my compliments to the Chevalier, D. Carlo [Dassio] and all my friends, and I have the honour to subscribe myself

Your Reverence's most humble, devoted, and obliged servant,

Giov. Bach.

London, 1 July 1763.

As he does not mention the appointment, it must be concluded that Bach was not yet Music Master in the Queen's Household.[4] Certainly he was in office before 1 February 1764; for the title-page of his Six Sonatas (Op. II), published on that date, describes him as 'Maitre de Musique de S.M. la Reine d'Angleterre'. The position was not a sinecure. Both sovereigns were musical: Charlotte, Haydn remarked, 'played quite well, for a Queen'; George played the violin and flute, and, during his insanity, Charlotte, entering his room, found him seated at a harpsichord singing a hymn to his own accompaniment.[5]   Bach was in regular attendance at Court, and, as the royal children grew up, they too became his pupils. 'The schoolroom at Court', writes Mrs. Papendiek of a later year, 'was one of gaiety and cheerfulness. The masters were . . . for music, our dear and valued friend, Johann Christian Bach. He also gave lessons to the Queen; and of evenings, by appointment, he attended the King's accompaniment to the pianoforte by the flute'.[6] Mrs. Delany, who frequented the 'Queen's Lodge' when

---

[1] Mainwaring's *Memoirs*, published in 1760.

[2] *Harmonics, or the Philosophy of Musical Sounds*, by Robert Smith (1749). An enlarged edition appeared in 1759, and a *Postscript upon the changeable Harpsichord* in 1762.

[3] 'poter andare in Italia'.

[4] A search of Queen Charlotte's papers in the Lord Chamberlain's charge and among the Add. MSS. in the British Museum has failed to discover any details regarding Bach.

[5] Jesse iii. 581.   [6] Papendiek i. 64.

the royal children were young, usually found the King on the floor playing with his family, while in the next room the royal band received his directions as to what they should play, Handel having his preference.[1] The servant of sympathetic masters, Bach won the esteem of his royal mistress, whom he served till his death, as much by his character as his ability. If his letters to Martini divulge little more than his assiduity as a student, the circumstances of his career indicate his possession of qualities which attracted the affectionate regard of those who knew him best. The friendship of Martini and Litta, the solicitude of a brother whose nature was not otherwise generous, the kindly recollections of Henry Angelo, and the almost filial affection of the Papendieks, all combine to reveal a personality genial and modest, open, light-hearted, and friendly.

The Mattei's farewell to London turned Bach adrift in search of a lodging; for, upon his arrival, he had been received into her house in Jermyn Street.[2] Her departure sent him northward to Soho, where he spent the rest of his days, and into a partnership, broken only by his marriage, with one closely linked with him by associations and birth. In February 1764 he advertised a concert in collaboration with Carl Friedrich Abel, the first of a series that continued without interruption for nearly twenty years, inviting the public to procure tickets, at half-a-guinea each, 'at Mr. Bach and Mr. Abel's Lodgings, in Meard's-street, St. Ann's, Soho'.[3] This retired thoroughfare, named after its designer,[4] had recently been built; it retains to-day something of the quiet aloofness that made it agreeable when the two friends frequented it. Here, in a furnished room at five shillings a week, had lived Bet Flint, who a few years before (1758) paid the stern penalty for stealing a counterpane therefrom. Here, too, lived pretty Miss Catherine Fourmantel, Lawrence Sterne's 'Pretty Kitty', and Batty Langley, the architect.[5] Bach and his friend did not long share its associations.

Born at Cöthen in 1725, Carl Friedrich Abel was ten years Bach's senior; throughout their joint tenancies his name only appears on the Rate-books.[6] His father, Christian Ferdinand Abel, was

[1] Jesse ii. 523.
[2] Bach's Op. I. was advertised on 17 March 1763 as 'to be had of him at Signora Mattei's, in Germyn-Street, St. James's'.
[3] P.A. 29 Feb. 1764.
[4] A stone let into the wall at the Dean Street end bears the date 1732. Cf. Rimbault, p. 127.
[5] Wheatley, ii. 518.
[6] The Rate-books for 1760–6 are lost; it is therefore impossible to identify the house in Meard's Street occupied by Bach and Abel.

Chamber musician and violinist in the Cöthen Capelle during the Capellmeistership of Sebastian Bach,[1] under whom, the music-lexikons state, Carl Friedrich was brought up at the Leipzig Thomasschule. If so, his London friendship with Sebastian's son had a juvenile foundation. The list of *alumni* during Sebastian's Cantorship does not include Abel's name, however;[2] and, since his father ended his days elsewhere, it is improbable that he attended the Thomasschule as an *externus*. But, as he entered the Dresden Electoral Capelle in 1748, he may have been acquainted with the great Cantor in his capacity as Hofcomponist, and, like his father, have played under him. Till the Prussian invasion of Saxony in the Seven Years War, Abel remained in Dresden, and, upon the dissolution of the Capelle, made his way to England in search of a livelihood. On 27 March 1759 he announced his arrival in London with a notice of his intention to give a concert of vocal and instru-mental music in the Great Room, Dean Street, Soho, on Thursday 5 April, at seven o'clock,[3] at which he displayed his surprising versatility by performing on the viola da gamba, harpsichord, and pentachord, an instrument newly invented in England, several pieces, all composed by himself. But it was as a gambist that his pre-eminent skill was admitted. Like Bach, he became a member of the Queen's Chamber Band, and as a composer was hardly less prolific. He was in constant request at public concerts, and from changing addresses in Soho announced his own. In 1760 he was lodging at the Golden Dove and Acorn, in Greek Street, and from 1761 to 1763 in the Golden Dial, in the same thoroughfare. He was residing there when Bach arrived in England, and moved thence to Meard's Street when the two set up their joint house-hold.

Meanwhile, under the new *impresaria* a season of Opera, dull and uneventful, opened on Saturday 26 November 1763 with *Cleonice*, a pasticcio announced as 'by several eminent Masters',[4] but mainly by Galuppi and Giardini, who, notwithstanding his promises, had secured for his singers none of conspicuous distinction—his part-ner Regina Mingotti, 'in the decline of her favour', Angiola Sartori, Signora Baini, and, for the male parts, Giuseppe Antonio Mazziotti,

[1] T.B. p. 120.
[2] Cf. B.–J. 1907, pp. 66 f.
[3] P.A. 27 March 1759. The Dean Street Great Concert Room was a large house in Dean Street (No. 17) and Frith Street (No. 67), once the residence of the Venetian ambassador. Later it became an auction mart, a dancing academy, and eventually was adapted for the use of St. Ann's schools. Cf. Rimbault, p. 183.
[4] P.A. 26 Nov. 1763.

and Guglietti.[1] Burney found little merit in the production, but praised the duet, 'Tu parti, mio ben', which he attributed to the Venetian composer Ferdinando Giuseppe Bertoni, perhaps correctly. Bach also, however, set the words as a duet,[2] probably for this occasion. The pasticcio was succeeded on Tuesday 13 December by *Siroe*, advertised[3] as 'entirely new, excepting in the three favourite Airs of Signora Mingotti'. Giardini, in fact, furnished the greater part[4] of the work, which was moderately successful. The first production of the new year, *Leucippo* (Tuesday 10 January 1764), introduced a new composer to the Haymarket, Matthias Vento, a Neapolitan of Bach's age, whom Giardini invited to England[5] in much the same circumstances as attended Bach's arrival in 1762, and who, like Bach, was encouraged to settle in London thereafter as a popular and successful teacher.[6] Described as 'an heroic Pastoral . . . intirely a new Composition of Mr. Vento, a Neapolitan Master',[7] the opera satisfied the public; Burney found its melody 'graceful and pleasing'. A 'command' performance of it was given on Saturday 21 January, on the occasion of the marriage of the King's sister, Princess Augusta, to the Hereditary Prince of Brunswick, when the attendance was so great that 'the Coaches of the Quality could not come near the Door, which obliged the Ladies to get out and walk to the House. Four Parts in five of the Number of genteel Persons were obliged to go back again, after being in the most eminent Danger of being crushed to Death'.[8] *Senocrita*,[9] by Piccinni and Davide Perez, followed on 21 February, and a 'new' opera, *Alessandro nell' Indie*, on Tuesday 13 March. Burney does not mention the latter, nor do the public news-sheets indicate its composer. It is therefore improbable that Bach's version was presented. On Saturday, May 5, the last novelty of the season was staged, Giardini's *Enea e Lavinia*, whose short run brought an inauspicious season to an end and terminated Giardini and his partner's management.[10]

While the season pursued its languid course, Bach and Abel

[1] Bur. iv. 484, who, however, has 'Marrietti' and 'Peretti'.
[2] *Infra*, p. 253.
[3] P.A. 13 Dec. 1763.
[4] Bur. iv. 484.
[5] *Ibid.*, Burney gives the operas in incorrect order.
[6] He died in London in 1776.
[7] Cast: *Narete*, Signore Guglietti; *Leucippo*, Antonio Mazziotti; *Dafne*, Regina Mingotti; *Tirsi*, Giuseppe Giustinelli; *Climene*, Angiola Sartori; *Aminta*, Signora Baini; Ballet Master, Pietro Sodi (Bott. 907 i. 10/3).
[8] P.A. 24 Jan. 1764.
[9] Burney incorrectly makes *Leucippo* and *Senocrita* a single opera under the title *Leucippe e Zenocrita*.
[10] Bur. iv. 484.

inaugurated their partnership with a concert on 29 February 1764, thus announced in the *Public Advertiser*:

For the Benefit of Mr. Bach and Mr. Abel:
Great Room in Spring Gardens, near St. James's Park,
This Day, February 29
A New Serenata in two Acts Composed by Mr. Bach. To which will be added several new Pieces of Instrumental Music by Mr. Abel. To begin exactly at Half an Hour after Six. Tickets at Half-a-Guinea each to be had at Mr. Bach and Mr. Abel's Lodgings, in Meard's-street, St. Ann's, Soho.

The concert is not otherwise recorded. A few days earlier (February 1) Bach had published his six Trios (Op. II) for harpsichord and strings, one or more of which he perhaps introduced on the occasion. The Serenata must have been either a composition no longer extant, or *Endimione*, which Bach revived many years later.[1] His popularity as a composer, and the necessity to protect himself against the piracy of unlicensed printers, are evident from the following Warrant:[2]

GEORGE R.

Whereas our trusty and well-beloved John Christian Bach, gent., has by his petition humbly represented unto Us that he hath, with great study, labour and expense composed divers works consisting of Vocal and Instrumental Music, and being desirous to print the same, and apprehending, unless he can obtain our Royal Licence and Privilege, other persons may be induced to print and publish the said works, and so invade his property therein, he hath therefore most humbly prayed Us to grant him our Royal Licence and Privilege for the sole printing and publishing the above mentioned Works for the term of fourteen years agreable to the Statute in that case made and provided. We, being willing to give all due encouragement to this his undertaking, are graciously pleased to condescend to his request, and We do therefore, by these Presents, so far as may be agreable to the Statute in that behalf made and provided, grant unto him, the said John Christian Bach, his Executors, Administrators, and Assigns, Our Licence for the sole printing and publishing the said Works for the term of fourteen years, to be computed from date hereof, strictly forbidding all our subjects within our Kingdom and Dominions, to reprint, abridge, copy out in writing for sale, or publish the same, either in the like or in any other size or manner whatsoever, or to import, buy, vend, utter or distribute any copy or copies thereof, reprinted or written, for sale beyond the seas, during the aforesaid term of fourteen years, without the approbation or consent of the said John Christian Bach, his Executors, Administrators, or Assigns, under their hands and seals first had and obtained, or they will answer the contrary at their perils, whereof the Commissioners and other Officers of our Customs, the Master Wardens and Company of Stationers are to take notice, that due obedience

---

[1] *Infra*, p. 123.
[2] State Paper, P.R.O. Home Office. Entry Book 375.

may be rendered to our Will and Pleasure herein declared. Given at our Court at St. James the 15th day of December 1763, in the fourth year of our Reign.

By His Majesty's Command.
Sandwich.

The reasons that moved Bach to invoke protection are revealed by the writer of a letter from London in April 1783:[1] 'You need not be surprised to see the works of Bach and Abel frequently printed in a manner that in Germany would be regarded as unworthy of these famous men. The fact is, that while they entrusted their compositions for public use to be engraved by Bremner[2] and Welcker,[3] who paid well for the privilege, other products of their pen, procured by underhand means, got into print without their knowledge or permission. For there are people, unable to obtain, or unwilling to pay for, compositions by these masters, who made it their business to collect, engrave, and sell pieces written for their pupils. No sooner were these in print than they were copied and circulated as authentic, especially Bach's, whose reputation suffered in consequence'.

Looking back across the years, we can discover the musical event of chief interest in 1764 to have been the sojourn in London of a youthful prodigy not yet past his ninth year. In April Wolfgang Amadeus Mozart, with his father and sister, arrived from Paris and took lodgings in Cecil Court, St. Martin's Lane. Vienna and Paris already had done homage to 'the little Wizard', who was hardly arrived before he and his sister were summoned to Buckingham House. They were treated with a graciousness their father reported as 'unbeschreiblich', and, driving through St. James's Park a week later, were recognized from the royal carriage with unceremonious heartiness; the King let down the window-sash, and with nodding head and waving hand greeted Master Wolfgang. The youthful master's first public performance was proposed for May 17 at Hickford's Room,[4] Brewer Street, when the violoncellist Graziani promised a 'Concerto on the Harpsichord by Master Mozart, who is a real Prodigy for his Age'. Mozart's indisposition postponed the concert till May 22, when he was again too unwell to appear. His indisposition had not prevented him from obeying a second command to the palace on May 19, when the King tested his powers with compositions by Wagenseil, Bach, Abel, and

[1] Cramer, 1783, p. 546.
[2] Robert Bremner came to London from Edinburgh in 1762. His shop was at ' The Harp and Hautboy', opposite Somerset House, in the Strand.
[3] Peter Welcker's shop was in Gerrard Street, Soho.
[4] It still exists.

Handel, all of which he read 'prima vista', Leopold Mozart reported to his wife. Wolfgang also played on the King's organ, and astonished his audience even more than by his skill on the harpsichord. He accompanied the Queen in an aria, and improvised a melody on the continuo of one of Handel's airs. On June 5 the two children at length were presented to the public at a mid-day concert in the Spring Gardens Room, and three weeks later (June 29) Wolfgang appeared at Ranelagh as 'the most extraordinary Prodigy, and most amazing Genius that has appeared in any Age'.[1]

When, at the end of June, Leopold Mozart withdrew his family to Tunbridge Wells, among those whom Wolfgang had met, none left a happier impression on his memory than Bach, who, as the Queen's Music Master, was officially concerned with the arrangements for the young visitor's appearances at Court. The attractive, unspoilt genius of the boy captured the older master, who, with Wolfgang on his lap,[2] played the harpsichord, each in turn taking a bar, and then a fugue, which Bach began and Wolfgang completed. Upon the young genius Bach impressed more than the memory of an agreeable personality. Mozart came to England a child, superbly gifted, precocious, but unformed. He left it, after more than a year's sojourn, equipped at every point in the technique of his art. Among the influences that moulded his genius, Bach's example must be counted vital. From him and Manzuoli Mozart learnt the secrets of vocal technique. The later symphonies he composed in London were directly inspired by Bach's. Leopold's first letter from London (28 May 1764) speaks of his son 'seated at the harpsichord preparing to play one of Bach's Trios'. In the domain of Opera Bach's elegance, melodic purity, inclination to subordinate dramatic expression to sheer beauty of phrase, were characteristics he imparted to his young disciple, who added the qualities of his own flaming genius. If less permanent, Bach's influence also affected Mozart's instrumental style, conveying the characteristics of his own—an almost feminine sweetness, and in his *Andantes* a rare and spontaneous beauty. Elegant rather than profound, Bach's effects were gained in large measure by the contrasts Burney observed as distinctive of his style—the alternation of *forte* and *piano*, transmission of a subject from one instrument to another, and, in general, a happy mixture of plan and improvisation—music of an elegant charm which made an ineffaceable appeal to Mozart, though his genius raised his own art to a plane above it.

[1] The statements in the text are taken from the *Public Advertiser*. Cf. for Mozart's London visit Pohl, pp. 93 f.; Jahn. i. 58 f.; Wyzewa, i. 89 f.
[2] Cf. Grimm's letter in Wyzewa, i. 164, and *ibid.*, i. 91.

Italy, who had laid her spell already on the older master, through him touched the pen of his precocious friend.[1]

The season of 1764–5 restored Bach's association with the King's Theatre and raised the Opera to a plane of favour and prosperity it had rarely known. The welcome conclusion of the Seven Years War contributed to this result. But the chief contriver of the surprising miracle was the *castrato* Giovanni Manzuoli, who recently had carried Madrid by storm and now arrived in London to repeat his triumph. Ungraceful in figure, and deficient in the finer technique of his art, his voice was of such beauty as extorted enthusiasm; the sensations he excited seemed to Burney[2] 'more irresistible and universal than I have ever been witness to in any theatre'. He was supported by Ferdinando Tenducci,[3] Bach's intimate friend, who had come to England in 1758, and though not recently engaged— for a large part of 1760 he was in prison for debt[4]—was popular with London playgoers. Ercole Ciprandi and Leopoldo Micheli completed the male cast, the former an excellent tenor who had first sung in the King's Theatre in 1754. The women were the constant Clementina Cremonini, Teresa Scotti, and Polly Young, a niece of Mrs Arne; she later married François-Hippolyte Barthélémon, who came to London in 1764 as leader of the Opera orchestra.

Though its prospects were encouraging, the season's opening was attended by anxiety and friction—doubts regarding the new management, dissension among the singers, in which Bach was involved, and other impediments. A few weeks before the first performance Mrs. Harris writes (19 October 1764) from Whitehall to her son at Oxford:[5] 'I can give you no better information as to the Opera than what I told you before; Giardini must go on, if he can, for none else can take it.' On the following day she was able to send fuller news: 'As you want to know about operas, I can inform you of what Tenducci says, who has just been here, and brought with him Manzolini.[6] I got him [Manzuoli] to sing one song; he has a most charming voice, particularly in the upper notes . . . Giardini is gone quite away; so his partner, one Fermier, and Crawford will manage it [the Opera]. Manzolini has made a

---

[1] For Bach's influence on Mozart cf. Wyzewa, i. 89 f., 117 f.
[2] Bur. iv. 485.   [3] Illustration No. 26.
[4] On 13 Jan. 1761 he advertised (in the *Public Advertiser*) a concert for Jan. 28, entreating 'the distinguished Benevolence of the Nobility and Gentry of this Kingdom' after eight months detention in the prison of the King's Bench.
[5] Harris, i. 115. Mrs. Harris's son James became the first Earl of Malmesbury. Her husband was a Lord of the Treasury 1763–5 and M.P. for Christchurch 1761–80.
[6] i.e. Manzuoli.

vow never to sing what Bach had composed; but that quarrel is now made up, and Bach is to compose one opera; but what they are to do for hands I cannot learn. I know almost all the old orchestra are engaged to the playhouses, and so are the dancers. Tenducci is to have £150 from Mossop for singing and acting two months, and a benefit besides.' On October 25 Mrs. Harris writes again: ' All Manzolini's clothes and finery are seized and carried to the Customs House, so he has sent a petition to the Lords of the Treasury to have them redeemed. This event diverts Lord North, as he says that not one of the Treasury know a note of music or care one farthing what becomes of Manzolini, except Mr. Harris. He says your father has told so moving a story to Mr. Grenville about it, that he thinks it may affect him. There have been some droll scenes between Mr. Harris, Manzolini, and Tenducci, who is interpreter, and who swears at every word he speaks, sometimes a little French, then English, and poor Manzolini stands by shrugging up his broad shoulders.'

Manzuoli having recovered his properties, the season opened on Saturday 24 November 1764 with the pasticcio *Ezio*, announced as a 'new serious Opera, the Music by different Masters'.[1] Manzuoli's fame drew so large a crowd that Burney, 'after waiting two hours at the door',[2] with difficulty obtained a seat. His praise of the entertainment was unstinted; Manzuoli's voice he declared 'the most powerful and voluminous soprano that had been heard on our stage since the time of Farinelli,[3] and his manner of singing was grand and full of taste and dignity'. The critics were unanimous in praising his voice and talents, while the audience applauded in a manner so spontaneous and enthusiastic that their clapping seemed 'a universal thunder'. Teresa Scotti (*prima donna*), with an elegant figure and attractive face, showed great flexibility and expression in her singing, though her voice lacked power. Tenducci (*secondo uomo*) revealed himself much improved since his previous engagement, while Cremonini once more showed herself a musician of sound technique, 'but almost without voice'. For Ciprandi Bach provided his popular aria 'Non so d'onde viene', originally composed for Raaf at Naples, and in it he was 'very deservedly applauded and generally encored'.[4]   The opera was frequently re-

[1] Cast: *Valentiniano III*, Ferdinando Tenducci; *Ezio*, Giovanni Manzuoli; *Massimo*, Ercole Ciprandi; *Varo*, Leopoldo Micheli; *Fulvia*, Teresa Scotti; *Onoria*, Clementina Cremonini; *Darce*, Polly Young. Ballet-master, Signore Gherardi (Bott. 907 i. 10/2).
[2] Bur. iv. 485.
[3] Carlo Broschi Farinelli, the finest *castrato* of his generation, visited London in 1734.
[4] Bur. iv. 485.

peated during the season, a circumstance which supports Burney's eulogy against Horace Walpole's less enthusiastic judgement. 'It was our first Opera', he wrote on the following day (November 25) to the Earl of Hertford, 'and I went to town to hear Manzuoli, who did not quite answer my expectation, though a very fine singer, but his voice *has been* younger, and wants the touching tones of Elisi.[1] However, the audience was not so nice, but applauded him immoderately and *encored* three of his songs. The first woman[2] was advertised for a perfect beauty with no voice; but her beauty and voice are by no means so unequally balanced: she has a pretty little small pipe, and only a pretty little small person and share of beauty, and does not act ill. There is Tenducci, a moderate singer, and the rest intolerable. The dances were not only hissed, as they deserved to be, but the gallery, à-la-Drury-Lane, cried out "off! off!".'

Ezio's success rendered a new production unnecessary until 1 January 1765, when *Berenice* was performed. The pasticcio, to which Vento and Abel, among others, contributed,[3] was little admired; of its arias only Bach's 'Confusa, smarrita',[4] sung by the beautiful but feeble-voiced Teresa Scotti, found popular approval.[5] He had so far been heard only in old material, and infrequently. But on Saturday, 26 January 1765, he produced his third London opera *Adriano in Siria*, with the following cast:[6]

Adriano	.	.	. Ferdinando Tenducci.
Osroa	.	.	. Ercole Ciprandi.
Farnaspe	.	.	. Giovanni Manzuoli.
Aquilio	.	.	. Leopoldo Micheli.
Emirena	.	.	. Teresa Scotti.
Sabina	.	.	. Clementina Cremonini.
Barsene	.	.	. Polly Young.

The subject—Hadrian's campaign in Syria and stern repression of the Jewish rising—was a favourite with composers in Metastasio's libretto. It had not been employed in England since 1750, however, when Legrenzio Vincenzo Ciampi presented it. Its novelty, and the conjunction of Bach and Manzuoli, drew an audience which even surpassed that of the opening night of the season, and occasioned such a throng at the doors as had seldom been seen there. Not a third of those who assembled found seats,[7] while the auditorium was so packed that many were obliged to stand behind

---

[1] Filippo Elisi.   [2] Teresa Scotti.
[3] Bur. iv. 486. Burney misstates the order in which the operas were produced during this season.
[4] *Supra*, p. 54.   [5] Bur. iv.486.   [6] Bott. 1342 c. 16/9.
[7] Bur. iv. 486.

the scenes throughout the performance.[1] Probably these incon-
veniences affected both singers and audience, or public anticipation
had been heightened to an unreasonable pitch. 'Every one seemed
to come out of the theatre disappointed', Burney declared, though
Walpole described the performance as 'prodigious'. The opera was
performed seven times,[2] while its songs, published by Welcker,[3]
were sung at concerts 'with great applause, and found, as detached
airs, excellent, though they had been unfortunate in their totality'.[4]
Possibly Burney reveals a major cause of Bach's disappointment in
his remark, that the opera's comparative failure 'seemed matter
of great triumph to the Italians'. The Opera was an Italian preserve, the intrusion of a German, though Italianized, disagreeable.
Manzuoli's original refusal to sing Bach's music perhaps was
founded on the narrow prejudice. The prominence of Bach and
others of his compatriots in the musical life of the metropolis
was another grievance, aggravated by the Court's patronage of
them.

Vento, now domiciled in London, provided the next opera
Demofoonte, produced on Saturday 2 March 1765. Burney found
it 'natural, graceful, and pleasing, always free from vulgarity, but
never very new or learned'.[5] It was frequently repeated. Meanwhile, the two principal male singers took their 'benefits' with
unequal gains. On Thursday, March 7, Manzuoli revived Giardini's
Il Re Pastore,[6] with new airs for himself.[7] The theatre doors
needed to be opened at four o'clock,[8] so great was the throng, and
the singer reaped a rich harvest. 'Signor Mangoli [*sic*], the Italian
singer at the Haymarket', the *Gentleman's Magazine* for the following week recorded,[9] 'got no less, after paying all charges of every
kind, by his benefit last week, than 1,000 guineas. This, added to
a sum of 1,500, which he has already saved, and the remaining
profits of the season, is surely an undoubted proof of British
generosity; one patriotic lady, we are told, complimented the above
gentleman with a 200 *l*. bill for a single ticket on that occasion.'
Leopold Mozart, now settled with his family at Mr. Williamson's,
21 Thrift Street,[10] had already (8 Feb. 1765) reported enviously to
his wife, that 'No one makes much money this winter except
Manzoli and some others at the Opera'; he computed the singer's

[1] Horace Walpole to the Earl of Hertford, 27 Jan. 1765.
[2] Not 'but two or three times', as Burney writes.   [3] *Infra*, p. 211.
[4] Bur. iv. 487.   [5] *Ibid*.   [6] First produced in 1755.
[7] Cast: *Aminta*, Giovanni Manzuoli; *Alessandro*, Ercole Ciprandi; *Elisa*, Teresa
Scotti; *Agenore*, Ferdinando Tenducci; *Tamiri*, Clementina Cremonini (Bott.
907 i. 10/6).   [8] Pohl, p. 76.   [9] Vol. xxxv, p. 141.
[10] Rimbault, p. 100. Now Frith Street.

earnings at '20,000 Teutsche gulden'.[1] Less acclaimed and rewarded, Tenducci took his 'benefit', on Thursday March 28, in the
pasticcio *Antigonus*, 'by different Masters'.[2]

An Italian and a German had been permitted to provide an
opera for Manzuoli, a privilege, Burney declares, 'every composer
now in London' was ambitious to win. To show their impartiality
the managers next accorded the favour to Arne, whose *Artaxerxes*
at Covent Garden in 1763 had been a success. He chose Metastasio's *L'Olimpiade* as his libretto and produced it on Saturday
27 April 1765.[3] It encountered not merely the prejudice which
had recently damped Bach's success, but also the comment that the
composer's technique was unequal to his opportunity. Burney remarked severely,[4] that Arne had 'written for vulgar singers and
hearers too long to be able to comport himself properly at the
Opera-house, in the first circle of taste and fashion. . . . The common play-house and ballad passages, which occurred in almost
every air in his opera, made the audience wonder how they got
there. A tarnished Monmouth-street suit of cloaths in the side
boxes would not have surprised them more. . . . A different language, different singers, and a different audience and style of Music
from his own, carried him out of his usual element, where he
mangled the Italian poetry, energies, and accents, nearly as much
as a native of Italy just arrived in London would English, in a
similar situation'. Yet, the composer of 'Where the bee sucks' has
outlived the reputation of those with whom Burney disadvantage-
ously contrasted him.

The pasticcio *Il Solimano*, produced on Tuesday 14 May 1765,
was the last opera of the season, and Manzuoli's success in it
created a problem for those whose desire to hear him conflicted
with the social tradition which held Tuesday performances unfashionable. Their dilemma found expression in an amusing letter:[5]

Sir,
My People tell me you are the Man I must send to for Redress in an
Affair of great Consequence, and which I shall obtain if you but print
my Letter. I therefore insist upon your doing it Tomorrow. Now, dont

[1] Schiedermair, iv. 242.
[2] Cast: *Demetrius*, Giovanni Manzuoli; *Alexander*, Ferdinando Tenducci;
Antigonus, Ercole Ciprandi; *Clearcus*, Leopoldo Micheli; *Berenice*, Teresa
Scotti; *Ismene*, Clementina Cremonini; *Eudice*, Polly Young (P.A. 28 March
1765).
[3] Cast: *Clistene*, Ercole Ciprandi; *Megacle*, Giovanni Manzuoli; *Licida*, Ferdinando Tenducci; *Aminta*, Leopoldo Micheli; *Aristea*, Teresa Scotti; *Argene*,
Clementina Cremonini; *Nice*, Polly Young (Bott. 907 i. 11/5).
[4] Bur. iv. 486.
[5] P.A. 17 May 1765.

trifle with me, Mr. Woodfall,[1] for, should you, I know not to what Length
my Rage may carry me. You must know I was at the great Concert
Yesterday, and was not more pleased with it (though a fine Entertainment)
than I was with the Account of the new Opera, *Solimano*. You will guess,
ere this (if you are not very stupid), I am a Woman of Fashion, consequently fond of an Italian Opera, and in course an Admirer of the Manzoli;
but I am in the greatest Dilemma imaginable, for they tell me it is not to
be done again till *Tuesday*. Now you know (if you know any thing) as it
is impossible there can be what we call *a good Opera on a Tuesday*. I cannot go—No; positively cannot go. You perhaps will be stupid enough
to suppose Manzoli does not sing so well *on that day as on a Saturday*;
but you have no Business to suppose. How should a Man that lives in
Pater-noster-Row know any thing of these Matters? Suffice it—'tis unfashionable to go to any but a *Saturday's Opera*. I desire therefore you
will go to the Manager with my Compliments and desire we may have
Solimano for the *Saturday's Opera*; and as the dear Manzoli may not
probably sing above six Times more in public, request he may only
perform on those Days, or we People of Fashion shall be deprived of
hearing him above three Times. If the Manager should not comply, as
I have *a great Rout on Tuesday*, I will take the Opinion of my Company,
if I can go to a *Tuesday's Opera* without risking my Reputation in point
of *Taste*.

                                            Yours, ARAMINTHA.
New Norfolk-street. Thursday Noon[2]

Tuesday had made her moan in an earlier year:[3]

The Opera-Tuesday's Complaint to her sister Saturday.

By Mr. J. L.[4]

Sister! so proud you're grown, such Scorn you dart,
The Women must despise you in their Heart;
Impartial, they confess your Face is fair,
Lovely your Form, and elegant your Air;
That Fire and Genius sparkle in your Eye:
These Charms you boast; and (SISTER!) these have I.

Add, that the Beauties of the magic Scene
Glow in the Colours of your *Francischin*,[5]
That light as Fawns th' Italian Dancers bound;
Whilst, like Diana, *Asselin* swims around;
That in *Gallini's* Attitudes we trace
Ease, Fancy, Spirit, Harmony and Grace;
That in *Calori's*[6] Accents, sweet and clear,
The Warblings of the Nightingale we hear;
That, on the Soul whilst soft *Tenducci* steals,
Each noble Sentiment *Quilici* feels:

---

[1] Henry Woodfall, the printer of the *Public Advertiser* and author of *Darby
and Joan*.
[2] May 16.
[4] ? John Lockman.   [3] P.A. 25 April 1760.
                                           [5] Scene-painter.
[6] Angiola Calori; she came to London in 1758.

That *Cornacchini*[1] ev'ry Note refines;
Whilst, over All, the lov'd MATTEI shines,
Her Powers of Voice increasing *Cocchi's* Praise;
Her Action strengthening *Metastasio's* Lays.

Born Twins, one Star did at our Birth preside,
Whence, sure, an equal Lot should both betide:
Explain then this strange Paradox:—why you
Attract a Croud of Suitors;—I, so few?

'Tis owing to—yes 'tis—I have it now!—
To FASHION, Goddess, to whom all Things bow:
Fashion, from whose Caprice Disorder springs,
Reversing the Propriety of Things;
Depressing Genius, or exalting Fools,
Just as the instantaneous Whimsey rules.

I'll to the Goddess haste, and, in her Fane
Prostrate, my crying Grievances explain,
With smoothest Flatt'ry her proud Name invoke,
(When we for Favours sue, the Master-Stroke):
If she but smile, o'erjoy'd, I shall no more
The Fate of my neglected Charms deplore;
But rival you, (vain SISTER!) in your Arts;
And thenceforth be proclaim'd joint QUEEN OF HEARTS.

In fact, the rivalry persisted. Meanwhile, the season reached its close on Saturday 22 June 1765. Cremonini had taken her 'benefit' at Hickford's Room on Friday May 17, at noon, in a 'Concert of Music composed and directed by Mr. Bach', assisted by Abel, Barthélémon, and Cirri, the violoncellist.[2] The Mozarts made their *adieux* to London, and Manzuoli faded for ever from the English sky. For Bach also the year was a milestone. Henceforward his association with the King's Theatre was intermittent; the purpose which had brought him to London was subordinated to activities in another sphere, in which, till he died, his pre-eminence was not challenged.

[1] Emanuele Cornacchini, of Milan.   [2] P.A. 17 May 1765.

CHAPTER IV

SOHO AND HAYMARKET

WHILE the season of 1764–5 ran its course, Bach and Abel removed from Meard's Street to the closer neighbourhood of congenial society in King's Square Court, now Carlisle Street, Soho Square.[1] Bounded by Tyburn (Oxford) Street on the north, the district was London's most recent suburb. Soho Fields, an expanse of open country north of St. Martin's, was surveyed between 1675 and 1680 by Gregory King, Rouge Dragon, who laid out Soho Square; it long bore his name. Its substantial houses fronted a formal garden, in whose centre figures representing the Thames, Trent, Humber, and Severn supported a water-basin. The sculptor Nollekens saw iron railings erected round the garden in 1748, and watched the water pouring from the jugs of the river-gods into the basin at the foot of a statue of Charles II. From the first the Square was an aristocratic quarter. In 1693 the Earls of Bolingbroke, Carlisle, Fauconberg, Yarmouth, Sir Richard Onslow, and others had houses in it. The ill-fated Duke of Monmouth built a fine mansion there, and, when Nollekens frequented it, four foreign ambassadors gave it dignity.[2] Monmouth House, its most imposing residence, stood on the south side of the quadrangle, where Bateman's Buildings were erected later. Designed by Sir Christopher Wren, it is said, the mansion was begun in 1681 on a scale of magnificence. Bach would pass it on his way to the Roman Catholic Chapel in Duke Street, Lincoln's Inn Fields, and certainly watched its demolition about 1775. Stone piers surmounted by the Monmouth crest supported massive wrought iron gates admitting to a spacious courtyard, whence steps ascended to the entrance hall. Eight rooms filled the ground floor, of which the principal apartment, the dining-room, looked to the south from windows between carved and gilded panels bearing whole-length portraits, while the corners of the ornamental ceiling, and the mantel above the chimney, displayed the arms of the ducal builder. An oak staircase, with shallow steps and tessellated landings of variegated woods, ascended to the first storey, and from brackets on its walls the busts of Seneca, Caracalla, Trajan, Hadrian, and others

---

[1] Bach's Op. III, published in 1765, was announced as being on sale at his house in King's Square Court, Dean Street, Soho.
[2] Cf. Kingsford, p. 69; Rimbault, chap. 2, and Illustrations Nos. 15 and 16.

looked down. The principal room on the first floor was superbly decorated with pheasants and other birds, figured in gold on a ground of blue satin, while its chimney-piece was richly carved to represent fruit and foliage, a recess within a wreath of oak-leaves awaiting a bust of Lucy Walter's luckless son. The panels of the lofty window-shutters were gilt, and the piers between them supported great mirrors. The garden extended to Queen Street, which its 'dirty and ill-kept' walls bounded.[1]

On the east side of the square, north of Sutton Street,[2] stood Fauconberg House, or the White House.[3] Here once lived Mary Cromwell, Lady Fauconberg (d. 1712), the Protector's daughter. The gallant Sir Cloudesley Shovel and the Dutch adventurer Ripperda also occupied it. When Bach passed its door, it was the residence of Count de Fuentes, the Spanish Ambassador, in whose suite was the astounding Joseph Merlin, whose 'magical inventions' provided interest, mingled with tremors, to the inhabitants of the Square. One of his novelties was a pair of skates contrived to run on wheels. With them on his feet, and a violin and bow in his hands, the wizard once attended Mrs. Cornelys' refined assembly in the Square, gyrating nimbly as he played; but, having invented no brake to retard his velocity, dashed with great force into a costly mirror, damaging himself severely and the furniture irreparably. His master vacated the house before 1776, when it became the property of Thomas Hooper, and as 'Hooper's Hotel' won unsavoury notoriety. Next to it stood a handsome house, with ceilings by Angelica Kauffmann and Biagio Rebecca. The Duke of Argyll, victor at Sheriffmuir in 1715, lived in it, and the famous Speaker Arthur Onslow held his Parliamentary levees in its drawing-room till his retirement in 1761.[4] Not far distant in the Square, at the corner of Greek Street, Alderman Beckford was living in 1765; Bach may have been one of a curious crowd in April 1770 gazing at the exterior of the house, which displayed the word LIBERTY in white letters three feet high.[5] General Oglethorpe, the subject of Pope's panegyric, was another householder at this time,[6] while the Rate-books for Christmas 1766–Michaelmas 1767 indicate others of distinction: the French Ambassador, Lord Pigot, Sir John

---

[1] For Monmouth House see Rimbault, pp. 20 f.; Kingsford, p. 69. It is clearly seen on the plan of Soho Square, Illustration No. 16.
[2] See Illustration No. 15.
[3] Now No. 20 and in the occupation of Messrs. Crosse & Blackwell.
[4] Like the neighbouring White House, the site is now occupied by the premises of Messrs. Crosse & Blackwell. Cf. Rimbault, p. 27.
[5] Rimbault, p. 30. [6] *Ibid.*, p. 35.

Palmer, Bart., the Duke of Argyll, Sir Stephen Theodore Jansen, Bart., the Duchess of Wharton, and the Venetian Resident.[1]

In a locality so distinguished it was proper that a house of entertainment, if it intruded, should function under direction competent to organize decorous and exclusive recreation. Such, until her fall from grace, was the Carlisle House of Mrs. Teresa Cornelys, the Aganippe of Soho's Golden Age:

> Where Carlisle House attracts the light and gay,
> And countless tapers emulate the day,
> There youth and beauty chase the hours along,
> And aid Time's flight by revelry and song;
> There masques and dancers bound on footsteps light,
> To jocund strains that echo through the night,
> Till morning's rosy beam darts full on all
> Who leave, though loath, this gorgeous Festival;
> Then, worn with pleasure, forth the revellers stray,
> And hail with languid looks the new-born day;
> They seek their homes;—there, weary with *ennui*,
> Joyless and dull is all they hear and see;
> Spiritless and void, of every charm bereft,
> Unlike that scene of magic they have left.
> They chide the lingering hours that move so slow,
> Till the night comes, when they again can go
> And mingle in the enchantments of Soho.[2]

Carlisle House stood at the south corner of Sutton Street,[3] on the east side of the Square; the site of its ball-room is occupied to-day by St. Patrick's Roman Catholic Chapel.[4] It owed its name to the third Earl of Carlisle, who, attracted by the amenities of the newly laid-out site, deserted his mansion in King's Square Court and, about 1692, built a new one within sight of it. His widow lived in the old house until 1752. She was the authoress of *Maxims for Young Ladies, before and after Marriage, but chiefly for the Latter*, a manual published too late (1790) to instruct the patrons of the new house under Mrs. Cornelys' tenancy. Carlisle House in Soho Square was still in possession of the Howards in 1756, and Mrs. Cornelys soon after succeeded them.[5]

Teresa Cornelys was born at Venice in 1723, an actor's daughter. Her early life is veiled, its details scanty.[6] On 7 January 1746 she sang under the name Pompeati in Gluck's *La Caduta de' Giganti* at the King's Theatre, in the presence of the Duke of Cumberland, before he set out to quell the Jacobite rebellion at Culloden, when

---

[1] The Rate-books for 1760–6 are lost.　　　　　　　　　[2] Mac Kinlay.
[3] See the plan and picture, Illustrations Nos. 15 and 17.
[4] Wheatley, i. 329.　　　　　　　　　　　　　　　　[5] Rimbault, p. 25.
[6] Cf. Rimbault, chap. 3; Mac Kinlay; and the article in the *Dictionary of National Biography*. See Illustration No. 18.

Burney noted in her 'such a masculine and violent manner of singing, that few female symptoms were perceptible'. Thereafter, as Signora Pompeati, she appears to have visited Vienna,[1] and at Amsterdam married Cornelis de Rigerboos, under whose name she returned to London in or before 1760. In February 1761 she sang in the Little Haymarket Theatre as 'Mrs. Cornelles' and 'Mrs. Cornelious',[2] and, as 'Signora Corneli', in Arne's *Judith*.[3] Already she had planned the entertainments which for ten years drew the world of fashion; for, on 30 December 1760, the *Public Advertiser* announced to 'the Nobility and Gentry, Subscribers to the Society in Soho-square', that its third and fourth meetings would be held on Thursdays, 1 and 15 January 1761, at seven o'clock.[4] After her occupation of it, the mansion and the ballroom at its rear were connected by a 'Chinese Bridge', while its interior decorations were claimed to make it 'the most magnificent place of public entertainment in Europe'. Its saloons, hung with blue and yellow satin, entertained sometimes six hundred dancers at two guineas a head.[5] Balls, masquerades, and cards were its principal lures until, in 1765, Bach and Abel were summoned to extend its attractions to another sphere.[6]

Upon the western side of the Square, King's Square Street (now Carlisle Street) connected it with Dean Street and led across that thoroughfare to King's Square Court.[7] Strype described the latter in 1720 as 'a handsome broad court fronting King's Square; 'tis a place well built and inhabited, and hath one very large House which takes up all the West end or front; by which is a little passage leading into waste ground betwixt Wardour Street and the backside of Dean Street: which ground is designed to be built upon, there being a street laid out, and some houses built'.[8] The 'one very large House' was the original Carlisle House, a Restoration building planned by Sir Christopher Wren after the creation of the Carlisle earldom in 1669. It still stands, dignified and regular, in three storeys of red brick, no longer within its cherry garden, but internally preserving the amenities with which Bach was familiar—a spacious marble-floored hall, grand staircase, lofty panelled rooms, rich ceilings; these remain to attest its former grandeur.[9] The third Earl's widow, authoress of the polite *Maxims*

---

[1] Gerber, ii. 171, mentions a Signora Pompeati as singing in Paris in 1756 'mit grossem Beyfalle'.
[2] P.A., 9 and 16 Feb. 1761.   [3] *Ibid.*, 18 Feb. 1761.
[4] *Ibid.*, 30 Dec. 1761.   [5] Rimbault, pp. 46, 167.
[6] Mrs. Cornelys' Carlisle House was pulled down *circa* 1803 (Wheatley i. 329).
[7] See Illustration No. 14.   [8] Rimbault, p. 67.
[9] See Illustrations Nos. 19 and 20. The house is now occupied by Keeble, Ltd.

already mentioned, died in it in 1752, and nine years later it passed by purchase to Domenico Angelo,[1] riding and fencing master, who, on 7 January 1763, advertised his intention to build 'a Riding House and Stables upon the large Square of Ground' between the house and Wardour Street, offering riding lessons to subscribers at one guinea a month of twelve lessons, with a subscription of ten guineas, and to non-subscribers at two guineas a month, with an entrance fee of three. His fencing school also was announced to open 'on the usual terms'.[2] Angelo continued to reside at what, in 1782, he described as 'No. 1, Carlisle Street' until nearly the end of the century, and died at Eton in 1802, after a career which had made him known to most of the celebrities of the day.

Into this 'handsome broad court' Bach and Abel moved in or before 1765. Henry Angelo, Domenico's son, then a boy of ten, asserts that the friends 'for some time were inmates at our house',[3] probably while the neighbouring one was awaiting their occupation, or later, when their tenancy of it ceased. In all, the Court contained thirteen houses.[4] On its north side lived Ignatius Geohegan, Joseph Campbell (two houses), and Mrs. How; on the south, William Wright, Thomas Stillingfleet, Susanna Jones, Mary Hache, and Lucy Courteille; one house, later occupied by Sir James Brown, Bart., was empty. Bach's was on the west side of the Court, north of and next to Carlisle House, from which it was separated by the latter's garden. The adjoining house on the other (northern) side was rented by John Miller. Carlisle House was rated at £165, Geohegan's at £64, Bach's at £32, third in size among them all. Till Michaelmas 1771, when he and Abel moved elsewhere, there were few changes in the occupancy of the thirteen houses, the only one of palpable interest being the arrival of the sculptor Carlini, at Michaelmas 1770, in the house formerly tenanted by Mrs. How on the north side of the Court.

Angelo kept open house. Garrick, Colman, Sheridan, Wilkes, Horn Tooke, Sir Joshua Reynolds, Gainsborough, Bartolozzi, Zoffany, Cipriani, the Chevalier D'Eon, and others were his frequent guests,[5] into whose company Bach and Abel were welcomed. 'Well do I remember', writes Henry Angelo, 'the delight-

---

[1] In the memoir attached to the 1904 edition of Henry Angelo's *Reminiscences* (p. xiii) the deed of sale of Carlisle House gives 29 Sept. 1761 as the date of Angelo's purchase. It was bought from Lord Delaval in the name of Archibald Fraser, probably Angelo's attorney. See Illustrations Nos. 21 and 22.
[2] Rimbault, p. 68.
[3] Angelo, i. 19.
[4] I follow the Rate-books for Christmas 1766–Lady Day 1767. The books for 1760–6 are lost.
[5] Rimbault, p. 26.

ful evenings which for years were frequent under my paternal roof, when they, with Bartolozzi and Cipriani, formed a little friendly party, and amused themselves with drawing, music, and conversation, until long after midnight.' Mrs. Angelo, with her gentle voice, delighted to sing Allan Ramsay's 'Patie' to Bach's accompaniment, to which Abel would add his viola da gamba. Both were connoisseurs of pictures and prints, but the excursions of Gainsborough, who painted them both,[1] into their own art were a cause of merriment, occasionally of exasperation.[2] The painter was eager to purchase Giardini's violin, or Abel's viola, supposing that with them he could acquire their owner's skill. Fischer's oboe also attracted him; but his bassoon chiefly tested the endurance of his friends. Calling at his lodging in Pall Mall, Bach once found him practising that instrument, his cheeks puffed, his face round and red as a harvest moon. 'Pote it away, man; pote it away,' shouted Bach above the horrid sounds; 'do you want to burst yourself, like the frog in the fable? De defil! it is only fit for the lungs of a country blackschmidt'. 'No, no,' Gainsborough protested, 'it is the richest bass in the world. Now, do listen again.' 'Listen', yelled Bach, 'I did listen at your door, and py all the powers above, as I hobe to be saved, it is just for all the vorld as the veritable praying of a jackass.' 'Damn it,' said Gainsborough, 'you have no ear, man, no more than an adder', and resumed his blowing. Bach stopped his ears: 'Baw, baw! vorse and vorse! no more of your *canarding*! Tis as a duck, by Gar! tis vorse as a goose.' At Angelo's the painter would display his skill on the harpsichord, now in Purcell's chant, now in a specimen of Byrd. 'Dat is debelish fine', Bach would say ironically. 'Now for a touch of Kent and old Henry Lawes', Gainsborough would proceed, till, pushing the artist from the instrument, Bach exclaims, 'Now dat is too pad! Dere is no law, by goles! why the gompany is to listen to your murder of all these ancient gomposers'.[3]

Horn Tooke, who lived in Richmond's Buildings, Dean Street, within a hundred yards of Carlisle House, was a frequent visitor; he used to amuse Tom Sheridan by singing a parody of 'God save the King', and his pamphlet warfare with Wilkes divided the company into two camps. Bach professed to side with Tooke, Abel with Wilkes, though Abel, 'who had more dry humour than Bach', says Angelo, used to call the controversy 'the squabbles of Bot and Geddle'. The affair of Dr. William Dodd, hanged at Tyburn in 1777 for forging a bond on his former pupil, Lord Chesterfield, also divided Angelo's neighbours, 'these waggish

[1] Illustrations Nos. 1, 13, 32.   [2] Angelo, i. 19 f.   [3] *Ibid.*, i. 184 f.

musicians'. Like Dr. Johnson, Abel pleaded for Dodd's pardon,
while Bach took the other view. 'What de debbel do you talk of
Tocdor Todd being in debt,' he objected; 'am nod I always in
debt? and is it prober and right, pecause of dat, I am to commit
forgery?'[1] Abel's sympathy carried him to Tyburn to witness the
doctor's execution, a scene from which he returned in tears.
'Baw, baw! mine friendt,' said Bach, 'I am thankful for note being
a sentimendalist. I gannot mineself boast of mine fine feelings, God
help me! Pote, mine dear Mister Abel, excuse me, for though you
cry to the amount of a prim-full pail of tears, I gannot admire the
man who shall take a front seat in the Tyburn boxes to behold
a human being die like a dog in a string.'[2] Abel insinuated that,
if forgery was a hanging crime, he and Bach, as forgers of another
kind of note, equally deserved the doctor's fate! 'Dat is not
chendeel of you, mine tear Abel', said Bach; 'it is not bolite to
hurl the *argumentum ad hominem* at mine head.' Abel maintained
his point: 'every comboser is a notorious forger of notes; *ergo*,
mine tear friend Bach, you must be hanged.' 'To be sure, friend
Abel,' Bach concurred, 'us gombosers are birates, and blagiarists,
and forgers of nodes; pote', he added, 'some gombosers forge
false nodes, and I only forge true.'[3]

Such anecdotes, if they bear marks of editorial embellishment,
construct for us, as they recalled to Henry Angelo, the happy
fellowship that frequented Carlisle House. Bach and Abel were
inseparable, 'with almost as large an acquaintance among the great
folks as [Domenico] Angelo himself';[4] though Dr. Johnson once
asked Burney: 'Pray, sir, who is Bach? is he a piper?'[5] The
doctor's ignorance was affected, and, if not, inexcusable. For,
in 1765, Bach's ability, and the enterprize of Mrs. Cornelys, introduced to London a musical experience to which it was almost
a stranger. Public concerts seem to have begun in England with
those provided by John Banister between 1672 and 1678. Thomas
Britton, the 'musical small-coal man', continued them in Handel's
day, offering his patrons weekly concerts for ten shillings a year,
with a dish of coffee at one penny. In 1731 Francesco Geminiani
organized subscription concerts in Hickford's Room, and, for a
short season, Giardini succeeded him in 1751. Meanwhile, the
Concert spirituel, founded by Philidor in Paris, had started (1725)
on a prosperous course which invited imitation and attracted
Mrs. Cornelys' observant eye. A programme of subscription
concerts was proposed, Bach was invited to provide them, and on

---

[1] Angelo, i. 57–60, 455.   [2] *Ibid*. i. 467.   [3] *Ibid*. i. 458.
[4] *Ibid*., i. 189.   [5] Burney (F.), ii. 156.

23 January 1765 Carlisle House announced a series of six, at five guineas subscription, to be conducted alternately by Bach and Abel.[1] Their programmes have not survived, and no details are revealed in the public press; Bach's early Symphonies (Op. III) were certainly heard at them. Thus the 'Wednesday Subscription Concert' was launched, and Mrs. Cornelys was indefatigable in her zeal for the comfort of its patrons. She promised them 'Tea below stairs and ventilators above', whereby, she advertised, 'the present complaints of excessive heat will be obviated, without subjecting the Subscribers to the least danger of catching cold'. She was understood to have expended £2,000 on embellishments and furniture, and, amongst her other 'elegant alterations', to have devised 'the most curious, singular, and superb ceiling to one of the rooms that ever was executed or even thought of'.[2]

The world of fashion, which turned its back on the Haymarket on Tuesdays, flocked to Soho on Wednesdays. So popular was the 'Soho Concert' that the number of meetings in 1766 was increased to fifteen.[3] As many were provided in 1767,[4] evidently without diminution of interest; for, at the close of the season, Bach and Abel announced[5] that, 'to avoid the Inconvenience of so great a Crowd as was at their last Year's Concert, the Number of Subscribers for the Future will be limited to 4 Hundred, viz: two hundred Gentlemen and two hundred Ladies'. The edict caused disappointment; so, faced with the alternatives of losing subscribers or deserting Soho, the partners gave notice that their concerts in 1768 would be held in 'Mr. Almack's Great Room' in King Street, St. James's.[6] Their decision was unwelcome to Mrs. Cornelys, between whom and Almack's some rivalry existed, though, in March 1764, she had contradicted a rumour, 'industriously reported', that she disapproved of the project 'to build a large Room in opposition to hers'.[7] The lavish expenditure upon her own establishment was due in measure to fear of her competitor, and her association with Bach and Abel probably was inspired by the same incentive. For Almack's opened its doors early in 1765, under the management of an exclusive committee of ladies, offering a weekly ball and supper for three months at a subscription of ten guineas. Its 'large Room', finished in December 1767,[8] opportunely invited Bach and his partner to transfer their concerts

---

[1] Bach conducted on Jan. 23, Feb. 6, Mar. 6, and Mar. 19; Abel, on Jan. 30 and Mar. 27. See P.A. for the dates named.
[2] Rimbault, p. 47.   [3] P.A., 8 Jan. and 7 May 1766.
[4] P.A., 14 Jan. and 13 May 1767.   [5] Ibid., 24 June 1767.
[6] Ibid., 26 Dec. 1767.   [7] Rimbault, p. 45.
[8] Wheatley, i. 37. See Illustration No. 25.

to its platform, severing themselves from the Soho mansion, on which the breath of scandal and ill-repute was about to fall.[1]

Meanwhile, Bach's versatility introduced him to another audience. Vaux, or Fox, Hall had been a resort of pleasure on the south bank of the Thames for a hundred years since Pepys found its fiddles, harp, 'Jew's trump', and fine people 'mighty diverting'. Jonathan Tyers, who got a lease of it in 1730, added a kiosk,[2] in which he placed an organ and orchestra, engaging Arne as composer. His two sons succeeded him, in 1767, in the management of 'that excellent place of publick amusement', Boswell found it,[3] 'which must ever be an estate to its proprietor, as it is peculiarly adapted to the taste of the English nation; there being a mixture of curious show, gay exhibition, musick, vocal and instrumental, not too refined for the general ear; for all which only a shilling is paid; and, though last, not least, good eating and drinking for those who choose to purchase that regale'. Though he held no official position in it, Bach's songs were popular with its audiences, and three sets of them were published during his lifetime. Probably in 1765 Welcker issued, from his premises in Gerrard Street, Bach's first collection of Vauxhall songs, four tuneful ditties sung by Mrs. Weichsell, the wife of Carl Weichsell, principal oboist at the Opera. She was a pupil of Bach's and the mother of Mrs. Billington, who, when only six years old (c. 1774), played a duet with him in public.[4] A second collection of Vauxhall songs was announced in 1767[5] as sung by Mrs. Weichsell and Mrs. Pinto. The latter, as Charlotte Brent, had recently married Thomas Pinto, leader at the Opera. A pupil of Arne's, she had shown herself a notable Polly in The Beggar's Opera, and achieved the summit of her reputation in Arne's Artaxerxes, in the part of Mandane expressly written for her. In 1765 she was associated with Bach on another stage, to which he so far had not been admitted.

English Opera at Covent Garden opened a chapter of particular brilliance on the accession of John Beard to management in 1761. Himself an eminent singer, he engaged the most successful English

---

[1] Bach's banking account with Drummond's, Charing Cross, reveals the following payments to Almack: £546 (1769), £567 (1770), £504 (1771), £520 (1772), £693 (1773). Bach evidently managed the concerts, for the account is debited with large payments to Abel. The receipts were considerable: £4,579 (1771), £3,595 (1774), £2,341 (1777), £1,058 (1779). The diminishing revenue in the late '70's supports Pohl's statement (A.D.B. i. 747) that the concerts were latterly financed by Lord Abingdon. The earlier series undoubtedly gave the partners a considerable income. Abel drew £273 in 1768, £270 in 1770, £400 in 1771, £450 in 1772, £743 in 1773, £527 in 1774, nothing in 1775, £375 in 1776, £100 in 1777, £200 in 1778, £175 in 1779.
[2] See Illustrations Nos. 23 and 24.　　　[3] Life of Johnson, ed. Dent. iv. 344.
[4] Papendiek, i. 233.　　　[5] P.A., 24 Aug. 1767.

composers, Arnold, Arne, Dibdin, and gathered round them native singers whose reputations challenged the rival institution in the Haymarket—Mrs. Weichsell, Charlotte Brent, Polly Young, Charles Dibdin, and others. In 1765 Bach was drawn into association with him in the production of a light opera. On Thursday, January 31, a few days after the *première* of Bach's *Adriano* at the King's Theatre, Covent Garden opened its doors with *The Maid of the Mill*, a 'comic opera', its libretto by Isaac Bickerstaff, to music by various composers, including Arnold[1] and Bach. Beard, Dibdin, and Charlotte Brent were in the cast, and for the last Bach provided both the songs he contributed to the opera— 'Trust me, would you taste true pleasure', and 'My life, my joy, my blessing'; in the second of which, a duet, Mattocks also took part.[2] Simple ditties with a right English flavour, both contributed to the success of an entertainment to whose excellence and popularity 'A Friend to Merit wherever he meets it' gave public testimony:[3]

Mr. Woodfall,
    On Saturday last I was at the Comic Opera, The Maid of the Mill, for the Twelfth Time, and I am not ashamed to own that my Liking was increased at every Representation. Yes, Mr. Woodfall, your Criticks, these Gentlemen of *vast Taste and Abilities*, may cry *Sing Song* as long and loud as they please; but I maintain that *The Maid of the Mill*, whether we consider it with regard to Plot, Character, Dialogue, Humour or Sentiment, is the best Dramatic Piece that has appeared on the English Stage for Twenty Years.
    But I want to say a Word or two to the Author, with regard to his Music. I love fine Compositions as well as any Man, and I think that of The Maid of the Mill is infinitely superior to any we have yet had on our Stage. In a Word, its Fault is that it is *too good.* Now, if this agreeable Author ever favours us with another Piece of the same Kind, suppose that he was not intirely to reject the higher Stile of Music, but here and there to throw in a few of our more familiar English Airs; which would, I apprehend, season it better to the Taste of a *London* Audience. I only mention this as wishing him to succeed as much as possible; nor would I have him at all daunted at the Clamours of a few incomprehensible Blockheads: For if a Comic Opera is really in itself so absurd, puerile, and contemptible an Entertainment as they would represent it, the greater his Merit, who has contrived to render it not only charming, but respectable.

Meanwhile, the King's Theatre had again passed under new management. For the season of 1765–6 Messrs. Gordon, Vincent, and Crawford undertook the 'opera regency', in Burney's phrase.[4]

---

[1] This was Arnold's first opera. He received £12 for its 'compilation'. Cf. Wyndham, i. 157.
[2] Cf. *infra*, p. 245.   [3] P.A., 7 May 1765.   [4] Bur. iv. 487.

The first two were 'experienced professors', while Crawford had acted as treasurer under many managers. Thomas Vincent, the principal partner in a venture that resulted in the customary losses, was a pupil of Sammartini, whose proficiency as an oboist gained him a situation in the King's and Queen's Bands.[1] He had enjoyed the favour of George III's father, acquired a considerable income in the practice of his profession, and augmented it by marriage. The withdrawal of Mingotti and Giardini had inspired the ambition to direct the Opera-house and 'turned his head and his purse inside out'. Gordon, according to Burney, was the son of a Norfolk clergyman and a good violoncellist. He may be identified with the John Gordon who, in 1775, was a member of the King's and Queen's Bands of Musick.[2] His father probably was William Gordon, elected to a Norwich scholarship at Corpus Christi College, Cambridge, in 1744, who held the Norfolk living of Blickling from 1756 to 1796.[3]

The season opened on 23 November 1765 with the pasticcio *Eumene*, under the direction of Cocchi, who, since his supersession by Bach, had settled in London, and now resumed his former situation. Excepting Elisi, the cast[4] contained no singer of distinction. The music, drawn from Hasse, Galuppi, Sacchini, Jommelli, and Cocchi himself, 'was not much noticed on the stage, or thought worth printing'.[5] Hence, on Tuesday, December 3, Cocchi revived his *La Clemenza di Tito*,[6] originally produced at the King's Theatre in 1760, when Burney discovered in it 'no new resources in this composer'. It now received new airs for Elisi, the original Sesto, whom Burney then praised as a great singer and greater actor, majestic, with a great vocal compass, and 'fond of distant intervals, of fourteen or fifteen notes'. These accomplishments now failed to win success. The opera was neglected by public and publishers alike, 'and is neither to be found in any memory or shop whatever'.[7]

At the moment Bach was either *persona non grata* to the managers or indifferent to their plans. Therefore, to provide a

[1] Thomas Vincent is named as a member in 1775.
[2] Court, pp. 71, 86.
[3] I owe the information to Dr. J. M. Bulloch, the historian of the House of Gordon.
[4] Cast: *Eumene*, Filippo Elisi; *Leonato*, Gasparo Savoi; *Antigene*, Ercole Ciprandi; *Artemisia*, Clementina Spagnoli; *Laodicea*, Giulia Visconti; *Peuceste*, Giacinta Ghiretti (Bott. 907 i. 10/4).
[5] Bur. iv. 472, 488.
[6] Cast: *Tito Vespasiano*, Ercole Ciprandi; *Sesto*, Filippo Elisi; *Annio*, Gasparo Savoi; *Vitellia*, Clementina Spagnoli; *Servilia*, Giulia Visconti; *Publio*, Giacinta Ghiretti (Bott. 1174 b. 39/2).
[7] Bur. iv. 488.

novelty in a dull season, Matthias Vento, who, like Cocchi, was domiciled in London, was called in. On Tuesday, 21 January 1766, he produced his *Sofonisba*,[1] to Bottarelli's libretto. The subject being historical, the author begged the audience, in respect to 'whatever I have added to the truth of history, either of my own invention, or in imitation of other authors', to 'look upon it as done to give this Drama that degree of probability which my talents were permitted to give it'. In fact, Bottarelli's facile pen contributed to a success of which the management was much in need. The opera had about fifteen performances, was heard more frequently than any other during the season, while the songs, published by Welcker, 'were long after in favour at concerts and public places, as well as among lisping misses and dilettanti'.[2] Burney's eulogy is confirmed by the rare criticisms of a member of the audience. On January 25 the *Public Advertiser* printed the following letter:

Sir,
    I am one of Those to whom an Oratorio, or an Opera (whether Italian or English) gives exquisite Delight, and therefore am glad that, as the Town is now full, those Entertainments will, very probably, be crouded, and thus amply repay the several Managers for the great Risk they run, as to their Property, as well as for the vast Pains they take to amuse us; for the Labour employed on these Occasions is infinitely greater than it is usually imagined.
    The Italian Opera has suffered considerably, this Season, by the Inability of Signora Spagnoli to exert her Musical Talents, owing to a most severe Cold; but as she has now recovered her Voice, 'tis presumed that she will be a Source of as great Pleasure among us, to Persons of a Musical Ear and who have a true Taste for that Species of Dramas, as she was in her native Country, where she was always heard with Applause.
    I myself find great Charms in the Entertainments as now exhibiting in the King's Theatre. For, besides Signora Spagnoli's Taste, I do not perceive the least Diminution in Signor Elisi's Voice or Action;[3] both which pleased us so much two to three Years ago. Ciprandi appears to me a fine Player as well as Singer; and with regard to Signor Savoi, he is generally thought to have a pleasing Voice.
    Nothing is objected to the *Orchestra*, it being known to consist (to speak in general) of the ablest Hands in the Kingdom; and this forming so very considerable a Part of the Dramas in Question, must consequently be one great Spring of Delight to all Lovers of fine Music.

[1] Cast: *Sofonisba*, Clementina Spagnoli; *Syphax*, Filippo Elisi; *Scipio*, Ercole Ciprandi; *Massinissa*, Gasparo Savoi; *Cyrene*, Giulia Visconti; *Lelius*, Giacinta Ghiretti; *Arideus*, Alessandro Maczura. Ballet master: Pietro Sodi; Ballet: Signori Adriani, Monari, Micheli; Signore Fabris Monari, Santoli, Capitani (Bott. 907 i. 10/5.)
[2] Bur. iv. 488.
[3] Bur. (iv. 488) says that 'Savoi's fine voice was now the more noticed, as Elisi's was upon the decline'.

The principal *Dancers* are likewise acknowledged to have considerable
Merit. The Gracefulness and Ease of Signor Adriani are very pleasing,
as is the elegant Agility of Signora Fabris Monari. Be this said without
detracting from the Talents of the other Dancers, whose Names are seen
in the Opera Books. Signor Sodi has so often diverted us by his Compositions as Ballet-Master, that it were superfluous to bestow any Encomium
on him in this Place.

I shall say no more as to the Musical Merit of Sophonisba (the Opera
now performing) than to observe that it was received very favourably
by the Audience last Tuesday. And, indeed, the Town had no small
Expectations from the future Compositions of the Author of Demofonte
last Winter. And, with regard to the Poet, he assures us that he had
exerted his utmost Endeavours to give all the Probability possible to his
Story.

The Elegance of the Scenery and of the Dresses speak for themselves;
and it is evident that the Managers have done all in their Power to embellish their House and to make it commodious. . . .

MUSIDORUS.

Vincent and his colleagues, in fact, had found it necessary, or
agreeable, to redecorate the theatre, whose interior, on other
nights than Tuesday and Saturday, was used for balls, routs, and
assemblies. The entrance formed a fine amphitheatre, ornamented
with sconces and glass lustres; the boxes were fronted with panels
painted and gilded; while the stage, hung with crimson damask
laced with gold, exhibited sideboards and 'sweetmeat tables', each
of them 'emblematically ornamented in a new Taste.'[1] Meanwhile,
Sofonisba drew the town, and continued to receive fresh plaudits:[2]

Sir,

Being extremely fond of Operas (and indeed of Music in general), it
was with singular Pleasure I saw the Pit and Boxes . . . filled with Persons
of Distinction last Saturday Night, and especially when I heard the great
Applause bestowed universally on Signor Elisi.

I always thought him a very graceful Player, and a most accomplished
Singer; but he seemed to excel himself the Night I am speaking of, in
the character of Syphax.

How did his Action charm in the Recitative accompanied at the Close
of the first Act; as well as in the Song which followed it. The sad Distress
in which the Poet has represented the Captive Syphax is most beautifully
heightened by the harmonious Sounds of Signor Vento; and Elisi has
done Justice to the Poet and musical Composer, by the Delicacy of his
Taste in Singing and the Pathos of his Action. The same may be observed
with Regard to the Recitative accompanied previous to the tender Duetto
which ends the second Act.

While I am endeavouring to do Justice to Elisi's Merit, I would in no
Manner forget Signora Scotti,[3] who delighted us in the Scene when she

---

[1] These details are found in a letter signed 'Atticus', printed in P.A., 25 Feb.
1766.
[2] P.A., 19 Mar. 1766.
[3] Teresa Scotti. Evidently she replaced Spagnoli.

is supposed to drink Poison. Her sweetly plaintive Accents in the Song *Che bramate, o giusti Dei*, heightened by Mr. Vincent's hautboy, worked powerfully on every One, as was evident from the high Applause. . . .

The little Encouragement given to Italian Operas at the Beginning and during Part of the Winter (owing to a violent Cold caught by Signora Spagnuoli, who otherwise would have charmed the Town) made me apprehensive that this most elegant of Entertainments would have been lost to this Country; but the Multitudes who have frequented the Opera for several Saturdays past makes me hope. . . .

I have ever considered the Italian Opera among us as the great School of Music to which all should resort who delight in exquisite Performances of that Kind, or are desirous of refining their Taste, in like Manner as those who would excel in the noble Art of *Designing* closely attend the Academy in St. Martin's Lane. Several excellent musical Compositions given by Masters of our Country prove what I have here asserted; and I doubt not but that Italian Operas (those beautiful Exotics) may, by proper and studious Culture, be naturalized here and flourish; and become a Spring of sweet Pleasure to Multitudes of my Countrymen. This is very much the wish of Mr. Woodfall's

most humble Servant,

March 17.   AMPHION

Meanwhile, on Thursday, 20 February 1766, the managers revived *Artaserse*, an opera, chiefly by Hasse, heard in London in 1734, which now received a few performances. Galuppi's *L'Eroe cinese* followed on Saturday, April 12. Neither caught the public taste, while the second was marked during its brief currency by an event whose more frequent occurrence is perhaps concealed in the laconic columns of a reticent press. 'As a Lover and Frequenter of Musical Entertainments', wrote Mr. Woodfall's humble servant 'Musicante' in the *Public Advertiser* of April 30:

my Curiosity was rais'd by a singular Advertisement, and I was induc'd to make my second Appearance on Saturday last to see and hear Signor Savoi perform the first Woman's Part in *L'Eroe Cinese*, and was agreeably surprized to find him exceed my Expectations and outdo his former Performance of the character of the Mandarin in the same Opera.

When I enter'd the House, a printed Hand Bill was presented to me which immediately accounted for the mutilated Condition in which I afterwards found the Opera, informing the Public, that, in the Morning of that Day in which the Opera was to be perform'd, Signora Visconti *positively* refused acting in it under Signor Savoi. But I was not a little pleas'd to find her malicious Purposes frustrated by the admirable Endeavours of Miss Young, who, tho' she had but a few Hours to read over the Part, justly gain'd more universal Applause than Visconti could raise in the *studied* Performance of that or any other Character she has appear'd in this Season. And tho' she endeavour'd to brazen it out in the very Centre of the Gallery, I should suppose she felt no small Mortification at the public Testimony that was given of her Insignificance. How great then must be her *Assurance* to even *hint* a *Desire* to attempt the *first* Character in an Opera, when she has appear'd so contemptible even in a lower Part.

Let me therefore ask any Friend of yours in the Law, Mr. Printer, whether Visconti is not guilty, by such Refusal, of Breach of Contract, and subject thereupon to Pains and Penalties agreeable to a Law made within these few Years, relative to Journeymen and People under Condition to perform any particular Thing? If so, I hope the Managers will treat her in the severest Manner, as I think it the highest Insult upon the Frequentors of those Entertainments, and a cruel Thing to see a Set of Gentlemen, and our *own Countrymen*, indefatigably studying every Method and generously sparing no Expence to support the Grandeur of these Entertainments, and restore the Dignity of that noble Theatre, which has been reduc'd to the lowest Ebb for many Years past, under the various foreign Undertakers whose whole Study was to make the most Money of the Town, by starving the Performance and cramming Night after Night the same dull Dish, or any Thing, down their Audiences' Throats. Surely then, the Nobility and Gentry, who are ever ready to patronize real Merit, must easily see thro' these mean and flagrant Artifices, and will treat them with the just Contempt they deserve.

The relevance of this outburst to the Visconti's rebellious gesture is not palpable. That the public at large was indifferent to the fact that English managers had superseded an Italian impresaria is evident from Amphion's letter already quoted. That the relations of the management and its singers were consequently unharmonious is possible; for Vincent and his partners' disinclination to favour the foreigner is evident in their choice of composers who, though un-English by birth, were at least domiciled in London. Cocchi and Vento had already been brought forward, and for the final production of the season, on Saturday, 24 May 1766, Barthélémon, leader of the orchestra, was invited to introduce his *Pelopida*.[1] Burney found in it 'traits of genius and bold modulation, which promised, with experience in writing for the voice, and a more perfect acquaintance with the Italian language and stage, future works of great worth and abilities'.[2] The anticipation was realized. Meanwhile, Barthélémon's first opera brought an adventurous season to an inconspicuous end.

Undaunted by their losses, or spurred to recover them, Vincent and his partners announced[3] a new season at the King's Theatre, to commence on 21 October 1766. A plan had been devised, which, it was hoped, would restore to Tuesday the vogue of her more frequented sister Saturday. During the vacation, accordingly, Gordon visited Italy to secure two bodies of singers, a 'serious troop' for Saturdays, and a *burletta* cast to supply the 'lyric theatre' on Tuesdays. The former included Signore Grassi,

---

[1] Cast: *Pelopida*, Ercole Ciprandi; *Clitus*, Filippo Elisi; *Egistus*, Gasparo Savoi; *Aspasia*, Teresa Scotti; *Ismene*, Polly Young; *Orestes*, Giacinta Ghiretti Bott. (907 i. 10/8).

[2] Bur. iv. 488.

[3] P.A., 27 Sept. 1766.

Piatti, Ponce, and Tommaso Guarducci, along with Savoi, Micheli, and Miss Young (Mrs. Barthélemon), who were again engaged. The burletta company consisted of Giovanni Lovattini, Pietro Morigi, Signore Guadagni, Quercioli, and Piatti, with the occasional support of Savoi and Micheli.[1] Of the newcomers the most notable were Guarducci and Grassi. The former, a pupil of Bernacchi at Bologna, was already in high repute throughout Italy. Tall, awkward, inanimate, ugly, and unfortunate in arriving before the memory of Manzuoli's superior art had faded, he impressed Burney as 'one of the most correct singers I ever heard', the possessor of a voice clear and sweet, of finished technique, and equipped with all the vocal embellishments of Italy.[2]

Cecilia Grassi, born at Milan in 1746, was now in her twenty-first year. Her engagement as 'first woman' at so early an age must indicate exceptional talent. Burney, however, found her abilities mediocre, her person unattractive, her acting inanimate; yet 'there was a truth of intonation, with a plaintive sweetness of voice and innocence of expression, that gave great pleasure to all hearers who did not expect or want to be surprized'.[3] Bach either met her now for the first time, or renewed acquaintance with one whom he had last seen as a girl.[4] Angelo makes the incredible statement,[5] that Cecilia forthwith became Abel's mistress, and that he established her in Frith Street. His narrative is circumstantial: Bach and Abel were connoisseurs of pictures and prints; both possessed examples of Bartolozzi and Cipriani, while Abel had many by Gainsborough.[6] Several of them, says Angelo, Abel parted with 'for the indulgence of that vanity which led many a wiser man than Abel to keep a mistress'. They decorated the drawing-room of his Dulcinea, who, 'though no beauty, was a wit'; she called the apartment her 'Painted Paradise'. Abel once brought Gainsborough's son-in-law Fischer with him to the Frith Street *ménage*. 'Abel, you are a fool,' he exclaimed, as they left, 'and mine fader Gainsborough is a plockhead; for the only painted thing in the house is mine lady's cat-face!' a reproof Abel acknowledged with 'a most grave and profound bow'. After Abel's death, Angelo proceeds, 'his Dulcinea going abroad, she parted with the house and furniture, together with this collection of

---

[1] Bur. iv. 489. The names of Signore Zamparini and Gibetti and others also appear in the programmes of the season.
[2] *Ibid*. iv. 490.   [3] *Ibid*. iv. 491.
[4] *Supra*, p. 52.   [5] Angelo, i. 190.
[6] D.N.B. i. 33, says that Abel covered his walls with drawings by Gainsborough, which the painter gave him in exchange for his music. Gainsborough twice painted him. See Illustration No. 13.

Gainsborough's, which were sold by auction, if I can trust my memory, at Langford's Rooms, now [1828] occupied by Messrs. Robins, in the Piazza, Covent Garden'.[1]

It is impossible to reconcile Angelo's statement with the known facts of Cecilia Grassi's career. He asserts that Abel 'supplied this Dulcinea with a handsome house before he had one of his own'. If so, he installed her in Frith Street before her arrival in England! He adds that the *liaison* continued till Abel's death. That event took place in 1787, five years after Cecilia became Bach's widow. She must therefore have been Abel's mistress while she was Bach's wife, an inference vetoed by the relations of the two men, and by the consideration Cecilia received from the Queen when her husband died. Angelo apparently associated two memories, and on them fabricated an unfounded innuendo. Apart from his virtuosity, Abel was remembered for his drunken habits and generous nature. Mrs. Papendiek declares[2] that, when Bach died, Abel 'lost also much of his power of exertion from grief, and often had recourse to stimulants that overdid his intention'. She adds that he was able to conceal his excesses, even on the platform. Before one of the Musical Fund concerts, at which he was engaged to play, his friends dined with him in order to conduct him to the platform sober. But they did not succeed in checking his 'supposed necessitous error'; he was led to the stage, his instrument, ready tuned, was placed in his hands, and he played 'almost better than ever'. But, when the concerto was finished, the curtain was dropped, for Abel could not rise from his seat. By reason of his failing he was 'not received in the higher circles of society as a visitor', and, when the end came, was buried 'without any honours conferred by the profession, but followed to his grave by a few select friends, of whom Mr. Papendiek was one'. Yet Abel's obituary notice[3] declared that, 'if he had a fault, it was too much generosity'. His last public appearance was at Mrs. Billington's concert in the Hanover Square Rooms, because he felt she had been unfairly treated 'at the Ancient Music'. His generosity would not be withheld from his friend's widow, particularly if her means were slender. Hence, it is probable that, after Bach's death, he gave Cecilia the shelter of his house till she returned to Italy. Angelo remembered their association, but, misled by the tradition of Abel's dissoluteness, misrepresented its nature. It might be

---

[1] Angelo's memory is accurate as to the locality of the sale. But the effects sold were those of Abel himself. The Gainsborough drawings were chiefly in chalk. E. F. Rimbault's father was a large purchaser of them. Cf. *Notes and Queries*, Series IV, vol. ix. 39.

[2] Vol. i. 154.   [3] Gent. Mag., vol. lvii (1787), p. 549.

supposed that he confused Cecilia with another, but for the fact that he refers to her as a woman of 'no beauty' who sold her belongings and went abroad. That he forgot her relationship to Bach is less surprising when we observe that he invariably calls Bach by his father's name—Sebastian. Mrs. Papendiek, who knew Cecilia well, expressly speaks of her as 'of good character and well-regulated conduct.'[1] Certainly she would not have so described her if Cecilia's relations with Abel were as Angelo's hazy recollection imagined them.

The Opera opened on Tuesday, 21 October 1766, with the burletta *Gli Stravaganti, o sia I Matrimoni alla moda*,[2] an entertainment moderately successful; for, though it contained airs by Piccinni, his reputation was not yet so established in London as to win for them particular attention. The performance was punctuated with disturbances, which drew from the management the intimation,[3] that the gallery was henceforth closed against chairmen and lackeys of subscribers, for whose accommodation a 'large, warm, and commodious apartment' would be provided, in which they could escape the irksome privilege of sharing their masters' relaxations. A week later, on Saturday, November 1, Grassi and Guarducci made their first appearance in *Trakebarne, Gran Mogul*, 'without impressing the public with very favourable ideas of their talents', Burney remarks,[4] or redeeming the season from the dullness which oppressed it. But, on Tuesday, December 9, Piccinni was introduced to an English audience in a work which, since its first production at Rome, had been acclaimed on every stage in Italy as the most popular *opera buffa* of its generation. Passing through Rome in 1760, Piccinni was importuned to compose a comic opera for the Teatro delle Dame, which had encountered misfortune. At short notice Goldoni adapted his comedy *Pamela*, and *La Cecchina, ossia La buona Figliuola* was forthwith launched upon a rising tide of acclamation. Among those singing at the Haymarket in 1766, Lovattini, Morigi, and Savoi took part in its first production, while Signora Guadagni had since performed the name-part with applause on several Italian stages.[5] London[6] confirmed the verdict of Italy; the lively

---

[1] Papendiek, i. 109.
[2] Cast: *Fastidio*, Pietro Morigi; *Alessio*, Giovanni Lovattini; *Cariglion*, Signore Zamparini; *Federico*, Leopoldo Micheli; *Aurora*, Signora Zamparini; *Faustina*, Signora Piatti; *Lisetta*, Signora Gibetti (Bott. 11775 e. 3/3).
[3] P.A., 23 Oct. 1766. [4] Bur. iv. 489. [5] *Ibid*. iv. 490.
[6] Cast: *Lucinda*, Signora Quercioli; *Armidoro*, Gasparo Savoi; *Marchese della Conchiglia*, Giovanni Lovattini; *Tagliaferro*, Pietro Morigi; *Paoluccia*, Signora Maggiore; *Cecchina*, Signora Guadagni; *Sandrina*, Signora Piatti; *Mengotto*, Leopoldo Micheli (Bott. 11714 aa. 22/5).

airs and instrumentation delightfully reproduced the sparkle of
a libretto purged of the ribald buffoonery characteristic of Italian
burletta. Lovattini's 'sweet and well-toned tenor' won him warm
and constant applause, and the under-parts were adequately filled.[1]
Tuesday regained its popularity at a bound, and till the end of
January Piccinni filled its bill.

The season had run half its course before the 'serious' cast
recovered for Saturday some of the *éclat* of which Piccinni
deprived it. Announced as a 'favourite serious opera, the music
by several celebrated composers', *Ezio* was revived on Saturday,
20 December 1766, by 'command'. Probably Bach's 'Non so
d'onde viene' and 'Se il ciel mi divide' again won popularity in
the mouths of Guarducci and Grassi, and heightened public
anticipation of his fourth London opera, *Carattaco*, which received
its first performance on Saturday, 14 February 1767, with the
following cast:[2]

Silurians

Teomanzio	.	.	.	.	Pietro Morigi
Carattaco	.	.	.	.	Tommaso Guarducci
Cassibelane	.	.	.	.	Signora Ponce
Trinobanta	.	.	.	.	Signora Piatti

Brigantians

Cartismandua	.	.	.	Signora Moser
Prasutago	.	.	.	Signore Grassi
Guideria	.	.	.	Mrs. Barthélemon

Romans

Claudio Caesar	.	.	.	Pietro Morigi
Publio Ostorio	.	.	.	Gasparo Savoi
Marco Ostorio	.	.	.	Leopoldo Micheli

Chorus of Druids, Silurians, Brigantians, Roman soldiers.
Ballet Master: Pietro Sodi.
Principal Dancers: Signore Adriani, Mr. Slingsby, Mons. Hamoir
(Amour), Signore Radicati, Santoli, Mlle Hamoir (Amour).
Scene-painter and Machinist: Signore Bigari, Signore Conti.

The opera pleased. Eulogizing its 'correct and rich harmony',
Burney declared it 'well entitled to favour'.[3] A complimentary
critic remarked that 'the masterly Stile of the Music, and particularly the Grandeur of the Chorusses, makes it to be wished that
Signor Bach may meet with further Encouragement, as his Genius
and Judgment seem admirably calculated to reform the present
corrupted Taste of our modern Music, and, like a second Handel,
once again restore that Elegance and Perfection we have for some

---

[1] Bur. iv. 490.   [2] Bott. 907 i. 10/10.   [3] Bur. iv. 490.

Time been Strangers to'. 'Harmonicus' indulged in more detailed eulogy:[1]

It was with singular Pleasure I saw every Part of the Opera House so full last Saturday at *Carattaco*, as it had been the previous Saturday [Feb. 14]. The just Applause it met with on both those Nights prov'd that a Love for Serious Opera is not lessened among us. . . .

Methinks the Poet, Author of *Carattaco*, deserves Commendation for bringing before us a Hero whose Memory does Honour to the English Name, and who thence must be dear to Englishmen. Encomiums here on Mr. Bach would be superfluous, as he has already distinguished himself so much among us by the Invention, the Spirit, and Dignity of his Compositions. . . . His Chorusses elevate the Soul and put us in mind of those of the immortal Handel, and of his own favourite *Orione*. With regard to his Airs, several of them are in the noblest Style of Music, and others very pleasing.

But many object to some of the Performers, as unworthy of Mr. Bach's Lyre. Tis certain they are not Guarduccis . . . as very few possess his exquisite Talent. Surely Sweetness flows from his Lips, and his Voice steals on the Ear, delicious as the Accents of the Æolian Harp, or the undulating Sounds of the Musical Glasses. An Enthusiast would compare it to the feign'd Harmony of the Spheres, of which Poets speak with Rapture. . . . The Scenes, the Dresses, and every other decorative Part, seem elegant and proper, and diversify the whole agreeably. They strike the more, as they call up (as it were) from the Dead, Times vastly remote; which are the more curious as those Times differed so widely from the present. One Scene is very magnificent, I mean that of the Imperial Palace in Rome, which forms a noble Piece of Perspective.

Bach's selection of an English theme accorded with the inclinations of an English board of managers, and marked an endeavour to break from the turgid, artificial conventions which were bringing 'serious opera' into disfavour.[2] The 'just Applause' it received on that account particularly gratified 'Harmonicus', who, a month later, communicated to Mr. Woodfall his further reflections upon it:[3]

Tis the property of all good Music to please the more it is heard. This I experienced the other Night at *Carattaco* . . . When Carattaco sung the Air at his leaving England [there was] profound Silence. . . . And tho' the Silence was not so deep while the Chorusses were performing, they seem'd to administer vast Pleasure, by the Applause they met with.

Being not a Stranger to the Italian Tongue, I was affected by many Parts of the Drama—an English King; his Magnanimity; his Love of Liberty and his native Country; his Abhorrence of Slavery; his Misfortunes, as drawn from Tacitus. How sweetly plaintive is the Air sung by Carattaco when fled from his Enemies to a Cavern! And how deliciously are both the Eye and Ear entertained when the ill-fated Monarch is a Prisoner in the Court of the Imperial Palace at Rome! When the Emperor, seated in a triumphal Car, advances, attended by sorrowing English Captives, by Priests, and by Roman Soldiers! . . . The

---

[1] P.A., 28 Feb. 1767.   [2] Cf. *infra*, p. 130.   [3] P.A., 14 Mar. 1767.

Noble Style of Architecture . . . the Splendor of the Lights; with the distant View of Rome; All these, with Carattaco singing his last Air, and the concluding Chorus, formed so sweet an Illusion that . . . will raise some Persons to Rapture, and disengage them, as it were, in certain Moments, so much from their corporeal Part, that they seem all Mind. They are conveyed into Elysium, and the whole is Inchantment.

Cecilia Grassi was not in the cast. Indisposition prevented her from taking part in a performance of *Ezio* earlier in the season (December 27), nor could she appear at Guarducci's 'benefit' in March. Evidently she had not recovered, and yielded her part to Signora Moser. That she was not friendless in a foreign country is suggested by the fact that the part of Prasutago in Bach's opera was sung by Signore Grassi, probably her brother, who may perhaps be identified with Luigi Grassi, engaged at Berlin from 1768 to 1788, who died at Pisa in 1789.[1] Meanwhile, *Carattaco* was honoured by repeated royal 'commands' and the presence of the Prince of Wales, not yet five years old, who a few weeks earlier paid his first visit to the theatre at Covent Garden, where an operetta was played by children for his entertainment, entitled *The Fairy Favour*, the libretto by the comedian Thomas Hull, the music by 'the celebrated Bach'.[2]

The last 'serious' opera of the season, Vento's *La Conquista del Messico*, was produced on Saturday, 4 April 1767. Burney praised its 'elegant and graceful melody',[3] but the 'lyric' stage had already presented a second opera by Piccinni, *La buona Figliuola maritata*,[4] which had its first performance on Saturday, January 31, and roused public interest to the highest pitch. The theatre was thronged; but the general impression was one of disappointment. The music exhibited all the qualities of its predecessor except simplicity. Indeed, it was so difficult, particularly for the orchestra, that the performers 'forgot it was winter' and were glad to return to Piccinni's earlier score 'for their own ease and relief from a too serious attention'.[5]

The customary 'benefits' brought the season to an end. On Thursday, 5 March 1767, Guarducci invited his patrons to the pasticcio *Sifare*,[6] to which Bach contributed two songs,[7] while the

---

[1] Schneider, i. 159.   [2] *Court Miscellany*, Jan. 1767, p. 45.   [3] Bur. iv. 490.
[4] Cast: *Il Marchese*, Giovanni Lovattini; *Il Cavaliere*, Gasparo Savoi; *Tagliaferro*, Pietro Morigi; *Mengotto*, Leopoldo Micheli; *Il Colonnello*, Pietro Morigi; *La Marchesa*, Signora Zamparini; *Lucinda*, Mrs. Barthélémon; *Sandrina*, Signora Piatti; *Paoluccia*, Signora Gibetti (Bott. 11714 aa. 13/6).
[5] Bur. iv. 492.
[6] Cast: *Sifare*, Tommaso Guarducci; *Mitridate*, Signore Grassi; *Monimia*, Signora Ponce; *Pharnaces*, Gasparo Savoi; *Laodice*, Mrs. Barthélémon; *Arbates*, Leopoldo Micheli (Bott. 907 i. 10/9).
[7] *Infra*, p. 238. In the edition of favourite songs the opera is called 'Sifari'.

bénéficiaire introduced an *Aria cantabile*, accompanied by Abel on the viola da gamba.[1] Guarducci cleared one thousand guineas, and invited public disapproval. 'This is the gentleman', the *Court Miscellany* commented severely,[2] 'who is paid £55 a night for singing at this distressful season, while the whole nation is complaining of oppressive taxes and insupportable poverty.' A week later (March 12) Lovattini took his 'benefit' in *Il Signor Dottore*, a 'new Comic Opera' by Domenico Fischietti, Hof-Capellmeister at Dresden.[3] Zamparini, a very pretty woman, but affected as a singer,[4] on Thursday, April 2, offered her admirers *L'Innamorata del Cicisbeo*, introducing 'new Cloathes in the Venetian Character', and, in the second Act, a song 'accompanied by the Mandolino by herself'. Morigi, the handy man of the cast, adventurously revived *La buona Figliuola maritata* a week later (April 9), and, with it, Jommelli's *Don Trustullo*.

Bach's resolution to transfer his concerts from Soho to Almack's coincided with the termination of the season. That careful investigator, Carl Ferdinand Pohl,[5] declares, but adduces no evidence, that the year 1767 witnessed Bach's marriage to Cecilia Grassi. He is certainly mistaken, both on the evidence of Cecilia's movements and of Bach's domicile. After her appearance in *Ezio*, in December 1766, illness appears to have prevented her from singing again till the spring of 1767, when she was heard in *Carattaco* and *La Conquista del Messico*, with more applause than rewarded her before Christmas.[6] She was not engaged for the seasons 1767–8, 1768–9, and for that of 1769–70 was announced as a 'new Performer'.[7] It must therefore be inferred that she left England with her brother (?) in the summer of 1767, though, till her return two years later, there is no trace of her movements, save that on 12 January 1769 she sang in San Carlo at Naples in a cantata by Pasquale Cafaro.[8] Her marriage to Bach, therefore, cannot have taken place before the latter part of 1769, and other circumstances postpone it to a later date. In May 1770 she was lodging with Mrs. Margaret Burner, grocer, at the corner of Panton Street, Leicester Fields.[9] Three years later she was still living in that locality, at Mr. Grey's, jeweller, in Lisle Street.[10]

[1] P.A., 4 Mar. 1767. The air, 'Frena le belle lagrime', was by Abel himself.
[2] Mar. 1767, p. 166.
[3] Cast: *Clarice*, Mrs. Barthélémon; *Rosina*, Signora Zamparini; *Pasquina*, Signora Piatti; *Don Alberto*, Gasparo Savoi; *Beltrame*, Pietro Morigi; *Bernardino*, Giovanni Lovattini; *Fabrizio*, Leopoldo Micheli (Bott. 907 i. 12/1). Slingsby, the dancer, also took his 'benefit' in this opera on Apr. 30.
[4] Bur. iv. 492.   [5] A.D.B. i. 748.   [6] Bur. iv. 490.
[7] P.A., 5 Sept. 1769.   [8] Florimo, iv. 241.   [9] P.A., 10 May 1770.
[10] *Ibid.*, 17 May 1773.

Moreover, Bach's account with Drummond's shows that on 28 May 1772 he paid £105 to 'Mrs. Grassi', evidently her fee for the recent *Endimione* and other performances. Thus, her marriage was subsequent to May 1773, and Bach's association with Abel leads to the same conclusion. The friends left King's Square Court at Michaelmas 1771, and in January 1772 announced their concert season from 'their house' in Queen Street, Golden Square. They repeated the notice in January 1773, but at some period in that year broke up their joint household; for, in January 1774, their concert tickets were announced for sale 'at Mr. Bach's, 80 Newman Street'. The marriage therefore probably took place in the latter part of 1773 or the early months of 1774. No record of it has yet come to light.

Before the season ended in the summer of 1767, Crawford intimated[1] that he 'declined carrying on Operas after the Expiration of the present Season', and that his partners, Vincent and Gordon, would continue jointly to do so. The latter, accordingly, on the eve of the new season, announced[2] that they had again engaged a 'serious' and 'comic' troop, for the most part those employed in the past season. As composers, Pietro Guglielmi and Felice Alessandri were promised, the first a musician whose most recent successes had been won in Dresden and Brunswick, while the second, the husband of Signora Guadagni, had produced his first opera at Verona only a few months before. A new leader was engaged in Gaetano Pugnani, a pupil of Tartini, and a new *danseuse* in Signora Coradini. Grassi had departed to sunnier skies, and though Guarducci's expensive attractions were again offered, the programme was clearly controlled by the need for economy.

The pasticcio *Tigrane* opened the season on Tuesday, 27 October 1767, notable as containing an aria, 'Cara luce', by Antonio Sacchini, his first music heard on the English stage, says Burney.[3] It was succeeded, on November 7, by Piccinni's *La Schiava*, which exhibited the talents of Signora Guadagni, a good singer and graceful actress;[4] it agreeably satisfied the public taste, was frequently repeated, and drew an ecstatic letter from an admirer:[5]

What a strange Fate is that which attends the Italian Opera, laughed at and ridiculed in every Country, yet in every Country making the chief Entertainment of the Great, Wealthy, and Elegant! How have the Wits of England exercised their Pens against it from the Days of Nicolini,[6]

[1] P.A., 19 May 1767.   [2] *Ibid.*, 11 Sept. 1767.
[3] Bur. iv. 492. The statement is incorrect. Cf. *supra*, p. 98.
[4] *Ibid.*   [5] P.A., 15 Nov. 1767.
[6] Nicolino Grimaldi visited England in 1708.

and what has been the Consequence? The Italian Opera is upon a better Footing in England this Day than ever it was since the King's Theatre has been confined to that Sort of musical Performance; from whence we may fairly conclude, that the Wits have been playing the Fool; that the Ridicule endeavoured to be thrown upon it was unjust, and that the Italian Opera has at least the Power of pleasing the Generality, in Spite of the bad Humour and ill directed Pleasantry of a few.

La Schiava . . . is the Composition of the celebrated Piccinni, in my Opinion preferable to his Buona Figliuola,[1] and the Company undoubtedly the best that ever appeared in this Kingdom. Indeed, we never could boast before of having the Flower of Italy in one Exhibition, as is the Case at present; Guadagni, the first Actress and Singer there, Lovatini, the first Man, and in all Probability the best Male Singer upon Earth. The same may be said of Morigi, and so of the rest in their several Classes.

The Managers have been at great Expence in Decorations and Dresses; in these Particulars indeed it exceeds any Thing I remember to have seen, and I apprehend that every Time the Opera is performed it will acquire new Admirers. But this was not designed the Purport of this Letter. I meant only to intreat the Audience not to encore so many of the Songs, which, however they may deserve it, renders the Entertainment long, and prevents such of the Auditers as like myself live in the City from getting home in Time. And so, Mr. Woodfall, I wish you well.

After a revival of *Sifare* (8 December 1767), Guglielmi made his *début* in his *Ifigenia in Aulide* on Saturday, 16 January 1768.[2] A man of forty, he came to London with a high reputation, which his earliest opera, produced at Turin in 1755, had founded, and his subsequent activities in Italy and Germany enhanced. Yet, his talents were not of the first order, and he was unhappy in the circumstances of his visit. For two seasons London had feasted on Piccinni's more attractive art, while his intrusion was resented by the partisans of Bach and the other London composers. Hence, though Guglielmi 'brought over the new and fashionable musical phrases from Italy',[3] he had no conspicuous success, while the frequent calls upon his pen refused him opportunity to do his talents justice. Felice Alessandri introduced himself in the burletta *La Moglie fedele* on Saturday, February 27. A young man of twenty-one, he owed his invitation, perhaps, rather to the services of his wife than his own reputation, though his opera

[1] Both *La buona Figliuola* and *La buona Figliuola maritata* were repeated during the season.
[2] Cast: *Agamemnon*, Signore Moser; *Ifigenia* (daughter of Agamemnon), Signora Campolini; *Ifigenia* (daughter of Theseus), Signora Quercioli; *Achille*, Tommaso Guarducci; *Aiace*, Gasparo Savoi; *Irene*, Signora Maggiore; *Euribate*, Pietro Morigi. Ballet-master, Pietro Sodi; Principal Dancers, Mr. Slingsby, Signore Adriani, M. Amour, Signore Santoli, Radicati, Coradini (Bott. 11714 aa. 21/8).
[3] Bur. iv. 493.

pleased and was repeated on several occasions. But the rest of
the season was Guglielmi's.[1] On Thursday, March 10, his
Sesostri was given for his and Signora Campolini's joint 'benefit'.[2]
Announced as 'entirely new', it had in fact been produced at
Venice in 1767, though Zeno's libretto was now 'alter'd and
adapted to the present Taste' by Bottarelli. A fortnight later
(Saturday, March 26) Guglielmi's 'new comic Opera' *Il Ratto
della Sposa*[3] was presented,[4] while the last production of the
season was his *I Viaggiatori ridicoli tornati in Italia*, produced on
Tuesday, 24 May 1768.[5] The opera served for the rest of the
season,[6] which was brought to an end on Thursday, June 30.

The visit of the King of Denmark in the summer reopened the
doors of the King's Theatre for a few inconvenient performances.
Guarducci having left the country, no 'capital singers' remained
to entertain the potentate with 'serious' opera.[7] He arrived at
St. James's on Thursday, 11 August 1768,[8] upon a visit which won
him the hand of the King's sister. On the following Saturday
La buona Figliuola was played for his entertainment, and it was
repeated on August 16. *La Schiava* was given on Tuesday,
September 27, and on Tuesday, October 11, two days before the
sovereign's departure,[9] *Ariana e Teseo*, a 'new serious Opera',
was performed with Signore Luciani and Signora Giacomazzi as
the principal characters.[10]

The Danish visit, no doubt, demanded Bach's frequent
attendance at Court. Otherwise, in the summer of 1768, he is
associated with another event of historical importance. Unlike
his father and Berlin brother, recently removed to Hamburg, Bach
declared a preference for the pianoforte over the harpsichord. His
arrival in London consequently stimulated the experts of the
capital to experiment in the manufacture of the newer instrument;
throughout the decade 1765–75 London held the first place in the

---

[1] *Il Filosofo di Campagna* had a few performances in April.
[2] Cast: *Sesostri*, Tommaso Guarducci; *Amasis*, Signore Moser; *Artenices*,
Signora Campolini; *Nitocris*, Signora Quercioli; *Fanetes*, Gasparo Savoi;
Orgontes, Pietro Morigi (Bott. 907 i. 12/3).
[3] Riemann, p. 458, ignorant of the English production, dates its first performance at Genoa in 1769.
[4] Cast: *Aurora*, Signora Guadagni; *Ortensia*, Signora Maggiore; *Biondino*,
Gasparo Savoi; *Dorina*, Signora Piatti; *Gaudenzio*, Giovanni Lovattini; *Polidoro*,
Pietro Morigi; *Gentilino*, Leopoldo Micheli (Bott. 11714 aa. 21/4).
[5] Riemann, p. 593, dates its first performance at Naples in 1772.
[6] Cast: *La Marchesa*, Signora Guadagni; *Gandolfo*, Giovanni Lovattini;
Don Fabrizio, Pietro Morigi; *Giacinto*, Leopoldo Micheli. The singers of the
parts *Donna Emilia*, *Livietta*, and *Il Conte* are not named (Bott. 11714 aa. 13/7).
[7] Bur. iv. 494.   [8] Gent. Mag., vol. xxxviii (1768), p. 394.
[9] Ibid., p. 492.   [10] Bur. iv. 494.

technique of a craft[1] of which Burkat Shudi (Burkhardt Tschudi), founder of the Broadwood factory, Johannes Zumpe, and Americus Backers were pioneers. Bach's reaction to these opportunities can be observed. His Opus I, published in 1763, is definitely 'pour le Clavecin'. His Opus II, published in 1764, is for the same instrument. His Opus III and Opus IV are not of a nature to indicate his preference. But Opus V, published in 1768, is 'pour le Clavecin ou le Piano Forte', and thereafter both instruments are invariably named in his compositions for the keyboard. His 'Progressive Lessons' are similarly designed. The earliest public use of the pianoforte is revealed in an advertisement of Miss Brickler's 'benefit' at Covent Garden on 16 May 1767: 'End of Act I [of the *Beggar's Opera*] Miss Brickler will sing a favourite Song from JUDITH, accompanied by Mr. Dibdin on a new Instrument call'd a Piano Forte'.[2] But the distinction of having first exhibited it to an English audience as a solo instrument belongs to Bach. On 2 June 1768 Johann Christian Fischer, who afterwards married Mary Gainsborough, announced his arrival in this country at a concert in the Thatched House, an assembly room which, from 1711 to about 1843, stood on the site of the present Conservative club-house in St. James's Street.[3] The *Public Advertiser* of that date printed the following advertisement: 'For the benefit of Mr. Fisher. At the Large Room, Thatch'd House, St. James's-street, This Day, June the 2nd., will be performed a Grand Concert of Vocal and Instrumental Music. First Violin and Concerto by Sig. Pugnani. Concerto on the German Flute,[4] Mr. Tacet. Concerto on the Hautbois by Mr. Fisher. Songs by Sig. Guarducci. Solo on the Viola di Gamba by Mr. Abel. Solo on the Piano Forte by Mr. Bach. Tickets to be had of Mr. Fisher at Mr. Stidman's, Peruke maker in Frith street, Soho; and at Welcker's Music Shop, Gerrard street, Soho, at 10/6 each.' That Bach used one of Zumpe's instruments can be stated positively; his banking account with Drummond's shows him to have paid £50 to Zumpe in this very month. The new instrument awaited Clementi's completer exposition of its technique, but Bach prepared the way; one or more of the simple, tuneful Sonatas of his Opus V were certainly heard for the first time at Fischer's historic concert.

The declining vogue of conventional 'serious' opera, whose

[1] Grove, iv. 157; Rees, *Cyclopaedia*, vol. xvii, *s.v.* 'Harpsichord'.
[2] The theatre-bill for 16 May 1767 is reproduced in Northcott, p. 5.
[3] Wheatley, iii. 370.
[4] The eighteenth-century name for the *traverso*, as distinct from the flageolet or *flûte à bec*.

absurdities awaited Gluck's correction, along with the genius of Piccinni created a situation which had already moved the managers no longer to exclude *opera buffa* from their Saturday programmes. Vincent and his partners had been driven to provide a double cast, and, being unable to repeat the extravagance for the season 1768–9, engaged only a 'comic' troop to satisfy their patrons. For the most part it was composed of singers already engaged and accessible. But Signore Bassanese and Signora Gori were newcomers; Signore Ricciardi replaced Sodi as Ballet-master; Signore Cattaneo and Signora Sarmetti appeared as the principal dancers; and Mr. Canter acted as painter and machinist. The season opened on Tuesday, 8 November 1768,[1] with Galuppi's *Gli Amanti ridicoli*,[2] under the direction of Felice Alessandri, with the addition of a third act, for which he was responsible. A month later (Tuesday, December 13) Piccinni's *Le Donne vendicate*,[3] originally produced at Naples in 1759, was given under Alessandri's direction, with an additional act. *Il Mercato di Malmantile*, by Galuppi and Fischietti, followed on Saturday, 28 January 1769, and on Thursday, March 2, for Lovattini's 'benefit', Alessandri brought forward his *Il Re alla Caccia*; while, on Saturday, April 8, Pugnani, leader of the orchestra, was permitted to produce his *Nanetta e Lubino*,[4] to a libretto by Carlo Francesco Badini. Burney thought little of it, concluding that Pugnani, though an excellent violinist, had taken to composition too late to attain excellence in 'lyric' music.[5] The opera, however, pleased more than its predecessors, and was succeeded, on Saturday, May 6, by *Lo Speziale*, an 'entirely new comic Opera' by Fischietti and Pallavicini. On Saturday, June 3, the last novelty of the season was staged, Traetta's *Le Serve rivali*,[6] under Alessandri's direction. Several productions of past seasons also were repeated, including Guglielmi's *I Viaggiatori ridicoli*, which introduced Signora

[1] Cast: *Orontes*, Leopoldo Micheli; *Ridolfo*, Giovanni Lovattini; *Onofrio*, Pietro Morigi; *Rombo*, Signore Bassanese; *Stella*, Signora Guadagni; *Franchetta*, Signora Gori; *Rosina*, Signora Gibetti (Bott. 907 i. 12/2).
[2] P.A. 8 Nov. 1768.
[3] Cast: *Violante*, Signora Giacomazzi; *Lindora*, Signora Guadagni; *Aurelia*, Signora Gori; *Dorina*, Signora Gibetti; *Ricardo*, Signor Luciani; *Bellezza*, Giovanni Lovattini; *Ferramonte*, Pietro Morigi; *Tiburzio*, Signore Bassanese (Bott. 907 i. 12/4).
[4] Cast: *Acasto*, Signore Luciani; *Il Podestà*, Pietro Morigi; *Giocondo*, Leopoldo Micheli; *Lubin*, Giovanni Lovattini; *Alpin*, Signore Bassanese; *Selmira (Erminia)*, Signora Giacomazzi; *Isabella*, Signora Gibetti; *Nanette*, Signora Guadagni; *Silvia*, Signora Gori (Bott. 907 i. 13/1).
[5] Bur. iv. 494.
[6] Cast: *Rosalba*, Signora Giacomazzi; *Leandro*, Signore Luciani; *Letanzio*, Pietro Morigi; *Giannino*, Giovanni Lovattini; *Giacinta*, Signora Guadagni; *Palmetta*, Signora Gori; *Grillone*, Signore Bassanese (Bott. 907 i. 13/3).

Giacomazzi to the Haymarket stage and drew from the *Court Miscellany*[1] a criticism of brutal frankness. Remarking that the opera was 'the only new Composition, in the comic way, made on purpose for [the King's Theatre], that we remember to have had any degree of merit', the writer continued: '[it] shews the principal performers, the powerful Lovatini and the elegant Guadagni, to the greatest advantage. Signora Giacomazzi made her first appearance in this opera: her voice is the sweetest and most agreeable that can be imagined. . . . But the new man [Luciani] is almost the reverse of this, indeed there is something so disgusting in his appearance that his voice could not please, was it of a kind to do so.' Neither he nor the more agreeable Giacomazzi were long associated with a company which the exigencies of finance tended to constitute as a 'stock' or permanent staff.

While Guglielmi and Alessandri occupied his former position in the conductor's seat at the King's Theatre, Bach and his partner established themselves in public favour at Almack's. The new locality was convenient, and the building well-adapted to musical entertainments; Bach's concerts appear to have been given there exclusively at this period. Under his direction, Anton Kammel, a pupil of Tartini, made his London *début* there on 6 May 1768.[2] On 25 May 1769 Bach, Abel, Tacet, Fischer, Crossdill, and Mrs. Barthélemon drew an audience there 'for the Benefit of a Family under great Difficulties', whose identity had been revealed, and its necessities partly relieved, at an earlier concert in the same hall. The *Public Advertiser* of 23 February 1769 announced it

For the Relief of Lady Dorothy Du Bois, eldest lawful Daughter of Richard the last Earl of Anglesey. Under the Direction of Messrs. Bach and Abel, who, on this Occasion, show they are as conspicuously endowed with soft Compassion as unequalled Harmony and Superiority of Genius, having with Chearfulness not only consented to exhibit their own Excellence, but also so warmly interest themselves for oppressed Innocence, as to incline many others who engage the Admiration of the Public, to follow their generous Example, viz. Mr. Pugnani will play a Solo on the Violin, and Mr. Fischer a Solo on the Hautboy.

> Involv'd in Law, and lawful Right with-held,
> By sad encreasing Want at last compell'd
> To make her Troubles known—the Mother's led
> By pow'rful Nature to solicit Bread
> For her poor Innocents—and hopes to find
> The Public to relieve their Wants inclin'd.
> Hard Case!—And with Expectancies so great,
> But who, alas! can counter act their Fate?

[1] Dec. 1768, p. 611.
[2] Riemann, *Musik-Lexikon*, i. 855, dates his London visit 1774.

Lady Dorothy, victim of her father's matrimonial irregularities, was the child of his secret marriage to a wealthy Dublin clothier's daughter, before whose death he contracted another union, which, if valid, cheated Lady Dorothy and her sisters of their 'Expectancies'. The legitimacy of their half-brother, claimant to the title, was subsequently disallowed and the earldom lapsed. Bach's charitable interest in Lady Dorothy was due to her marriage to Dubois, a violinist, who, on 8 February 1770, himself took part in a concert organized by Bach for his family's relief.

The season of 1769–70 revealed a reaction against the tendency of its predecessors to exalt *opera buffa* to the exclusion of her 'serious' sister. Crawford again associated himself with the management,[1] while the engagement of Gaetano Guadagni as 'first man' introduced a spirit of enterprise which manifested itself in the activities of an adventurous season. He had visited London twenty years before, as 'a full and well-toned countertenor'. Though a careless singer, his voice had attracted the notice of Handel, who allotted him the parts in the *Messiah* and *Samson* originally composed for Mrs. Cibber. After leaving England in 1753 his voice changed to a soprano, thin and feeble by comparison with its former state, but of a beauty which, combined with his good looks, graceful gestures, and noble bearing, assured him no diminution of his plaudits as a singer. His strong resentments and caprice, however, made relations with him uneasy, even alienated the goodwill of those who most admired his art; while, on the stage, his conduct was often so provocative that he excited hisses rather than applause.[2] Cecilia Grassi, after two years' absence, was now associated with him as 'first woman', with Guglielmi as composer and director.

Piccinni's *Le Contadine bizarre*[3] opened the season on Tuesday, 7 November 1769. Guglielmi had submitted the opera to some revision (its original title was *La Contadina bizarra*), while Piatti, in the character of Lucio, introduced a song by Bach.[4] Guadagni made his *rentrée* on Saturday, November 11, in the pasticcio *L'Olimpiade*, to which Bach contributed the favourite song,[5] 'Quel labbro adorato', sung by Guadagni.[6] *Il Padre ed il Figlio*

---

[1] P.A., 5 Sept. 1769.   [2] Bur. iv. 495.

[3] Cast: *Rosalba*, Signora Piatti; *Lucio*, Signore Piatti; *Auretta*, Anna Zamparini; *Fiorina*, Signora Guadagni; *Nardone*, Giovanni Lovattini; *Gianfriso* Pietro Morigi; *Masino*, Signore Bianchi; *Livietta*, Antonia Zamparini. Balletmaster, Signore Campioni; Principal dancers, Mr. Slingsby, Signore Galeotti, M. Simonin, M. Delsire, Signora Radicati, Signora Guidi, Mlle. Gardel (Bott. 907 i. 12/6).

[4] Cf. *infra*, p. 231.   [5] Bur. iv. 496.   [6] *Infra*, p. 231.

rivali,[1] a new 'comic Opera', followed on December 5. Its composer, Tommaso Giordani, who for some years had been producing Italian opera at Dublin, probably owed his admission to the King's Theatre to Tenducci's association with him in the Irish capital. Grassi made her *rentrée* on Saturday, 13 January 1770, in Guglielmi's *Ezio*,[2] and, after a series of revivals, London at length was privileged to hear Gluck's *Orfeo ed Euridice*, now nearly eight years old.[3] Produced on Saturday, April 7, the opera was not given in its original form, but owed its presentation to the co-operation of Bach and Guglielmi, who were permitted to expand Gluck's original score. The title-page of the programme-book[4] announced, and excused, the mutilation of a classic:

ORFEO ED EURIDICE
ORPHEUS AND EURYDICE

An

Opera, in the Grecian Taste
As Perform'd at the

KING'S THEATRE

in the

HAY-MARKET.

The Music as originally composed by Signor GLUCH, to which, in order to make the Performance of a necessary length for an evening's entertainment, Signor BACH has very kindly condescended to add of his own new composition all such chorusses, airs, and recitatives, as are marked with inverted commas,[5] except those which are sung by Signora *Guglielmi*, and they are likewise an entire new production of Signor GUGLIELMI, her husband.

The Poetry is from Signor CALZABIGI,[6] with additions by G. G. BOTTARELLI of all that Messrs. *Bach* and *Guglielmi* have enriched this Performance by their Music.

Inmites potuit flectere cantibus umbrarum Dominos,
Eurydicen dum repetit suam.

[1] Cast: *Clarice*, Antonia Zamparini; *Asdrubale*, Giovanni Lovattini; *Ernesto*, Signore Piatti; *Giannetta*, Signora Guadagni; *Fabrizio*, Signore Bianchi; *Nannina* Anna Zamparini; *Il Barone*, Pietro Morigi; *Carlotta*, Signora Piatti (Bott. 907 i. 12/5).
[2] Cast: *Valentiano III*, Signore Piatti; *Ezio*, Gaetano Guadagni; *Massimo*, Signore Bianchi; *Fulvia*, Cecilia Grassi; *Onoria*, Achiapati Guglielmi; *Varo*, Pietro Morigi. The libretto is bound up with the text of *Orfeo ed Euridice* in a volume in the library of the Royal College of Music (xxi. A. 5).
[3] Produced at Vienna, 5 Oct. 1762.
[4] Bott. 11714 aa. 21/5.
[5] *Infra*, p. 235.
[6] Gluck's original librettist.

DRAMATIS PERSONAE

Eagrus, King of Cicony, Father of Orpheus . .	Signor Bianchi
Orpheus	Signor Guadagni
Eurydice	Signora Grassi
Egina, Sister to Eurydice, and Happy Ghost .	Signora Guglielmi
Love	Signor Giustinelli
Pluto	Signor Morigi

Chorus of Youths, with Orpheus; of Happy Ghosts, with Eurydice; of Furies and Specters, with Pluto; Guards with Eagrus; Damsels with Egina.

Ballet Master . . . . Signor Galeotti

Principal Dancers

Mr. Slingsby	Signora Guidi
Signor Galeotti. . . .	Madem. Gardel
Monsieur Simonin . . .	Signora Radicati

Monsieur Delsire
Painter and Machinist
Signor Bigari

Guadagni revealed his responsibility for the production in a Preface to the programme-book:

To the Nobility and Gentry:

Illustrious Patrons, The taste which the English Nation has always shown (in a superior degree to almost any other) for true harmony, engaged me to propose the performance of this Opera, to the Gentlemen Managers of the King's-Theatre, not doubting but its excellent composition, added to the classical merit of the drama, would afford something beyond what is usually seen, to gratify real judges; to whom, in your Persons, it is particularly dedicated.

The original Composer made himself a perfect master of his author's meaning; and infused the genius of the poetry into his music, in which he followed the example of my great master Handel, the phœnix of our age; who in all modes of musical expression, where sense was to be conveyed, excelled beyond our praise. In order to the more immediate observation of this beauty, resulting from a happy coalition between the writer and composer of an Opera, I most earnestly wish that such Ladies and Gentlemen, as propose to honour the exhibition of this drama with their presence, would read the piece, before they see it performed; I believe they will not find their attention ill repaid; and, as a small, but zealous instance of humble gratitude for long enjoyed countenance, and repeated favours, I flatter myself, the supporters of the Italian drama in England will condescend to accept this dedication of the Opera of Orpheus, and his warmest endeavours to contribute to their entertainment, from their most obliged, and most obedient, humble servant,

Gaetano Guadagni.

Burney justly remarks,[1] that the simplicity, unity, and dramatic excellence of Gluck's masterpiece were gravely prejudiced by the intrusion of other composers and alien styles. Their interpola-

[1] Bur. iv. 496.

tions occasioned delays and impeded the action, with the result
that the opera was judged, not upon the beauties which won it
acclamation at Vienna, but as a medium by which to test the merits
of the performers. Bach, the chief offender, contributed, besides
the choruses, seven airs to Bremner's 'Favourite Songs' of the
opera,[1] a collection of fifteen in which Gluck was represented
by only five! Guadagni, in the character of Orfeo, by his
impassioned acting, no less than his masterly singing, won great
applause and favour, which he sacrificed, owing to a subsequent
altercation over the preference of one of the Zamparini sisters
before his sister, Alessandri's wife, but chiefly from his refusal
to lower the dignity of his dramatic character by responding to the
audience's applause, or to gratify it by repeating an encored air at
the end of the scene. The customary 'benefits' concluded the
season, Grassi taking hers at a repetition of *L'Olimpiade*, for which
she solicited 'the kind Protection of the Nobility and Gentry, and
hopes the Subscribers to the Boxes will not think her remiss in
not waiting on them in Person, she being a Stranger in the Method
how to proceed, therefore most humbly desires they will send their
Orders for the Boxes to the Office of the said Theatre'.[2]

Guadagni's former association with Handel perhaps suggested
to Bach the unfortunate enterprise he organized in Lent 1770.
While his annual series of concerts was in progress at Almack's,[3]
he was rashly induced to engage the King's Theatre in competition
with Covent Garden and Drury Lane, in a sacred entertainment
with which the other theatres were more popularly associated.
Beginning on Friday, March 2, and continuing till the Friday
in Passion Week (April 6), both Covent Garden and Drury Lane,
on Wednesdays and Fridays, the off-nights at the Opera, gave
performances of Oratorio. Drury Lane offered Handel exclusively
—*Samson*, *Judas Maccabaeus*, *Acis and Galatea*, *Alexander's Feast*,
Gideon, and the *Messiah*. Covent Garden, besides the *Messiah*,
Judas Maccabaeus, *Samson*, and *Israel in Babylon*,[4] performed
Jommelli's *La Passione*, Piccinni's *Death of Abel*, and *The Resurrection*, a new work by Dr. Arne. Of the last the *Town and Country
Magazine*[5] remarked: 'As this is the first season Oratorios have,
for several years, been performed at both houses, where they now
are exhibited at reduced prices, an emulation has been kindled
between them, to which, in some degree, we may attribute a new
sacred oratorio that was performed, for the first time, on the

[1] *Infra*, p. 234.
[2] P.A., 10 May 1770.
[3] From 17 Jan. to 16 May 1770.
[4] A perversion of *Israel in Egypt*.
[5] March 1770, p. 155.

9th [March] inst. at Covent-Garden, under the direction of the gentlemen who conducted these entertainments at the Haymarket last year. This piece is called the *Resurrection*; the principal vocal performers in which are Signor Tenducci, Mr. Vernon, Mr. Du Bellamy, Mrs. Barthélemon, and Mrs. Mattocks. . . . The entertainment was still farther heightened by Mr. Giardini's performance on the violin, notwithstanding some pretended connoissenti testified their disapprobation of his introducing the air of *Rural Felicity* in his concerto.'

Into this competition Bach was induced to enter, by providing a series of performances at the King's Theatre on the five Thursdays in March (1, 8, 15, 22, 29) and the first in April (April 5) 1770. On March 1 he gave Jommelli's popular *La Passione*, with Guadagni, Bianchi, Cecilia Grassi, Signora Guglielmi as his vocalists, and interludes by Jean-Joseph Rodolphe,[1] solo horn player at the Paris Opera, and Jean-Pierre Duport, the eminent violoncellist. On March 8 and 15 the first act of Jommelli's work was repeated, with Pergolesi's *Stabat Mater*, while on the last three Thursdays Bach presented his only oratorio, *Gioas, Re di Giuda*, with the following cast:[2]

Sebia (Soprano)	.	.	.	Cecilia Grassi
Gioiada (Tenor)	.	.	.	Signor Bianchi
Gioas (Alto)	.	.	.	Gaetano Guadagni
Atalia (Alto)	.	.	.	Signora Guglielmi
Matan (Bass)	.	.	.	Pietro Morigi

The oratorio, in effect an unacted opera on a Biblical subject, pleased and was repeated in 1771. Bach, however, was less well advised to introduce himself at the Lenten performances as a soloist on the organ,[3] challenging the reputation of Charles John Stanley, the blind organist of the Temple Church, who for some years had been associated with John Christopher Smith in continuing at Covent Garden the oratorio performances formerly directed by Handel. Bach, however, was too much out of practice on the instrument to assert superiority over Stanley, or to satisfy those who remembered Handel. He had composed for the occasion,' writes Mrs. Papendiek,[4] 'and played between the acts, his second concerto.[5]   A modern piece was usual, but as it was to be heard on the organ it was ill chosen; for, though beautiful in itself, it did not accord with the sacred performance, and Bach

---

[1] Rodolphe drew £136 on Bach's account at Drummond's in 1770.
[2] P.A., 22 March 1770. Owing to her indisposition, Grassi's place was taken by Gasparo Savoi, the sopranist, on Mar. 22. Tenducci replaced Guadagni on March 29 and April 5.
[3] Bur. iv. 497.   [4] Papendiek, i. 107.   [5] *Infra*, p. 297.

being no organ player, the whole thing rather tended to detract from the success of the evening.'

The season was therefore neither flattering nor profitable. The King and Queen more than once honoured Bach with their presence, but were unable to draw the public to an entertainment for which they were accustomed to look elsewhere. The oratorios were thinly attended, and the theatre usually presented a depressing vista of empty boxes. 'Do you go to the oratorio in the Haymarket this evening?' said General Fitzpatrick, meeting James Hare, the witty friend of Charles James Fox. 'Oh, no,' Hare replied, 'I have no wish to intrude on His Majesty's privacy.'[1]

Guadagni's departure at the end of the season left his position as the principal star of the musical firmament to Ferdinando Tenducci, who had first been heard in London under Colomba Mattei's management, when Burney judged him 'a singer of the second or third class'.[2] Notorious for vanity and extravagance, his arrival in London put the Channel between himself and his Italian creditors. But he spent the greater part of 1760 in prison, and on 13 January 1761 published an affecting appeal for charity in the *Public Advertiser*.

The Petition of Ferdinando Tenducci, Musician, most humbly sheweth: That he was arrested for a Debt contracted in Italy, and has been detained in the Prison of the King's Bench eight Months, great Part of that Time confined to a Sick-bed, where he must have perished for Want of Necessaries and Attendance, had he not been relieved by the Charity of the Humane. That being destitute of Friends, and reduced to the utmost Indigence and Misery, he begs Leave to fly to the distinguished Benevolence of the Nobility and Gentry of this Kingdom, imploring their Compassion towards an unfortunate Stranger in Distress, and intreating the Honour of their Company at the Great Music-Room in Dean-street, Soho, where, on Wednesday, the 28th of January 1761, some of the best Professors of Music will generously perform for his Benefit.

The compulsion that moved Tenducci from Italy to London probably also propelled him from London to Dublin, where, in 1766, he married a girl with a considerable fortune, and, in 1767, 'renounced the Errors of Popery'.[3] His conversion conveniently anticipated his migration to Edinburgh, where he spent the season of 1768 and 1769. Thence he returned to London, and, on 15 December 1769, produced at Covent Garden the English opera *Amintas*, his adaptation of *The Royal Shepherd*,[4] first given at Dublin in 1765. His friendship with Bach dated from this

---

[1] Parke, i. 55. Bur. (iv. 497) also comments on the ill-success of the venture.
[2] Bur. iv. 497.   [3] P.A., 11 July 1767.   [4] *Ibid.*, 15 Dec. 1769.

period.[1] But in 1776 his extravagance again compelled him to evade his creditors by flight to the continent, where Bach met him in 1778. He found means to return to England, and until Bach's death their friendship was not interrupted. Its continuance too clearly indicates a similarity of tastes to permit Bach's biographer to challenge the tradition of his hero's extravagance.

Meanwhile, Tenducci was invited by Crawford and his partners[2] to fill Guadagni's position as 'first man' for the season 1770–1, along with Grassi and a cast which contained several newcomers. Their programme was unambitious and few 'serious' operas were presented.[3] The pasticcio Le Vicende della Sorte[4] (November 6), Cosroe (November 24), Astarto (December 13), a 'new serious Opera',[5] and Gli Ucellatori[6] (December 18) were given before Christmas, and in the second part of the season, on Tuesday 30 April 1771, Orfeo was revived, 'by command of their Majesties', with Guadagni again in the title-part. The opera was 'new dressed [with] new Scenes and new Dances', while, in the form of a letter to Sir Watkin Williams Wynn, Guadagni prefaced the programme-book with an assurance that the revival expressed to the British public his gratitude, 'of all the virtues that which is most congenial to human nature'. 'Permit me to boast', he concluded, 'that, in performing the part of Orpheus, I require no other bribe, or reward, than the pleasure of shewing you a ready obedience'.[7]

Meanwhile, the Bach-Abel concerts filled Almack's weekly from January 9 to 8 May 1771, while on Thursday, January 10, Bach's Gioas was revived, with Tenducci, Grassi, Savoi, Morigi, Signora Guglielmi, and Mrs. Barthélemon in the principal parts.

---

[1] In Aug. 1770, on the occasion of the Queen's brother's birthday, they appeared at Court, and so charmed their Majesties that Tenducci received 100 guineas and Bach, 'who composed the music for the above occasion, an elegant piece of plate'.
[2] P.A., 27 Oct. 1770.   [3] Bur. iv. 497.
[4] Cast: Celidoro, Giovanni Lovattini; Ruggiero, Giovanni Ristorini; Berto, Michele del Zanca; Calimone, Andrea Morigi; Lisaura, Mrs. Barthélemon; Coccolina, Catterina Ristorini; Ruspolina, Marianna Demena (Bott. 907 i. 13/4).
[5] Cast: Elisa, Signora Guglielmi; Sidonia, Signora Romani; Astarto, Ferdinando Tenducci; Phoenicio, Giovanni Ristorini; Nino, Gasparo Savoi; Agenor, Andrea Morigi (Bott. 907 i. 13/5).
[6] Cast: Marchese di Bel Fiore, Gasparo Savoi; Contessa Armelinda, Mrs. Barthélemon; Roccolina, Catterina Ristorini; Cecchino, Giovanni Lovattini; Mariannina, Marianna Demena; Pierotto, Michele del Zanca; Toniolo, Andrea Morigi (Bott. 907 i. 13/3).
[7] (Bott. 907 i. 11/7.) Cast: Orfeo, Gaetano Guadagni; Eagrus, Giovanni Ristorini; Tiresia, Gasparo Savoi; Amore, Giuseppe Giustinelli; Pluto, Andrea Morigi; Eurydice, Cecilia Grassi; Egina, and First Happy Ghost, Signora Guglielmi; Second Happy Ghost, Gasparo Savoi. Ballet-master, Signore Galeotti; Principal dancers, M. Grocet, Signore Como, Signore Guidi, Radicati, Chollet.

Duport, as before, provided an interlude between the acts, while in Act II Maddalena Lombardini Sirmen, Tartini's pupil, made her London *début* as a violinist.[1] But, for Bach himself, the most interesting event of the season was the visit of Johann Baptist Wendling, '1st German Flute to H.S.H. the Elector Palatine', the husband of Dorothea Spurni, 'the German Melpomene of Mannheim's Golden Age'. That Bach owed his invitation to Mannheim in 1772 to Wendling's recommendation is the more probable seeing that he was Bach's guest in King's Square Court when he and Duport, directed by Bach and Abel, held a joint 'benefit' on 15 May 1771, with the assistance of Signora Sirmen and Nikolaus Joseph Hüllmandel, musician to the Comte de Guînes.[2]

The season 1770–1 imposed the last straw upon the straining finances of Crawford and his colleagues. Serious opera was in precarious state; its patrons flocked to the theatre 'more for the gratification of the eye than the ear', enticed by the seductions of Anna Heinel, a dancer 'whose grace and execution were so perfect as to eclipse all other excellence'. Her extraordinary talent received an extraordinary recompense—a salary of £600 and a 'regallo' of £600 more from the Maccaroni Club. 'How curious it is', remarked Cocchi, 'that the English value nothing but what they pay a big price for.'[3] Bach and Abel, however, with increasing profits, continued to draw the town to Almack's, where they gave their annual series of concerts from January 22 to 20 May 1772; while on April 6, at the King's Theatre, Bach presented his *Endimione*, described as a 'Serenata with grand Chorusses', with the following singers:

Diana	Cecilia Grassi
Nice	Signora Carpara
Amore	Gasparo Savoi
Endimione	Giovanni Lovattini

The cantata was repeated later at Mannheim.[4] It is therefore noteworthy that Wendling took part in the London performance, and in some measure appears to have been responsible for it; for the advertisement[5] announced that tickets could be procured from him 'at Mr. Bach's in Queen Street, Golden Square', where Bach and Abel were now installed.

Shortly after the performance of *Endimione* the foreign colony of musicians in London was augmented by the arrival of one who eventually succeeded to Bach's office at court, and, in the last decade of his life, challenged Bach's vogue on his peculiar instru-

[1] P.A., 10 Jan. 1771.
[2] P.A., 15 May 1771.
[3] Bur. iv. 498. Heinel married the elder Vestris.
[4] *Infra*, p. 129.
[5] P.A., 6 Apr. 1772.

ment. Johann Samuel Schroeter made his first bow to a London
audience at the Thatched House on 2 May 1772, in a concert under
Bach and Abel's direction. 'A young man, fascinating, fawning,
and suave', remarks Mrs. Papendiek,[1] Schroeter in a short time
became the popular 'teacher for the belles, company for the
mode', the recognized master of the pianoforte, on which he was
heard at his first concert, an instrument whose use was now
general for solo playing, though the harpsichord was retained in
the theatres to accompany the voice. 'Bach perceived his excellence in his profession', adds Mrs. Papendiek, 'and assisted him
as a friend, for his heart was too good to know the littleness of
envy. He gave Schroeter advice from his experience of this
country, and was also of great use to him in the theory of his
profession.[2] He loved him almost as a son, looking upon his
talent with delight, and deploring that his disposition was such
as must, in the end, work to his bane. Schroeter was truly an
enchanting player, and so prepossessing that, after hearing him
once, one could not but regret any lost opportunity of hearing
him again. He did little or no good to his fraternity in music. He
played when called upon,[3] but took no interest to forward or
assist any individual, and left no immediate scholar, though John
Cramer studied under him upon the decline of dear Bach.'

January 1773 found Bach and Abel again at Almack's for the
opening of their season. But their house in Queen Street had
closed after the Schroeter concert; for the two friends went their
separate ways to the continent. Abel, called thither by his private
affairs, conducted young Henry Angelo to Paris to place him in
'an orderly family'. Bach and Wendling took the road to Mannheim, where, in November 1772, Bach produced his *Temistocle*
and, belatedly, fell in love.

[1] Papendiek, i. 134.
[2] ABCD, p. 44, declares that Bach wrote the accompaniments for his
published concertos.
[3] His marriage made him independent.

CHAPTER V

MANNHEIM AND PARIS

IN the seventies of the eighteenth century Germany neither asserted nor was conceded the musical primacy which, from the advent of Haydn, Mozart, and Beethoven, was universally accorded her. Though she had recently boasted Bach and Handel, and still exhibited Gluck and Carl Philipp Emanuel Bach, Burney[1] deliberately concluded that her people were musicians by cultivation rather than instinct, quoting with approval 'an accurate observer of human nature', who admitted their application and perseverance, but denied them innate genius. The journal of his German tour (1772) constantly records his animadversions on untuned organs, clumsy orchestral playing, and indelicate church singing.

Mannheim provided a conspicuous exception to these experiences. The town was the capital of the Palatinate since Elector Carl Philipp, abandoning Heidelberg in 1720, planned his prodigious palace, and built an Opera House, one of the largest in Europe; it seated 5,000 persons, and at each performance consumed £40 worth of wax candles for its illumination.[2] Under his successor, Carl Theodor, Mannheim enjoyed her golden age. His court, lavish and magnificent, removed in the summer months to Schwetzingen, a country retreat Carl Theodor sought to make a second Versailles, embellishing its gardens with temples, statues, grottoes, and fountains. A theatre was added for the performance of light opera in 1752,[3] and in the village a retinue of 1,500 persons attended the sovereign, among them such a number of musicians that their instruments were heard from every window, 'at one house a fine player on the violin; at another, a German flute; here an excellent oboe; there a bassoon, a clarionet, a violoncello, or a concert of several instruments together.'[4] Schwetzingen, remarked Schubart, was a magician's island 'wo alles klang und sang'.[5] For here, as at Mannheim, concerts and Opera were the Elector's chief and most constant enjoyment.

Mannheim's reputation as a musician's paradise reached its apogee in the decennium 1767–77, following the disastrous wars. The court orchestra, under Christian Cannabich, attained to a degree of virtuosity which placed it on a platform of its own. In

[1] Burney, p. 190. [2] *Ibid.*, p. 109. [3] Walter, pp. 105–7.
[4] Burney, p. 107. [5] Schubart, p. 130.

size ranking below the largest—Paris's numbered 63, Milan's 66—
it contained from 40 to 50 players: 20 to 22 violins, 4 violas,
4 violoncelli, 3 or 4 contrabassi, 3 or 4 flutes, 3 oboes, 3 or 4
clarinets, 4 bassoons, 6 horns, trumpets, and timpani.[1] While
the traditions of Sebastian Bach's time still obtained at other
German courts,[2] whose orchestras were largely haphazard collections of palace officials, the Mannheim Capelle was a body of
professional players, whose technique no other approached. Containing, Burney observed,[3] 'more solo players, and good composers, than perhaps any other orchestra in Europe', it was
'an army of generals, equally fit to plan a battle, as to fight it',
and, under Cannabich, exhibited a perfection of finish till then
unknown. Composers, consequently, were offered a new technique; the Overture, which had served merely as an usher to
demand silence for the vocalist, was advanced to importance as
a work to be listened to; the directions *crescendo* and *diminuendo*
received usage and attention, while the indications *forte* and
piano were now discovered to be pigments as capable of giving
colour to the score as those of the artist's palette to his canvas.
Moreover, the proportion of wood wind to strings was contrary
to usage. A new relationship consequently was set up between
the two families, and delicate shading was rendered possible
where before only a contrast of dynamics was attempted. The
conductor, too, ceased to be a time-beater and became the controlling mind of a mobile instrument. No orchestra in the world,
Schubart considered, approached Mannheim's in plasticity: its
forte was a thunder-roll, its *crescendo* a cataract, its *diminuendo*
a dying ripple of sound, its *piano* the murmur of spring.[4] Burney
detected only one defect in an organization otherwise perfect—
the faulty intonation of the wind instruments, especially the oboes
and bassoons, which, beginning too sharp, tended to sharpen as
the performance proceeded, a blemish too common to all orchestras
of the period to make the censure severe.[5]

To this musician's El Dorado Bach introduced himself in

[1] Walter, p. 108. The violins, violas, and violoncelli were disposed on the right
of the conductor, the contrabassi and wood-wind on his left, while the trumpets
and timpani occupied an elevated platform. Ballets and symphonies were
conducted by the leader (Concertmeister) from his desk; at performances of
Opera the Capellmeister took his place, seated at a harpsichord in the middle
of his players.
[2] Cf. T.B., p. 11.   [3] Burney, p. 110.
[4] 'Kein Orchester der Welt hat es je in der Ausführung dem Mannheimer
zuvorgethan. Sein Forte ist ein Donner, sein Crescendo ein Cataract, sein
Diminuendo ein in die Ferne hin plätschernder Krystallfluss, sein Piano ein
Frühlingshauch' (Schubart, p. 130. Cf. Jahn, i. 563).   [5] Burney, p. 110.

August or September 1772.[1] Its season opened in November, when the Elector's name-day received a gala performance, which Bach was invited to provide. The selection of a German, albeit expatriated, administered a check to Italy's hitherto unchallenged monopoly, and, according to Junker,[2] revealed the Elector's inclination to vary its monotony. For Carl Theodor, like his contemporary at Berlin, was a musical amateur, proficient on the German flute and violoncello, though his prowess was less publicly displayed than Frederic's.[3] Nor did he exhibit Frederic's narrow preference. Mannheim, declared Schubart,[4] was 'ein Odeum' in which the listener could satisfy an eclectic taste more readily than at any other musical centre in Europe.

Their recent association in London suggests that Bach was the guest of Wendling at Mannheim. His host was an Alsatian, a flautist of European repute, who had been in the Elector's service for nearly twenty years, and in their course exhibited his talent in London, Paris, and other capitals. His wife, Dorothea, a woman of thirty-five, was the daughter of Spurni, a court musician at Stuttgart; since 1752 she was engaged as a soprano at Mannheim, where she married Wendling in 1756. Employed at first as 'second woman', she was promoted to be *prima donna* in the early 60's by the retirement of Rosa Gabrieli-Bleckmann, and thenceforward was the star of Mannheim's musical sky, adding to an attractive person high powers as an actress in 'serious' and 'comic' roles, and a voice of singular beauty. She sang, remarked Wieland, with her heart and soul, and Mozart both admired and wrote for her. Her attractions adorned her daughter Augusta, a girl of fifteen or sixteen in 1772, who subsequently became Carl Theodor's mistress.[5] Bach also succumbed to her charms and wished to make her his wife. In a postscript to Wolfgang's letter, written at Mannheim on 20 November 1777, Frau Mozart relates that she and Wolfgang had dined with the Wendlings the previous day, and adds: 'They have an only daughter who is very beautiful, whom the English Bach wanted to marry.'[6] The

---

[1] 'Mr. J. Bach was daily expected here from London, when [in August] I was at Mannheim' (Burney, p. 109).
[2] 'Wenn J. Bach zur Schöpfung einer Oper nach Mannheim gerufen wird, so macht diess in meinen Augen dem Kurfürsten, der, des zu einseitigen Geschmacks müde ist, mehr Ehre, als Bachen selbst' (Junker, p. 15).
[3] Burney, pp. 109, 111.
[4] Schubart, p. 129.
[5] Walter, pp. 235 f.
[6] 'Göstern als an Elisabetha Tag hab ich und der Wolfgang bey Herrn und Madame Wendling gespeiset, nemlich bey den Flautraversisten, der Wolfgang

'natural coldness of her character',[1] however, repelled her from a man some twenty years her elder, and drove Bach to the maturer consolations of Cecilia Grassi.[2] Franz Anton Wendling and his wife were also in the circle of Bach's intimate Mannheim acquaintances. The former, a violinist in the Capelle, was Johann Baptist's brother; his wife, Elisabeth Auguste, was a daughter of Peter Sarselli, the Mannheim tenor, and, like her sister-in-law, on the Opera establishment, in which, however, she assumed only minor roles.[3]

After ten years' absence, Bach would revisit his native land with pleasure. His steps may have turned to Bückeburg, where his elder brother was still in service, inviting the return visit the latter paid to London a few years later.[4] Leipzig, too, where his two sisters were living in dire poverty, may have called him. But Mannheim summoned him to compose the opera he was commissioned to produce.[5] He chose for his libretto Metastasio's *Temistocle*, which exhibited the conventional play of human passion on a classic background. On Thursday, 5 November 1772, the opening night of the season, it was performed in the presence of the court with gala pomp and ceremonial. At four in the afternoon a procession was formed in the ante-room of the Electress's apartments in the left wing of the Schloss, whence, under the blare of trumpets, their Electoral Serenities were conducted to a box in the middle of the first tier. Persons of distinction graced the occasion and made their compliments; the young Margraves of Baden, with their suites, were accommodated in a large box on the third tier; the Crown Prince and Princess of Hessen-Cassel, in the 'loge grillée' on the right of the parterre; the Prince and Princess of Nassau-Weilburg, the Countess of Neipperg, and the three Princes Radziwill, in the corresponding box opposite. Several foreign ladies of rank received places formerly reserved for the Jesuits, while other parts of the huge building were occupied by such a concourse of visitors that the townspeople, usually

gilt alles bey ihnen. Sie haben eine einzige Tochter die sehr schön ist, und die der Bach in England hat wollen heurathen' (Schiedermair, iv. 324).
[1] Schubart's words. Cf. Walter, p. 236.
[2] When I wrote the article 'Johann Christian Bach' in *Grove*, I accepted the year 1767 as the date of Bach's marriage to Cecilia Grassi. As Augusta Wendling was then about ten years old, I concluded that Frau Mozart was mistaken, and that Bach had known and admired her mother before she married Wendling. I was able to correct my error in the reprint of 1928.
[3] Walter, p. 236.
[4] *Infra*, p. 159.
[5] That Bach composed his Mannheim operas at Mannheim is established by Mozart's letter of 13 Nov. 1777: 'Bach hat hier [Mannheim] zwei Opern geschrieben' (Schiedermair, i. 113).

admitted to the parterre, were unable to gain admission.[1] The audience was brilliant, the cast distinguished:[2]

Temistocle	Anton Raaf
Xerxes	Giovanni Battista Zonca
Lysimachus.	Silvio Giorgetti
Aspasia	Dorothea Wendling
Neocles	Francesco Roncaglia
Roxane	Elisabeth Wendling
Sebastes	Vincenzo Mucciolo

One of the finest tenors of his generation, Raaf had a voice of the purest quality and great range, round, full, and clean.[3] Zonca, an admirable bass, who had been in the Elector's service since 1769, was further commended to his employer by his proficiency on the harmonica.[4] Giorgetti made his *début* at Mannheim in 1766, and was useful in both 'serious' and 'comic' roles, though Burney, who heard him in 1772, thought his voice weak; he retired in 1776.[5] Roncaglia, a soprano *castrato*, who afterwards appeared in London,[6] made his *début* at Mannheim in Bach's opera.[7] Mucciolo, an altist, also was a newcomer.[8] Characteristically melodious,[9] *Temistocle* was followed by two ballets: *Roger dans l'isle d'Alcine*, arranged by Hoftanzmeister Étienne Lauchery, which represented the release of an English Prince Astolf and of Roger, a Saracen knight, from the sorceries of Alcine; and *Medea und Jason*, a tragic dance based on Ovid's legend. Madame Micheroux was the *prima ballerina* of both pieces, the music of the first being by Carlo Giuseppe Toëschi, the Mannheim Concertmeister since 1759, and of the second by Cannabich.

Bach's London engagements did not permit him to prolong his visit or to take lengthy advantage of the Elector's courtesies. But his opera survived his departure; it again provided the gala performance in November 1773,[10] and its popularity invited future contributions from his pen. In 1774 *Endimione*, already heard in London,[11] was produced at Mannheim. Described as 'azione drammatico teatrale',[12] and on the Darmstadt score as 'Serenata a quattro', the work was a setting, in two parts, of Metastasio's version of the legend of Diana and Endymion. Though not recorded, the cast probably was as follows:

Endimione	Anton Raaf
Diana	Dorothea Wendling
Nice	Francesco Roncaglia
Amore	Elisabeth Wendling.

[1] Walter, p. 104.   [2] *Ibid.*, p. 141.   [3] Cf. Schubart, p. 136.
[4] Gerber, ii. 856. Cf. Walter, p. 234.   [5] Walter, p. 229.
[6] *Infra*, p. 153.   [7] Walter, p. 229.   [8] *Ibid.*
[9] Cf. *Infra*, p. 238.   Cf. Walter, pp. 141, 162.   [10] Walter, p. 141.
[11] *Supra*, p. 123.   [12] Walter, p. 142.

The programme was completed by an elaborate mythological ballet by Laucherey and Cannabich, entitled *Achille reconnu par Ulisse dans l'isle de Scyros*.[1] For Dorothea Wendling Bach also wrote, in August 1774, a one-act pastoral cantata entitled *Amor Vincitore*.[2] Performed at Schwetzingen, it contained two characters, both soprano voices, the nymph Dalisa, and the hunter Alcidoro (Roncaglia).[3]

If Bach was inclined to maintain his associations with Mannheim, Mannheim was as willing to hear his music. The late summer of 1776, therefore, found him again in the sparkling capital, where the production of his *Lucio Silla*, on November 20, celebrated the Electress's name-day. The libretto, by Hofdichter Mattia Verazi, was based on Giovanni da Camera's text, which Mozart had already used at Vienna (1772), while the cast, with one exception, was that for which Bach had composed on his first visit:[4]

Lucio Silla .	. . . .	Anton Raaf
Giunia	. . . .	Dorothea Wendling
Celia .	. . . .	Elisabeth Wendling
Cecilio	. . . .	Francesco Roncaglia
Cinna .	. . . .	Giovanni Battista Zonca
Aufidio	. . . .	Pietro Paolo Carnoli [5]

The opera pleased less than its predecessor; Bach did not write again for the Mannheim stage.[6] But his comparative failure was only partially due to the demerits of his score. With one exception, *Lucio Silla* was the last Italian opera produced at the Electoral Court,[7] where, as elsewhere, a sturdy reaction had been preparing against its conventional artificiality. The tyranny of *castrati* and *prime donne* had made it a platform for the exhibition of their virtuosity, in a monotonous sequence of arias, infrequently broken by a duet or trio, and devoid of choral *ensembles*. Public taste had outlived its venerable *clichés*, its classic heroes, magic gardens, imprisoned princesses, knightly paladins, and wearisome *réchauffage* of the classics. Metastasio's pompous platitudes fell heavily

---

[1] Walter, p. 162.   [2] *Ibid.*, p. 142.
[3] Of this cantata Vogler writes: 'Diese Cantata besteht aus zwei Arien und zwei Recitativen. Die verschiedene Leidenschaften, Gemählde, Caractere, so darin herrschen, geben dem Sänger, wenn sie bedeutend ausgedrückt und vorgetragen werden, Gelegenheit sich sowohl im sanften und zärtlichen, als auch im pathetischen und feurigen zu zeigen' (*Betrachtungen*, p. 63).
[4] Walter, p. 141.
[5] Carnoli had been singing subordinate tenor roles at Mannheim since 1752–3. Cf. Walter, p. 231.
[6] Mozart writes from Mannheim on 13 Nov. 1777: 'Bach hat hier zwei Opern geschrieben, wofon die erste besser gefallen als die 2te' (Schiedermair, i. 113).
[7] Walter, pp. 141, 156, 367.

on the ears of a generation ready to find diversion, romance, and
distraction in the characters of a society, or the happenings of an
age, less remote, finding the strutting of a Themistocles or Lucius
Silla less agreeable than the gaiety of a Figaro, and the outwitting
of a jealous husband more to its taste than the crude politics of
a Persian or Roman general. That Bach preferred the traditions
of the older school is evident from the themes that attracted his
pen. Yet his conservatism did not abate the regard in which
Mannheim held him. While he deplored Bach's addiction to 'the
disappearing taste for antiquity', Abt Vogler named him in 1778
'one of the greatest composers, a man of whom Germany may be
proud', detecting in his music a compound of Italian, German,
French, and English styles not elsewhere exhibited.[1]

Mannheim introduced Bach to Paris. On the last day of 1777[2]
the Elector Carl Theodor was called to the throne of Bavaria,
and the most capable of his Capelle followed him to Munich.
Mannheim's golden age was at end. Meanwhile, public mourning
closed the theatres, and in June 1778 Anton Raaf made his *début*
at Paris at one of the Concerts spirituels. He introduced himself
with Bach's 'Non so d'onde viene', Mozart's 'favourite piece', as
Wolfgang, then in Paris, informed his father (12 June 1778).[3]
Hence, there would appear to be a connexion between Raaf's
advertisement of Bach's genius and the arrival of Bach himself
in the French capital. Mozart writes on 9 July 1778:[4] 'Baron Bach
[an illuminating exaggeration] is expected here very shortly. I
am glad for many reasons.'

Bach arrived about the middle of August. On the 27th Mozart
writes again:[5]

Mr. Bach of London has been here a fortnight, having been commissioned to write a French opera. He has come over to listen to the singers,
and will return to London to compose the work, revisiting Paris later for
its production. Our joy at meeting again you may imagine, and if,
perhaps, his satisfaction is not so genuine as mine, we must remember
that he is a man of position and must comport himself with persons of
less importance. I love him, as you know, with all my heart and have
great regard for him. That his affection for me is real and unfeigned I

[1] *Betrachtungen*, pp. 63–6.   [2] Walter, p. 312.
[3] 'Hier endlich als er [Raaf] im Concert spirituell debutierte, sang er die Scene
von Bach, *Non so d'onde viene*, welches ohnedem meine favorit Sache ist, und
da hab ich ihn das erstemahl singen gehört' (Schiedermair, i. 198). On the
previous day (June 11) Mozart's ballet, *Les petits riens*, was produced along with
an *opera buffa* by Piccinni (Prod'homme, p. 87).
[4] Schiedermair, i. 211.
[5] *Ibid.* i. 246. Tenducci also was in Paris. Mozart calls him 'der Herzens-
freund von Bach.'

know, because he has told me, and others too; and that is sufficient proof, surely.

Bach's invitation to Paris involved him in a feud as bitter as that of Capulet and Montague. Four years before (19 April 1774), with the countenance of his patroness and former pupil, the Dauphiness Marie-Antoinette, Gluck had produced his *Iphigénie en Aulide* at the Paris Opera House. The principles inspiring this revolutionary work are set forth in the Abbé Arnaud's paraphrase of the dedication prefixed by Gluck to the score of his *Alceste*:[1]

When I undertook to set the opera *Alceste* to music, I resolved to avoid all those abuses which had crept into Italian opera, through the mistaken vanity of singers and the unwise compliance of composers, which had rendered it wearisome and ridiculous, instead of being, as it once was, the grandest and most imposing stage of modern times. I endeavoured to reduce music to its proper function, that of seconding poetry by enforcing the expression of the sentiment, and the interest of the situations, without interrupting the action, or weakening it by superfluous ornament. My idea was that the relation of music to poetry was much the same as that of harmonious colouring and well-disposed light and shade to an accurate drawing, which animates the figures without altering their outlines. I have therefore been very careful never to interrupt a singer in the heat of a dialogue in order to introduce a tedious *ritornello*, nor to stop him in the middle of a piece, either for the purpose of displaying the flexibility of his voice on some favourable vowel, or that the orchestra might give him time to take breath before a long-sustained note. Furthermore, I have not thought it right to hurry through the second part of a song, if the words happened to be the most important of the whole, in order to repeat the first part regularly four times over, or to finish the air where the sense does not end, in order to allow the singer to exhibit his power of varying the passage at pleasure. In fact, my object was to put an end to abuses against which good taste and good sense have long protested in vain.

My idea was that the overture ought to indicate the subject and prepare the spectators for the character of the piece they are about to see; that the instruments ought to be introduced in proportion to the degree of interest and passion in the words; and that it was necessary, above all, to avoid making too great a disparity between the recitative and the air of a dialogue, so as not to break the sense of a period, or awkwardly interrupt the movement and animation of a scene. I also thought that my chief endeavour should be to attain a grand simplicity, and consequently I have avoided making a parade of difficulties at the cost of clearness. I have set no value on novelty as such, unless it was naturally suggested by the situation and suited to the expression; in short, there was no rule which I did not consider myself bound to sacrifice for the sake of effect.

Challenging the traditions of Lully and Rameau, Gluck's heresies provoked a lively controversy and summoned his opponents to find a champion to battle for orthodoxy. Piccinni's

[1] Quoted in Grove, ii. 401.

triumphs at Rome, Naples, and elsewhere marked him for the purpose, and, in December 1776, the lure of a large salary drew him to Paris. His ignorance of the French language imposed a difficulty and postponed the production of *Roland*, his first French opera, until 27 January 1778. Meanwhile, four months earlier, his rival's *Armide* had roused almost frenzied enthusiasm (23 September 1777), confuting the critics who declared Gluck's powers restricted to tragedy. Stimulated by the violence of public passion, the Director of the Opera proposed a test on which judgement could be conveniently pronounced—he invited both masters to compose a work on the same subject, *Iphigénie en Tauride*. The challenge was accepted, but the libretto supplied to Piccinni was so poor that, after composing two acts, he preferred to have it completely rewritten. Consequently, Gluck's opera was ready first, and was produced with triumphant success on 18 May 1779. Piccinni's was not performed until 23 January 1781, and, in the interval, Bach made his first appearance on the Paris stage.

Posed with the choice of a subject, Bach sensibly withdrew himself from the strenuous controversy by avoiding a classical theme. In selecting the character of Amadis of Gaul, he at the same time touched the patriotic sense of his audience; for much of his text was derived from the French romances of the Round Table. The legend, indeed, had already been presented on the Paris stage; Lully had produced Philippe Quinault's *Amadis de Gaule*, in five acts and a prelude, on 18 January 1684,[1] while, more recently, on 26 November 1771, Quinault's text had again been performed, to music by Rameau's pupil, Jean-Benjamin de la Borde.[2] Thus, in accepting Quinault's libretto, Bach associated himself with the traditions that Gluck challenged, having the intention to commend them by his more elaborate canvas. His *Amadis des Gaules* was produced on 14[3] December 1779, upon a scale which dwarfs his earlier operas: the orchestra was a large one—strings, 2 flutes, 2 oboes, 2 clarinets, 2 bassoons, 2 trumpets, 2 horns, 3 trombones, timpani; the recitatives are fully accompanied; the arias exhibit Bach's melodic facility, and indicate that the French language presented none of the difficulties which had daunted Piccinni; *ensembles* are introduced; and the score contains ballet movements which can without disparagement be put beside those of Gluck's *Orfeo*. The opera excited lively interest, but drew the fire of Gluckists and Piccinnists alike. 'The

[1] Prod'homme, p. 67.　　　　　　　　　　　　　　　　[2] *Ibid.*, p. 85.
[3] The printed score gives the incorrect date 'le Quinze décembre'.

Amadis of M. Bach', Baron von Grimm noted in his *Correspondance*,[1] 'so long looked for to reopen or end the war between the Piccinnists and Gluckists, had its *première* on Tuesday, the 14th [December], and failed to fulfil our expectations. M. Bach's style exhales pure and sustained harmony; his instrumentation is rich and delicate; yet, if the result is always good, it never rises to a higher level. In this particular work, at any rate, we cannot hide from ourselves the conclusion that his music lacks warmth and effectiveness. The Gluckists fail to detect in it Gluck's originality and sublime *élan*; the Piccinnists are unable to discover the charm or variety of Piccinni; while the Lully and Rameau school, inveterate punsters, have decided that the Opera House needed a *bridge* and not a *ferry*.[2] The libretto of *Amadis* has been arranged by M. de Vismes, an artillery officer, brother of M. le Directeur de l'Opéra, and how? He has pitilessly abridged the first act of Quinault's text, and has compressed the fourth and fifth into one. However, excepting the Corisande-Florestan episode, he has retained all the characteristic situations, having sacrificed the links and motives that bind them; an ingenious compensation, no doubt, but the proceeding of a man who, in order to strengthen a building, should knock off the roof and dig up the foundations.'[3]

Bach's position as a pioneer of the pianoforte's vogue has already been remarked.[4] His Paris visit apparently established a partnership the fruit of which was one of the earliest instruction-books for that instrument. Pasquale Ricci, a man approaching his fiftieth year, is mentioned by Leopold Mozart in 1778 among the 'kleine Lichter, Halbcomponisten' of his generation.[5] Born at Como, of whose cathedral he became *maestro di cappella*, he had written a good deal of music which had got into print,[6] and now, either directly or through Pierre Leduc, the publisher, was brought into touch with Bach, whose co-operation he desired in the compilation of a manual of pianoforte instruction for the use of the Naples Conservatorio. Bach about this time published a set of 'Four Progressive Lessons for the Harpsichord or Piano-forte', a circumstance which, along with his prominence as a public exponent of the new instrument, explains Ricci's desire to secure

---

[1] Grimm, Part II, v. 59.　　　　　　　　　　　　　　　　　　　[2] *Fr.* bac.
[3] Bach received 10,000 francs for the work (Eitner, i. 263). Jean-Georges Siéber printed the score, a fine example of the printer's art. The British Museum copy belonged to J. B. Cramer and bears his autograph. According to Grove, iv. 752, Siéber took over Huberty's business as a printer and publisher on Bach's advice. I have not found the authority for this statement.
[4] *Supra*, p. 112.　　　　　　　　　　　　　　　　　　　　　[5] Jahn, i. 609.
[6] Gerber, ii. 278. His Op. 4 (six trios) was published by Welcker in 1768 (B.M. g, 279b).

his co-operation in a manual, published by Leduc, which bore
the following title:

Méthode où Recueil de connoissances élémentaires pour le Forte-
Piano où Clavecin. Œuvre mêlé de Théorie et de Pratique. Divisé en
deux Parties. Composé pour le Conservatoire de Naple par J. C. Bach
et F. P. Ricci. Prix 12. A Paris. Chez Le Duc, successeur de La-
chevardiere, au Magazin de Musique et d'Instrumens, Rue du Roule,
à la Croix d'Or, No. 6, ou 290. Et Rue Neuve des Petits Champs No. 1286,
vis à vis la Trésorerie.

The Introduction, written in the first person, is in French; the
Exercises that follow are annotated in French and Italian. Part I
contains 100 simple Exercises with supplementary violin accompaniments; Part II provides eighteen of a more advanced and
agreeable character. The Introduction, evidently by Ricci, affords
elementary instruction, planned in the opening paragraph: 'Dans
une pièce de Musique, pour le Forte-Piano, il y a principalement
à considérer, I. Le Ton. II. Le Mode. III. La Clef, et sa position.
IV. L'Espèce de la Mesure. V. Le Mouvement. VI. Le Lieu ou
la Position de chaque Note. VII. La Figure, qui détermine la
valeur de la Note. VIII. Les Accidens qui peuvent l'accom-
pagner. IX. Les Signes communément reçus. X. Les Nuances
des Forts et des Doux. XI. L'ensemble. XII. L'exécution
régulière.' Throughout the Introduction the pupil is referred to
Examples in Part I only, while the writer breaks off his exposition
of *basso continuo* with the remark, 'Comme je traite cette Partie de
Musique dans un autre Écrit, je me dispense d'en parler plus
amplement sous cet Article, qui n'est déjà que trop prolixe'.
Part II, therefore, was evidently an addendum, and is prefaced by
a page bearing only the words 'Seconde Partie'. On examination
this section is found to be identical with Bach's 'Six Progressive
Lessons', published by William Forster in 1783. Their character
may be judged by the example which concludes this Chapter.

Whether Bach's Exercises were originally written for use at
Naples, or were appended to Ricci's Manual for French circulation, cannot be determined; the second alternative is the more
probable. But Leduc's imprint, and the readiness with which
Bach's later works found French publishers, indicate that his
intrusion into the Gluck–Piccinni controversy left more than a
fleeting impression of his ability.

Tempo di minuetto.

CHAPTER VI

THE LAST YEARS

AUGUSTA WENDLING'S cold beauty was a tantalizing memory when Bach returned to London from Mannheim in the last weeks of 1772. Yet, twelve months or so later, he married Cecilia Grassi, a woman of twenty-seven, eleven years his junior. The evidence is wholly inferential: At Michaelmas 1771 Abel's name disappears from the Rate-book as tenant of the house in King's Square Court; Bach and he transferred their bachelor household to Queen Street, Golden Square, whence, in January 1772, they issued the annual notice of their concerts. In January 1773 the announcement was repeated from that address, and for the last time; for, in January 1774, subscribers were invited to obtain their tickets at 'Mr. Bach's, 80 Newman Street'.[1] Only Bach's marriage can satisfactorily explain the severance of his domestic relations with Abel, and circumstances point to the latter part of 1773 as the period of its occurrence.[2] Mrs. Papendiek[3] infers that Cecilia's savings, some £2,000, attracted him. But his account with Drummond's for 1774 shows a full list of five hundred subscribers to the Bach-Abel concerts, a revenue of £3,595, and a relatively small pay-sheet. If Cecilia's moderate attractions could not secure a husband, nor her savings contribute to his relief, a practical reason for their partnership may be found in her ability to assist him in labour from which his income chiefly was derived. The Bach-Abel concerts put a few hundreds into his pocket, while his position at Court brought him only £300 a year.[4] As a public singer, Cecilia was now in moderate demand,[5] and would be the more willing to place her experience at her husband's disposal in the instruction of his pupils. Mrs. Papendiek,[6] who speaks of her at this period as 'rather *passée* for a *prima-donna*, and singing, therefore, now only at concerts, public and private', positively indicates this relationship. She mentions Miss Cantelo,[7] afterwards Mrs. Samuel Harrison, as 'their' articled pupil, adding that after Sheridan's marriage to Miss Linley (13 April 1773), which

---

[1] Bach either occupied only part of the house, or was a subtenant. According to the Rate-book, John Daniel Smith was the tenant, at a rental of £30.
[2] Cf. *supra*, p. 109.   [3] Papendiek, i. 109.   [4] Cramer, 1783, p. 552.
[5] Her last engagement at the Opera was for the season 1772–73. Cf. *supra*, p. 123.
[6] Papendiek, i. 109.
[7] Lady Whitelegge, her descendant, owns a miniature of Anne Cantelo, by Cosway.

prevented the latter from 'coming any longer as a singer to the Queen's House,[1] Madame Bach's and Miss Cantelo's attendance [there] was established'.

Bach is silent upon his domestic circumstances in a letter to Martini which breaks an apparently long interval:

Very reverend Father and most honoured patron,
Mr. Waterhouse,[2] an Englishman in the service of H.R.H. the Duke of Cumberland, desires an introduction to you. I have ventured to grant it, remembering your inimitable kindness to me on all occasions. He is an expert violoncellist and very anxious to make the aquaintance of so celebrated a personage as yourself. So, I beg you will grant him your friendship, and let him hear some of your music. Anticipating your grant of this favour, and with deep respect, I sign myself
Your Reverence's most humble and devoted servant,
G. C. Bach.[3]

London, 18 September 1773.

For their 1774 season, which lasted from January 12 to May 4, Bach and Abel removed their concerts from Almack's to Carlisle House, whose glories had been extinguished by the decline of its presiding genius. Mrs. Cornelys was gazetted a bankrupt in 1772, when, by order of the assignees, the contents of her 'extensive, commodious, and magnificent House in Soho Square', with its 'rich and elegant Furniture, Decorations, China, &c.', were put up to auction.[4] Bach may have been attracted to the empty house by the prospect of cheaper accommodation than Almack's afforded; his banking account shows that in 1773 he paid Almack £693, nearly £190 more than in 1771, and over £120 in excess of any past season. The Soho room, also, though smaller than Almack's, was probably better adapted to Bach's purposes. Mrs. Harris was of that opinion She writes to her son on 14 January 1774:[5] 'In the evening [of January 12] I went to Carlysle House, which Bach has taken for his concerts; the furniture, like Mrs. Cornelys, is much on the decline, but it is in my opinion better for the concert than Almack's.' Bach's tenancy, however, was brief.[6] Emerging from her eclipse before the end of the year, Mrs. Cornelys again invited her Nobility and Gentry to their familiar haunts,[7] compelling Bach and his partner to find other accommodation, in quarters which served them without interruption till Bach's death eight years later.

In the summer of 1774 Bach and Abel entered into partnership

[1] Buckingham House, in St. James's Park.
[2] William Waterhouse was a member of Cumberland's Band of Musick.
[3] Bach writes in Italian.   [4] Rimbault, p. 58.   [5] Harris, i. 278.
[6] Either now, or more probably for his earlier season at Carlisle House, Bach commissioned Cipriani to design the concert ticket figured in Illustration No. 29.
[7] Rimbault, p. 59.

for the erection of a concert room which continued in regular usage for exactly a century. The site of this historic building was on the east side of Hanover Square, at the corner of Hanover Street, a plot of ground described in a deed of 2 July 1773 as 'in breadth, from N. to S., in the front next the Sq., as well as in the rear, 40 feet of assize, more or less; and in depth, from W. to E., on the N. side as well as the S., 135 ft., more or less; together with the messuage or tenement, garden, stables, coach-house and buildings, then in the occupation of the Right Hon. Matthew[1] Lord Dillon.' The freehold belonged to Lord Plymouth, who sold it for £5,000 on 28 June 1774 to Philip Viscount Wenham, who, on the same date, conveyed the whole to John Andrea Gallini, John Christian Bach, and Charles Frederic Abel, Gallini contributing one-half and the other two each one-quarter of the capital.[2] Gallini,[3] a Swiss-Italian, who had made a fortune as stage-manager at the King's Theatre and as a dancing-master, was residing at this time at 55 Harley Street.[4] The Rate-book reveals that the Hanover Square premises, though in Lord Dillon's occupancy, were vacant throughout 1774 and, when completed for the purpose Gallini and his partners had in view, were rated at £400, whereas Dillon's house was assessed at only £140. The trebled assessment indicates the magnitude of the alterations which followed the change of ownership. They involved the erection over the garden, at the rear of the house, of a new building, whose principal apartment, 95 feet long by 35 feet wide, ran parallel to Hanover Street, which its heavy sashed windows overlooked, and to which Dillon's house continued to give admission.[5]

Gallini proposed to entertain his patrons with music, masquerades, and balls, disturbing the aristocratic seclusion of the Square with the noisy revels of Soho. Among its residents were the Earl of Tyrconnel; Viscount Hillsborough, a prominent politician, lately Colonial Secretary; Mary Lady Shelburne, widow of the second Earl; Susan Lady Westmorland, widow of the fifteenth Earl; Sir John Frederick; Sir John Danvers; Margaret Lady Leicester, widow of the nineteenth Earl; and the Duke of Roxburghe, the bibliophile.[6] If none of them welcomed the in-

---

[1] This appears to be inaccurate. Henry, 11th Viscount Dillon, succeeded to the title in 1741 and was buried at St. Pancras in 1787.
[2] Cocks, p. 4.
[3] He was subsequently knighted by the Pope.
[4] A note on the blotting-paper of the Rate-book for 1775 reveals the fact.
[5] See Illustrations Nos. 27 and 28. The Hanover Square door was reserved for 'chairs only'. A new door in Hanover Street was eventually opened 'for the Figured [i.e. Sedan] Chairs'. Cf. Edwards, p. 28.
[6] These names appear in the Rate-book.

truders, Lord Hillsborough was active in demonstrating his very lively indignation. One of the earliest occupants of the Square, a man of artistic tastes, who many years before had organized a society of musical amateurs,[1] he now invoked the law to preserve his privacy. Mrs. Harris writes to her son on 3 February 1775:[2] 'Lord Hillsborough, Sir James Porter, and some others have entered into a subscription to prosecute Bach for a nuisance, and I was told the jury had found a bill against him. One would scarce imagine his house could molest either of these men, for Bach's is at the corner of Hanover Street. Poor Sam Clarke may complain, but the others can have no reason.' The inhibition was not conceded. On 31 December 1774 Bach announced[3] a series of fifteen concerts in the new room, and on Wednesday, 1 February 1775, formally inaugurated it with the first of them.

Bach and Abel had proposed to open their season a week earlier, but were compelled, on 23 January 1775, to advertise that 'they are obliged to postpone their First Concert to Wednesday the 1st of February, on account of some unexpected Disappointments of Part of the Furniture and Ornaments of their new Room.'[4] Mr. Harris attended the opening concert, and Mrs. Harris gave her son an account of it:[5] 'Your father and Gertrude attended Bach's Concert, Wednesday. It was the opening of his new room, which by all accounts is by much the most elegant room in town; it is larger than that at Almack's. The statue of Apollo is placed just behind the orchestra, but it is thought too large and clumsy. There are ten other figures or pictures, bigger than life. They are painted by some of our most eminent artists: such as West, Gainsborough, Cipriani, &c. These pictures are all transparent, and are lighted behind; and that light is sufficient to illuminate the room without lustres or any candles appearing. The ceiling is domed, and beautifully painted with alto-relievos in all the piers. The pictures are chiefly fanciful; a Comic Muse, painted by Gainsborough, is most highly spoken of. 'Tis a great stroke of Bach's to entertain the town so very elegantly.'

Bach's prominence in the partnership is evident. Handsome, popular, accomplished, he drew the public eye. He was the author, too, of a witty *bon mot* which pleased the town. Though the effect of the new transparencies was brilliant and agreeable, and the pictures themselves were finely executed, they so copiously reflected their mingled colours upon the powdered *chevelures* of the company, that their removal was demanded. Unaware of the change, a 'Lady of Quality', entering the room at the next concert, ex-

---

[1] Wheatley, ii. 188.   [2] Harris, i. 288.   [3] P.A., 31 Dec. 1774.
[4] *Ibid.*, 23 Jan. 1775.   [5] Harris, i. 287.

claimed to Bach, 'What! Apollo and the Muses gone?' 'They
have quitted their late station, madame,' he replied, 'but have not
absolutely deserted us. When the performance begins, I hope
your ladyship will hear them all.'[1]

Samuel Wesley, within a few weeks of his ninth birthday when
the first of them was held, was a juvenile attendant at Bach's
concerts in the new room, and once remarked that he was 'much
satisfied both with the compositions and performers, but the
musical pieces were ill-arranged, as four had been played succes-
sively which were all of the same key'.[2] He lived to become a
boisterous champion of Sebastian Bach, but has been quoted
as authorizing a statement which dishonours Sebastian's son.
Mr. F. G. Edwards asserts[3] that 'Samuel Wesley records that
J. C. Bach called his father "the Old Wig"'. The phrase is
Wesley's own; and it occurs in a letter to Benjamin Jacob:[4]
'Huzza! Old Wig for ever, and confusion of Face to Pig Tails and
Mountebanks!' Himself a youthful prodigy, it is probable that
Wesley was personally known to Bach; but he was barely sixteen
when the latter died, and that he received disparaging remarks of
Bach's father from Sebastian's son is altogether improbable.

Gallini's direction was as inventive as that which controlled the
establishment in Soho. 'There was a new thing last night at
Bach's room in Hanover Square, called the Festino,'[5] Mrs. Harris
writes to her son[6] on 17 February 1775: 'tis under the direction of
Gallini and is to be weekly, like Almack's. As I understand, the
plan is a dinner for gentlemen. At eight or nine the ladies are
to come, then catches and glees till supper, and after, dancing.'
These activities proved more lucrative than those of Gallini's
partners. Bach's account at Drummond's shows a drop in receipts
of more than £600 in 1775, while those for 1776 appear as £1,505
against £3,595 in 1774. Moreover, the accounts for 1776–9 reveal
large annual payments to Gabriel Buntebart, an intimate friend,[7]
totalling nearly £1,050, which may represent either a personal loan
or, more probably, capital advanced to finance the partnership with
Gallini in 1774. Abel, too, disappears from Bach's cheque-book
for the year 1775, an omission which also appears to relate to the
partnership, for their share of whose capital Bach probably made
himself responsible. Abel at the moment was training Signora
Georgi, a young Venetian engaged at the Pantheon, who visited

---

[1] Busby (2), ii. 111.   [2] Daines Barrington, p. 303.
[3] *Musical Times*, Sept. 1896, p. 585.
[4] *Letters relating to the Works of John Sebastian Bach* (London, 1878), p. 41.
[5] *i. e.* Entertainment.   [6] Harris, i. 292.
[7] He was one of the four persons who attended Bach's funeral.

him at his lodgings in Fulham, a locality which gave one of her countrymen reason to remark, that it was difficult to find Abel in town, for he was always going to 'Foolish'.[1] Hence, after two seasons, Gallini either desired to secure entire control of the undertaking, or Bach and Abel were not prepared to put further capital into it. On 12 November 1776 the partnership was dissolved, and Gallini proceeded to enlarge and embellish the Rooms, which assumed the form they retained until 1804.[2] Meanwhile, for their five remaining seasons the Bach-Abel concerts continued to be given in Hanover Square, but with dwindling revenue[3] and waning popularity. The Earl of Abingdon, whose daughter married Gallini, is declared to have expended £1,600 in the attempt to support them.[4] On the other hand, only Bach's death prevented their continuance.[5]

After his return to London from Mannheim, till the spring of 1777, Bach's association with the King's Theatre was rare and intermittent. The Gluck-Piccinni controversy had its London counterpart in the jealous animosities of a batch of resident foreigners, Cocchi, Guglielmi, Vento, and Bach,[6] whose cabals distracted the managers, and disposed them to seek composers from abroad, to satisfy a public whose prejudices had not been stirred in advance. At this time, too, 'Dancing seemed first to gain the ascendant over Music, by the superior talents of Mademoiselle Heinel, whose grace and execution were so perfect as to eclipse all other excellence'.[7] Moreover, Mrs. Cornelys now instituted her 'Harmonic Meeting',[8] which, though it was speedily suppressed, opposed Carlisle House in direct rivalry with the Haymarket, and, so long as it continued, caused the latter much anxiety. 'Giardini's Opera at Mrs. Cornelys'', Mrs. Harris writes[9] on 12 January 1771, 'really fills, and undoubtedly will greatly injure that of Mr. Hobart's,[10] in the Haymarket; but fine ladies are so very capricious, 'tis hard to say what they would have.'

Thus, from the production of *Orfeo* in April 1771 till the arrival of Giuseppe Millico in 1772, 'serious' opera was not attempted at the King's Theatre. The newcomer, a sopranist of whom Gluck

[1] Bur. iv. 507. [2] Cocks, p. 4.
[3] Bach's accounts show receipts: 1777, £2,832; 1778, £1,961; 1779, £1,101. The account was closed on 2 Nov. 1780 with a sum of £43 18s. 11s. to extinguish an overdraft. [4] *Dictionary of Musicians* (1827), i. 4.
[5] *Infra*, p. 167. For the seasons 1776–82 tickets were obtainable from Mr. Lee, whose address is given variously as 2 Suffolk Street, 41 Suffolk Street, 22 Edward Street, and 'Mr. Hill's, Glover, Pall Mall'. [6] Cf. Bur. iv. 498.
[7] *Ibid.* [8] Rimbault, p. 57. [9] Harris, i. 211.
[10] The Hon. George Hobart, afterwards third Earl of Buckinghamshire; he had succeeded Vincent and his partners in the Opera directorship.

had the highest opinion, was at first received coldly by a public
which contained prejudiced admirers of Tenducci and Guadagni.
But, during his engagement, prolonged till 1774, he so completely
reversed the earlier verdict upon his abilities, that his critics,
Burney remarks,[1] 'would have given a hundred pounds if they
could have recalled their words, or made their acquaintance forget
they had been guilty of such manifest injustice and absurdity'.
The season opened on Saturday, 14 November 1772, with a
revival of Vento's *Sofonisba*.[2] Millico took Elisi's part as Syphax,
while the *prima donna* was Signora Girelli Aguilar, who had won
applause at Milan in 1771, in Mozart's music for the wedding of
Archduke Ferdinand, but whose voice was now in decay and her
intonation inaccurate.[3] The prevailing craze was satisfied by the
presentation of a 'new Grand Ballet' after the last act, and the
engagement of Mlle Grenier and M. Fierville, who made their
first appearances in association with Slingsby.[4] Giordani's
Artaserse was produced on December 5.[5] Burney[6] particularly
commended Millico's singing of the favourite air 'Infelice, ah dove
io vado'. But Lord Mount Edgcumbe, visiting the Opera for the
first time, was chiefly struck by the singer's appearance: 'Being
then quite a child, I could not in the least judge of his performance;
but his face and figure were too entirely remarkable not to make
an impression never to be entirely effaced, being of a singularly
dark complexion, ill made, and uncommonly plain in features'.[7]
Mount Edgcumbe, however, was not too young to remark that
Savoi's voice was of singular quality; in after years he recognized
it during the performance of Mass at Siena.[8]

The second part of the season introduced a new composer,
Antonio Maria Sacchini, whose continental fame secured him a
welcome which his talents confirmed. Though his habits were
irregular and dissolute, he established such a hold upon English
audiences as eclipsed his competitors. Competent to please not
only in 'serious' Opera, but also in the lighter form that public
taste preferred, Sacchini was in regular demand at the King's
Theatre for the remainder of Bach's life, and ousted him from
the first place in public favour. London had heard none of his

---

[1] Bur. iv. 498.   [2] *Supra*, p. 99.   [3] Bur. iv. 499.
[4] P.A., 14 Nov. 1772. Subscriptions for the season were invited 'to Mr. Crawford at his dwelling adjacent to the Theatre'.
[5] Cast: *Artaserse*, Gasparo Savoi; *Artabano*, Catterina Ristorini; *Arbace*,
Giuseppe Millico; *Megabise*, Pietro Morigi; *Mandane*, Cecilia Grassi; *Semira*,
Signora Giordani (Bott. 907. i. 15/1).   [6] Bur. iv. 498.
[7] Mount Edgcumbe, p. 13. Burney remarks that Millico 'was not an Adonis
in person'.   [8] Mount Edgcumbe, p. 18.

music, since the production of his opera *Tigrane* in 1767.[1] Arriving in England in 1772, he had leisure to study the standards of English taste, and, on Tuesday, 19 January 1773, produced his *Il Cid*,[2] to Bottarelli's text, a revision of his *Chimena*, performed at Rome in 1762.[3] Burney found the opera 'full of taste, elegance, and knowledge of stage effects'.[4] It was frequently repeated and completely established Sacchini's popularity with the London public. Otherwise, the production was remarkable for the signal failure of Maddalena Sirmen to maintain as a singer her reputation won as a violinist. 'She degraded herself', remarks Burney, 'by assuming a character in which, though not destitute of voice and taste, she had no claim to superiority'. Tuesday, March 9, was notable for the production of Gluck's *Orfeo* in its original Vienna form, unencumbered with Bach's additions. Millico was the Orfeo, Girelli Aguilar the Eurydice, and Sirmen the Amore.[5] It was preceded by the Pastoral *Il Trionfo d'Amore*, in which Ristorini played Melibeo, Signora Carara Amarilli, and Savoi Titiro. Gaetano Pugnani, who had last been heard in April 1769,[6] produced his *Apollo ed Issea* on Tuesday, March 30, and five weeks later (Thursday, May 6) Sacchini made a second appearance with his *Tamerlano*, to Bottarelli's libretto.[7] It achieved the success of its predecessor, and the season ended with two revivals, the Gluck-Bach version of *Orfeo* (May 25), and Piccinni's *La buona Figliuola* (June 1), with the Sirmen in the principal part.

Sacchini's agreeable genius and the fascination of the expensive Heinel failed to reward the managers with a satisfactory balance-sheet. Hobart, going the way of his predecessors, surrendered control to two ladies, Mrs. Yates and Mrs. Brook, the former of whom, at the opening of the new season, on Saturday, 20 November 1773, delivered 'A Poetical Exordium',[8] in which she made the significant announcement that, besides Opera, she proposed to produce plays and entertain the public 'with singing and declamation, alternately'. The innovation challenged vested interests

---

[1] Cf. *Supra*, p. 110.
[2] Cast: *Fernando*, Signore Ristorini; *Rodrigo*, Giuseppe Millico; *Duarte*, Gasparo Savoi; *Armindo*, Leopoldo Micheli; *Cymene*, Signora Girelli Aguilar; *Elvyra*, Maddalena Lombardini Sirmen (Bott. 11714. aa. 21/7.)
[3] Riemann, p. 74.   [4] Bur. iv. 499.
[5] The programme-book names M. d'Auvigny as Ballet-master, and as principal dancers MM. Fierville, Slingsby, Lepy, Asselin, and Mlles Heinel, Grenier, Crespi, and Lafond. Painter and designer of the dresses, M. Mönch (Bott. 907, i. 14/6).   [6] *Supra*, p. 114.
[7] Cast: *Serpane*, Signora Girelli Aguilar; *Cyrene*, Signora Carara; *Tamerlano*, Giovanni Ristorini; *Dasipe*, Giuseppe Millico; *Molise*, Gasparo Savoi; *Onimo*, Leopoldo Micheli (Bott. 11725, b. 23).
[8] P.A., 20 Nov. 1773. Cf. Bur. iv. 499.

outside, and the law, which had already corrected Mrs. Cornelys's trespass on the domain of Opera, impartially intervened to keep the Opera within bounds; the Lord Chamberlain refused his licence, and the new managers continued along the orthodox paths.

Sacchini's *Lucio Vero* opened the season, on Saturday, 20 November 1773.[1] Grassi had disappeared entirely from the operatic stage; the occasion was memorable for the appearance of Cecilia Davies, her elder by eight years, already distinguished as the only English-woman whom the Italians had admitted to their stage as a *prima donna*. Known by them as 'L'Inglesina', their admiration of her talents was so great that they regarded Gabrielli alone as her superior. Burney found her more admirable in *bravura* than *cantabile* singing, but in the former declared that, if he had 'as many hands as Briareus, they would have been all employed in her applause'.[2] Signora Galli, who played the part of 'second man', had made her *début* in London thirty years before. She was reputed to be a favourite pupil of Handel, and won applause in 1746 for her singing in *Judas Maccabaeus*. Her voice being a contralto, and her figure rather large and masculine, she was frequently invited to sing male parts,[3] as on this occasion. After a pasticcio *Il Puntiglio amoroso*, by Galuppi and others, produced on Tuesday, December 7, Florian Leopold Gassmann's *La Contessina*, described as a 'new comic Opera', was presented (11 January 1774), eleven days before its composer's death at Vienna.[4] Though the Marchetti exhibited 'a brilliant toned voice, *bel metallo di voce*',[5] Gassmann's comedy failed to make an impression, a disappointment compensated by the success of the resourceful Sacchini's 'new serious Opera' *Perseo*, produced on Saturday, January 29.[6] Beyond Burney's praise of the work as 'admirable', there is no record of its reception. But the frequency of its repetition attests its popularity. *Antigono*, by Giordani and others, followed on Tuesday, March 8, after which Sacchini presented his third opera for the season (Tuesday, April 19), *Nitteti*, to a libretto adapted from Metastasio by Bottarelli.[7] The pasticcio

[1] *Vologesus*, Giuseppe Millico; *Lucio Vero*, Signore Schiroli; *Berenice*, Cecilia Davies; *Lucilla*, Stella Lodi; *Anicetus*, Signora Galli; *Flavius*, Leopoldo Micheli (Bott. 907, i. 15/2.)   [2] Bur. iv. 500.   [3] Mount Edgcumbe, p. 18.
[4] Cast: *La Contessina*, Signora Marchetti; *Vespina*, Stella Lodi; *Lindoro*, Signore Schiroli; *Pancrazio*, Signore Fochetti; *Conte Baccellone* (Samuel?) Webbe; *Gazzetta*, ? (Bott. 162, g. 19).   [5] Bur. iv. 500.
[6] Cast: *Perseo*, Giuseppe Millico; *Cepheus*, Signore Schiroli; *Anfrisius* and *Mercury*, Leopoldo Micheli; *Andromeda*, Cecilia Davies; *Tomiris*, Signora Gardi; *Barsene*, Signora Galli (Bott. 907, k. 1/5).
[7] Cast: *Nitteti*, Signora Marchetti; *Amenosi*, Signora Galli; *Beroe*, Cecilia Davies; *Amasi*, Signore Schiroli; *Sammete*, Giuseppe Millico; *Bubaste*, Leopoldo Micheli (Bott. 907, i. 14/7).

L'Olimpiade (Friday, June 3), directed by Giordani, brought the season's productions to an end.

The season 1774–5 brought to London a singer whose attractive personality, fine voice, and gifts as a teacher added another rival to Bach at this critical stage of his career. Venanzio Rauzzini was exceptionally handsome, a good composer, possessed of a remarkable voice, sweet, clear, and flexible, rather than strong, and, as an actor, animated and intelligent.[1] Like Schroeter, he found in London a lucrative field for his talents; together they seriously menaced the profitable monopoly Bach had so long enjoyed. He brought with him his pupil, Marianne Schindler, a young, good-looking German, elegant and graceful, though her voice, in Burney's opinion,[2] was 'a mere thread, for the weakness of which there was neither taste nor knowledge to compensate'. Mount Edgcumbe,[3] also, thought her 'a weak and moderate performer', though Germany, in after years, held her one of the best singers on her national stage.[4] The newcomers made their *début* on Tuesday, 8 November 1774, in the pasticcio *Armida*,[5] under the direction of Giordani, who was again in the conductor's chair. One member of the audience[6] praised the performance with undiluted eulogy, commended Rauzzini as 'the Italian Roscius', thought the Schindlerin the best actress that had appeared 'on *our* Italian stage', considered the tenor Pasini 'the best since Amorevoli', and the 'second woman', Farinella, 'superior to any we have heard'. Repeated later in the season, the pasticcio received a number of new airs contributed by Sacchini, Vento, and Bach, who provided Pasini with the *scena* 'Ebben si vada',[7] which included the melodious air afterwards introduced into *The Flitch of Bacon*:

Io   ti   la - scio, e que - sto ad - di - o

se   sia   l'ul - ti - mo, non sò

<hr />

[1] Cf. Bur. iv. 501.   [2] *Ibid.*   [3] Mount Edgcumbe, p. 15.
[4] In the theatre-bills and elsewhere she is named 'Schindlerin'—the *in* being a conventional feminine suffix in the eighteenth century. Cf. Gerber, ii. 430.
[5] Cast: *Armida*, Marianne Schindler; *Rinaldo*, Venanzio Rauzzini; *Tancredi*, Signore Pasini; *Erminia*, Signora Farinella; *Rambaldo*, Signora Galli; *Dano*, Vincenzio Sestini (Bott. 907, i. 14/9).
[6] P.A., 22 Nov. 1774.   [7] *Infra*, p. 250.

Notwithstanding the encomium of the *Advertiser's* correspondent, *Armida* was only moderately successful. The pasticcio, in fact, exaggerated the characteristics of *opera seria* which least commended it to a generation beginning to tire of its conventionalities. An entertainment to which each singer brought his own selected *scena* for the display of his peculiar talent was unlikely to present a balanced proportion, but rather, in the words of the *Advertiser's* correspondent, to exhibit 'the general Defect of all Pasticcios, the Want of proper Light and Shade in the Disposition of the Songs'.

For their second production the managers commissioned a young composer better known in Edinburgh than in London, and elsewhere not at all. Domenico Corri, born at Rome in 1746, a pupil of Porpora, had found his way to the Scottish capital in 1771 to conduct the Musical Society, an institution which patriotically instructed Edinburgh's musical taste throughout the century, but preferred the guidance of Italian directors. His ability as a singing-master and gift of composition gave him a reputation in his own community. But elsewhere, Burney remarks,[1] 'his name was not sufficiently blazoned to give his opera much éclat'. His invitation to write for the London stage he may have owed to Rauzzini's recommendation. Both were of Roman birth, of the same age, and, perhaps, contemporaries among Porpora's pupils in the last years of the master's life. Feeling it safer to exhibit the old *clichés*, or too inexperienced to venture into new paths, Corri chose Metastasio's *Alessandro nell' Indie*,[2] as arranged by Bottarelli, and produced it on Saturday, 3 December 1774.

The second part of the season provided six novelties. On Tuesday, 7 February 1775, the fertile Sacchini produced his *Montezuma*. A month later (March 7) Pasquale Anfossi, who had lately experienced the fickle taste of the Roman public, produced his *La Marchesa Giardiniera*, which introduced two new comers, Signora Spiletta and Signora Sestini. Burney[3] praised the latter for her good looks, elegant figure, and the 'considerable agility' of her singing. She contributed to the opera's success; it was frequently repeated. Rauzzini revived[4] his *Piramo e Tisbe* on March 23 for the 'benefit' of his pupil.[5] A week later, Giovanni Lovattini, who

---

[1] Bur. iv. 501.
[2] Cast: *Alessandro*, Signore Pasini; *Poro*, Venanzio Rauzzini; *Timagene*, Vincenzio Sestini; *Cleofide*, Marianne Schindler; *Erissena*, Signora Farinella; *Gandarte*, Signora Galli (Bott. 11715, aaa. 29).   [3] Bur. iv. 502.
[4] First performed at Munich in 1769 (Riemann, p. 451).
[5] Cast: *Piramo*, Venanzio Rauzzini; *Tisbe*, Marianne Schindler; *Eupalte*, Signore Pasini; *Corbeo*, Signora Galli (Bott. 907, i. 14/11.)

had enjoyed public favour for eight years,[1] took his in Guglielmi's
I Viaggiatori ridicoli, in which, as Gandolfo, he had been successful
in 1768.[2] Two pasticcios brought the season to an end; *La Difesa
d'Amore*,[3] adapted by Badini from Metastasio (Saturday, May 6),
and *La Donna di Spirito*[4] (Tuesday, May 23).

The season 1775-6 introduced to London the notorious
Catterina Gabrielli, whose eccentricities[5] excited as much curiosity
as her vocal art promised pleasure. In neither did she fulfil
anticipation. The 'freaks and espiegleries' which had founded her
reputation were so subdued, that Burney actually discovered in
her deportment the dignity and restraint of a Roman matron.
Nor did her singing support her reputation; her admirers declared
that she never appeared at her best, while her detractors insisted
that caprice and ill-humour prevented her from exhibiting it.
'It was thought she never gave herself the trouble to exert her
great powers before an English audience,' Lord Mount Edgcumbe
remarks;[6] 'certain it is, that, whether from that, or some other
cause, she was less enthusiastically admired here than she had
been in various parts of the Continent, and her success was so
moderate that she stayed only for one season.' Rauzzini, deprived
of his pupil's support, remained; while Lovattini's place was taken
by Giuseppe Trebbi, whose humour lacked the 'risible'[7] quality
which had made Lovattini popular.

Neither Gabrielli nor Rauzzini was heard in the first opera of
the season, the pasticcio *La Sposa fedele*, presented on Tuesday,
31 October 1775, under the direction of Vento, who replaced
Giordani as conductor for the season. The entertainment served,
however, to introduce Catterina's sister Francesca, 'a miserable
performer', in Mount Edgcumbe's opinion,[8] 'whom she carried
everywhere to act as the *seconda donna*, and occasionally as her
double'. Catterina made her *entrée* on Saturday, November 11,
in *Didone abbandonata*, chiefly by Sacchini,[9] a performance which
left a singular impression on one of her audience. 'I can remember
seeing [Catterina] once in the opera of *Didone*,' Mount Edgcumbe

[1] Bur. iv. 502.   [2] *Supra*, p. 112.
[3] Cast: *Cupid*, Venanzio Rauzzini; *Venus*, Marianne Schindler; *Mars*, Signore
Pasini; *Mercury*, Signora Galli; *Pallas*, Signora Farinella (Bott. 907, i. 14/10).
[4] Cast: *Isabella*, Signora Sestini; *Carillon*, Giovanni Lovattini; *Carciofolo*,
Signore Fochetti; *Lindoro*, Signora Galli; *Geltruda*, Signora Farinella; *Pastosa*,
Signora Spiletta; *Moschino*, Vincenzio Sestini (Bott. 907, i. 14/8).
[5] *Supra*, p. 53.   [6] Mount Edgcumbe, p. 15.   [7] Bur. iv. 502
[8] Mount Edgcumbe, p. 16.
[9] Cast: *Dido*, Catterina Gabrielli; *Selene*, Francesca Gabrielli; *Osmida*, Vincenzio Sestini; *Aeneas*, Venanzio Rauzzini; *Jarba*, Signore Onofrio; *Araspe*,
Gasparo Savoi (Bott. 907, i. 15/14).

recalled,[1] 'but can say nothing of her performance. All I can recollect of it being the care with which she tucked up her great hoop as she sidled into the flames of Carthage.' She was not heard in a new production until the following February. Meanwhile, on Tuesday, 9 January 1776, Vento provided a new 'comic' opera, *Il Bacio*, eked out by ballets, which were prominent in the season's programmes.[2] A month later (Tuesday, February 6) he presented another novelty, his *La Vestale*, to a libretto by Badini dedicated to Catterina herself.[3] Notwithstanding the compliment, Catterina affected to be indisposed at the performance at which Mount Edgcumbe was present, and obliged her sister Francesca to take her part.[4] Out of humour with the climate and her audiences, there was a confirmed belief that she often feigned sickness, with the result that her genuine ailments were under suspicion, while the impression that she deliberately refrained from singing her best created an opinion that her best was below the standard of rumour.

On Thursday, 29 December 1776, Rauzzini again came forward as a composer with the opera *Le Ali d'Amore*, described as a 'New Pastoral Entertainment', written by Badini and dedicated to the Duke of Dorset, chiefly interesting for the *début* of the youngest member of the cast.[5] Though she had already appeared (15 April 1774) at a concert given by the harpist Evans, Anna Storace, described as 'a Child 8 Years of Age', played her first part on the operatic stage on this occasion; she, no doubt, already was Rauzzini's pupil. Two new 'comic' operas followed, Sacchini's *L'Isola d'Amore* (March 12), and Giuseppe Gazzaniga's *Alcina* (March 28), which probably owed its performance to Sacchini, whose influence had secured for its composer a hearing of his first opera at Vienna in 1770. *Caio Mario*, an early work by Piccinni, but now described as 'new', followed on Saturday, April 20,[6] and two revivals brought the season to a close, Pergolesi's *La Serva*

---

[1] Mount Edgcumbe, p. 16.
[2] Bur. iv. 504 says that the dancing this season was attractive. He names Fierville, Baccelli, and 'the two Valouys in *demi-caractère*'.
[3] Cast: *Æmilia*, Catterina Gabrielli; *Pomponia*, Francesca Gabrielli; *Venus*, Signora Cardarelli; *Pinaria Maxima*, Signora Galli; *Celer*, Venanzio Rauzzini; *Domitian*, Giuseppe Trebbi; *Licinius*, Gasparo Savoi (Bott. 907, i. 15/3).
[4] Mount Edgcumbe, p. 16.
[5] Cast: *Damone*, Giuseppe Trebbi; *Fileno*, Venanzio Rauzzini; *Erasto*, Gasparo Savoi; *Silvano*, Signore Peretti; *Amarilli*, Catterina Gabrielli; *Clori*, Francesca Gabrielli; *Lucida*, Vincenzio Sestini; *Cupid*, Anna Selina Storace (Bott. 907, i. 15/5).
[6] Cast: *Caio Mario*, Giuseppe Trebbi; *Annio*, Venanzio Rauzzini; *Lucio*, Gasparo Savoi; *Aquilio*, Vincenzio Sestini; *Marcia*, Catterina Gabrielli; *Rhodope*, Francesca Gabrielli (Bott. 907, i. 14/12).

Padrona (Tuesday, 23 April), and *Antigono* (Saturday, May 18),
first performed in March 1774.

That Bach was not in close touch with the King's Theatre at
this period is evident. Vento, Sacchini, and Giordani were
employed, but Bach did not receive a similar compliment till 1777.
Burney makes no reference to him after the disastrous season of
1770, nor even records the production of his last London opera
in 1778. As a German, no doubt, he needed to battle for his
opportunities in the preserves of Italian musicians, but that his
reputation was high abroad is evident from his invitations to
Mannheim and Paris, while a flattering request for his portrait
from Martini as clearly indicates his continental renown. Bach
replied as follows:

> Very reverend Father and most honoured patron,
> I had the honour to receive your much esteemed letter, though long
> after Mr. Parsons'[1] arrival, who, I think, had forgotten it. You do me
> too much honour in desiring to place my portrait among persons so
> celebrated, of whose company I do not think my own worthy. Still, my
> respect for your commands compels me to obey without question. The
> portrait is already finished, and only awaits an opportunity to come to
> you, along with some music. Begging for the continuance of your good
> esteem, I subscribe myself
> Your Reverence's most humble, devoted, and obliged servant,
> G. C. Bach.

London, 22 May 1776.

Gainsborough's portrait[2] waited for two years before Bach found
opportunity to dispatch it.[3] Meanwhile, his duties as teacher of
the royal children removed him from London to the nearer
vicinity of the Court at Richmond Lodge. He took a house at
Richmond,[4] not distant from the Alberts,[5] Mrs. Papendiek's
parents, who, in 1776, bought a house at the corner of Richmond
Green, in which the Queen's Chamber Band—Bach, Abel,
Simpson (oboe), and F. Nicolai (violin)[6]—found it convenient to
rehearse, Bach having provided a small pianoforte for the purpose.
Abel usually came down to 'Bach's agreeable establishment at
Richmond' on Wednesdays, in readiness for next day's rehearsal,
when it was the rule for him and Bach alternately to produce a new
composition or arrangement. On one occasion Mrs. Papendiek,

---

[1] William Parsons, later Master of the Musick. He was returning from Italy,
where he had been completing his musical education.
[2] The frontispiece to this volume. Gainsborough made a copy of the picture for
Bach himself. It now belongs to Lord Hillingdon. See Illustration No. 32.
[3] *Infra*, p. 160.   [4] Papendiek, i. 65.
[5] Frederick Albert accompanied Queen Charlotte to England.
[6] Court, 1775, p. 86.

then a child of eleven or twelve, recalled that Bach, who had
forgotten it was his turn, sat down after dinner and wrote 'an
enchanting first movement of a quintett in three flats. He sent
off for two copyists, who wrote down the parts from score over
his shoulders, while he wrote the harmony, after having composed
the melody'.[1] The quintet, Mrs. Papendiek added, 'is ranked
among the best of his compositions, and the melody is sweetly
soothing'.[2]

The little sketch serves to indicate an aspect of Bach's life at
this period more regular than the intermittent service of the
Haymarket, where, at the moment, Sacchini's reign was almost
undisputed, and he himself 'so firmly established in the public
favour, that he was not to be supplanted by a composer in the
same style.'[3] His vogue compromised the prospects of the distinguished Neapolitan Tommaso Traetta, whom the management
invited as guest-composer for the season 1776-7, a man now in his
fiftieth year, of an earlier generation than Bach, Vento, and
Sacchini, and by Burney compared with them to his disadvantage.[4]
The Gabrielli had returned to the Continent, after a season in
which she was accorded less than her usual applause. Her place
was taken by Anna Pozzi, young, handsome, possessed of a brilliant
voice, but so inexperienced that she was immediately replaced as
'first woman' by Cecilia Davies, who had recently sung with
Millico.[5] Giardini, who succeeded Vento as conductor, opened
the season, on Saturday, 2 November 1776, with the pasticcio
Astarto. Though his name was not on the programme, Bach
contributed the overture, which had served elsewhere already as
the prelude to *Catone*.[6] Marianna Farnese and Anna Pozzi were
the only new comers in the cast, and the latter's inexperience was
so obvious that she made no appearance until the end of the season.
Paisiello's *La Fraschetana*, originally produced at Venice in 1774,
followed on Tuesday, November 5, with Trebbi,[7] Fochetti, Savoi,
Micheli, Signore Sestini,[8] Prudom,[9] and Farnese in the cast.
Cecilia Davies made her *rentrée* in Traetta's first opera, *Germondo*,
on Tuesday, 21 January 1777, with Rauzzini in the principal role.
Anfossi's *Il Geloso in Cimento* followed (February 4), and on

[1] Papendiek, i. 75-6.
[2] The quintet is No. 4 of the six dedicated to the Elector Palatine. *Infra*, p. 303.
[3] Bur. iv. 505.   [4] *Ibid.*
[5] *Ibid*. Mount Edgcumbe, p. 16, agrees with Burney that, as 'second woman',
Pozzi was superlatively good.
[6] *Infra*, p. 277.   [7] A *buffo*. Cf. Mount Edgcumbe, p. 34.
[8] Mount Edgcumbe, p. 33, says she was popular with the public, but not
approved by connoisseurs. She died in England in great poverty.
[9] Bur. iv. 514 describes her as young and insufficiently trained.

Saturday, 15 March, Traetta produced his second opera, *Telemaco*. April was given up to revivals,[1] and on Tuesday, May 13, Traetta presented his last work, *I Capricci del Sesso*. Bach brought the productions of the season to an end with his *Orione*, announced as a 'new Serious Opera. With grand Chorusses.' The work had not been heard since its production in 1763, and Bach appears to have subjected it to some revision.[2] It was given on Saturday, 24 May, and was repeated 'by command' a week later.

The season 1777–8 brought to London Bach's Mannheim friend, Francesco Roncaglia, who was accompanied by Francesca Danzi, daughter of Innocenz Danzi, principal violoncellist in the Mannheim Capelle. Her extraordinary powers as a mimic detracted from her effectiveness as a singer. She had been, writes Burney,[3] so 'constantly imitating the tone and difficulties of instruments, that her chief labour and ambition had been to surprise, concluding, perhaps, that wonder, however excited, includes pleasure, and forgetting that, though an ounce of salt may make a soup or *ragoût* sufficiently savoury, yet that two ounces will spoil it; in short, forgetting that she is not a bird in a bush or a cage, and that from a human figure, representing a princess or great personage, it is natural for an audience to expect human passions to be expressed in such tones, and with such art and energy, as will not degrade an individual of our own species into a being of an inferior order'.[4] She married Ludwig August Lebrun, the oboist, and, after a triumphant tour of the European capitals, returned with him to London as *prima donna* in the autumn of 1779. Meanwhile, associated with her for the present season were Guglielmo Jermoli and his wife, Antonio Rossi, Giuseppe Coppola,[5] Luiza Todi, Valentino Adamberger, and Carlo Rovedino. Adamberger, who won Mozart's affection and applause, came to London from Munich, where he was in the Elector's service. Burney[6] admired his technique rather than his tenor voice. Luiza Todi, a Portuguese, failed to reveal to London the qualities which created a sensation in Paris a year later. Mount Edgcumbe was not attracted by her voice, and Burney[7] supposed that she either much improved after her London

---

[1] Piccinni's *La Schiava* (Tuesday, April 1) and Gazzaniga's *Alcina* (Thursday, April 17), for Signora Sestini's 'benefit'.
[2] Cf. *infra*, p. 235.　　　　　　　　　　　　　　　　　[3] Bur. iv. 508.
[4] Mount Edgcumbe, p. 21, who evidently refreshed his memory with Burney's *History*, also remarks that she sang 'too much *alla Tedesca*'.
[5] 'a languid and uninteresting Soprano' (Bur. iv. 514).
[6] Bur. iv. 514. Mount Edgcumbe, p. 27, remarks that Adamberger had 'a disagreeable nasal voice'.
[7] Bur. iv. 509.

season, 'or we treated her very unworthily'. She was, in fact, idolized in St. Petersburg and Berlin, and died extremely wealthy. Rovedino, a young bass singer, was a pupil of Leopoldo Micheli;[1] he was employed at the Opera henceforward until he quitted the stage. One of his daughters married Charles Weichsell, Mrs. Billington's brother.[2]

The new season opened on Tuesday, 4 November 1777, with Paisiello's *Le due Contesse*, under Giordani. The opera, produced at Vienna the previous year (November), had a moderate success, and served merely to create an atmosphere for the staging of a new work by the popular Sacchini, *Creso*,[3] a few days later (November 8). Roncaglia, Danzi, and Adamberger made their *début* in it, and the first so pleased by his performance that he was at once engaged for the season 1779–80, before it was known how his immediate successor, the renowned Pacchierotti, would satisfy the public taste.[4] Piccinni's *Vittorina*[5] followed on Tuesday, December 16,[6] at a moment when its composer was wrestling in Paris with the unfamiliarities of the French tongue.[7] The three operas sufficed until Tuesday, 20 January 1778, when Anfossi's *La vera Costanza*[8] was staged. Produced originally at Rome (1776), under another title, it was given at Vienna in the Hoftheater on 12 January 1777 in preference to Haydn's score, which was subsequently performed at Esterház. The appearance of Jermoli in the London cast therefore has significance. The opera was only moderately successful, and, on Saturday, February 7, was succeeded by the prolific Sacchini's *Erifile*.[9] In March two *opere buffe* were added to the repertory : Gassmann's *L'Amore Artigiano* (Tuesday,

---

[1] Micheli was an all-round man; Burney (Bur. iv. 514) describes him as 'for all work'.
[2] Mount Edgcumbe, p. 27.
[3] Cast: *Creso*, Valentino Adamberger; *Ariene*, Francesca Danzi; *Euriso*, Francesco Roncaglia; *Cratina*, Signora Prudom; *Ciro*, Giuseppe Coppola; *Sibari*, Leopoldo Micheli (Bott. 907, i. 15/7).
[4] Mount Edgcumbe, p. 36.
[5] Cast: *La Marchesa*, Signora Prudom; *Il Cavaliere*, Guglielmo Jermoli; *Vittorina*, Luiza Todi; *Il Conte di Ripalta*, Giuseppe Coppola; *Il Barone di Sarzane*, Antonio Rossi; *Donna Isabella*, Signora Buroni; *Roberto*, Leopoldo Micheli (Bott. 907, i. 16/3). Jermoli is described in the programme-book as 'Virtuoso di Camera' to Prince Esterhazy.
[6] Ignorant of the English performance, Riemann, p. 599, dates the opera 'ca. 1790'.
[7] *Supra*, p. 133.
[8] Cast: *Ernesto*, Giuseppe Coppola; *Enrico*, Guglielmo Jermoli; *Villotto*, Antonio Rossi; *Masino*, Leopoldo Micheli; *Irene*, Signora Prudom; *Lisetta*, Signora Jermoli; *Rosina*, Anna Pozzi (Bott. 907, i. 16/6).
[9] Cast: *Erifile*, Francesca Danzi; *Hermione*, Signora Prudom; *Cleomenes*, Francesco Roncaglia; *Learchus*, Valentino Adamberger; *Cresphontes*, Giuseppe Coppola (Bott. 1342, m. 4).

March 3),[1] and the pasticcio *Il Marchese Villano*[2] (Thursday, March 26), the former of which had a few repetitions.

Strongly as he was attracted to opera in early manhood, and though his reputation as a composer of Opera brought him to England, it is remarkable that Bach's output, compared with that of his popular contemporaries and competitors, was small—*Orione* and *Zanaida* in 1763; *Adriano in Siria* in 1765; *Carattaco* in 1767; *Gioas* in 1770; *Temistocle* in 1772; *Lucio Silla* in 1776. He contributed none to the English stage from 1767 until 1778, nor were any of those he wrote for foreign theatres reproduced in London. The fact is curious and not clearly explicable. His operas, like those of Sacchini and other rivals, have vanished into the dark cupboard that conceals forgotten masterpieces. But, whatever may have been their standard, it is evident that Bach's was as high as they, and in particulars higher. Burney's testimony to his gifts on his first coming to England is not exceeded in warmth by his appreciation of the successive Italians who sought the applause of the London public. But, amid the influences of his Italian upbringing, Bach retained a measure of the Teutonic seriousness which had disposed his father to despise the more frivolous manifestations of the operatic stage. It cannot be an accident that all his operas were inspired by tragic subjects; there is not a single *opera buffa* among them. Yet, public taste inclined increasingly to the lighter form, and Piccinni, Sacchini, Vento, and others satisfied it to the full. But, apart from the qualities of his work, it cannot be doubted that his own deliberate choice rejected opportunities which his rivals more willingly exploited. Though there is not a tittle of evidence that taints his character with sordidness, it may be doubted whether the composition of operas brought wealth to any but the particular 'star' of the season. Bach's tastes were expensive, even extravagant, not to be satisfied by such precarious revenues as the operatic stage afforded the composer. Nor, until his last years, had he need to covet them. His personality, reinforced by the advantages of his Court connexion, made him, for most of his life in England, one of the most popular and fashionable teachers in the metropolis. In his later years his monopoly was challenged, especially by Schroeter and Rauzzini. But his infrequent association with the King's Theatre from 1767 to 1778

---

[1] Cast: *Costanza*, Signora Prudom; *Rosina*, Luiza Todi; *Angiolina*, Signora Jermoli; *Girò*, Leopoldo Micheli; *Giannino*, Guglielmo Jermoli; *Titta*, Carlo Rovedino; *Bernardo*, Antonio Rossi (Bott. 907, i. 16/5).
[2] Probably the opera, in the main, was Galuppi's, produced at Venice in 1762. But the 'Finales and Airs' were announced (1778) as being by Piccinni and Paisiello.

was due as much to his disinclination to disturb his chief activities as to the tastes of the public, while his services in the concert-room were so uninterruptedly in demand, that there was neither time nor necessity to exhibit his genius, save intermittently, on another stage.

But it is evident that, for the last four or five years of his life, Bach's circumstances no longer exhibited their former prosperity, and that he was disposed to resume connexions he had suffered to relax. His visit to Paris in the summer of 1778 followed the production of his fifth and last opera for the Haymarket. On Saturday, 4 April 1778, his *La Clemenza di Scipione*, described as a 'new Serious Opera, with Grand Chorusses', was given, with the following cast:[1]

Scipio	.	.	.	.	Valentino Adamberger
Luceius	.	.	.	.	Francesco Roncaglia
Marcius		.	.	.	Giuseppe Coppola
Arsinda	.	.	.	.	Francesca Danzi
Idalba	.	.	.	.	Signora Prudom.

For the production M. Simonet, the ballet-master, invented new dances; at the end of Act I a *divertissement* by M. and Mlle Banti, M. Valouy the younger, and Mlle Baccelli; at the end of Act II a pastoral ballet, planned by Simonet and Banti, entitled *La Surprise de Daphnis et Céphise*, danced by the Bantis and M. and Mme Zuchelli; and, to conclude, 'A new grand Serious Ballet', *Les Amans unis par l'Hymen*. 'Magnificent new Scenes, Dresses, and Decorations, both for the Opera and Dances', were promised, while in Act II the Danzi introduced an air accompanied on the violin, violoncello, flute, and oboe, by Cramer, James Cervetto, Florio, and her husband[2] Lebrun. The silence of the public news-sheets in regard to them significantly indicates the exclusive public to which the opera and frequent concerts made an appeal. The student of London music at this period must find his materials on the front (advertisement) sheet of the *Public Advertiser*, which announces the opera and, sometimes, the cast. For he searches vainly for a notice or criticism of the event. The newspaper was neither staffed for that purpose, nor did its readers look to it to instruct them. Such information as can be gleaned is afforded by infrequent letters to Henry Woodfall, from persons interested to whip lethargic patrons, or whose standing secured them the favour of publication. Bach's last English opera invited a contribution of this character to the *Public Advertiser's* 'Operatical Intelligence'.[3]

---

[1] Bott. 907, i. 16/4.　　[2] The date of the marriage is not established.
[3] P.A., 6 April, 1778.

After remarking that the libretto was believed to be the work of a foreign Ambassador to the Court of St. James's, 'a Person of Taste and Learning, who softens the Cares of Negotiation by sacrificing in secret to the Muses', the writer continued:

The Fame of Signor Bach, as a Musical Composer, is already well known in Europe; Were it not so, this last Composition would be sufficient to stamp him an Author of the first Merit in his Profession. Signor Sacchini and Signor Bach are undoubtedly two of the best Composers now existing for Serious Opera; and the Managers of the King's Theatre, by engaging both, have occasioned an Emulation between them, and given a Spur to their Invention, which cannot fail of adding considerably to the Amusement and Satisfaction of all Lovers of Music.

La Clemenza di Scipione is the third new Serious Opera produced this Season at the King's Theatre. They are all excellent in their Kind. *Creso* is remarkable for its Melody, *Erifile* for Harmony: We do not mean to enter into invidious Comparisons, but Signor Bach seems to have paid a proper Attention to both, though chiefly to the Melody of the Airs, which are finely adapted to the Voices, and are composed with great Learning, Taste, Feeling, Novelty, and Variety. That beautiful Air in the second Act, 'Frena le belle lacrime', sung by Signor Roncaglia, is charmingly pathetic, and well suited to his Voice; as is likewise the one in Act III, 'Nel partir, idolo mio'; and that of Signora Danzi in Act I, 'Dal dolor cotanto oppressa'. The most capital Air, however, is that of Signora Danzi in the Second Act,[1] accompanied by the Violin, Violoncello, German Flute, and Hautboy. This is truly a *Chef d'œuvre* in every Respect, and Signor Bach is extremely fortunate in the amazing Execution of Signora Danzi, and the masterly Accompanyment of Messrs. Cramer, Cervetto, Florio, and Le Brun. Indeed, it is but common Justice to acknowledge, that the present Opera *Orchestra* is infinitely superior to any in Europe.

The *Duetto* at the End of Act I is most delightful,[2] the Words are extremely pathetic, and the Sound echoes the Sense. The *Terzetto*[2] at the End of Act II is also admirably composed, and pleased much, though it had the Disadvantage of coming after the very capital Air of Signora Danzi. The Chorus of Priests in Act III breathes the true Spirit of clear Harmony. As to the Drama (though it is the *Fashion* not to pay much Attention to it), yet it must be confessed, that the Language is both correct and poetical, and that it is free from the Turgidity and Bombast which is the Bane of most Italian Operas.

The opera received a second performance on April 11, inviting another communication from the same ecstatic, though not profound, pen:[3]

On Saturday last the new Opera of *La Clemenza di Scipione*, composed by Mr. Bach, was performed for the second Time, with the greatest Applause, to a crowded and brilliant Audience. We congratulate the present Managers on finishing their Reign with such a *Chef d'œuvre* as this admirable Opera; and we most earnestly recommend it to their

[1] 'Infelice in van m'affano'. Cf. *infra*, p. 230.
[2] *Infra*, p. 229.   [3] P.A., 13 April, 1778.

Successors, never to let a Winter pass without employing this great Master in composing at least one Opera; this being, in the Painter's Stile, '*the best Time of the Master*'. We could likewise advise the future Managers, at any Rate, to employ Mr. Cramer for the first Fiddle; as he leads the Orchestra with a Force, a Precision and Attention very rarely, if ever, to be found.

La Clemenza di Scipione received six other performances. But the best testimony to its qualities is afforded by the fact that in 1805, nearly thirty years later, Mrs. Billington, the daughter of Mrs. Weichsell, Bach's pupil, revived it at her 'benefit'. The *Morning Post*[1] anticipated the event with a preliminary paragraph:

There was a grand rehearsal on Friday last at the Opera House of *La Clemenza di Scipione*, the opera which Mrs. Billington produces at her Benefit. Many of the first and most distinguished amateurs were present, and pronounced the music to be a *chef d'œuvre*. It is the production of Bach, whose compositions are so justly famed for blending the force and energy of the German school with the simplicity and beautiful cantilena of the Italian. Her Majesty was particularly partial to his music, and he had the distinguished honour of being her musical instructor.

On Thursday, 28 March 1805 the performance took place, and on the following day the *Morning Post* reported:

The Grand Serious Opera entitled *La Clemenza di Scipione* was produced last night for Mrs. Billington's benefit. The scenery and decorations are truly splendid, and, to use a theatrical term, the Opera is got up with all the pomp the subject demands. The dresses were elegant and characteristic; and the music may, indeed, be said to be a *chef d'œuvre*, bold, impressive, and tasteful. Among the most prominent pieces were a bravura by Mrs. Billington,[2] sung with the greatest neatness and with the most happy effect; a duet, and a trio in the first act. In the second act, Mrs. Billington's obligato song, accompanied by Mr. Weichsel[3] on the violin, Harrington on the oboë, Lindley[4] on the —cello, and Ashe[4] on the flute, afforded a most delectable treat; the rapidity of her execution in this divine composition baffles all description, and decidedly ranks her the first bravura singer in the world. She introduced the beautiful Rondo of *Se ti perdo*, which she sung with exquisite taste, and was rapturously applauded by a brilliant and discerning audience.

Before the season closed, on July 20, the opera had been frequently repeated, and was revived again on the following December 28.

Meanwhile, following Bach's *chef d'œuvre*, the season of 1777–8 concluded with the staging of two other operas by London

---

[1] Of 25 March 1805.　　　　　　　　　　[2] 'Dal dolor cotanto oppressa'.
[3] Charles, Mrs. Billington's brother.
[4] Robert Lindley, pupil of Cervetto, who accompanied Francesca Danzi in the song in 1778.
[5] Andrew Ashe; he took part in the Hanover Square concerts at which Haydn's symphonies were produced.

composers—Sacchini's *L'Amore Soldato*[1] (Tuesday, May 5), and Giardini's *Il Re Pastore* (Saturday, May 30).[2] They were witnessed, no doubt, by Bach's Bückeburg brother and his son Wilhelm Friedrich Ernst, who timed their visit, it would appear, to coincide with the run of *La Clemenza di Scipione*. Leave of absence from Bückeburg was granted on April 15,[3] and, as the journey was broken at Hamburg, where Carl Philipp Emanuel welcomed his relatives, the travellers probably reached London early in May. Bach's visit to Paris,[4] no doubt, coincided with his brother's return. But Wilhelm Friedrich Ernst, just turned nineteen, remained in London to receive his uncle's tuition, returning to Germany after his death, when he took home a bust of John Christian from among the effects dispersed at his sale.[5]

Meanwhile, Martini still awaited Bach's promised portrait, and at the beginning of 1778 sent a reminder of his request through Burney, who, on 22 June 1778, replied:[6]

Most reverend Father and honoured patron,
    As I hold no more cherished memory than that of your Reverence, I should not have left your letter of January 13 unanswered had I not been immersed in unavoidable business of various kinds. But as I am now somewhat less engaged, and can take advantage of the civility of Signore Roncaglia, who proposes shortly to start for Bologna, I should indeed be failing in proper feeling were I to neglect the opportunity to assure you of my respect and veneration, and to thank you, as the present deserves, for the most esteemed gift of your *Saggio di Contrapunto*,[7] to whose arrival I look forward with the utmost impatience. The copy entrusted to Signore Vergani for me has not yet come to hand, but I hope shortly to receive it, as I urgently require it, since the booksellers can supply it only after several months' delay. The third volume of your learned and indispensable *Storia*[8] would vastly aid me in the composition of my own History were it already in print. I trust that the public's impatience, and my own, will soon be allayed by the appearance of that invaluable work.

Had I been sooner informed of Signore Roncaglia's intention to

---

[1] Cast: *Don Faustino*, Guglielmo Jermoli; *Don Anselmo*, Antonio Rossi; *Pasquino*, Leopoldo Micheli; *Ottavina*, Luiza Todi; *Lisandrina*, Signora Jermoli; *Semplicina*, Signora Prudom (Bott. 907, i. 16/9).
[2] Cast: *Alessandro*, Valentino Adamberger; *Aminta*, Francesco Roncaglia; *Agenore*, Giuseppe Coppola; *Eliza*, Francesca Danzi; *Tamiri*, Signora Prudom (Bott. 907, i. 16/7). Francesca Danzi was now advertised as 'Madame Lebrun (late Mademoiselle Danzi)'.
[3] B.-J. 1914, p. 105.   [4] *Supra*, p. 131.
[5] Gerber, ii. Anhang 68, mentions, among the busts and statues of celebrated musicians: 'Bach (Johann Christian) in Gyps zu London verfertiget, besitzt der Herr Conzertmeister Bach in Bückeburg'. I have failed to discover the present locality of the bust.
[6] The original, in Italian, is in the Liceo Musicale, Bologna. I am indebted to Signore Vatielli for a copy of it.
[7] Published at Bologna in two volumes, 1774, 1775.
[8] Published in 1781.

proceed direct to Bologna, I should have felt highly honoured in acceding to your flattering request for my portrait. Before long, however, I hope to find occasion to send you a likeness of some sort. Meanwhile, I have delivered your message to Signore Bach, who, as he promised, has had himself painted.

Be assured, reverend sir, of my prayers, along with those of every lover of music, learning, and virtue, that Providence may grant you life, health, and endurance to complete your tremendous labours, and thereby make your name and fame known to posterity, as they are to-day, most reverend and distinguished Father, to

your most humble, devoted, and obliged servant

London, 22 June 1778.   Carlo Burney.

Belatedly, on the eve of his visit to Paris, Bach dispatched Gainsborough's portrait to Bologna, and, with it, his last letter to his old teacher:

Most reverend Father and honoured patron,
   I have placed in Signore Roncaglia's charge an excellent portrait of myself by one of our best painters. He is passing through Bologna and, no doubt, will deliver it into your hands. I beg you graciously to accept it as a small token of my heavy debt to you, and pray that, when you look at it, you will give a thought to one who has the honour to be

Your Reverence's most humble and devoted servant,

London, 28 July 1778.   G. C. Bach.

P.S.—I should like to know when the third volume of your *Istoria della musica* will appear.

While Bach was preparing his *Amadis* for the Paris stage, the King's Theatre engaged fresh singers and a new composer. Gasparo Pacchierotti, who took Roncaglia's place, one of the great artists of the century, now made his first appearance in England. His powers can be gauged by Burney's eulogy:[1] 'I eagerly attended the first general rehearsal, in which, though he sung *sotto voce* under a bad cold in extreme severe weather, my pleasure was such as I had never experienced before'.[2] Of Antonia Bernasconi, who replaced Mme Lebrun, Burney has little to say, except that she had 'a neat and elegant manner of singing, though with a voice that was feeble and in decay'.[3] She deserves another sentence, however; Gluck had written *Alceste* for her at Vienna in 1764, and, six years later, the youthful Mozart composed airs for her in his *Mitridate* at Milan. The new composer, Ferdinando Bertoni, was a pupil of Father Martini's, but ten years Bach's senior, a writer to

[1] Bur. iv. 510. He devotes nearly four pages to Pacchierotti's career and circumstances.
[2] Mount Edgcumbe, p. 23, confirms Burney's estimate and shows the singer to have been an attractive personality.
[3] Bur. iv. 509. Mount Edgcumbe, p. 27, agrees that she was past her prime, but praises her as a good actress.

whom his venturesome charge of plagiarism against Gluck had given notoriety. Burney[1] was not impressed by his abilities, but allowed that Sacchini was in too high favour for a stranger's success to be considerable.

Sacchini opened the new season on Tuesday, 24 November 1778, with his 'New Comic Opera', *L'Avaro deluso*,[2] which failed to win its author his usual success. Bertoni made his *début* four days later (Saturday, November 28) in *Demofoonte*,[3] 'a well selected and agreeable pasticcio,'[4] which introduced Pacchierotti and incidentally exhibited the heterogeneous character of this kind of composition: he sang four songs in different styles by as many composers, and by his versatility at once established his reputation.[5] Among them was Bach's 'Misero pargoletto', originally written for Elisi at Milan, with which he won his first operatic success.[6] The reception of the pasticcio was favourable, and after the new year Bertoni presented (Saturday, 23 January 1779) his *Artaserse*, in which Manzoletto, 'a very tolerable singer',[7] made his *entrée* as 'second man'. André Grétry's *Zemira ed Azore* followed on Tuesday, February 23, described as 'a new Comic Opera never performed', but actually seven years old. In it Signora Polone made her first appearance on any stage. Sacchini's *Enea e Lavinia* was given on March 25, Bertoni's *La Governante* on Saturday, May 15, and the season's productions concluded with the pasticcio *L'Olimpiade* (Saturday, May 29), by Bertoni 'and other eminent Masters', including, probably, Bach, whose 'Quel labbro adorato' was one of the successes of the pasticcio when produced in 1769.

In the spring of 1779 Tenducci, having placated his creditors, returned to London, where he announced on Saturday, April 17, a concert[8] in which he was assisted by Bach, whose cheque-book had already relieved his friend's necessities.[9] Abel, Fischer, Crossdill, and Giardini contributed solos, while Abel's pupil, Signora Georgi, and Signora Marchetti added songs. Bach

---

[1] Bur. iv. 513.
[2] Cast: *Gervasio*, Guglielmo Jermoli; *Agapito*, Carlo Rovedino; *Calandrano*, Antonio Rossi; *Lazzarina*, Anna Pozzi; *Zerbinetta*, Signora Sestini; *Modesta*, Signora Jermoli (Bott. 907, i. 16/10).
[3] Cast: *Demofoonte*, Valentino Adamberger; *Timantes*, Gasparo Pachierotti; *Cherintus*, Giuseppe Coppola; *Adrastus*, Leopoldo Micheli; *Dircea*, Antonia Bernasconi; *Creusa*, Anna Pozzi; *Matusius*, Carlo Rovedino (Bott. 907, i. 16/8).
[4] Bur. iv. 509.   [5] Mount Edgcumbe, p. 27.
[6] *Supra*, p. 33. A copy of this song at Schwerin describes it as 'aus Demofoonte'.   [7] Mount Edgcumbe, p. 29.
[8] The concert was advertised on Apr. 17 to take place on Apr. 29. It was postponed to May 10. Tenducci lodged at 7 Prince's Street, Leicester Fields.
[9] In June 1778 Bach paid Tenducci £15 10s., and in Feb. 1779 four sums totalling £115 3s.

introduced his *Amor Vincitore*[1] and 'a new Quartetto for a Violin, Oboe, Violoncello, and Piano Forte',[2] in which Crossdill, Fischer, and Giardini also took part.

Bach's household at Richmond was broken up at this period, in circumstances which reveal the delicate state of his finances. He employed a housekeeper, whom he furnished with money month by month to pay the local tradesmen. The woman was dishonest, forged receipts to deceive her employer, and appropriated the money she should have disbursed. Her fraud might have escaped detection longer, had not a rumour of Bach's intention to leave Richmond made his creditors alert and suspicious. The facts were revealed, his housekeeper absconded, and Bach was called on to furnish £1,100 or £1,200, of which she had defrauded him. 'This shook him,' remarks Mrs. Papendiek,[3] 'and other troubles followed.' But, for the moment, his situation was not critical; Mrs. Papendiek's journals indicate no interruption of the agreeable amenities of the society in which Bach and his wife moved. The Zoffanys were added to the circle,[4] and Bach was on intimate terms with them; Mary Zoffany witnessed his last Will and Testament.[5]

The success of his *Scipione* invited the managers to advertise Bach's name among the composers engaged for the Opera season of 1779–80. He perhaps co-operated in the pasticcio *Alessandro nell' Indie*,[6] with which the season opened on Saturday, 27 November 1779, though not actively; he was at the moment in Paris superintending the rehearsals of his *Amadis*. Sacchini's *La Contadina in Corte* followed on Tuesday, December 14, and Bertoni's *Quinto Fabio*[7] on Saturday, 22 January 1780, in which Pacchierotti repeated the success he had achieved in and for the opera at Padua in 1778. Sacchini provided the next opera, his *Rinaldo*,[8] on Saturday, April 22, in which Pachierotti particularly excelled.[9] But the rest of the season was Bertoni's; his *Il Duca d'Atene*[10] was

---

[1] *Supra*, p. 130.   [2] It is not possible to identify the work.
[3] Papendiek, i. 106.   [4] *Ibid.*, i. 109.   [5] *Infra*, p. 166.
[6] Cast: *Alessandro*, Giuseppe Trebbi; *Poro*, Gasparo Pacchierotti; *Gandarte*, Signore Manzoletto; *Timagene*, Leopoldo Micheli; *Cleofide*, Francesca Lebrun; *Erissena*, Anna Pozzi (Bott. 907, i. 17/1).
[7] Cast: *Quinto Fabio*, Gasparo Pacchierotti; *Emilia*, Francesca Lebrun; *Lucio Papirio*, Giuseppe Trebbi; *Volumnio*, Signore Manzoletto; *Fausta*, Anna Pozzi; *Marco Fabio*, Carlo Rovedino (Bott. 11714, cc. 4).
[8] Cast: *Rinaldo*, Gasparo Pacchierotti; *Ubaldo*, Giuseppe Trebbi; *Idreno*, Signore Sampieri; *Clotarco*, Leopoldo Micheli; *Armida*, Francesca Lebrun; *Zelmira*, Anna Pozzi (Bott. 907, i. 17/3).   [9] Bur. iv. 513.
[10] Cast: *Il Duca*, Signore Manzoletto; *La Duchessa*, Anna Pozzi; *Capocchio*, Giuseppe Trebbi; *M. de l'Allumette*, Signore Gherardi; *Violetta*, Signora Prudom; *Capricorno*, ?; *Gionchiglia*, Antonia Bernasconi (Bott. 907, i. 17/2).

staged on Tuesday, May 9, while, on the last day of that month, his *Orfeo*, originally produced in 1776, was performed for one night only 'in the Manner of an Oratorio', with Pacchierotti as Orfeo, Mme Lebrun as Eurydice, and Trebbi as Hymen.

Pacchierotti's popularity could readily have secured him re-engagement. But the managers had already arranged for the return of Roncaglia,[1] who, following Pacchierotti, was now voted insipid, while the new 'second man', Giovanni Ansani, a comparatively unknown singer,[2] so eclipsed his leader, that their quarrels on and off the stage disturbed the harmonies of the new season. Ansani was peevish and assertive, Roncaglia 'saucy and conceited'; neither could brook the superiority asserted by the other. Ansani, in fact, threw up his engagement, and for want of him, Mount Edgcumbe remarked,[3] the season moved heavily. Mme Lebrun was retained, and Mrs. Barthélémon made her *rentrée*.

The season opened on Saturday, 25 November 1780, with the comedy-pasticcio, *L'Arcifanfano*, probably based on Galuppi's opera of that title, with Trebbi, Manzoletto, Gherardi, Micheli, Mrs. Barthélémon, Signora Prudom, and Signora Sestini in the cast. Roncaglia and Ansani made their first appearance on Saturday, December 2, in *Ricimero*, a pasticcio arranged by Francesco Bianchi, who conducted throughout the season.[4] It was moderately successful. But, on December 16, the first appearance of the elder Vestris diverted enthusiasm from the singers to the ballet. The dancing of the younger Vestris and Mlle Baccelli had already given pleasure; but pleasure, remarks Burney,[5] was now 'sublimed into ecstacy' by the newcomer's genius. He adds an illuminative comment, but without reproof: 'Pacchierotti had been heard so frequently, that his singing was no impediment to conversation, or even to animated narrative and debate; but while the elder Vestris was on the stage, if during a *pas seul* any of his admirers forgot themselves so much as to applaud him with their hands, there was an instant check put to his rapture by a choral hu—sh! For those lovers of Music who talked the loudest when Pacchierotti was singing a pathetic air, or making an exquisite close, were now thrown into agonies of displeasure, lest the graceful movements *du dieu de la danse*, or the attention of his votaries, should be disturbed by audible approbation. Since that time, the

[1] *Supra*, p. 154. Sacchini's *Rinaldo* was given on 22 April 1780.
[2] Burney (Bur. iv. 515) declares that Ansani had 'one of the best Tenor voices I ever heard on our Opera stage'. [3] Mount Edgcumbe, p. 29.
[4] This early visit of Bianchi to London has been overlooked by the music lexicons. He settled in England later and died at Hammersmith in 1810.
[5] Bur. iv. 518.

most mute and respectful attention has been given to the manly grace of Le Picq, and light fantastic toe of the younger Vestris, to the Rossis, the Theodores, the Coulons, and the Hilligsburgs, while the poor singers have been disturbed, not by the violence of applause, but the clamour of inattention.'

Traetta's *Le Serve rivali* was given on Tuesday, 19 December 1780, and on New Year's Day, 1781, Sacchini's *Rinaldo* was revived, with Roncaglia and Ansani for the last time in association, a production of which the ballet was the most conspicuous feature.[1] Sacchini was again called upon for the next production, his *Mitridate*,[2] presented on Tuesday, January 23, and the remaining weeks were filled with revivals: Piccinni's *Il Barone di Torre Forte*[3] (Thursday, February 22), for the 'benefit' of Vestris; Rauzzini's *Piramo e Tisbe* (Thursday, March 29); and Paisiello's *La Fraschetana* (Thursday, April 5). Rauzzini made his reappearance on Tuesday, June 5, in *L'Ommaggio*, a Pastoral, of which Bianchi and Giardini were his fellow-authors. The voluble Sacchini's *Euriso*,[4] on Saturday, June 23, brought the season's productions to an end.

Though he made no other effort to contest Sacchini's popularity, Bach's *La Clemenza di Scipione* clearly restored the reputation his earliest operas had won him more than twenty years before among the Opera-going public. In every season thereafter he was retained by the managers, though no other original work came from his pen. On 27 October 1781 Crawford again announced his composers for the imminent season—Bach, Bertoni, Bianchi, and Rauzzini.[5] But Bach had made his last music. He was still in the prime of life, and, if Gainsborough's portrait is a true likeness, robust in appearance. His premature death therefore invited allegations against his character. Macfarren[6] did not scruple to assert, that while Bach's marriage to Cecilia Grassi may have cured him of his gallantries, it did not check his propensity to drink, and that, in his last years, 'he rarely wrote save under spirituous excitement'. There is not a tittle of evidence to support either reckless accusa-

[1] Writing to the *Public Advertiser* of 2 Jan. 1781, 'A Frequenter of the Opera' expressed a doubt 'whether it is possible to carry the Art of Dancing to a higher Degree of Perfection'. The dancers were Vestris, Baccelli, Slingsby, Simonet, and Signora Tantini.
[2] Cast: *Mitridate*, Giuseppe Trebbi; *Pharnace*, Francesco Roncaglia; *Fabio*, Signore Manzoletto; *Oronte*, Leopoldo Micheli; *Almira*, Francesca Lebrun; *Irene*, Signora Prudom (Bott. 907, i. 15/9).
[3] Cast: *Armidoro*, Giuseppe Trebbi; *Il Barone*, Signore Gherardi; *Lucinda*, Signora Sestini; *Serpina*, Signora Prudom (Bott. 907, i. 17/6).
[4] 'Music composed (with Improvements)' by Sacchini.
[5] P.A., 27 Oct. 1781.
[6] *The Imperial Dictionary of Universal Biography*, s.v. J. C. Bach.

tion. Mrs. Papendiek appears to attribute Bach's premature death in chief measure to financial worries and declining popularity. They would hardly depress a constitution inherently robust. His younger sister predeceased him in August 1781, and both may have inherited in lesser degree the physical disability which carried off so many of their elders in the old Leipzig home.

Still, Bach's last year of life was not wholly clouded. In the spring of 1781 the Court's residence at Kew, to await the prorogation of Parliament, invited agreeable gaieties. On fine afternoons a procession of boats on the river escorted the Prince of Wales, recently declared of age, to the promenade at Richmond. The Zoffanys owned a decked yacht, 'elegantly and conveniently fitted up', on board of which the Bachs and their pupil, Miss Cantelo, were frequent guests. Bach was anxious to give the latter every opportunity of being heard, and she often sang with Madame Bach, 'whose voice sounded beautiful on the water'. There were musical parties, morning and evening, in which members of the King's Band of Musick took part, and Mrs. Papendiek herself played with Bach his admired duet for two performers on one pianoforte.[1] The Prince of Wales, residing at the Lodge, added another centre of jollity. He was fond of music, sang well, played the violoncello, joined in the quartet parties, and even adapted music for them. Bach and his associates were received at the Lodge, and their good-humoured pranks afforded him amusement. On one occasion Bach bet Fischer five guineas that he could not play his own minuet on his own instrument, the oboe. Fischer sat down confidently to win the wager. Allowing him to proceed for a few bars, Bach stood in front of him, munching a lemon whose juice trickled from his mouth. Fischer's filled sympathetically at the sight; he vainly tried to stem the flood, and confessed himself the loser.[2]

On Wednesday, 9 May 1781, Bach gave the last of the Bach-Abel concerts in the Hanover Square Rooms. His health already disturbed his friends, and evidently his affairs were in a disordered state. His account with Drummond's was overdrawn £43 18s. 11d. for 1779; the overdraft was not made good until 2 November 1780, and nothing was paid into the account in 1781. Financial anxiety weighed on his health and spirits, and in the course of the year he removed to Paddington for change of air.[3] Here, on 14 November 1781, he executed his Will, in the following terms:[4]

This is the last will and testament of me John Christian Bach of the

---

[1] Papendiek, i. 138, 142. [2] Ibid., i. 131, 142. [3] Ibid., i. 150.
[4] The original is at Somerset House.

parish of St. Mary le bone in the County of Middlesex, Music Master to Her Most Gracious Majesty Queen Charlotte. I give, devise and bequeath unto my dear wife Cecilia Bach, late Cecilia Grassi, all my real and personal estate whatsoever to hold to her, her heirs, executors, administrators, and assigns for ever, but subject nevertheless to the payment of my debts and funeral expenses. And of this my will I do appoint my said dear wife Cecilia sole executrix. In witness whereof I the said John Christian Bach have hereunto set my hand and seal this fourteenth day of November 1781.

The witnesses were Mary Zoffany, Francis Mecci, and Augur Greenland. Mecci was an acquaintance of some standing: his name appears in Bach's banking account in 1770 and 1773 as receiving £40 and £30 respectively. Augur Greenland was probably the father of Miss Greenland, or Greenlands, to whom Bach dedicated his Op. 16. They were among the 'kind friends' who never forsook him in his last days of sickness and sinking fortune; 'and I believe', Mrs. Papendiek adds,[1] 'few days passed without one or other of our family seeing him. The Zoffanys, poor Abel, and others supplied him entirely with provisions sent ready prepared. Mr. Papendiek saw him every day, and assisted him by many kind acts, which are all the more comforting when done by the hand of one we love. Here, I urged him to close the eyes of his beloved friend[2] by offering marriage to his *protégée*, Miss Cantelo, but on that subject Mr. Papendiek was deaf to entreaty. The last visit we paid was together with my father and mother.[3] Bach, on taking a final leave, joined our[4] hands. I think now I see his enchanting smile. Not a word was said; we were motionless. On retiring, we could not get Mr. Papendiek away, but at last my father prevailed upon him to hasten to the Queen, with the news of Bach being so near his end. This roused him, and after this painful mission, he obtained leave to return to his friend, who had just passed away when he reached this room of mourning.'

Bach died on Tuesday, 1 January 1782. The *Public Advertiser* for the following Saturday announced the event as having taken place 'at his House in Soho'. The paragraph added an intimation of Schroeter's appointment to succeed him in the Queen's service, an announcement lacking decorum: for Bach was not yet buried. The ceremony took place on Sunday, January 6, in the churchyard of St. Pancras,[5] where three eminent musicians later laid their bones—Stephen Paxton (*d.* 1787), John Danby (*d.* 1798), and

---

[1] Papendiek, i. 150.
[2] Papendiek was Bach's pupil. Cf. Papendiek, i. 154.
[3] Mr. and Mrs. Albert.
[4] Papendiek and his fiancée, Miss Albert.
[5] The St. Pancras Register merely records the name and date.

Samuel Webbe (*d.* 1816).[1] It was a sad, unceremonious passing. Schroeter, Cramer, and others had called at the house of mourning to express their concern. But only four of his friends attended Bach to his grave—Albert, Papendiek, Zoffany, and Buntebart.[2] Nor did his death evoke any public expression of regret and appreciation, though in one breast it roused a memory and drew a compliment. 'No doubt you know that the English Bach is dead,' writes Mozart from Vienna on 10 April 1782; 'a sad day for the world of music!' [3]

Bach's death revealed the disordered state of his affairs. Notwithstanding the success of his *Scipione* in 1778, he no longer enjoyed the vogue and popularity of his earlier years. Younger men had replaced him as a teacher, Sacchini's facile genius reigned in the Haymarket, and, though the favour of the Court was not withdrawn, it was not adequate to support a household whose extravagance had become too habitual to be abated. His creditors flocked to the house when his death was known, and only the vigilance of Papendiek and the forcible resistance of Bach's coachman, who had been in his service since his first coming to England, prevented them from 'disturbing the corpse'.[4] Bach's legacy to his widow, in fact, were debts amounting to £4,000.[5] Her immediate necessities were relieved by the Queen, who sent money by the hand of Mr. Albert to buy mourning for her and Miss Cantelo. The Queen also paid the cost of the funeral, and restored to the faithful coachman a sum of £100 lent by him to his master. But, 'finding how things were', she was unable to discharge the heavy debt which weighed on Bach's widow, who consequently surrendered everything she had to satisfy those creditors 'who would not relinquish their claims'. Parting from Miss Cantelo, who removed to Rauzzini's charge at Bath, she was received by friends until her return to Italy.[6]

Bach's death was so little expected, that, on the very day it occurred, the *Public Advertiser* intimated the resumption of the Bach–Abel Concerts in the Hanover Square Rooms on 23 January 1782, an announcement amended a week later (January 8) by the notice: 'The above Concerts are continued for the joint Benefit of Mr. Abel and the Widow of his late worthy Friend Mr. Bach.' But Abel's abilities were inadequate to the task of controlling an organization of which Bach had been the managing partner. With the encouragement of friends, Cecilia was unhappily led to

[1] *Musical Times*, 1896, p. 585.   [2] Papendiek, i. 151.
[3] Schiedermair, ii. 163.   [4] Papendiek, i. 151.
[5] Gerber, i. 84.   [6] Papendiek, i. 152.

arrange a 'benefit' in her behalf in the King's Theatre. It took place on Monday, 27 May 1782, when Anfossi's *I Viaggiatori felici* was presented as 'a new Comic Opera'. A 'new Serious Dance', *Le triomphe de l'amour conjugal*, followed Act I, while a new Pantomime Ballet, *Rinaldo ed Armida*, was danced after Act II. 'Tickets, Half a Guinea each, to be had of Mrs. Bach, at Mr. Zoffany's, in Albemarle street, Piccadilly, and at the Office in Union Court.'

The programme was planned with delicate regard to the circumstances. Apart from the implication of its title, Anfossi's opera had been performed on the evening of Bach's death, and was repeated with the same cast;[1] the Pantomime Ballet was upon a subject Bach himself had treated, while the 'serious' dance paid a compliment to the *bénéficiaire*. But the public response was disappointing; Bach's name no longer evoked enthusiasm, his death stirred no emotion; the curtain rose before an audience insufficient to pay the ordinary expenses of the evening, though both singers and orchestra gave their services. The Queen's generosity again intervened: a present of £100 enabled Cecilia Bach to return to her native Italy, accompanied by the faithful coachman and a single friend; from the same source she continued to receive an annual pension of £200 for the few years that remained to her of life.

Thus, Mrs. Papendiek reflected sadly,[2] 'this man of ability in his profession, of liberal kindness in it, of general attention to friends, and of worthy character, was forgotten almost before he was called to the doom of us all, and every recollection of him seems buried in oblivion'.[3] Bach descended into the shadows which still shrouded his colossal father. His operas left no impress upon a generation that outlived their technique. His ditties lie on dusty shelves, swelling the library of forgotten things. His symphonies, sonatas, and chamber music were eclipsed by the more perfect art of an era whose threshold only he approached. Uniting the formulas of the sixteenth and seventeenth centuries, his father

---

[1] The principal characters were taken by Signori Viganoni, Morigi, Manzoletto, Micheli, Signore Lorenzini, Salpietro, and Allegranti.

[2] Papendiek, i. 152.

[3] Tenducci, however, commemorated Bach at his concert in the Hanover Square Rooms on 17 May 1786 by performing certain pieces of that 'justly celebrated master' which remained in manuscript. The vocal pieces included 'the favourite Cantata', *Rinaldo ed Armida*, and 'the distinguished Cantata' *Aurora*, both for three voices. Tenducci was assisted by Miss Maddan and Madame Mara. The *Public Advertiser* of 22 May 1786 declared that 'the angelic genius of Bach appeared to inspire the performers in a superlative degree'. The characters in *Rinaldo* are named as Rinaldo, Ubalda, and Armida; and in *Aurora* as Aurora, Cesala, and Procri. See *infra*, pp. 247, 250.

and Handel had set music upon a new course, while preserving
the ancient tradition of composite harmony. Haydn, Mozart, and
Beethoven controlled the stream into fresh channels, yet drew
from the same fount. Craving new modes of utterance, they
perfected the Symphony and Sonata, and through them fulfilled
the high purpose of their art—the comfort and illumination of the
human soul. Bach inhabited the borderland between these two
dispensations, the old and the new. His stature is not gigantic;
but he was prominent and respected in his generation, a pioneer
in the exploration of new idioms, and honoured by the giants who
perfected them. The man whose death Mozart deplored as a loss
to the world of music may not be lightly belittled, nor will
instructed minds pronounce that his parentage alone rescues his
memory from oblivion. On the platform of his generation Bach
owes his honourable position, not to the inheritance of a great
name, but to his own eclectic genius and indomitable industry.

CHAPTER VII

BACH'S INSTRUMENTAL COMPOSITIONS

TO the public of his generation Bach was chiefly known as an instrumental composer. Of his operas, only *Amadis* and *Scipione* got themselves completely into print, at the end of his career, though the favourite songs of his earlier operas, and his Vauxhall collections, were readily accessible. But, from the moment of his arrival in London, his instrumental music was eagerly sought by publishers. Gerber mentions twenty separate issues between 1765 and 1779, a total which corresponds with the list in Forkel's *Almanach*. Of these, all but three bear opus numbers, 1 to 17, omitting an Op. 12, which is identified neither by Forkel nor Cramer. All three catalogues, in fact, are incomplete. Before framing a comprehensive one, it must be observed that (1) confusion is caused by the lack of correspondence between English and continental editions of the same work; (2) the opus numbers generally distinguish only instrumental publications, though the first set of Canzonette and the score of *Scipione* bear the numbers 4 and 14 respectively; while a set of Symphonies and the second set of Canzonette bear the indicator 6 in common. Where the English and continental editions are not uniformly labelled, it is reasonable to assume that the English numeration is correct. The same inference can be drawn when they vary in their contents. The continental editions were published at Berlin, Amsterdam, Paris, the Hague, Riga, Vienna, and Offenbach.

Bach was fertile in every form of instrumental music popular in his period—symphonies, opera overtures, concertos, chamber music (sextets, quintets, quartets, trios), pianoforte and violin sonatas, violin duets, pianoforte sonatas, and military marches. The following bear an opus number :

Opus.	Date.	Description.
1.	1763.	*Six Harpsichord Concertos.* Dedicated to the Queen. Hummell published an edition in 1765, which Cramer and Forkel mention. Others are indicated in the Thematic Catalogue, *infra*.
2.	1763.	*Six Trios for Harpsichord*, Violin (Flute) and Violoncello. Dedicated to Princess Augusta of Brunswick-Lüneburg, sister of George III. Johann André (Offenbach) published a Quartet in G as Op. 2. See also Op. 4, *infra*.

Opus.	Date.	Description.

3. 1765. *Six Symphonies.*
Dedicated to the Duke of York. Cramer and Forkel
mention the Amsterdam edition. For others, see T.C.,
infra. André published a Sextet as Op. 3.

4. 1765. *Six Canzonets.*
Dedicated to Lady Glenorchy. Cramer and Forkel
name Six Trios as Op. 4, indicating a set published by
Huberty (Paris) as Op. 2, but not identical with Op. 2
supra.

5. 1768. *Six Sonatas for Harpsichord or Pianoforte.*
Dedicated to the Duke of Mecklenburg-Strelitz, the
Queen's brother. Cramer and Forkel mention the
Amsterdam edition. The English editions are dated
?1770 and ?1775 in the British Museum Catalogue.

6. 1770. *Six Canzonets*, second set.
Dedicated to Duke Joseph Friedrich of Sachsen-
Hildburghausen. Cramer and Forkel distinguish as
Op. 6 a set of Six Symphonies published by Huberty
(Paris), dated 1770. Hummel published a set of
Symphonies as Op. 6, with a French title-page. See
T.C., and also Op. 17, *infra*.

7. 1770–5. *Six Harpsichord or Pianoforte Concertos.*
Dedicated to the Queen. Cramer and Forkel mention
the Amsterdam edition. For others, see T.C., and also
Op. 10, *infra*. Torricella (Vienna) published Nos.
1–3 of this set, dedicating them to the Countess
of Fünfkirchen. Welcker's (*c.* 1770) was the earlier
English edition.

8. 1770–5. *Six Instrumental Quartets.*
Dedicated to Sir William Young, Bart. The set was
published at the Hague as Op. 9, and in a different
order. Under this opus number Markordt (Amsterdam)
published Six Periodic Symphonies.

9. 1770–5. *Three Symphonies.*
Cramer and Forkel mention the Amsterdam edition.

10. 1770–5. *Six Sonatas for Harpsichord (or Pianoforte) and Violin.*
Dedicated to Lady Melbourne. Huberty (Vienna)
published the set as Op. 7.

11. 1772–7. *Six Instrumental Quintets.*
Dedicated to the Elector Palatine. Cramer and Forkel
mention the Amsterdam edition and Cramer dis-
tinguishes it as Op. 11. Welcker gives no opus number.

12. 1772–7. Cramer and Forkel do not indicate an Op. 12. But see
Op. 13 and 17, *infra*.

Opus.	Date.	Description.
13.	1777.	*Third Set of Harpsichord or Pianoforte Concertos.* Dedicated to Mrs. Pelham. Hummel published the set in two parts as Op. 12 and 13. Unaware of Welcker's edition, Cramer and Forkel attach this opus number to 'Trois grands Concerts pour le Clavecin'. There is much confusion here. See Thematic Catalogue, and also Op. 14.
14.	1778.	*La Clemenza di Scipione.* Cramer and Forkel attach this opus number to 'Trois grands Concerts pour le Clavecin'. As in Op. 13, there is much confusion here. Schmitt (Amsterdam) published Welcker's Op. 13 as Op. 14.
15.	1779.	*Four Sonatas and two Duets for Harpsichord (Pianoforte) and Violin.* Dedicated to the Countess of Abingdon. Cramer and Forkel name the Berlin (Hummel) edition, and Forkel dates it 1779.
16.	1779.	*Six Sonatas for Harpsichord (Pianoforte) and Violin (Flute).* Dedicated to Miss Greenland. Cramer and Forkel mention the Berlin (Hummel) edition.
17.	1779.	*Six Sonatas for Harpsichord or Pianoforte.* Cramer and Forkel mention the Hummel edition and date it 1779. Siéber's edition is marked Op. 12; Huberty's as Op. 6. Hummel's edition is dedicated to Princess Julie of Hessen-Philippstahl.
18.	1781.	*Six grand Overtures.* Under this opus number a set of Sonatas and Duets for Harpsichord (Pianoforte) and Violin was published at Berlin and Paris.
19.	posthumous.	*Four Instrumental Quartets.* Composed for the Earl of Abingdon. See *infra*, p. Under this opus number Freeman published Six Sonatas for Pianoforte (Harpsichord) and Flute (Violin).
20.	„	*Three Sonatas for Pianoforte (Harpsichord) and Violin.*
21.	„	*Three Favourite Overtures.* Under this opus number Bonin published Three Pianoforte Sonatas.
22.	„	*Two Quintets.* Ed. Hummel.

The Symphonies.

When Bach arrived in Italy the Symphony was a composition sufficiently independent to be listened to for its own sake, and no longer the conventional prelude to an opera (*Sinfonia avanti l'opera*). The French tradition of the eighteenth century had been

superseded by Italian usage; unlike the Suite or Partita, the
Symphony made its effect by the dexterous treatment of thematic
material, not as a series of contrasted dance measures. In structure,
long before Mozart and Haydn penned their early essays, the
Symphony conformed to the Sonata's example, though the
Minuet and Trio, which became its regular sections, recalled the
pattern it had superseded. By the middle of the eighteenth century the Symphony was an orchestral Sonata, almost invariably
in three movements—the first, a busy *Allegro*, the second an
Andante or *Largo*, and the third a lively *Vivace* or *Allegro*—for
the most part written for a chamber orchestra in eight parts—two
violins, viola, bass, two flutes (or oboes), and two horns (*Cor de
chasse: corno da caccia*). Structure rather than orchestral colouring was the chief consideration; the chief burden rested on the
strings, the flutes and oboes reinforced them, after the manner of
the *ripieni* in the earlier Concertos, while the horns generally
sustained the harmony.

These conventions Bach's Symphonies, with their wide
European vogue, did much to establish, affording a model to the
youthful Mozart, as to others. Twenty-one of them were published in his lifetime as Op. 3, 6, (8), 9; further examples were
provided by his Overtures in Op. 18 and 21, and by other editions
bearing no opus number. With rare exceptions, they are cast in
the three-movement mould. The exceptions are: (1) A Sinfonie
concertante in A major, published by Siéber, which contains only
two movements, an *Andante di molto*

followed by a Rondo (*Allegro assai*); (2) The first of two 'Sinfonies
à Grande Orchestre', published by Schmitt as Op. 18, also
restricted to two movements, an opening *Allegro assai*

followed by an *Andante*; (3) An unpublished Symphony at
Einsiedeln, which consists of an opening *Largo assai*

followed by a Minuet; (4) A Symphony in E flat in MS. at
Wernigerode

in four movements—*Adagio, Allegro molto, Allegretto, Minuetto*;
(5) A concerted Symphony in F at Berlin for oboe and orchestra,
which contains only two movements, an *Allegro moderato*

followed by a *Minuet*. These infrequent exceptions to a general
rule are further distinguished by the fact that Nos. 1, 3, 4, 5 were
written for concerted instruments, while the second was the overture to *Scipione*, which, in the score, is printed as a single movement. Thus, Bach definitely adopted the three-movement form
for the concert Symphony.

Bach also accepted the *Allegro—Andante—Allegro* (*Rondo*)
formula, but with exceptions to his general practice. The most
striking are three instances in which his opening movement is
marked *Adagio* or *Largo*, after the example of the French Ouverture. Two of the three are indicated in the preceding paragraph.
The third, altogether abnormal, is in the opening Sinfonia of the
oratorio *Gioas*, which consists of an *Allegro* and *Allegretto*, preceded in each case by a short *Largo*, such as Sebastian Bach and
Handel wrote. The reason for its introduction is apparent when
it is observed that the *Allegro* and *Allegretto* were originally written
for the royal birthday Ode, *Happy morn, auspicious rise*, and
demanded such an introductory note of solemnity as the short
Largo provided.[1]

Greater importance attaches to Bach's use of the Minuet.
Unlike the other dance measures which furnished the movements
of the Suite, the Minuet survived in its successor. In Haydn's
use it was a normal part of the four-movement Symphony. Bach's
Symphonies exhibit no similar instance, but there are several in
which a *Tempo di Minuetto* takes the place of the concluding
Presto: e.g. Op. 3, No. 4; Op. 18, No. 5; Op. 21, No. 2; Op. (8),
No. 4; the Einsiedeln E flat Symphony already mentioned; a MS.
Concerto in E flat in the Berlin Library;

[1] See also a Sinfonie concertante in C major, *infra*, p. 286.

another in MS. in the same collection;

and the Wernigerode Symphony in four movements already mentioned. It is observable that Bach's Minuets anticipate Haydn's usage: they are brisk, obviously *Allegro*, while the Wernigerode example is definitely marked *Presto*.

Bach's Symphony orchestra was the normal instrument of his period—strings, flutes or oboes, and horns. His flute was the German flute, i.e. the *flauto traverso*, or modern flute, as distinguished from the older flageolet; his horn is usually named as *corno da caccia*. Though he was not an innovator of Gluck's originality, he was undoubtedly a pioneer. The experimental spirit in him, which preferred the pianoforte to the harpsichord, is evident in his introduction of the clarinet into the English Opera orchestra, though he was less disposed to admit the instrument into the Symphony. It is found in Op. 18; in a Wolfenbüttel MS. of Op. 21, No. 2; in a Symphony in C major at Basel,

also in a set of Symphonies in MS. at Bückeburg (*infra*, p. 285); and in the two-movement Einsiedeln Symphony already mentioned. But, of these, Op. 18 and 21 are Opera overtures, while in the Basel MS. the indication of the instrument is not positively clear.

Bach's first set of Symphonies (Op. 3) was published in 1765 and performed at the Carlisle House concerts in that year. Scored for the normal Symphony orchestra, they won instant popularity, attested by their speedy publication at Paris (Huberty) and Amsterdam (Hummel). A reviewer of them in the *Hamburger Unterhaltungen*[1] remarked that their composer would have been

[1] Quoted in Tutenberg, p. 252; Schökel, p. 126. Both writers analyse the set.

taken for a foreigner but for his German name, adding that the
opening movements were spirited and good in the Italian style
('feurig und italienisch gut'), and the middle sections melodious
and agreeable ('singend und angenehm'). The critic's 'italienisch
gut' veiled a sneer, but his adjectives concisely express the qualities
of the set. It is, in fact, not unlikely that three of the six were
written in Italy; for Nos. 1, 3, and 5 are found in MS. in the Milan
Conservatorio. None of the slow movements exhibits Bach at his
best, but the opening *Allegro* of No. 2 is notable for the rhythmic
force of its opening theme:

The *spiccato* bowing is characteristic, and, along with other frequent evidences of Bach's attention to dynamics and phrasing,
indicates that, long before his introduction to Mannheim, he was
sensitive to the delicacies of orchestral playing. No. 3, whose
opening movement illustrates the form of the Viennese *ritornello*
Symphony, as clearly reveals the influences to which he had been
subjected under his brother's roof. Thus, though a North German
critic failed to recognize indigenous inspiration in Bach's Op. 3,
the set is instructive, since it discloses the principal characteristic
of his genius—the mingling of the German and Italian spirit.

Bach's second set of Symphonies (Op. 6) was published in
1770, five years after Op. 3. But, as a MS. of No. 1 of the set at
Kremsmünster is dated 1764,[1] while a copy of No. 2 is in the Milan
Conservatorio, it is probable that the publication does not exclusively represent Bach's activities after 1765. Yet, its superiority
to its predecessor is evident, and as a whole it pictures the Symphony at the level from which Mozart, Haydn, and Beethoven
raised a nobler structure.

About the year 1775 Markordt of Amsterdam published as
Op. 8 a set of six Periodical Symphonies. The title refers to the
scheme of publication, not to the work, and was used by Schmitt
of Amsterdam with the same signification. Nos. 1 and 6 of
Markordt's set are the same as Nos. 3 and 5 of Op. 6. Of the
remaining four, No. 4, in F major, is an example of Bach's highest
art in this form, and affords an agreeable example of his treatment
of the Minuet and Trio:

---

[1] Tutenberg, p. 268. He affords a detailed analysis of the set.

In the Trio the horns are silent:

The three Symphonies published by Hummel as Op. 9 in the late seventies seem to have lacked an English edition until after Bach's death. There is little doubt that they were written for the Hanover Square concerts; the monotony of their tonality—the whole nine movements are in two or three flats—suggests that they were the compositions on which the precocious Wesley offered his criticism.[1] But they exhibit a deftness of treatment, a sureness of touch, which place them among the best of their period, while their middle movements are Mozartian in melodious fluency; for example, that of No. 2:[2]

Tempo di minuetto.

The Overtures.

The earliest set of Bach's overtures was published about 1770 ('Six Favourite Overtures in VIII Parts') by William Randall, who had succeeded Walsh in 1766. By an audience which chattered and played cards while the singers were on the stage the Opera overture was likely to be as little regarded, nor were composers encouraged to take pains with a composition imperfectly heard. In his early years in London Bach not infrequently provided the overture for a pasticcio, but the contribution was deemed of too minor importance to be intimated. Nor did he share Gluck's view of the overture as an indicative prelude to the drama it preceded. The six in Randall's collection are so uniform in character that, though each bears the name of an opera, it would be as appropriate

[1] *Supra*, p. 142.
[2] The Thematic Catalogue reveals a small number of Symphonies published separately, and a larger number still in manuscript.

in another context. Besides the overture to *Artaserse*, of which,
no doubt, Bach made use at the King's Theatre, Randall included
that of *Orione* and others written under the Mingotti management
—*Il Tutore e la Pupilla* (1762), *Astarto* (1762), *La Cascina* (1763),
and *La Calamità* (1763). Three of them are in D major, a key to
which Bach was partial, and all are of the three-movement
Allegro—Andante—Allegro design. Walsh had already published
a set of Bach's overtures arranged 'for the Harpsichord or Organ',
which differs from Randall's by the omission of *La Calamità* and
Il Tutore, for which he substituted *Zanaida* (1763) and another,
in D major

Allegro con spirito.

which bears no indication of its source. Probably it belongs to
Adriano in Siria, the only one of Bach's early London operas whose
overture is not discoverable in Walsh's, Randall's, or a subsequent
publication.

Shortly before Bach's death, William Forster, who in the same
year (1781) contracted with Haydn for the purchase and publication of his compositions, issued 'Six Grand Overtures' by Bach,
three for a single, and three for a double, orchestra. Two of the
six record Bach's visits to Mannheim: No. 2 is the overture to
Lucio Silla (1776), No. 3 to *Endimione* (1774). The overture to
La Clemenza di Scipione (1778) was published by Schmitt, along
with Op. 18, No. 4, as 'Œuvre XVIII'. If the British Museum
Catalogue correctly dates Schmitt's edition (?1775), the overture
was not composed originally for *Scipione*. Of Bach's remaining
operas, *Carattaco* (1767) was published by Longman and Broderip
and did duty, in part, for *Temistocle* (1772); *Amadis* is found in
the full score of the opera; of the two *Catone* overtures the earlier
remained in manuscript,[1] the later, which also served for *Astarto*,
is No. 6 of Randall's collection. Thus, only the overture to *Alessandro nell' Indie* remains unidentified.

Concerted Symphonies.

Besides the symphonies and overtures, there are extant a few
compositions indifferently styled 'Sinfonie concertante', 'Concerto',
'Concert ou Symphonie'. The uniformity of their design, and the

[1] *Infra*, p. 277, Nos. 3 and 6.

maturity of their technique relate them to the period of the 'Grand
Overtures', i. e. to the last years of Bach's life; it may be concluded
with certainty that they were composed for the Hanover Square
concerts. The concerted instruments are the violin, viola, violoncello, and oboe. The players, consequently, were Cramer, Abel,
Crossdill, and Lebrun. A 'Concerto Toni B', which appears in
a Berlin MS. as a 'Concerto a Fagotto principale',[1] no doubt was
written for Fischer, while a 'Concerto a Flauto traverso' in D
may perhaps be associated with Wendling.[2]

Harpsichord and Pianoforte Concertos.

Bach's earliest essays were the five composed at Berlin under his
brother's supervision. He was not inactive at Milan in this form,
and in England wrote at least eighteen which found their way into
print. The MS. of a Concerto in E major at Dresden[3] definitely
attributes the composition to 'Sign. Bach in Meiland', and can be
assigned to, or near, the year 1760. Associated with it are two,
in A major and E flat major, published by Hartknock at Riga about
1770,[4] and, like it, for harpsichord and a quartet of strings. They
exhibit a technique much in advance of the Berlin essays, and show
the composer, under the influence of Martini and Italian models,
already exhibiting the melodic facility, which, imposed upon his
brother's teaching, produced the style which gave him his distinctive place among his contemporaries.[5]

It was natural that Bach should announce himself in this form
in his earliest published work in England. His engagement at
the King's Theatre was, originally, for a season's duration, and
his first inclination was to return to Italy on its conclusion. But
the favour of the Court, and the prospect of lucrative employment
as a teacher, decided him to abandon his original purpose. The
six Concertos published as Op. 1 in 1763 opportunely displayed his
talent, while their dedication to the Queen announced the high
patronage already accorded him. Burney correctly remarks the
simplicity and ease of these compositions for the harpsichord; they
were 'such as ladies can execute with little trouble'.[6] The Bass
line is figured, while the right hand is rarely invited to play a chord;
thirds and arpeggios make the extremest demand on the player's
execution. Still, Bach's Op. 1 not only represents the fruits of his

---

[1] *Infra*, p. 288.   [2] *Infra*, p. 286.   [3] *Infra*, p. 300, No. 13.   [4] *Infra*, p. 297.
[5] Cf. Schökel, p. 163; Schwarz, p. 434. Another MS. Concerto (A major) at
Berlin may date from the Milan period. Cf. *infra*, p. 300.
[6] Bur. iv. 482.

Italian discipline, but shows him a pioneer in a mode of handling the keyboard which anticipated the technique of the pianoforte.[1] Nos. 1, 2, 3, 5 are in two movements; it is noteworthy that Nos. 4 and 6, which are in three, are described as 'Concerto o Sinfonie', that is, are in the *Allegro—Andante—Allegro* form. But the six are uniform in their freshness and agreeable melody; the final movement of the sixth consists of very elementary variations on 'God save the King'.

As its title declares, Bach's first set of Concertos was written for the harpsichord. His second set (Op. 7), while designed for a similar trio of accompanying strings, is distinguished from its predecessor as being composed 'per il Cembalo o Piano e Forte'. Publication must therefore be assigned to the early seventies, shortly after Bach's demonstration of Zumpe's pianoforte in 1768.[2] Its contents otherwise exhibit no characteristics which distinguish it from its predecessor, while the composer is no nearer acceptance of the classical three-movement form established by Mozart; all but Nos. 5 and 6 of the set are in two movements.

Bach's third set of Concertos (Op. 13) appeared in 1777. Like its predecessors, only two (Nos. 2 and 4) of the six are in three movements. The fourth

Allegro.

was one of the most popular, as it is one of the finest that Bach wrote. A fondness for Scottish melodies he probably acquired through Tenducci; in the third movement of No. 4 he introduces 'The yellow haired laddie', treating it like the National Anthem in Op. 1. The Concerto pleased Haydn so much that he arranged it for pianoforte solo. As a whole, Bach's Concertos display complete mastery of the means at his disposal, and a resourcefulness and gift of melody which attracted Mozart and Haydn to study him in a sphere in which both owned their discipleship.

Chamber Music.

Bach's earliest publication in this form was a set of six Sonatas for harpsichord, violin (flute), and violoncello, dedicated to Princess Augusta and bearing the opus number 2. Announced in the *Public Advertiser* of 9 April 1763 as 'Six Sonatas or Notturnos', they are all in two movements, but otherwise without uniformity

[1] Cf. Schökel, pp. 167 f., for an analysis of the set.   [2] *Supra*, p. 113.

of design. The first movement is generally *Allegro*, in one case (No. 4) *Andante*, while the second is exceptionally in *Minuet* form. The strings do little more than accompany the harpsichord, and rarely have independent material of their own.

In the enumeration of Bach's Trios confusion is caused by the fact that Huberty labelled as Op. 2 another set of Trios, for two violins and viola ('ou Basse obligée'), which should, in fact, be distinguished as Op. 4. If, like Op. 2, the period of its composition be assigned to Milan, it exhibits in its contents a uniformity lacking in its predecessor. The six Trios are in two movements, the last invariably a Minuet and Trio, and the first in slow *tempo* (*Largo*, *Larghetto*, *Adagio*); an *Allegro* is lacking throughout. Yet the themes, particularly those of Nos. 1, 4, 5, 6, do not suggest a slow *tempo*, and would hardly be so interpreted, were not the direction evident to that effect.[1] That the set is accurately referred to the Milanese period is indicated by the large number of similar compositions in manuscript in the Milan Conservatorio which, exhibiting the same characteristics, are definitely labelled, 'Del Sig^re Bach in Milano'.[2] Some eighteen years after Bach's death, Theobald Monzani published a Trio by him 'composed for the Rig^t Honble Earl of Abingdon',[3] and therefore in Bach's English period. In it Bach follows the Sonata form: the first and last movements are *Allegros*, while the middle one, though not so described, is a Minuet. The British Museum owns another in manuscript, similar in construction,[4] which may be assigned to the same period. Another,[5] in E flat, at Carlsruhe, is also in three movements, though the middle *Adagio* is not in Minuet form. A third, also in E flat, is in private hands at Danzig.[6] It must be concluded, therefore, that, though Bach did not write much in the Trio form in England, he discarded the traditions which guided him at Milan, and had reached the stage from which Haydn carried the Trio to perfection.

Of Bach's Quartets only one set (Op. 8) was published in his lifetime. A second appeared posthumously as Op. 19 a few years after his death. Three quartets, in association with others by Abel and Giardini, were published by Napier in 1777; André published another (in G major)[7]—fourteen in all. Three more exist in arrangements made by John Christian Luther, and at Uppsala are two others in MS. which may be attributed to him. Schökel,[8] who indicates only nine of these nineteen compositions, refers those of Op. 8 to Bach's early residence in London. Their publication

[1] *Infra*, p. 314.   [2] *Infra*, p. 317.   [3] *Infra*, p. 317.   [4] *Infra*, p. 319.
[5] *Infra*, p. 320.   [6] *Infra*, p. 320.   [7] *Infra*, p. 311.   [8] p. 78.

may, indeed, be placed in the middle seventies, but their two-movement form connects them so closely with the early Trios that, like them, they may have been composed for Count Litta's *Cappella*; indeed, a manuscript of No. 1 in the Thomasschule, Leipzig, is inscribed 'del Sig: G. C. Bach, Milano'.[1] They exhibit little understanding of Trio technique, the first violin usually receives the melody, while the other instruments generally furnish an accompaniment. Even in the Minuetto con Variazioni of No. 4, a singularly beautiful theme:

----

[1] Edited by Riemann for Hermann Beyer's edition.

the variations, elementary in design, are exclusively presented by the first violin.

Op. 19 belongs to Bach's later English period. Its title-page declares it to have been composed for the Earl of Abingdon, a patron of the Bach–Abel concerts, while the fact that all four quartets are in Sonata form also dates it. They are very Haydnish in character, and the *Allegro assai* of the second is built upon a theme obviously reminiscent:

The set also differs from its predecessor in that it was not written for strings exclusively: the two upper parts are taken either by two flutes or a flute and oboe. The André Quartet was written for the harpsichord, violin, and two violoncelli, while those preserved in Luther's arrangements also admitted a keyboard instrument.

Bach's Quintets, nine in number, are found in his Op. 11, the posthumous Op. 22, and a single example in B flat published at Paris.[1] The dedication of Op. 11 to the Elector Palatine dates its composition about 1772; its association with the Hanover Square concerts may therefore be inferred. The two Quintets in Op. 22, being found in Luther's set already referred to, were therefore dedicated to the Earl of Abingdon and date from the same period. That all were designed for the concert platform rather than private performance is suggested by the grouping of the instruments (flute, oboe, violin, viola, bass) to form two bodies of tone, as in the Symphonies for two orchestras, or the harpsichord Sonata for four hands. Bach's only Sextet must also be associated with his activities as a concert-giver; it is written for harpsichord or pianoforte, oboe, violin, violoncello, and two horns.

Violin Music.

The taste of Bach's generation favoured pieces for the harpsichord or pianoforte 'with an accompaniment' for another instrument, generally the violin or German flute. Such compositions were in considerable request for domestic use, and Bach supplied them liberally. His Op. 10, 15, 16, (18), (19), 20 contain thirty-three compositions of this character. With two exceptions, they are in two movements, the second being almost invariably marked *Tempo di Minuetto* or *Rondeau*. Simplicity and tunefulness are their characteristics, and, inverting later usage, the violin is the

[1] *Infra*, p. 305.

accompanying, rather than the solo instrument, playing at the octave, in unison, or thirds, but rarely stating the theme alone. The dedication of Op. 16[1] to Miss Greenland indicates the purpose to which these simple pieces were put; they might usefully be revived. No. 2 of Op. 16 displays in its *Andante grazioso* the agreeable simplicity that marks them all:

It is interesting to observe that the opening bars of Op. 10, No. 3, quote Sebastian Bach's first Partita (B flat) in the first part of the *Clavierübung*.[2] Six Violin duets, published by Longmans and Lukey, *circa* 1775, though more advanced than the Pianoforte-Violin Sonatas, also must have been chiefly intended for use as exercises.

Pianoforte Works.

Having regard to Bach's popularity as a player and teacher, it is curious that so little of his published music was written for his peculiar instrument. His earliest set of harpsichord Sonatas (Op. 5) appeared in 1768. Op. 17, containing six more, was published eleven years later, while three others—making fifteen

[1] *Infra*, p. 325.   [2] B.G. iii. 46.

in all—were issued posthumously by Bonin (Paris). The Thematic
Catalogue indicates a considerable quantity of 'arrangements' of
other works for the instrument, and many unpublished pieces.
Otherwise, only two other prints call for notice—the two sets of
'Progressive Lessons', the later of which has already been dis-
cussed in connexion with the Bach–Ricci manual.[4]

It is at once evident that Bach, like his contemporaries, preferred the two-movement Sonata form, though in the 'Six Progressive Lessons' the three-movement scheme predominates, as
in Carl Philipp Emanuel Bach's Sonatas. But apart from form,
Bach's Sonatas reveal him completely master of the technique
of his instrument. They are consistently simple and almost invariably in two-part harmony; chording is rare in either hand, and
a sequence of thirds, generally speaking, is the utmost difficulty
that faces the player. There is neither depth of feeling nor pro-
fundity of expression in compositions which declare their peda-
gogic purpose on every page. The Andante of Op. 5, No. 2, may
serve as an example of their melodious simplicity:

Military Music.

Bach's many-sidedness faces us unexpectedly in a number of military marches written for regiments in Continental service. The Court's connexion with Hanover and Mecklenburg-Strelitz accounts for those he wrote for regiments on their establishments. Others are indicated in the Thematic Catalogue. They exhibit Bach's complete ability to furnish the kind of music required, but otherwise invite no comment.

CARL PHILIP EMANUEL BACH.

1. CARL PHILIP EMANUEL BACH

Prospect der Königlichen Opern-Hauses zu Berlin.

2. THE OPERA HOUSE, BERLIN, 1750

3. JOHN CHRISTIAN BACH, *circa* 1754

4. GIOVANNI BATTISTA MARTINI

Veduta della Chiesa di S. Francesco de' PP. Min. Conventuali in Bologna
Per Pergoli Int. for. Tom. 01..

5. CHIESA DI SAN FRANCESCO, BOLOGNA, 1760

6. JOHN CHRISTIAN BACH

Prospetto interiore della Chiesa di S. Fedele de' P.P.
della Compagnia di Giesu.

7. CHIESA DI SAN FEDELE, MILAN

8. BACH'S MUSICAL AUTOGRAPH, 1758
(*Magnificat in* C)

9. THE KING'S THEATRE, 1783

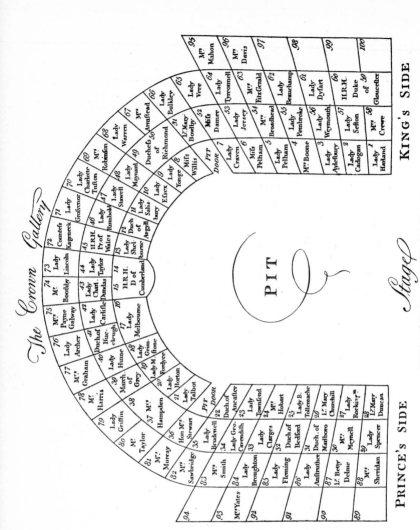

The Crown Gallery

PIT

Stage

Published 1st March 1785 by J. Fielding Pater Noster Row.

10. THE KING'S THEATRE, 1783.

KING'S SIDE

PRINCE'S SIDE

OPERA HOUSE or KINGS THEATRE in the HAY-MARKET.

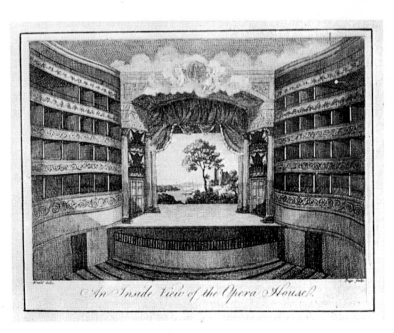

An Inside View of the Opera House.

11. THE KING'S THEATRE

12. CARL FRIEDRICH ABEL

13. SOHO SQUARE AND ITS ENVIRONS, 1763

14. SOHO OR KING'S SQUARE, LOOKING NORTH

A Merry Andrew Street.
B Thrift Street.

C Greg Street.
D Sutton Street.

Kings Square in Soho.

15. SOHO OR KING'S SQUARE, LOOKING SOUTH

16. THE NEW CARLISLE HOUSE, 1764

Mrs Teresa Cornelys.

17. TERESA CORNELYS

18. OLD CARLISLE HOUSE, MAIN STAIRCASE

19. OLD CARLISLE HOUSE, CONVERSAZIONE ROOM

20. DOMENICO ANGELO

21. MRS. ANGELO

22. OLD VAUXHALL GARDENS

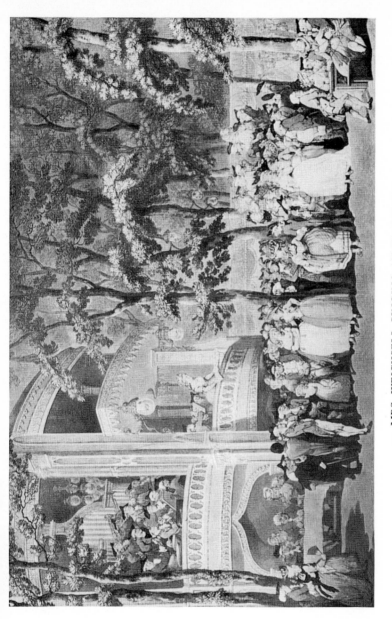

23. MRS. WEICHSELL SINGING AT VAUXHALL

24. ALMACK'S, 1767

Instruction of

Mʳ. TENDUCCI,
to his Scholars.

Publish'd by Longman & Broderip. Nº 26 Cheapside & 13 Haymarket.

25. FERDINANDO TENDUCCI

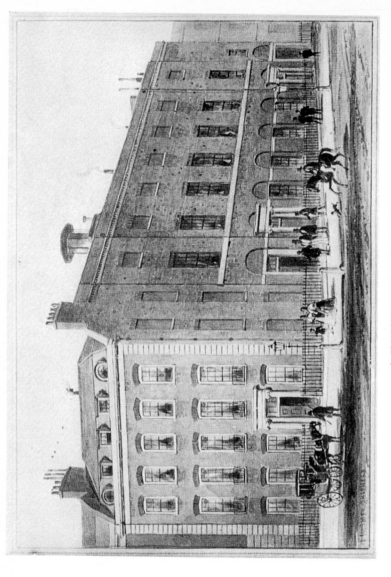

26. HANOVER SQUARE ROOMS

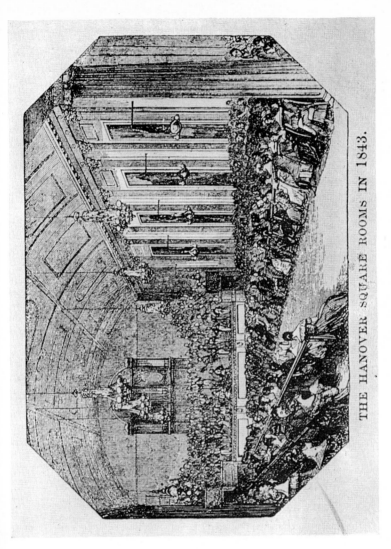

THE HANOVER SQUARE ROOMS IN 1843.

27. HANOVER SQUARE ROOMS, 1843

28a. A BACH-ABEL CONCERT TICKET

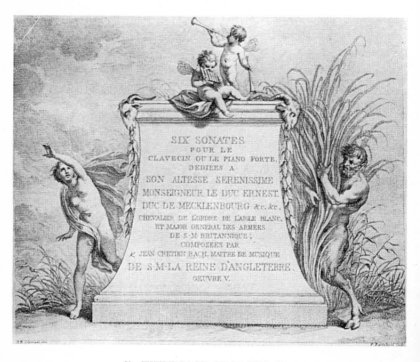

28b. TITLE-PAGE OF BACH'S OP. 5

MONS.ᴿ VESTRIS Jun.ʳ in the favorite Ballet
(call'd) LES AMANS SURPRIS.

29. M. VESTRIS, JUNIOR, 1781

Signora Baccelli in the Ballet (call'd) Les Amans Surpris

30. SIGNORA BACCELLI, 1781

31. JOHN CHRISTIAN BACH
(*the Hillingdon portrait*)

IOANNES CHRISTIANUS BACH,
SAXONIAE NATUS,
INSIGNIS MUSICAE MAGISTER
XLV.° AETATIS ANNO
OBIIT LONDINI.
KAL. IANUARII A.D. MDCCLXXXII

32. JOHN CHRISTIAN BACH

JOHN CHRISTIAN BACH'S WORKS
VOCAL AND INSTRUMENTAL
THEMATIC CATALOGUE

CONTENTS

VOCAL MUSIC

(a) Sacred

I. Church Music 199

(b) Secular

II. Operas 211
III. English Comedies and Cantatas . . . 243
IV. Italian Cantatas and Arias . . . 247
V. English Songs 254
VI. Vocal Duets 259

INSTRUMENTAL MUSIC

(c) Orchestral

VII. Symphonies and Overtures . . . 262
VIII. Concerted Symphonies 284
IX. Pianoforte Concertos 292

(d) Chamber Music

X. Sextets 302
XI. Quintets 303
XII. Quartets 306
XIII. Trios 313

(e) Violin Music

XIV. Violin and Pianoforte 322
XV. Violin Duets 335

(f) Pianoforte Music

XVI. Sonatas and Arrangements . . . 338

(g) Military Music

XVII. Marches 359
Index 363

SOURCES AND ABBREVIATIONS

AAR.	Aarhus, Statsbiblioteket.
BAS.	Basel, Universitätsbibliothek.
BER.	Berlin, Preussische Staatsbibliothek.
BER(H).	Berlin, Hochschule für Musik.
BER(S).	Berlin, Sing-Akademie.
BITT.	Bitterfeld, Kantoreigesellschaft.
BM.	London, British Museum.
BOL.	Bologna, Biblioteca del Liceo Musicale 'G. B. Martini'.
BONN.	Bonn, Universitätsbibliothek.
BRUN.	Brunswick, Landestheater.
BRUSS.	Brussels, Conservatoire Royal de Musique.
BUCK.	Bückeburg, Fürstl. Institut für Musikwissenschaft.
COP.	Copenhagen, Kongelige Bibliotek.
DAN.	Danzig, Stadtbibliothek.
DARM.	Darmstadt, Landesbibliothek.
DRES.	Dresden, Sächsische Landesbibliothek.
EINS.	Einsiedeln, Benediktiner Kloster.
FLO.	Florence, R. Conservatorio di Musica.
GOT.	Gotha, Herzogliche Bibliothek.
HAG(M).	The Hague, Muziek-Historisch Museum (D. F. Scheurleer).
HAMB.	Hamburg, Staats- und Universitätsbibliothek.
KARL.	Karlsruhe, Badische Landesbibliothek.
KON.	Königsberg, Staats- und Universitätsbibliothek.
KREMS.	Kremsmünster, Stifts-Musikarchiv.
LAMB.	Lambach, Stiftsbibliothek.
LEIPZ.	Leipzig, Stadtbibliothek.
LUB.	Lübeck, Stadtbibliothek.
LUN.	Lüneburg, Ratsbücherei.
MAIH.	Maihingen, Prinz Öttingen-Wallersteinsche (Universitäts-) Bibliothek.
MIL.	Milan, R. Conservatorio di Musica.
MUNCH.	Munich, Bayerische Staatsbibliothek.
MUNST.	Münster, Universitätsbibliothek.
NAP.	Naples, R. Conservatorio di Musica.
PAR.	Paris, Bibliothèque Nationale.
PAR(C).	Paris, Conservatoire National de Musique et de Déclamation.
PAR(Ste. G).	Paris, Bibliothèque Ste.-Geneviève.
RAM.	London, Royal Academy of Music.
RCM.	London, Royal College of Music.

REG.   Regensburg, Fürstl. Thurn und Taxissche Bibliothek.
ROS.   Rostock, Universitätsbibliothek.
SCHW.   Schwerin, Mecklenburgische Landesbibliothek.
STOCK.   Stockholm, Kungl. Musikaliska-Akademien.
TUB.   Tübingen, Universitätsbibliothek.
TUR.   Turin, Biblioteca Nazionale.
UPS.   Uppsala, Kungl. Universitetets Bibliotek.
WEI.   Weimar, Landesbibliothek.
WERNIG.   Wernigerode, Fürstl. Stolberg'sche Bibliothek.
WIEN.   Vienna, National-Bibliothek.
WIEN(M).   Vienna, Gesellschaft der Musikfreunde.
WOLF.   Wolfenbüttel, Herzog-August-Bibliothek.
ZWICK.   Zwickau, Ratsschulbibliothek.

VOCAL MUSIC

(a) SACRED

I. CHURCH MUSIC

LET THE SOLEMN ORGANS BLOW.   An Anthem for the use of Magdalen Chapel. By the Rev. W. Dodd, Chaplain to the King. Set to Music by Mr. Bach, Composer to Her Majesty [1765].

Let   the   so - lemn   or - gans   blow

'The Christian's Magazine; or, A Treasury of Divine Knowledge vol. vi, p. 140 (BM. PP. 324 n.).

In manuscript

AD COENAM AGNI

Allegro.

1

EINS. 389, 5 (Tenor, Strings).

Allegro.

2

EINS. 390, 5 (Tenor, Strings).

ATTENDITE MORTALES.   Motetto a Violino primo, Violino secondo, due Flauti, due Oboe, due Corni ex B et D, due Clarini ex D, Tympana, Viola, con Organo.

Recit.

At - ten - di - te   mor - ta - les,   vi - gi - la - te

Aria.

Cor - dis   di - lec - te spon - se,   di - lec - te   spon - se

Recit.

For - ti   er - go   fid - e ar - ma - ti

Allegro spiritoso.

Al - le - lu - ia

BER. Mus. MS. 30, 127 ('für Raaf in München componirt').

AVE CORPUS CHRISTI

Allegro.

A - ve cor - - pus Chris - ti

(See Operas, 'Temistocle', Atto I.)

EINS. 697, 10 (Soprano, Strings, Oboes, Horns, Bassoon).

AVE MARIS STELLA

Larghetto.

(See Italian Cantatas, 'Endimione', No. 6.)

EINS. 697, 17 (An operatic Aria: 'Grato sonno amato'). (Soprano, Strings, Flutes, Horns.)

BEATUS VIR

Allegro non tanto.

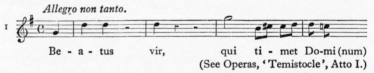

Be - a - tus vir, qui ti - met Do-mi (num)

(See Operas, 'Temistocle', Atto I.)

EINS. 697, 18 (Soprano, Strings, Flutes).

Andante.

Be - a - tus vir qui ti - met

(See Operas, 'Temistocle', Atto I.)

EINS. 697, 14 (Alto, Strings, Horns).

Allegro moderato.

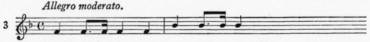

HAMB. MS. ND. vi. 540, No. 14 (Autograph: 'Milano 1758'); EINS. 391, 4 (S. A. T. B., Strings, Oboes, Horns, Organ).

BENEDICTUS

Andantino.

Bene - dic - tus Ma - ri - ae   Fi - li - us

(See Operas, 'Temistocle', Atto II.)

EINS. 697, 3 (Soprano duet, Strings, Oboes, Horns).

CHRISTUM REGEM ADORAMUS

Allegro.

Chri - stum,   Chri - - stum re - gem

(See Operas, 'Orfeo', No. 1.)

EINS. 697, 7 (Alto, Strings, Oboes, Horns).

CONFITEBOR

Andante.

1

Con - fi - te - bor   (See Operas, 'Temistocle', Atto II.)

EINS. 697, 19 (Tenor, Strings).

Allegretto.

2

EINS. 390, 1 (Alto, Tenor, Strings).

Andante.

3

Con - - fi - te - - bor ti - - bi
Bo - - ne pas - - tor pa - - nis

EINS. 391, 5 (Soprano duet, Strings, Oboes, Horns, Organ).

Tempo giusto.

4

(See Italian Arias, 'Oh dei'.)

EINS. 697, 12 (Soprano, Strings).

Andante con moto.

5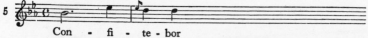

Con - fi - te - bor

(See Operas, 'Temistocle', Atto I.)

EINS. 697, 15 (Tenor, Strings, Clarinets, Horns).

Allegro moderato.

HAMB. MS. ND. 540, No. 8 (Autograph: '1759'); EINS. 390, 3; MUNCH.; PAR (C). (S. A. T. B., Strings, Oboes, Horns, Organ.)

COR MUNDUM

Largo.

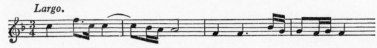

EINS. 389, 2 (Soprano, Strings, Horns).

CREDO

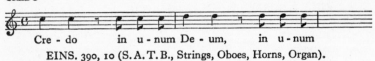

Cre - do   in u - num De - um,   in u - num

EINS. 390, 10 (S. A. T. B., Strings, Oboes, Horns, Organ).

DIES IRAE, a 8 Reali

Allegro moderato.

BER. Mus. MS. Bach 976; BOL.; DRES. 3374/D1; EINS. 388, 2; MUNCH (S. S. A. A. T. T. B. B., Strings, Oboes, Horns, Organ).

DISPERSIT

EINS. 389, 2 (S. A. T. B., Strings, Oboes, Horns).

DIXIT DOMINUS

Allegro vivace.

BOL.; EINS. 388, 5 (S. A. T. B., Strings, Oboes, Horns, Organ).

DOMINE AD ADIUVANDUM

Allegro spiritoso.

Allegro spiritoso.

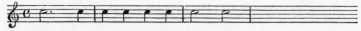

Do - mi - ne ad ad - iu - van - dum

BM. Royal Music, 24 a. 6 (S. A. T. B., Strings).

Allegro.

HAMB. MS. ND. vi. 540, No. 5 (Autograph: '1760'); EINS. 389, 3 and 391, 1 (S. A. T. B., Strings, Oboes, Horns, Organ).

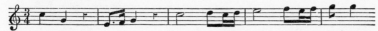

HAMB. MS. ND. vi. 540, No. 1 (Autograph: '1758').

DOMINE DEUS

Allegro con spirito.

EINS. 389, 2 (Soprano, Alto, Bass, Strings, Oboes, Horns, Organ).

ET SECUNDUM

Allegretto.

EINS. 389, 2 (Tenor, Strings).

EXULTET COELUM

Allegro.

EINS. 390, 6 (Alto, Strings).

Allegretto.

Ex-ul - tet coe - lum   lau-di-bus

(See Operas, 'Temistocle', Atto II.)

EINS. 697, 13 (Soprano, Strings).

GLORIA IN EXCELSIS

Allegro di molto.

1

Allegro di molto.

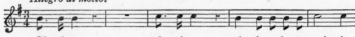

Glo-ri-a, - - glo-ri-a, - glo-ri-a in ex-cel-sis

BER. P. 385; DARM.; EINS. 388, 6; KON.; LEIPZ. III. 2. 16
(S. A. T. B., Strings, Oboes, Horns).

Allegro maestoso.

2

HAMB. MS. ND. vi. 540, No. 13 (Autograph: '1759'); EINS. 388,
1 (S. A. T. B., Strings, Oboes, Horns, Organ).

GLORIA PATRI (di ' Beatus vir ')

Andante.

EINS. 389, 3 (Tenor, Strings).

GRATIAS AGIMUS

Andante.

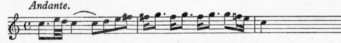

EINS. 389, 7 (Soprano, Strings, Oboes, Organ).

KYRIE

Con spirito (Messa a più voci)

1

BM. Royal Music, 24 a. 6 (S. A. T. B., Strings, Oboes).

(Messa in pastorale)

2

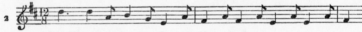

BM. Royal Music, 24 a. 6 (S. A. T. B., Strings).

Vivace.

3

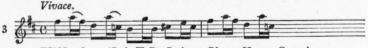

EINS. 389, 9 (S. A. T. B., Strings, Oboes, Horns, Organ).

LAETATUS SUM

Allegro.

EINS. 389, 8 (Soprano, Strings, Flutes, Clarinets).

LARVAE TREMENDAE

Allegro con brio.

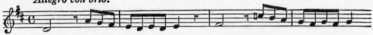

EINS. 389, 6 (Soprano, Strings, Oboes, Horns).

LAUDA JERUSALEM

Allegretto.

Lau - da Je - ru - sa-lem Do - mi-num

(See Cantatas, 'Endimione', No. 4.)

EINS. 697, 11 (Soprano, Strings, Clarinets, Horns).

LAUDA SION

Allegro.

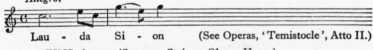

Lau - da   Si - on   (See Operas, 'Temistocle', Atto II.)

EINS. 697, 20 (Soprano, Strings, Oboes, Horns).

LAUDAMUS TE

Andante.

HAMB. MS. ND. vi. 540, No. 3 (Autograph: 'a 4 Conc. con Sinfonie, 1758').

LAUDATE PUERI

Andante.

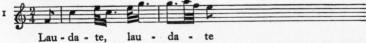

Lau - da - te,   lau - da - te

(See Operas, 'Temistocle', Atto III.)

EINS. 697, 6 (Soprano, Strings).

Allegro.

2

Lau - da - - - te pu - er - i,   lau - da - te

HAMB. MS. ND. 540, No. 12 (Autograph: '1760'); BER. P. 386;
DARM.; EINS. 389, 2 and 390, 9 (Soprano, Tenor, Strings, Oboes,
Horns).

Andante.

3

Lau - da - te   puer - i

(See Operas, 'Temistocle', Atto I.)

EINS. 697, 8 (Soprano, Strings).

4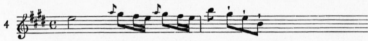

HAMB. MS. ND. vi. 540, No. 15 (Autograph: 'Milano 12 Ag. 1758').
(Soprano con Sinfonia.)

LEZIONI DEL OFFICIO PER GLI MORTI

Andante.   (Parce mihi, Domine)

1

HAMB. MS. ND. vi. 540, No. 11 (Autograph: '1757'); EINS. 388, 3
(Soprano, Strings, Oboes, Horns).

(Taedet animam meam)
Andante.

2

HAMB. MS. ND. vi. 540, No. 4 (Autograph: '1757'); EINS. 388, 3
(Bass, Strings, Horns).

(Manus tuae)
Adagio.

3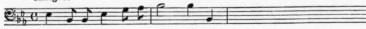

HAMB. MS. ND. vi. 540 No. 6 (Autograph: '1757'); EINS. 388, 3
(Soprano, Strings, Oboes, Horns, Organ).

LIBERA ME

Allegro.

Li - be - ra me de san-gui - ni - bus

EINS. 389, 2 (S.A.B., Strings, Oboes, Horns).

MAGNIFICAT

Adagio.   *Allegro moderato.*

Mag - ni - fi - cat,   Mag-ni - fi-cat a - ni-ma me-a Do-mi-num

BM. Royal Music, 22 a. 13 (Autograph: '1758'); RCM. No. 1656
(S. S. A. A. T. T. B. B., Strings, Trumpets, Organ).

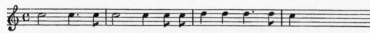

Mag - ni - fi - cat a - ni-ma me-a Do-mi - num

BM. Royal Music, 22 a. 11 (Autograph, incomplete: *c.* 1758) (S.S.A.A.
T. T. B. B., Strings, Organ).

Allegro.

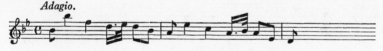

Mag - ni - fi - cat   a - ni-ma me-a   Do - mi - num

BM. Royal Music, 22 a. 12 (Autograph: '1760'); EINS. 391, 2 (S. A.
T. B., Strings, Oboes, Trombe da caccia, Horns, Organ).

MISERERE

Adagio.

HAMB. MS. ND. vi. 540, No. 10 (Autograph: '1757'); EINS. 391,
3; MUNCH. (S. A. T. B., Strings, Oboes, Horns, Organ).

NISI DOMINUS

Allegretto.

EINS. 390, 8 (Soprano, Tenor, Strings, Horns).

Andante.

Ni - si   Do - mi - nus

(See Operas, 'Temistocle', Atto III.)

EINS. 697, 16 (Soprano, Strings, Horns).

O GLORIOSA DOMINA

Allegro.

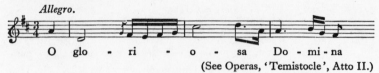

O glo - ri - o - sa   Do - mi - na

(See Operas, 'Temistocle', Atto II.)

EINS. 390, 13 (Alto, Strings, Oboes, Horns).

O IESU MI DILECTE

Larghetto.

O Iesu mi di - lec - te

(See Operas, 'Catone', Atto III.)

EINS. 697, 5 (Tenor, Strings, Oboe, Bassoon).

O LUX BEATA TRINITAS

Andantino.

EINS. 390, 12 (Alto, Strings, Oboes, Horns).

REGEM CUI OMNIA VIVUNT: Invitatorio

Re - - - gem cu - i om - - ni - a   vi - vunt

HAMB. MS. ND. vi. 540, No. 2 (Autograph: '1757'); EINS. 390, 7
(S. A. T. B., Strings, Oboes, Horns).

REQUIEM AND KYRIE ('Messa de' Morti')

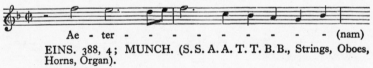

Ae - ter - - - - - - - - - (nam)

EINS. 388, 4; MUNCH. (S. S. A. A. T. T. B. B., Strings, Oboes,
Horns, Organ).

SALVE REGINA

Maestoso.

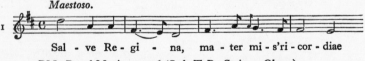

Sal - ve Re - gi - na,   ma - ter mi - s'ri - cor - diae

BM. Royal Music, 24 a. 6 (S. A. T. B., Strings, Oboes).

Largo.

WIEN. SA. 67 B. 36 (Soprano, Strings, Oboes, Horns).

Andante di molto.

Salve, sal - - ve Re - gi - na

(See Operas, 'Temistocle', Atto II.)

EINS. 697, 4 (Soprano, Strings).

Largo.

Largo.

Sal - ve Re - gi - na, ma - ter mis er - i - cor-di-ae

BM. Add. MSS. 29,293 (Autograph: ?1758) (Soprano, Strings, Oboes, Horns).

SI NOCTE TENEBROSA (Motetto)

Allegro.

Allegro.

Si noc - te te - ne - bro - sa

BM. Add. MSS. 14183, fol. 91; BER. Mus. MS. 30127 ('für Raaf componirt') (Soprano, Strings, Oboes, Trumpets; or Strings, Oboes, Horns, Organ).

TANTUM ERGO

Largo.

HAMB. MS. ND. vi. 540, No. 7 (Autograph: '1759'); EINS. 390, 14 (S. A. T. B., Strings, Flutes, Horns, Trumpets, Organ).

Largo.

Tantum tum, tan - tum

(See Operas, 'Temistocle', Atto I.)

EINS. 697, 9 (Soprano, Strings, Oboes, Horns).

Largo.

HAMB. MS. ND. vi. 540, No. 9 (Autograph: '1757'); EINS. 390, 11 (Soprano, Strings, Oboes, Horns).

TE DEUM

Te De - um lau-da-mus

BM. Royal Music, 22 a. 14 (Autograph: '1758') (S. S. A. A. T. T. B. B., Strings, Oboes, Horns, Trumpets, Timpani).

Allegro maestoso.

Allegro maestoso.

Te De-um lau-da-mus

BM. Royal Music, 22 a. 15 (Autograph: '1762'); EINS. 391, 6; MUNCH. (S. A. T. B., Strings, Oboes, Trumpets, Organ).

VOCAL MUSIC

(b) SECULAR

II. OPERAS

The Favourite Songs in the Opera Adriano in Siria. Composed by
Sig[r]. Bach. Price 7/6. [London: Welcker. ? 1765.]

Produced at the King's Theatre, London, 26 January 1765

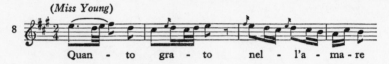

(*Miss Young*)

Quan - to   gra - to   nel - l'a - ma - re

Largo. (*Signore Manzuoli*)

Ca - - - ra,   ca - ra la dol - ce   fiam-ma

Andante. (*Signore Tenducci*)

Dal   lab - bro che t'ac - cen - de   di co - sì dol-ce ar - dor

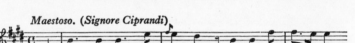

Maestoso. (*Signore Ciprandi*)

Le - on   pia - ga - to a   mor - te,   pia - ga-to a   mor - te

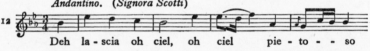

Andantino. (*Signora Scotti*)

Deh la - scia oh ciel, oh   ciel   pie - to - - so

BM. H. 348 c (1); BM. G. 760 b (4) (Nos. 1–4 only); BM. Royal Music, 3 copies; BER. Hausbibl. No. 130; BOL.; BRUSS. No. 5411; TUR.

In manuscript

Nos. 1–7: BER. Hausbibl. No. 137.
No. 2: WOLF. No. 14.

Alessandro nell' Indie

Produced at Naples, 20 January 1762

ATTO I

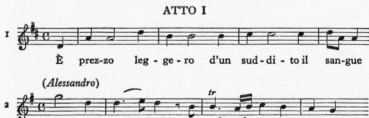

È   prez-zo   leg - ge - ro   d'un sud - di - to il   san-gue

(*Alessandro*)

Vil   tro - fe - o   d'un al - - ma im - bel - le
(Original in Tenor Clef.)

(*Timagene*)

3. O su-glie-sti-vi ar-do-ri   pla - - ci-da al sol
(Original in Tenor Clef.)

4. Se   mai   più   sa - rò . ge - lo - so

(*Cleofide*)

5. Se   mai tur - - bo   il tu - o   ri - po - so

(*Gandarte*)

6. Se pos - so - no   tan - to   due lu - ci   vez - zo - se

7. Com - pa - gni   nel - l'a - mo - re

(*Alessandro*)

8. Se a - mo - re a ques-to pet - to   non fos - se ig-no-to fat - to
(Original in Tenor Clef.)

(*Poro*) Recit.

9. Lo - de a gli de - i,   son per - sua-so al fi - ne
(Segue Aria.)

(*Cleofide : Poro*)

10. Se . . mai tur - bo il tuo . . ri - po - so

ATTO II

(*Erissena*)

11. Non sa - re - i   sì   sven - tu - ra - ta

12 (*Poro*)
Oh Di - o, la man mi tre - ma, pal - pi - ta il cor nel

13 (*Cleofide*)
Di - gli ch'io son fe - - de - le

14 (*Poro*)
De - strier ch'all'ar - mi u - sa - - - - - (to)

15 (*Alessandro*)
S'è ver che t'ac - cen - di di no - bi - li ar - do - ri
(Original in Tenor Clef.)

16 (*Cleofide*)
Se il ciel mi di - vi - de dal ca - ro mio spo - so

17
Di ren - der - mi la cal - - - - ma

ATTO III

18 (*Cleofide*)
Se trop - po cre - de al ci - glio

19 (*Alessandro*)
Non so . d'on - de vie - ne quel te - ne - ro af - fet - to
(Original in Tenor Clef.)

20
Tra - fig - ge - rò quel co - re che di per - fi - de

21 (*Gandarte*)
Mio ben, ri - cor - da - ti se av - vien ch'io mo - ra

(Erissena)

22

Son con - fu - sa pa - sto - rel - la

(Cleofide)

23

Om - bra del ca - ro, del ca - ro spo - so

In manuscript

Score: NAP.; PAR (C).
Nos. 2, 10, 16, 19: PAR (C) ('Airs: Partition d'orchestre').
No. 5: BRUSS. No. 3705; WEI. 349, fol. 59.
No. 6: BRUSS. No. 3706; RCM. No. 2068.
Nos. 9, 10: BOL.; BRUN. No. 47; COP.; DRES. 1/F./49, 9;
FLO. D. 1618; HAMB. BM. Royal Music, 23 d. 5/11 (as a Duet).
No. 12: RCM. No. 689.
No. 16: BM. Add. MSS. 14183, fol. 120. (See 'Ezio' *infra*.)
No. 19: BM. Add. MSS. 31817, fol. 77; 31578, fol. 33; BOL.;
DRES. 1/F./82, 2 ('aus Olimpiade, Palermo, 1764'); MUNCH.;
RCM. Nos. 2067, 2080. (See 'Ezio', *infra*.) As a Duet: BM. Royal
Music, 23 d. 5/11.

Amadis des Gaules. Tragedie lirique de Quinault, Reduite en
Trois Actes, Dediée a Monsieur de Caumartin, Grand Croix de
L'Ordre de St. Louis, Conseillier d'Etat, et Prevost des Mar-
chands de La Ville de Paris. Représentée pour la premiere fois au
théatre de l'Accademie Royale de Musique le Quinze [*sic*] decembre
1779. Mise en Musique par Jean Chretien Bach. Prix 30. [Paris:
Siéber. ? 1780.]

Produced at Paris, 14 December 1779

OVERTURE

1

(See Symphonies and Overtures.)

ACT I

Moderato. (*Arcabonne*)

2

Mon âme au-roit trop de pei - ne, trop de pei - ne

Allegro vivace. (*Arcabonne*)

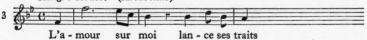

3

L'a - mour sur moi lan - ce ses traits

Allegro assai. (*Arcalaus*)

4
Ah! bri-sez vot-re chaî - ne

Allégro très vif. (*Arcabonne: Arcalaus*)

5
Qu'une hor-ri - ble ven - gean - ce   me con-sole en ce jour

Andante. (*Oriane: Amadis*)

6
Pour-quoi   me fuy-ez vous,   trop cru-el - le   Prin-ces-se

Larghetto. (*Amadis*)

7
Je ne ver-rai   plus ce   que   j'ai - me

(Original in Alto Clef.)

Andante. (*deux Coryphées*)

8
Mal - gré nous   l'A - mour nous en - chaî - ne

ACT II

Allegro di molto. (*Arcabonne*)

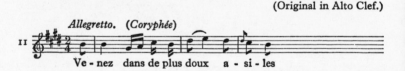

9
Bien-tôt l'en-ne-mi qui m'ou-tra - ge, l'en-ne-mi qui m'ou-tra-ge

Larghetto. (*Amadis*)

10
Ah   si votre â - me est at-ten - dri - e   par pi - tié

(Original in Alto Clef.)

Allegretto. (*Coryphée*)

11
Ve - nez   dans de plus doux   a - si - les

ACT III

Larghetto. (*Oriane*)

12
A qui pour-rai j'a - voir . . re - cours

(Arcabonne : Arcalaus)

Ah! quel plai - sir

Allegro assai. *(Arcalaus)*

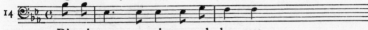

Dis - si - pons ces vai - nes al - lar - mes

BM. H. 740a; BRUSS. No. 1359; DARM.; PAR. Vm.² 478;
PAR (C); WIEN. SA. 83 B. 37.

In manuscript

Score: Musée de l'Opéra, Paris.
No. 7: STOCK.

Artaserse.

Produced at Turin, 1761

OVERTURE

Allegro di molto.

(See Symphonies and Overtures.)

ATTO I

Allegro di molto. *(Arbace)*

Fra cen - to af - fan - ni e cen - to

(Artaserse)

Per pie - tà, bel - l'i - - dol mi - o

Allegretto. *(Semira)*

Bra - mai di per - de-re per trop - po af - fet - to

Allegro. *(Semira)*

Tor - na inno - cen - te e po - i

Allegro. *(Mandane)*

Dim - mi ch'un em - pio sei

JOHN CHRISTIAN BACH

ATTO II

Allegro con espress. (Arbace)

10

Mi scac - ci sde - gna - to

Andante. (Mandane)

12

Se d'un a - - mor, a - mor . . ti - ran - no

Largo. (Arbace)

13

Per quel pa - ter - no am - ples - so per questo e - stremo

Allegro di molto. (Mandane)

14

Và, Và, Và tra le sel - ve ir - ca - ne

Allegro. (Semira)

15

Fra tan - ti miei tor - men - ti

Andante. (Artaserse)

16

Non co - no - sco in tal mo - men - to

(Artabano)

17

Co - sì stu - pi - sce e ca - de

ATTO III

Allegro. (Artaserse)

18

Nu - vo - letta op - posta al so - le

Allegro. (Megabise)

19

Ar - di - to ti ren - da, t'ac - cen - da di sde-gno

Allegro. (Artabano)

20

Fi - glio, se più non vi - vi

Allegro. (Mandane)

21

Mi cre-di spie-ta - ta, mi chia-mi cru - de - le

Larghetto. (Mandane and Arbace)

23

Tu voi ch'io vi - va, o ca - ra

In manuscript

Score: BM. Royal Music, 22 a. 18–20, 3 vols., each inscribed: 'This Volume belongs to the Queen 1788'.
No. 13: BOL. DD. 102; KON. No. 14028.
No. 17: BER. Mus. MS. Bach St. 286.

The Favorite Songs in the Opera Berenice. [London: Bremner. 1765.]

Produced at the King's Theatre, London, 1 January 1765

A Pasticcio, containing one Aria by Bach:

Andante espressivo. (Signora Scotti)

Con - fu - sa, smar - ri - ta spie - gar - ti vor - re - i

BM. G. 760 d (4); BER. Hausbibl. No. 131; BRUSS. No. 5425; TUR.; Paris, Bibl. de l'Arsenal, No. 95 ('Tremblante, mourante').

In manuscript

BM. Add. MSS. 14183, fol. 134; BER. Mus. MS. Bach St. 287 a; ROS. (See 'Catone', *infra*).

The Favourite Songs in the Opera Carattaco. Composed by John Christian Bach. [London: Welcker. 1768.]

Produced at the King's Theatre, London, 14 February 1767.

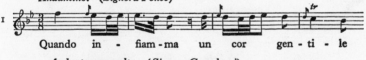

Andantino. (Signora Ponce)

1

Quando in - fiam - ma un cor gen - ti - le

Andante non molto. (Signore Guarducci)

2

Ca - ra spo - sa, a - ma - - ta fig - lia

Allegro. (Signora Piatti)

3

Ac - cen - der mi sen-to, d'ar - de - re di spe - me

BM. H. 740 c.; Royal Music, 2 copies; BER. Hausbibl. No. 132; BOL.
No. 2: published by Longman & Broderip (London) RCM.
No. 7: published by Hummel (Amsterdam) as 'Ariette italienne');
SCHW. (See English Songs).

In manuscript

Orchestral parts: BM. Royal Music 21 a. 11 and 12.
No. 1: BER. Bach Mus. MS. Bach St. 555.
Nos. 1-4, 9-12: BER. Hausbibl. No. 137.
No. 6: BER. Mus. MS. Bach St. 295; BER. Hausbibl. No. 140.
Nos. 7 and 8: BER. Hausbibl. No. 140.
No. 10: STOCK. (as 'Min Zephis'); WIEN. S. m. 3904.
No. 11: BER. Mus. MS. Bach St. 294.
No. 12: RCM. No. 769.

Carattaco.

Produced at the King's Theatre, London, 14 February 1767

The Manuscript contains the following movements which are not found in the 'Favourite Songs':

ATTO I

(*Coro*)

13   O - - Dio, giu - ra - mo

Allegro assai. (*Signora Moser*)

14   Per - fi - di,   per - fi - di, non o - sa - te

Andante maestoso. (*Signore Morigi*)

15   Al - lor che in cam-po ar-ma-to com-bat - te - rai più for-te

Allegretto. (*Mrs. Barthélemon*)

16   Se a quei   det - ti,   a quel - lo sde - gno

Allegro di molto. (*Signore Savoi*)

17   Va - no,   su - per - bo,   au - da - ce

Allegro. (*Coro*)

18   Vi - va O - stori - o   e vi-va Ro - ma

ATTO II

Andante. (*Cavatina*)

19   Trà l'or - ror   di tan - to   spa - ven - to

In manuscript

Score: BRUSS. No. 2039. (Each of the three volumes is inscribed:
'This volume belongs to the Queen 1788'. With other works from
that source it was acquired by Jean-Baptiste-Jules De Glimes (d. 1881),
whose large collection was bought by the Belgian Government for
the Conservatoire.)
Orchestral parts, BM. Royal Music, 21 a. 11 and 12.

Catone in Utica

Produced at Florence, 1761

OVERTURE

(See Symphonies and Overtures.)

ATTO I

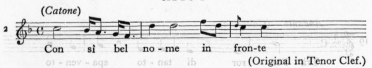

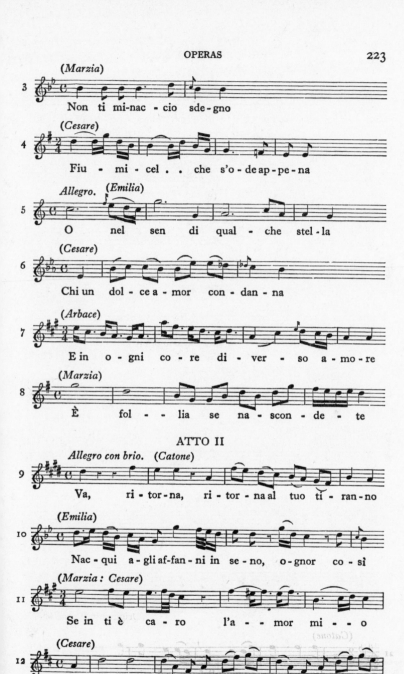

3 (*Marzia*)
Non ti mi-nac - cio sde-gno

4 (*Cesare*)
Fiu - mi - cel . . che s'o - de ap - pe - na

5 *Allegro.* (*Emilia*)
O nel sen di qual - che stel - la

6 (*Cesare*)
Chi un dol - ce a - mor con - dan - na

7 (*Arbace*)
E in o - gni co - re di - ver - so a - mo - re

8 (*Marzia*)
È fol - - lia se na - scon - de - te

ATTO II

9 *Allegro con brio.* (*Catone*)
Va, ri - tor - na, ri - tor - na al tuo ti - ran - no

10 (*Emilia*)
Nac - qui a - gli af - fan - ni in se - no, o - gnor co - sì

11 (*Marzia : Cesare*)
Se in ti è ca - ro l'a - - mor mi - - o

12 (*Cesare*)
Se in cam - po ar - - ma - to vuoi ci - men - tar - mi, vuoi ci - men -

13 (*Catone*)
Do - vea sve-nar-ti al - lo - ra che a - pri-sti al dì le
(Original in Tenor Clef.)

14 (*Marzia*)
So che go-den-do va - - i

15 (*Arbace*)
Co - sì . . ta - lor . . ri - mi - ra

ATTO III

16 (*Fulvio*)
La fron - - - da che cir - con - da
(Original in Tenor Clef.)

17 (*Marzia*)
Con - fu - sa, smar - ri - ta spie - gar - ti vor - re - i

18 (*Cesare*)
Quel - l'a - mor che po - co ac - cen - de

19 (*Marzia : Cesare : Emilia : Catone*)
Deh in vi - ta ti ser - ba

20 (*Catone*)
Vin - ce-sti i - ni - que stel - le
(Original in Tenor Clef.)

21 (*Catone*)
Per dar-vi al-cun pe-gno d'af-fet-to il mio co-re
(Original in Tenor Clef.)

In manuscript

Score: BRUN.; NAP.; PAR (C).
No. 1: BER. Hausbibl. No. 133.
No. 4: KON.; STOCK.
Nos. 5 and 6: DRES. 1 / F./82, 2.
No. 8: BER. Mus. MS. P. 846 ('Aria ad uso del Sig^re Antonio Muzio à Bronsvic, 1766').
No. 9: LUB. Mus. Q. 150.
No. 11: FLO. D. 1617.
No. 12: BOL.; STOCK.
No. 14, entitled 'Fra tanti miei tormenti': PAR (C).
No. 17: BM. Add. MSS. 14183, fol. 134; MIL. 958/4. (See 'Berenice', *supra*.)
No. 21: RCM. No. 691; MIL. 956/2; WIEN. S. m. 3903.
Nos. 2, 6, 9, 10, 17: BRUSS. Nos. 3698–70, 3702, 3709.

The Favorite Songs in the Opera Ezio. [London: Bremner. 1765.]

Produced at the King's Theatre, London, 24 November 1764

A Pasticcio, containing two Arias by Bach:

BM. H. 300 b; BER. Hausbibl. No. 139 (instrumental parts); BRUSS. No. 5450; HAMB.; TUR. (See 'Alessandro nell' Indie', *supra*.)

In manuscript

No. 1: BRUSS. No. 3703.

The favourite Songs and the Duett in the Oratori (*sic*) Gioas. Composed by John Christian Bach. Opera IX. Pr. 4s. [London: Welcker. 1770.]

Produced at the King's Theatre, London, 22 March 1770

Andantino. *(Signore Guadagni)*

T'a - do - ro,   te   so - lo,   pla - ca - to mio Di - o

Larghetto. *(Signora Grassi : Signore Guadagni)*

Guar - da-mi in volto o   ma - dre

BM. H. 348 c (3); Royal Music, 2 copies; BRUSS. No. 12137; RCM. No. 529.

In manuscript
No. 1: PAR (C) ('Airs et Duos, Partition d'orchestre').

Gioas Re di Giuda. Oratorio à 6 Voci con Cori. Compositione del Sig: Christiano Bach, Maestro di Sua Majesta La Regina della Gran Brettagna. In Londra 1770. Poesia del Sig. Metastasio

Produced at the King's Theatre, London, 22 March 1770

SINFONIA

[*Allegro.*]

Allegro.

Largo.

Allegretto.

PRIMA PARTE

Allegro commodo. *(Ismaele)*

Pian - ta   co - se - - co

3 Coro 1°.

Andantino. *(Gioas)*

Pen - sa nel tu - o - do - lor

5 *Allegro.* (*Sebia*)

Nel mi - rar le vo - glie, oh Di - o

6 *Allegro.* (*Gioiada*)

D'in - so - li - to va - lo - re sen - to

7 Coro 2do.

8 *Allegro.* (*Matan*)

Tem - pe - - ste il mar

9 *Andantino.* (*Atalia*)

Fi - gli - a, ra-sciu-ga il pian - to

10 *Allegro con spirito.* (*Sebia*)

Ven - di - ca e - ter - no Di - o

11 Coro 3°.

SECONDA PARTE

12 Coro 4to.

13 *Allegro.* (*Matan*)

Là nel suo tem - pio

14 *Allegro moderato.* (*Atalia*)

L'al - ma i - stes - sa che pal - pi - ta

15 *Allegretto.* (*Gioiada*)

Tu com - pir co - sì pro - cu - ra

16 *Allegro moderato.* (*Gioas*)

Sven - - tu - ra - to in van mi la - gno

Allegro moderato. (Ismaele)

Col - la . fe - de   il suo ca - mi - no

Larghetto. (Gioas and Sebia)

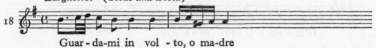

Guar - da - mi in vol - to, o ma - dre

19 Coro 5ᵗᵒ.

Allegretto. (Sebia)

Son . . pas - sa - - - ti lun - ghi af - fa - ni

Moderato. (Atalia)

Nel - l'or .. or   del - la . . . tem - pes - ta

22 Coro 6ᵗᵒ.

Andantino. (Gioas)

T'a - do - ro,   te so - lo,   pla - ca - to mio o - ro

24 Coro ultimo.

In manuscript

Score: WIEN S. m. 3091; WIEN (M). III. 14233; RCM. No. 24
(incomplete).
No. 1: See English Cantatas, 'Happy Morn'.
No. 9: See English Songs, 'No more with unavailing woe'.

The Favourite Songs in the Opera call'd La Calamità de Cuori.
[London: Walsh. 1763.]

Produced at the King's Theatre, London, 3 February 1763

A Pasticcio, containing one Aria by Bach:

Aria nell' Astarto [1762]. (*Signore Ciardini*) (*Signora de' Amicis*, 1763)

Pu - pil - la   vez - zo - sa   ch'il pi - an - to   stil - la

BM. G. 760 d (5).

La Clemenza di Scipione. A Favorite Opera as Perform'd at the
Kings Theatre. Composed by John Christian Bach, Music
Master to her Majesty and the Royal Family. Act I [II and III].
Opera XIV. [London: Welcker. 1778.]

Produced 4 April 1778

OVERTURE

Allegro assai.

(See Symphonies and Overtures.)

ACT I

Marcia.

Allegro moderato. (Signora Danzi)

Con - fu - - sa,   ab - ban - do - na - - ta

Andante. (Signora Prudom)

Al - lor che il vin - ci - to - re

Largo. (Signore Roncaglia)

Par - to,   ma serbo in men - te,   ma serbo in   men - te

Allegro maestoso. (Signore Adamberger)

Al - ma   na - ta   in   ri - va al Te - bro

Allegro. (Signore Coppola)

Pu - gna il guer - rier

Larghetto. (Signora Danzi)

Dal do - lor   co - tan - to op - pres - sa

Larghetto. (Signore Roncaglia : Signora Danzi)

Deh quel pian - to, o - mai ter - ge - te

ACT II

Allegretto. (*Signora Prudom*)

10

Nel - l'og - get - to che m'ac - cen - de

Allegro assai. (*Signore Adamberger*)

11

Frà le ca - te - ne av - vin - to

Larghetto. (*Signore Roncaglia*)

12

Fre - - - na le bel - - le la - gri - me

Allegro. (*Signore Coppola*)

13

Non o - di con - si - glio

Allegro maestoso. (*Signora Danzi*)

14

In - fe - li - ce, in van m'af - fan - no

Allegro. (*Signora Danzi, Signori Roncaglia, Adamberger*)

15

Tu mi di - vi - di al - te - ro, tu mi tra - dis - ci in - gra - ta

ACT III

Larghetto. (*Signore Roncaglia*)

16

De - i pie - to - si in tal ci - men - to

Andantino. (*Signore Roncaglia*)

17

Nel par - tir, bel - l'i - dol mi - o

Allegro assai. (*Signora Danzi*)

18

Ah si va - da, ma il pie - de va - cil - la

Maestoso. ('*March*')

(There are movements for Coro after Nos. 2, 10, 19.)

BM. H. 740; Royal Music, 11 a. 17; BRUSS. No. 2038 (Acts I and
II); HAMB.; PAR (C) (Act III only).
Nos. 2 and 19 are published together (London: Dale): BM. h. 62,
No. 16.
No. 4, published by Georg A. Walter (1919) as 'Wenn nach der
Stürme Toben'.
No. 9, published by Birchall (London): RCM. LXXI. 2. 12.
No. 14, published by Dale (London, ? 1785): BM. G. 811, No. 5.
No. 17, 'Sung by Miss Chann at Bath and at the Nobility's Concerts'
(London: Dale, ? 1785); BM. H. 345, No. 16; also in John Corri's
(Edinburgh) 'Select Collection of the Most Admired Songs', Vol. I,
p. 90; BM. I. 278; BRUSS. No. 17232; also, as 'En quittant l'objet
que j'aime', in the Bibl. de l'Arsenal, Paris, No. 95.

In manuscript

Score and parts: BRUN. No. 218.
No. 1: WOLF. No. 15.
No. 3: RCM. No. 25.
No. 9: BRUN. No. 219.
No. 14: WEI. 349, fol. 27.
No. 15: RAM.
No. 17: BRUN. No. 216; BUCK.
Coro 'S'oda il suon della tromba guerriera': BER. Mus. MS. 30015,
No. 9.

The Favorite Songs in the Opera Le Contadine Bizzarre. Del Sig^r.
Piccini. [London: Bremner. 1769.]

Produced at the King's Theatre, 7 Nov. 1769

Contains one Aria by Bach:

Allegro. (*Signore Piatti*)

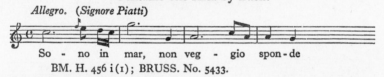

So - no in mar, non veg - gio spon - de

BM. H. 456 i (1); BRUSS. No. 5433.

The Favorite Songs in the Comic Opera L'Olimpiade. [London:
Bremner. 1770.]

Produced at the King's Theatre, London, 11 Nov. 1769

A Pasticcio, containing one Aria by Bach:

Andantino. (*Signore Guadagni*)

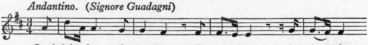

Quel lab - bro a - do - ra - to   m'è gra - to,   m'ac - cen - de

BM. 760 d (3); G. 760 f. (10–11); BRUSS. No. 5228; DARM. (See
English Songs, 'Farewell, ye soft scenes'.)

Lucio Silla

Produced at Mannheim, 20 Nov. 1776

OVERTURE

Allegro assai.

(See Symphonies and Overtures.)

ATTO I

(Cinna)

Vieni ove a - mor

(Cecilio)

Il te - - ne - ro .

(Celia)

Se tu in ghie - ra

(Giunia)

Dal - la spon-da te - ne - bro-sa

(Silla)

Nel - l'o - dio co - stan - to

(Original in Tenor Clef.)

ATTO II

(Aufidio)

Guer - rier che d'un ac(ciaro)

(Original in Tenor Clef.)

(Silla)

Anch' io per un' in(grata) (Original in Tenor Clef.)

(Celia)

Il lab - bro ti - mi-do

10 (Cinna)
Nel for - tu - na - to

11 (Silla)
D'o - gni pie - tà   mi spo - glio

(Original in Tenor Clef.)

12 (Cecilio)
Ah se a mo - rir, a morir

13 (Giunia)
Ah se il cru - del, cru - del . per

ATTO III

14 (Celia)
Stri - der sen - to

15 (Cinna)
Da' più su - per - bi il core

16 (Cecilio)
Pu - pil - la a - ma - ta

17 (Giunia)
Fra   i pen - sier   più fu - ne - sti

18 (Silla)
Se al ge - ne - ro-so ar - di - re

(Original in Tenor Clef.)

In manuscript

Score: DARM.
No. 2: WIEN. SA. 67 H. 60.

The Favourite Songs in the Opera Orfeo. [London: Bremner. 1770.]

Produced at the King's Theatre, London, 7 April 1770

Contains seven Airs by Bach:

BM. 760 a. 38; G. 760 e (1); BRUSS. No. 5472; PAR. Vm.⁴ 48.
Nos. 2 and 3 in 'A Valuable Collection of the most Favourite Songs, selected from the latest Italian Operas' [London: Welcker. 1776]; BM. g. 421 a (1).
No. 2, as 'Solfége emprunté à G. C. Bach', in 'Méthode de chant du Conservatoire de Musique . . . A Paris, A l'Imprimerie du Conservatoire de Musique. An 12'; BRUSS. No. 24058.

In manuscript

Instrumental parts: BER. Hausbibl. No. 134.
Nos. 1–3: BRUSS. Nos. 5225–27, 12,834.
No. 2: BER. Mus. MS. P. 389; KON.; PAR (C). ('Airs, Partition d'orchestre); WEI. 349, fol. 1.
No. 3: WEI. 349, fol. 11.
No. 5: BER. Mus. MS. Bach St. 292.

Orfeo ed Euridice, Orpheus and Euridice; An Opera, in the Grecian Taste. As Perform'd at the King's-Theatre in the Hay-
Market. [London: Griffin. 1770.]

'The Music as originally composed by Signor GLUCH, to which, in order
to make the Performance of a necessary length for an evening's entertainment, Signor BACH has very kindly condescended to add of his own new
composition, all such chorusses, airs, and recitatives, as are marked with
inverted commas, except those which are sung by Signora *Guglielmi*, and
they are likewise an entire new production of Signor GUGLIELMI, her
husband.

'The POETRY is from Signor CALZABIGI, with additions by G. G.
BOTTARELLI, of all that Messrs. *Bach* and *Guglielmi* have enriched
this Performance by their Music.
        Inmites potuit flectere cantibus umbrarum Dominos, Eurydicen
        dum repetit suam'

*1 'Non è ver il dir talora'
*2 'Per onor dell' offeso mio regno'
*3 'Chiari fonti, ermi ritiri'
*4 'Obbliar l'amato sposo'
*5 'Accorda amico il fato'
*6 'Dio d'Amor, de' plausi tuoi' (Coro)
*7 'Torna, o bella, al tuo consorte'

        Nos. 1, 3, 4, 5 are among the earlier published 'Favourite Songs' (q.v.).
        Bottarelli's libretto, which provides the text, but not the music of the
        rest, was prepared for the performance of the Opera on 7 April 1770.
        It was repeated several times in that year.

        BM. 11714 aa. 21/5; RCM XXI. A. 15.

The Favourite Songs in the Opera call'd Orione ossia Diana
vendicata. [London: Walsh. 1763.]

Produced at the King's Theatre, London, 19 February 1763

Andantino. (*Signore Ciardini*)

Be - ne a - do - ra - to, ad - di - o

2 *Allegretto.* (*Signora de' Amicis*)

Se ve - le - te e - ter - ni de - i

3 *Largo.* (*Signora de' Amicis*)

Di ques - t' al - ma de - so - la - ta

4 *Largo.* (*Signore Ciardini*)

Se mi è ca - - ro l' i - - dol mi - o

5 *Allegretto.* (*Signora Cremonini*)

A . . me ba - sta, o ca - - - ro Tir - si

6 *Allegro.* (*Signora de' Amicis*)

Si'l cor pen - sa un mar si - cu - ro

7 *Allegro assai.* (*Signora Segantini*)

Più ma - dre non so - no, o Per - so, il mio fi - glio

8 *Andante.* (*Signora Cremonini*)

An - drò dal col - le al pra - to le a - gnel - le a pa - sco - lar

BM. H. 348 c (2); Royal Music, 2 copies; BER. Hausbibl. No. 135;
BOL.; DARM.; HAMB.
The eight songs are also in ' Le Delizie dell' Opere ', Vol. 12 [London:
Walsh. 1776]; BM. G. 159.

In manuscript

BER. Hausbibl. No. 137.
No. 1: LUB. Mus. Q. 152.
No. 6: RCM. No. 2257; SCHW.
No. 8: LEIPZ. III. 15. 32.

Orione ossia Diana vendicata

Produced at the King's Theatre, London, 19 February 1763

Allegro con brio.

1

(See Symphonies and Overtures.)

Andante di molto. (*Enopione*)

2

Fre-ma cru-del - lo sdeg-no   del l'a-di-ra - ta
(Original in Tenor Clef.)

Largo ma non tanto. (*Candiope*)

3

Di ques - t'al - ma de - so-la - ta

4

Il fi-glio tu - o   la   de - a

Largo ma non tanto. (*Orione*)

5

Sì   mi è ca - - ro i - - dol mi - o

Allegro assai.

6

Più ma - dre non so - no,   o Per - so   il mio

Allegro maestoso.

7

Co - sì   stu-pi - scee ca - de

Allegro di molto.

8

Va   cru-de - le, va   ti-ran-no, no,   no che   pa - dre
(Original in Tenor Clef.)

Allegretto.

9

Se di - ri - so   dal   mio be - ne

In manuscript

Score: BM. Add. MSS. 31717. Another at St. Michael's College, Tenbury, No. 348. No. 9 (in the Tenbury Score) appears to be an addition: the words do not occur in Metastasio's libretto. A quartet and Coro intervene between Nos. 6 and 7.

No. 4: BM. Add. MSS. 31633, fol. 99 (assigned to a character 'Argia' and sung by Signora Carmignani).

The favourite Songs in the Opera Sifari. [London: Welcker. 1767.]

Produced at the King's Theatre, London, 5 March 1767

A Pasticcio, containing two Arias by Bach:

Fiu - mi - cel . . che s'o - de ap - pe - na

Se è ver che t'ac - cen - di   di   no - bi - li ar - do - ri

BM. H. 348 (5).

No. 1, in 'A Valuable Collection of the most Favourite Songs, selected from the latest Italian Operas' [London: Welcker. 1776]; BM. g. 421 a (1).

In manuscript

No. 1: STOCK.
Instrumental parts: BER. Hausbibl. No. 138.

Temistocle

Produced at Mannheim, 5 November 1772

OVERTURE

(See Symphonies and Overtures.)

ATTO I

Ch'io spe-ri,   ah,   ah, pa - dre a - ma - to,

Fo - sca nu - be   il   sol   ri - co-pra

(Original in Tenor Clef.)

Andante. *(Roxane)*

4

Ba - sta . dir . ch'io so - no a - man - te

Andante espress. *(Aspasia)*

5

Chi mai d'i - ni qua stel - la pro - va te-nor sì ri - o

Largo. *(Lysimachus)*

6

Ch'io par-ta, ch'io par-ta il co - man-do ta-cen-do ris-

Andante. *(Xerxes)*

7

Con - tra-sto as-sai . più deg - no, con - tra - sto as-sai . . più

Allegro. *(Temistocle)*

8

Non m'al-let - ta quel ri - so, quel ri - so fal - la - ce

(Original in Tenor Clef.)

ATTO II

Allegro. *(Sebastes)*

9

Si scor - de - - rà l'a - man - te

Andante. *(Xerxes)*

10

Del ter - re - no nel con - ca - vo se - no

Andante di molto. *(Aspasia)*

11

È spe - cie di tor - men - to, di tor - men - to

Allegro. *(Roxane)*

12

Or' a dan - ni d'un in - gra - to

Allegretto. (*Neocles*)

13

Nò,   quel . lab - bro   non par-mi ve - ra - ce

Andantino. (*Aspasia, Lysimachus*)

14

Se un   re - gno è pic-ciol van - to,   è pic-ciol van - to

Andante. (*Temistocle*)

15

Ser - be - rò .   fra cep - pi an - co - ra

(Original in Tenor Clef.)

Allegro moderato. (*Roxane, Aspasia, Neocles, Xerxes*)

16

Quel si - len - zio,   quel so - spi - ro

Larghetto. (*Aspasia*)

17

Co - sì   ad - don - ta   dal - l'em - pia mia sor - te

ATTO III

Andante. (*Lysimachus*)

18

A quei sen - si di glo - ria e d'o - no - re

Allegro maestoso. (*Temistocle*)

19

Ah   fre - na - te   il pian - to im - bel - le

(Original in Tenor Clef.)

Andante. (*Neocles*)

20

Di quel - la   fron - te,   di quel-la fron-te un rag-gio

Allegro con spirito. (*Aspasia*)

21

Ah si re - sti   o - nor mi   sgri-da

Cavatina. Largo. (Temistocle)

Ma di Ser - se   in petto a - mo - re

(Original in Tenor Clef.)

Tutti. Allegro. (Neocles)

Ah! fer - ma, ah! pa - dre, ah! pa - dre a - ma - to

In manuscript

Score: BER. P. 387 and 388; BER. Hausbibl. No. 129; DARM.;
DRES. 3374/F./1; PAR (C) (Atto I only).
Nos. 5, 8, 9: MIL.
Nos. 7 and 8: LEIPZ. III. 15. 32.
No. 9: WEI. 349, fol. 17.
No. 12: BRUSS. No. 3704.

The Favourite Songs in the Opera call'd Zanaida. By Sig[r]. Bach.
[London: Walsh. 1763.]

Produced at the King's Theatre, London, 7 May 1763

Allegro maestoso. (Signore Ciardini)

Se spie - go le pri - me ve - - - - - le

Larghetto. (Signora de' Amicis)

Par - to, ad - di - o, io va - do a mor - te

Andantino. (Signora de' Amicis)

Men - tre vol - go in torno il pie - de pal - (pitar)

Allegro moderato. (Signora de' Amicis)

Tor - - to - rel - la ab - ban - - do - na - ta

Allegretto. (Signora Cremonini)

Se del - le a - ni - me . fe - de - li

Allegretto. (*Signore Ciardini*)

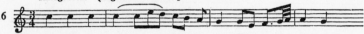

6

Pu - pil-le a - ma - - bi - li del ca - ro . be - ne

Andante. (*Signora de' Amicis*)

7

Che pie - tà   non sen - te al co - re

Andantino. (*Signore Ciardini*)

8

Im - pa - ra - i   dal   pri - - mo i-stan-te

BM. G. 136 b.; Royal Music, 11 a. 18; BER. Hausbibl. No. 136;
BOL.; BRUSS. No. 5496; HAMB.
The songs are also published in 'Le Delizie dell' Opere', Vol. 12
(London: Walsh. 1776); BM. G. 159.
No, 1: see English Songs ('See the kind indulgent gales ').

In manuscript

No. 2: PAR. Vm.⁷ 4877, fol. 43; BER. Hausbibl. No. 137; WIEN.
S. m. 3901.
No. 3: BER. Hausbibl. No. 137.
No. 4: SCHW.
Nos. 5–8: BER. Hausbibl. No. 137; WIEN. S. m. 3901.

III. ENGLISH COMEDIES AND CANTATAS

Happy Morn, auspicious rise!

SINFONIA

Allegro.

1

Andante.

(Coro)

2

Hap - py morn,   au - spi-cious rise

Andante. *(Soprano Solo)*

3

See,   see,   he   darts . a bright-er   ray

Allegro moderato. *(Tenor Recit. and Aria)*

4

Be mine   to gra-tu-late,   to gra-tu - late . . this hour

5. Eight-part *Coro* ('Such heart-form'd strains').

6. *Tenor Recit.* ('Approach, ye infant pledges').

Andantino. *(Duet, Soprano, Soprano)*

7

Blest to our   pa - rents be . . this   day .

Largo. *(Coro)*

8

May time long spare,   may time long spare our mo - narch from

In manuscript

Score: BM. Royal Music, 22 a. 16 (inscribed 'This Volume belongs to
the Queen 1788') (Soli, Chorus, Strings, Flutes, Clarinets, Bassoons,
Horns, Trumpets, Drums).

Bach used the opening Sinfonia also in 'Gioas, Re di Giuda' (1770) (see
Operas).

Manalcas: a Pastoral. The Words by James Harris Esqr. and by
him adapted to the most celebrated compositions. [*Circa* 1773]

Five numbers are by Bach:

(*Corydon*)

Re - lent - less Death, Oh! stay, stay, re - lent-less

(From 'Orione', q.v.)

(? *Corydon*)

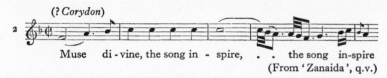

Muse di - vine, the song in - spire, . . the song in-spire

(From 'Zanaida', q.v.)

(*Chorus*)

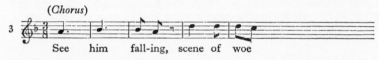

See him fall-ing, scene of woe

(*Manalcas*)

Cease, cease your tra - gic mea-sures

(From 'Orione', q.v.)

(*Chorus*)

Swaynes be gay while ye may, be gay while ye may

In manuscript
Score owned by Freiherr v. Waldthausen, Essen-Bredeney.

Thanks be to God who rules the Deep. An Ode on the auspicious
Arrival and Nuptials of Her present most gracious Majesty Queen
Charlotte, by John Lockman. Set to Music by Mr. Bach [1761]

Thanks be to God who rules the Deep

Allegro. (Coro)

O   see   one   u - ni - ver - sal   Smile

In manuscript

Score: BM. Royal Music, 22 a. 17 (inscribed 'This Vol^m belongs to the Queen. 1788'). (Solo, Chorus (S. A. B.), Violin, Continuo.)

The Flitch of Bacon, a Comic Opera, now performing with Universal Applause at the Theatre Royal in Covent Garden &c. Part of it Composed and Part Compiled by W. Shield. [London: Napier. 1778.]

Produced at the Haymarket Theatre, 17 August 1778; at Covent Garden Theatre, 7 January 1780

One Aria is by Bach:

Andante. (Sung by Mr. Johnstone, 1778)

No,   'twas nei - ther   shape   nor   fea - ture   Made   me   own

BM. E. 108 (see English Songs).

The Maid of the Mill. A Comic Opera. As it is Performed at the Theatre Royal in Covent Garden, for the Voice, Harpsichord, or Violin. [London: Bremner. 1765.]

Produced 31 January 1765

Two Arias are by Bach:

Allegretto. (Sung by Miss Brent)

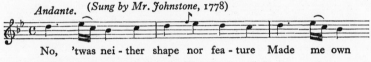

Trust   me,   trust me, would you   taste true   plea - sure

Andante. (Sung by Miss Brent and Mr. Mattocks)

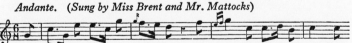

My   life, my   joy,   my   bless-ing,   in   thee each grace pos-ses-sing

BM. D. 273 (3).

The Summer's Tale. A Musical Comedy. As it is Perform'd at the Theatre Royal in Covent-Garden. The Music by Abel, Bach, Giardini, Lampugnani, Arne, Cocchi, Hasse, Richter, Arnold,

Ciampi, Howard, Russell, Boyce, C. St. Germain, Lampe, Stanley. For the Harpsichord, Voice, German Flute, or Violin. [London: Walsh. 1765.]

Produced 6 December 1765

Three Arias are by Bach:

Andante. (*Sung by Mr. Mattocks in Act 2*)

So pro-found an im-pres-sion I bear   of the maid who was

Andante. (*Sung by Mr. Beard and Miss Brent in Act 3*)

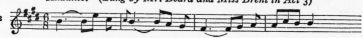

Yes, . . 'tis   plain . she sees . . me   trem - ble

Allegro moderato.   (*Sung by Miss Brent in Act 3*)

Na - ture, when she gave us   plea - - - - sure

BM. D. 273 (1).
No. 3.   For another version see English Songs.

In manuscript

No. 2: RCM. No. 2106.

IV. ITALIAN CANTATAS AND ARIAS

A Favorite Scene and Rondo on the Duke de Nivernois Air, sung by Mr. Tenducci, at Bath, the Pantheon, and Messrs. Bach and Abels Concerts. Composed by the late celebrated John Christian Bach. [London: Longman and Broderip. 1783.]

BM. H. 1648 a (1) (see 'La Clemenza di Scipione ').

Amor Vincitore. Cantata a Due Voci con Cori e Stromenti. Del Giovanni Cristiano Bach. 1774

In manuscript
Score: DARM.; PAR (C).

Aurora. A Favorite Cantata, Performed at the Vocal Concerts, Hanover Square, Composed by J. C. Bach. Adapted from the MS. Score, and Dedicated (by Permission) to Her Royal High[s]. The Duchess of Gloucester, by the Proprietor, C. Knyvett, jun[r]. Price 3/-. [London: at the Regent's Harmonic Institution.]

Recit. Andantino.

Già Fe-bo ri-con-du-ce

Aria. Larghetto. (*Aurora*)

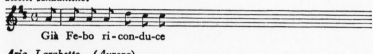

Vo   cer - can - do   in que-ste a - re - ne

BM. H. 1662, No. 6.

In manuscript

Score: BM. Add. MSS. 24310 (Soli, Strings, Flutes, Clarinets, Bassoon).

Endimione. Serenata a quattro. Del Giov. Crist. Bach. La poesia è del ... Metastasio. 1774.

OVERTURE

Allegro.

1

(See Symphonies and Overtures, Op. 18, No. 3.)

PARTE I

(*Nice*)

2

Non   te - mer, oh Dea fe - li-ce

(*Diana*)

3

Sem - pli - cet - to . an - cor

(*Endimione*)

4

Dim-mi che va - ga   se - i   (Original in Tenor Clef.)

(*Amore*)

5

Quel - l'al - ma   se - ve-ra

Cavatina. (*Endimione*)

6

Gra - - to son - no   (Original in Tenor Clef.)

PARTE II

Cavatina. (Diana)

7 — Or al pra-to ed or³ al fon-te

(Amore)

8 Se s'ac - cen-de in fiamme or

(Diana)

9 Se ti-ran-ni, oh

(Nice)

10 O fà che m'a-mi

(Endimione)

11 Va-do per un mo - men-to

(Original in Tenor Clef.)

(Amore)

12 Rob-bia, ros-sor di-spet-to

In manuscript

Score: DARM.
No. 4: MAIH.
No. 6: see Church Music, 'Ave maris'.
Nos. 10, 11: PAR (C) (in 'Airs et Duos. Partition d'Orchestre').

L'Olimpe. Chœur pour l'anniversaire du Jour de Naissance du Roi [? Frederick the Great: 1752 or 1753].

Allegretto.

1 Gloire à ja-mais au prin-ce bien ai-mé

Andantino.

2 Vei-llons sur ce roi ma-gna - ni - me, nos ver-tus

Allegro.

Chan-tons,   chan-tons   qu'a-vec nous tout s'u - ni - sse

In manuscript

Score: BER. Mus. MS. Bach 907 and SA. 600 (S. A. T. B., Strings, Clarinets, Horns).

Rinaldo ed Armida. Scena con Aria a 12 part. del Sig[r]. J. C. Bach (nach einer Abschrift seines Neffen W. Bach).

Recit. Allegro.

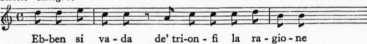

Eb-ben si va-da   de' tri-on - fi la ra - gio - ne

Recit. Andante.

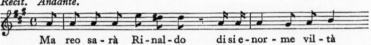

Ma reo sa - rà Ri - nal - do   di si e - nor - me vil - tà

Aria. Andante un poco Adagio.

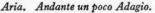

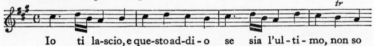

Io   ti la-scio, e que-sto ad-di - o   se sia l'ul - ti - mo, non so

In manuscript

Score: BM. Add. MSS. 32151, fol. 17. Another copy: BM. Add. MSS. 31578, fol. 1 ('The Favorite Rondeau sung by M[r]. Tenducci accompanied on the Pianoforte by M[r]. Bach, and on the Hautboy by M[r]. Fisher'); BRUSS. No. 3701; BUCK.; WIEN. No. 18568 and S. m. 3900 (see English Cantatas, 'The Flitch of Bacon')

Detached Arias (MS. unless a printed source is indicated)

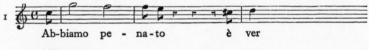

Ab-biamo pe - na-to   è ver

MIL. 957/3.

Allegretto.

Ac - cen - der mi   sen - to, d'ar-de - - re di spe-me

BM. Add. MSS. 29964, fol. 101 (see 'Carattaco').

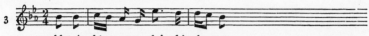

Al mio bè - ne a lei ch'a-do - ro

BUCK.
The Aria is included in John Corri's 'A Select Collection of the most Admired Songs' [Edinburgh], vol. i, p. 115; BM. I. 278; BRUSS. No. 17232. Also in 'Tonwerke alter deutscher Meister', No. 4 (Walter: 1919).

Largo.

Ca - - - ro, ca - ro mio be - ne ad - di - o

WIEN. S. m. 3902.

Largo.

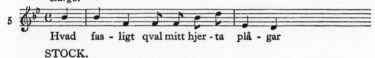

Hvad fas - ligt qval mitt hjer - ta plå - gar

STOCK.

La sor - te mia spie-ta - ta

BRUSS. No. 24058 (in 'Méthode de chant du Conservatoire de Musique, contenant les principes du chant' [Paris: An. 12], p. 204).

Recit.

La sven-tu - ra del fi - glio di te - ne-rez-za o-gnor

Coro.

Dal - suo be - ne al -l' ur-na in-tor - no

BER. Mus. MS. Bach P. 1153 ('Scena aus Egisto').

Recit.

Mi scor-do i tor - ti mie-i

Aria.

Dol - ci au - ret - te, ah! voi por - ta - te

BER. Mus. autogr. Bach No. 881 ('Scena con Rondo'); WEI. 349, fol. 43.

Andantino.

9

Mi - se - ra, mi - se - ra

STOCK.

10

Mi - se-ro   par - go - let - to

PAR. Vm.[4] 861; SCHW. ('Arie aus Demofoonte.')

Andante.

11

O Ve - ne - re vez - zo - sa

In 'Sei Ode di Oratio. Tradotte in Lingua Italiana da Giovan Gualberto Bottarelli. Messe in musica da Signori Bach, Giordani, Boroni, Vento, Barthelemon, è Holtzbaur' [London: Welcker. ?1775]; BM. G. 136 c; HAMB.

Recit.

12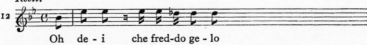

Oh de - i   che fred-do ge - lo

Aria.

Se ti - ran - ni, oh de - i, non sie - te

BER. Mus. MS. 30110; BUCK. ('Cantata in B del Signor Massimo Giugliano il 15 d'Ottobre 1777 del Signore Bach a Londra').

Maestoso.

13

Par - to, ma se tu m'a - mi,   ma se tu m'a - mi

BER. Mus. MS. Bach St. 293.

Recit. Andante sostenuto.

14

Prin-ci-pe,   non te - mer

Aria. *Allegro vivace.*

Con sì bel no - - - me in fron-te

BER. Mus. MS. No. 30127 ('Recit. und Aria 1758. Von der Hand des berühmten Bassisten [Ludwig] Fischer') (see 'Catone').

Andante grazioso.

15

Quel lab-bro a - do - ra - to m'è gra - to, m'ac-cen-de

LUB. Mus. Q. 151 ('Komponiert für das Pasticcio "L'Olimpiade",' q.v.).

Andante.

16

So - spi - ri del cor mi - o

LUB. Mus. Q. 153.

Larghetto.

17

Tu par - ti, o de - i

mio ben

BER. Mus. MS. Bach St. 285 ('Duetto dell' Opera "Cleonice"'; produced in London 1763).

Andante sostenuto.

18

U - - na sem - pli-ce a - - gnel - let - ta

BER. Mus. MS. Bach St. 287[b].

19
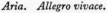

Wenn nach der Stür-me To - ben

In J. A. Hiller's 'Deutsche Arien und Duette' (Leipzig: Breitkopf: 1785) and 'Tonwerke alter deutscher Meister', No. 4 (Walter: 1919).

V. ENGLISH SONGS

A Collection of Favourite Songs Sung at Vaux Hall by Mrs. Weichsell. Compos'd by John Christian Bach. [London: Welcker. ? 1765.]

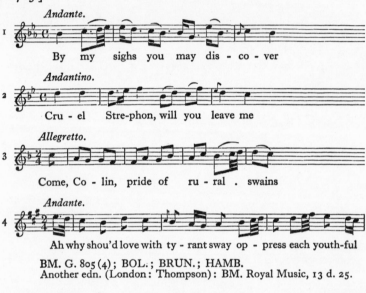

1 *Andante.*
By my sighs you may dis - co - ver

2 *Andantino.*
Cru - el Stre-phon, will you leave me

3 *Allegretto.*
Come, Co - lin, pride of ru - ral . swains

4 *Andante.*
Ah why shou'd love with ty - rant sway op - press each youth-ful

BM. G. 805 (4); BOL.; BRUN.; HAMB.
Another edn. (London: Thompson): BM. Royal Music, 13 d. 25.

A Second Collection of Favourite Songs. Sung at Vaux-Hall by Mrs. Pinto and Mrs. Weichsel. Composed by John Christian Bach. [London: Welcker. 1767.]

1 *Andante.*
In this sha - dy . . blest re - treat . .

2 *Andante.*
Smi - - ling Ve - nus, God - dess dear

3 *Andante.*
Ten - der vir - gins shun de - ceiv-ers

Love - ly   yet . un - grate - ful   swain

BM. G. 136; BOL.

No. 1: published separately BM. G. 805 e (13) (no title-page); BM. H. 1994 a (105) (London: Falkener. ? 1775); also in 'A Select Collection of the Most Admired Songs, Duets, etc. From Operas in the highest esteem, and from other Works' [Edinburgh: John Corri], Vol. iii, p. 23; BM. I. 278; BRUSS. No. 17232.

No. 2: published separately as 'The Intercession' (q.v.).

No. 3: see 'The London Lass', 'Blest with thee', and 'Carattaco', No. 7.

Another edn. (London: Longman & Broderip): BM. Royal Music, 13 d. 25.

A Third Collection of Favorite Songs. Sung at Vaux-Hall by Miss Cooper. Composed by John Christian Bach. [London: Welcker. ? 1775.]

Midst si - lent shades and pur -ling streams

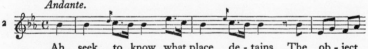

Ah   seek   to know what place   de - tains   The   ob - ject

Would   you   a   fe - male   heart   in-spire

Cease a - while, ye   winds, to   blow

BM. G. 136 a, No. 2.   No. 1: published separately, BM. G. 809, No. 7. No. 4: published separately as 'Cease a while' (q.v.). Another edn. (London: Longman & Broderip): BM. Royal Music, 13 d. 25.

Blest with thee, my Soul's Dear Treasure. A favorite Song, Composed by Sig^r. Bach. [London: Longman and Broderip. ? 1780.]

Andante.

Blest with thee, my soul's dear trea-sure

BM. G. 809, No. 6.   See 'Vauxhall Songs', Second Collection, No. 3; 'The London Lass'; and 'Carattaco', No. 7 ('Non è ver').

Cease a while, ye Winds, to blow. A favorite Rondo composed by Sig^r. Bach. [London: Longman, Clementi. ? 1800.]

Cease a . while, ye winds, to blow

BM. G. 809, No. 7.
Another edition (London: Falkener. ? 1770): BM. H. 1994 a. No. 126.
See 'Vauxhall Songs', Third Collection, No. 4.

In manuscript
HAMB.

Farewell, ye soft Scenes. A celebrated Air by Mr. Bach. [London: Preston. ? 1790.]

Fare - well, ye soft scenes, the plain, the brook

BM. G. 351 (1) ('The Beauties of Music and Poetry', Vol. I).
The melody is from the Opera 'L'Olimpiade', q.v.

Lochaber, a Favorite Scotch Song Sung by Mr. Tenducci, at the Pantheon, and Mr. Abel's Concert. The Instrumental Parts by the late Celebrated Mr. Bach. [London: Longman and Broderip. ? 1785.]

BM. G. 805 h (19).

Neptune. Composed for the satisfaction of Dido, to the addition of News, by Mr. Bach. [London. ? 1775.]

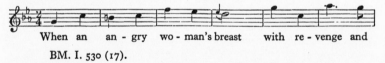

When an an - gry wo - man's breast with re - venge and

BM. I. 530 (17).

No more with Unavailing Woe. A Favorite Air from Gioas. Composed by J. C. Bach. Sung by Mrs. Bland, in the Oratorios, at Covent Garden. [London: Bland and Weller. ? 1795.]

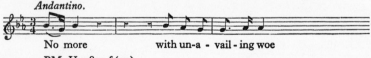

No more   with un-a - vail - ing woe

BM. H. 2830 f (10).
See Operas, 'Gioas'.

No, twas neither Shape nor Feature. Sung by Mr. Johnstone in The Flitch of Bacon [London: Goulding. 1778]

No, twas nei - ther shape nor fea - ture Made me own your

BM. G. 793 (110).
Also (to the words 'Gentle breezes, waft him over') in 'The Beauties of Music and Poetry', Vol. I (London: Preston. ? 1790); BM. G. 351 (1).
See also 'Pianoforte Sonatas': 'Four Progressive Lessons', No. 4 (Arioso con Variatione').

See the kind indulgent Gales. A Favourite Song sung by Mrs. Weichsell at Vaux Hall Gardens. Composed by John Christian Bach [London: Longman and Broderip. ? 1780]

See, see the kind in-dul-gent gales . . .

BM. G. 805 r. (3).
See 'Zanaida', No. 1; and 'The Summer's Tale', No. 3.

The Broom of Cowdenknows, a Favorite Scotch Song. Sung by Mr. Tenducci, at the Pantheon and Mr. Abel's Concert. The Instrumental Parts by the late Celebrated Mr. Bach [London: Thos. Cahusac. ? 1784]

BM. G. 308 (104).

The Intercession. Sung by Mrs. Weichsell at Vauxhall. Compos'd by Mr. Bach

Smi - ling Ve - nus, God - dess dear

RCM. 1375, fol. 21.
See 'Vauxhall Songs', Second Collection, No. 2.

The London Lass. To a favourite Rondeau in the Opera of
Carattaco by Sig[r]. Bach. Compleatly fitted for two German
Flutes [no title-page or imprint. ? 1768]

[*Andante*]

While Ce-ci - lia   we   ad - mire

BM. G. 313, No. 253.
See 'Vauxhall Songs', Second Collection, No. 3, and 'Carattaco',
No. 7.

VI. VOCAL DUETS

Sei Canzonette a due composte da Giovanni Cristiano Bach, e da
esso dedicate in segno di umilissimo ossequio, a sua eccellenza
Lady Glenorchy. Londra. Opera IV [1765.]

Allegretto.

6

As - col - ta mi, oh Clo-ri, l'of - fe - so son i - o

BM. 398 and 398 a (1); DRES. 3374/L./1; FLO. B. 706; HAMB.;
LEIPZ. III. 4. 63; PAR. (C).
No. 1: in Leuckardt's 'Orion', No. 24. Also in John Corri's 'A
Select Collection of the most Admired Songs, Duets, etc.', vol. 3,
p. 67; BM. I. 278; BRUSS. No. 17, 232.

Sei Canzonette a due, composte da Giovanni Cristiano Bach,
dedicate all' alt^za ser^ma di Giuseppe Federigo Duca di Sassonia
Hildburghausen, &c., &c., &c. Opera VI. [London: 1766]

Andantino.

1

Tor - na in quel l'on - da, in quel l'on-da - chia-ra

Andantino.

2

I - o lo so che il bel sem - bian - te

Allegro.

3

E pur fra le tem - pe - ste

E pur fra

Andantino.

4

Tro - va un sol mia bel - la Clo - ri

BM. 398 a. 2.
Another edition (London: Welcker. ? 1770): BM. A. 1340.

In manuscript

Nos. 1–6: DRES. 1/F./82, 2.
Nos. 1, 4, 6: WIEN. 18680.

INSTRUMENTAL MUSIC

(c) ORCHESTRAL

VII. SYMPHONIES AND OVERTURES

Six Simphonies a deux Violons, deux Hautbois, deux Cors de
Chasse, alto Viola, et Basse, Composées & tres humblement
dediées a son Altesse Royale Monseigneur le Duc de York &c.
Par Jean Chretien Bach, Maitre de Musique de S. M. la Reine de
la Grande Bretagne. Oeuvre III. London. Printed for the Author
and Sold at his House in King Square Court, Dean St. Soho [1765]

BM. g. 435 a.
Another edn. (London: Welcker): BM. h. 423 b; BM. Royal Music,
16 b. 12; LEIPZ. III. 10. 27; STOCK.
Another edn. (Amsterdam: Hummel): BER. Hausbibl. No. 151;
BER (S). ZD. 1383 b; BRUSS. No. 7230; COP. U. 150; EINS.
673. 1; HAMB. Nd. VI. 3190; STOCK.; UPS. i. tr. 114. 3.
Another edn. (Paris: Huberty): PAR. (C); STOCK.
Siéber (Paris) published Nos. 1 and 2 in his 'Six Simphonies à deux

Violons, Alto Viola, Basse, Hautbois et Cors—Composés par J. C.
Bach, Toesky, et Stamitz': STOCK.
Another edn. (London: Bremner): BM. Royal Music, 17 b. 1; RCM.
XXXVII. e. 32.

In manuscript

No. 1: DRES. 3374/N./1; 3374/N./2; MIL. 968/14; REG. C 26;
WERNIG. Ue 76 g.
No. 2: BAS. kr. iv. 16; REG. C XXXI. 5.
No. 3: MIL. 967/13; REG. C XIII. 3.
No. 4: BAS. kr. iv. 15; REG. C XXXI. 4.
No. 5: MIL. 971/17; REG. C XXXI. 3.
No. 6: DRES. 3374/N./1; 3374/N./2.

Six Simphonies a Deux Violons, Alto Viola et Basse. Deux Haut-
bois et Deux Cors de Chasse. Composées par Jean Chrétien Bach,
Maitre de Musique de S. M. La Reine de la Grande Bretagne.
Oeuvre VI. Prix f. 6. [Amsterdam: Hummel. No. 113] [?1770.]

BER. Mus. 9471; COP. N. 150; EINS. 673, 1; STOCK.
No. 3 is No. 1 of Op. 8 (*infra*). No. 4 is No. 5 of Op. 8 (*infra*).
No. 5: published as 'A Favorite Overture in Eight Parts' (London:
Welcker. ? 1775): BM g. 474. 15; and as 'Simphonie périodique à
8 Instruments' (Amsterdam: Markordt): BM. 474 b. 19. It is also
No. 6 of Markordt's edition of Op. 8 (*infra*). Also published by
Bremner, BM. Royal Music, 17 b. 1.

In manuscript

No. 1: KREMS. H. 31. 271 and 272.

No. 2: LAMB.; MIL. 969/15; WOLF. Vogel No. 11.

No. 3: REG. C XXX. 1; SCHW. No. 825; STOCK.

No. 4: BER. Hausbibl. No. 143; DRES. 3374/N./1; 3374/N. 2; REG. C XXX. 5; SCHW. No. 864.

No. 5: BER. Hausbibl. No. 145; BER. Mus. MS. Bach P. 938; EINS. 679. 8; MIL. 970/16; REG. C XXXI. 6; SCHW. No. 866; STOCK.

No. 6: WIEN (M). XIII. 17759. (See 'Six Simphonie périodique', *infra.*)

Another edn. (Paris: Huberty) omits Nos. 3 and 4 and substitutes:
   (1) the Overture to 'Il Tutore e la Pupilla' (*infra*); and
   (2) the following:

WIEN (M). XIII. 16890.

In manuscript

WERNIG. Ue. 76 h; (Strings, Oboes, Horns).

Six Simphonie périodique [*sic*] à 8 Instruments, deux Violons, Taille, et Basse, deux Hautbois, et deux Cors de Chasse. Composées par Jean Chretien Bach. Opera 8. Prix f. 6. [Amsterdam: S. Markordt]

Andante.   *Allegro assai.*

BM. Royal Music, 2 copies; RCM. XXXVII. e. 32.
No. 1 is No. 3 of Op. 6 (*supra*).
No. 5 is No. 4 of Op. 6 (*supra*).
No. 6: published as 'A Favorite Overture in Eight Parts' (London: Welcker. ?1775) BM. g. 474. 15)); as 'Simphonie périodique à 8 Instruments' (Amsterdam: Markordt? 1775) (BM. 474 b. 19); and as No. 5 of Hummel's edn. of Op. 6 (*supra*). Also an edn. by Bremner, BM. Royal Music, 17 b. 1.

In manuscript

No. 1: see Op. 6, No. 3.
No. 2: EINS. 679, 10; KREMS. H. 31. 270; REG. C 9, No. 2; WIEN (M). XIII. 17756.
No. 4: BAS. kr. iv. 13; BER. Mus. MS. P. 940; DRES. 3374/N./1; 3374/N./2; EINS. 678, 25; SCHW. No. 824.
No. 5: BER (S). ZD 1383°; DRES. 3374/N./1; 3374/N./2; See also Op. 6, No. 4.
No. 6: MIL. 970/16. (See Op. 6, No. 5, *supra*.)

Trois Simphonies a deux Violons, Taille & Basse, deux Flutes ou Hautbois et deux Cors de Chasse (ad Libitum). Composées par Jean Chretien Bach, Maitre de Musique de SM. la Reine de la Grande Bretagne. Oeuvre neuvieme. [La Haye: B. Hummel]

1   *Allegro con spirito.*

   Andante.

   Presto.

   Allegro.

2   *Allegro.*

   Andante con sordini.

   Allegro. (Tempo di Menuetto)

BM. h. 423 c; COP.; EINS. M. 673, 1; STOCK.; UPS. i. tr. 44. 3.
Another edn. as 'Three Favorite Overtures' (London: Longman &
Broderip) (as Op. 21. ? 1785): BM. h. 2770 (3); Royal Music, 17 b. 1;
EINS. 679, 5.
Another edn. (Longman & Lukey): RCM. LX. C. 17.
No. 2: in Siéber's (Paris) 'Trois Simphonies . . . par Mrs. Gossec,
Haydn et Bach': DARMS. Mus. 3939; BRUSS. 12, 903.
No. 3 is No. 2 of 'Six Overtures in 8 Parts . . . by Sigᵣ. Bach, Jomelli,
Galuppi, Perez' (London: Walsh): BM. g. 212 a; and No. 2 of
'Six Favourite Opera Overtures set for the Harpsichord or Organ
compos'd by Sigr. Bach' (London: Walsh) BM. e. 12 (2) BRUSS. 30.
218. It is the Overture to 'Zanaida', London 1763.

In manuscript

No. 1: BM. Royal Music, 21 d. 4; BAS. kr. ii. 1.
No. 2: BER (S). ZD. 1384; DRES. 3374/N./1; 3374/N./2;
STOCK.; UPS. i. tr. 44 3; WOLF.Vogel, No. 12 (also a Pianoforte
arrangement, No. 311).

Six Grand Overtures, three for a Single, and three for a Double
Orchestre, for Violins, Hautboys, Flutes, Clarinetts, Horns, Tenor
and Bass. Composed by John Christian Bach, Music Master to
Her Majesty and the Royal Family. Opera XVIII. Price £1 1s. 0d.
[London: William Forster. ? 1781]

* For double Orchestra.

(Overture to 'Lucio Silla'.)

(Overture to 'Endimione,' 1772.)

* For Double Orchestra.

BM. h. 3210 (1); Royal Music, 2 copies; AAR., BER. Hausbibl.
No. 141; DARM.
Another edn. (London: Walsh): BRUSS. No. 30218.
Nos. 1 and 2 in 'Deux Simphonies. La première à Grande Orchestre,
la Seconde à Double Orchestre, composée par J. C. Bach' (Berlin :
Hummel): BER (S). ZD. 1383ª; BRUSS. No. 7229; WERNIG.
Ue 76 m.
No. 2 as 'Sinfonie périodique à plusieurs Parties, Nro. IX. (Am-
sterdam: Schmitt. ? 1774): BM. h. 423 (2); BER (S). ZD. 1383ᶠ;
BITT.; SCHW. No. 826; also in Edn. Peters 3832.
No. 4 is No. 2 of Schmitt's 'Deux Sinfonies . . . Oeuvre XVIII'
(*infra*).
No. 2: Columbia Record L 2047.

In manuscript

No. 1: EINS. 679, 6; RCM. No. 1139; STOCK.; WIEN (M).
XIII. 27792.
Nos. 1 and 2 : BRUSS. No. 28. 447.
No. 2: DARM. Mus. 135; EINS. 679, 4; arr. for military band, BM.
Royal Music 21. d. 4.
No. 3: DARM. Mus. 5304
No. 4: DARM. Mus. 3033.

Deux Sinfonies à Grande Orchestre. Composés par J. C. Bach.
Maitre de Musique de S. M. la Reine de la Grande Bretangne.
Oeuvre XVIII. [Amsterdam: Joseph Schmitt.]

Overture to 'La Clemenza di Scipione', London, 1778 (Strings,
Flutes, Oboes, Bassoons, Horns). See Operas, *supra*.

Allegro con spirito.

(No. 4 of Forster's edn. of Op. 18, *supra*.)
BM. h. 423 (3); BITT.; EINS. 22, 2; TUB.

In manuscript
No. 1: DARM. Mus. 3033; WOLF. Vogel 16.

Six Favourite Overtures in VIII Parts for Violins, Hoboys, French Horns, with a Bass for the Harpsichord and Violoncello. Composed by Sig^r. Bach. [William Randall: London. ? 1770.]

Allegro con brio.

Andante.

Allegro.

'Orione', London, 1763.

Allegro assai.

Andante grazioso.

Presto.

'La Calamità', London, 1763.

Allegro di molto.   *Andante.*

Presto.

'Artaserse', Turin, 1761.

Allegro assai.

4

Andante.

Presto.

'Il Tutore e la Pupilla', London, 1762.

Allegro.

5

Andante.

Presto.

'La Cascina', London, 1763.

Allegro con spirito.

6

Andante.

Allegro assai.

'Astarto, Re di Tiro', London, 1762.

BM. g. 474. a (10); Royal Music, 17 b. 1; BRUSS. 30218; LEIPZ. III. 10. 27.

Another edn. (Walsh: London): RCM. LXXI. C. 4.

No. 4 is also in the Leduc (Paris) edn. of Op. 6 (*supra*).

In manuscript

No. 1: REG. C XIII. 1 (with a different middle and final movement).

No. 2: BER. Mus. MS. St. 489 (as overture to 'Artaserse'); BER (S). ZD. 1383ᵈ; EINS. 678, 27; REG. C XXX. 2; LEIPZ. III. 11. 1; MIL. 966/12; REG. C XXX. 2; SCHW. No. 827; STOCK.

No. 3; BER. Mus. MS. St. 613; DRES. 3374/N/1; 3374/N/2; EINS. 678, 26; MIL. 965/11; REG. C XIII. 4; SCHW. No. 823; WIEN (M). XIII. 17755.

No. 4: BAS. kr. iv. 14; EINS. 679, 3; LAMB.; MIL. 963/9.

No. 5: BAS. kr. iv. 11; DRES. 3374/N/1; 3374/N/2; EINS. 678, 24; ZWICK. II. 2.

No. 6: BER. Hausbibl. 133 ('Sinfonia nell' Opera Catone'); EINS. 679, 12; LAMB.

Six Favourite Opera Overtures set for the Harpsichord or Organ. Compos'd by Sigʳ. Bach. [London: Walsh. ? 1770.]

1 'Orione.' See *supra*.

2 'Zanaida.' See *supra*.

3 'Artaserse.' See *supra*.

4 'La Cascina.' See *supra* (Pf. arrangement, Ed. Bernouilli).

5 'Astarto.' See *supra*.

6

BM. e. 12 (2); Royal Music, 16 a. 15; BRUSS. No. 30218.

No. 6 is by Baldassare Galuppi.

Symphonie periodique No. XXVIII a deux Violons, Taille, et Basse, Flutes ou Hautbois et Cornes de Chasse. Composée par Sʳ. J. C. Bach. Prix f. 1. 10. [Amsterdam: Hummel.]

Andante.

Tempo di Gavotta. Allegro.

BER. Mus. 9470; STOCK.
Another edn. (London: Bremner): B.M.

In manuscript

DRES. 3374/N/1; 3374/N/2; REG. C 9, No. 4.

An Overture in Eight Parts. Composed by Sig[r]. Giovanni Cristian Bach. [London: Welcker. ? 1770.]

Allegro di molto.

Andante.

Allegro.

BM. g. 474 a (6); UPS. i. tr. 114. 2.
Also published by Bremner (London) (? 1790) as No. 15 of 'The Periodical Overture': BM. h. 3210 (21); Royal Music, 16 f. 16.

In manuscript

BAS. kr. iv. 10; BER. Mus. MS. St. 615; EINS. 678, 28; PAR. Vm.[7] 4787; REG. C 9, No. 1; SCHW. No. 865; WIEN (M). XIII. 17754.

The favorite Overture in the Opera of Carattaco in Eight Parts. Composed by Sig[r] J. C. Bach. Price 3s. 6d. [London: Longman and Broderip.]

Allegro di molto.

Andante.

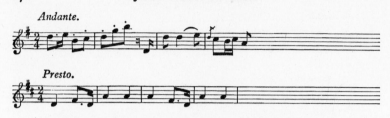

Presto.

BM. Royal Music, 17 b. 1 (Strings, Flutes or Oboes, Horns).
Another edn. (Amsterdam: Hummel): WERNIG. Ue 76. f.
Also overture to 'Temistocle', Mannheim, 1772.

In manuscript
BER. Mus. MS. P. 387–8; Hausbibl. 129; DARM. Mus. 130; DRES.
3374 F. 1; WOLF. Vogel 14.

In manuscript

Allegro.

1

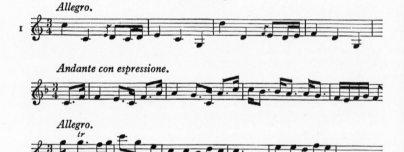

Andante con espressione.

Allegro.

EINS. 679, 9: REG. C XXX. 4 (Strings, Oboes, Horns).

Molto allegro.

2

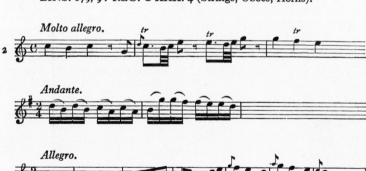

Andante.

Allegro.

BAS. kr. IV. 9 (Strings, Oboes, Clarini).

BER. Hausbibl. M. 133 ('Sinfonia nell' Opera Catone'). Also served as the Overture to 'Astarto' (see 'Six Favourite Overtures in VIII Parts' (*supra*)). This is not the original Overture to 'Catone'.

EINS. M. 678, 22 (Strings, Oboes, Horns).

UPS. as 'Sinfonia del Sign. Back' (? J. C. B.) (Strings).

Andante.

Allegro assai.

EINS. 679, 1; LAMB.; MIL. 964/10; REG. C XXXI. 2 (Strings, Oboes, Horns).   Score, NAP.
The original overture to 'Catone in Utica', Naples 1761.

Allegro di molto.   *Andante.*

7

Presto.

DARM. Overture to 'Temistocle', Mannheim, 1772.   See (middle movement) Op. 18, No. 4, and final movement of 'Carattaco' (*supra*).

8

Andante.

Tempo 1°.

Overture to 'Amadis des Gaules', Paris 1779.
BER. Mus. MS. Bach P985 (Strings, Flutes, Oboes, Clarinets, Trumpets, Horns, Bassoons, Timpani).   Also in printed score (*supra*, p. 215).

Allegro.   *Andante grazioso.*

9

Allegro.

WIEN. (M) XIII. 17751 ('de Sigre Giuseppe Pach') (Strings, Oboes, Horns).

WIEN. (M) 17752 ('del Sigre Giuseppe Baach') (Strings, Oboes, Horns).

EINS. 679, 11; REG. G. 9, No. 3 (Strings, Oboes, Horns).

BAS. No. 249; EINS. 678, 29 (Strings, Oboes, Trumpets).

UPS. as 'dell Sign. Back' (? J. C. B.) (Strings).

WIEN. (M) 17757 ('del Sigre Giuseppe Bach') (Strings, Flutes, Horns).

DRES. 3374 / N/1 ; 3374 / N/2 (Strings, Oboes, Horns).

Andante non troppo.

Presto.

BER. Hausbibl. No. 144; BER. Staatsbibl. Mus. MS. Bach St. 490;
EINS. 679, 2; REG. C XXX. 3; BER (S). ZD. 1383 e; BRUSS.
No. 7232; SCHWER. No. 863; WIEN (M). XIII. 17753 (Strings,
Oboes, or Horns).

Allegro.

17

Andante.

Tempo di Minuetto.

WIEN (M). 17758 ('del Sigre Giuseppe Baach) (Strings, Oboes,
Horns).

Vivace.   *Andante spiritoso.*

18

Prestissimo.

STOCK. (Strings, Oboes, Trumpets).

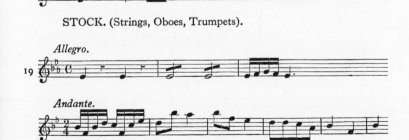

Allegro.

19

Andante.

Presto.

STOCK. (Strings, Oboes, Horns).

Allegro molto.   *Larghetto.*

20

Presto assai.

STOCK. (Strings, Oboes, Horns).

Largo assai.

21

Tempo di Minuetto, ma più tosto Allegro.

Da capo il primo Minuetto senza Ritornelli.

EINS. 679, 13 (Strings, Oboes, Horns); MIL. 972/18; STOCK.

Allegro.

22

Andante.

Allegro.

EINS. 678, 23 (Strings, Horns, Trombe di guerra).

Allegro.

23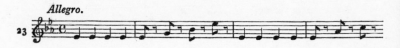

Andante.

Presto.

BER. Mus. MS. Bach St. 491 (Strings, Oboes, Horns).

Allegro assai.   *Andante grazioso.*

Presto con brio.

WOLF. Vogel 18 (Strings, Trumpets, Horns, Bassoons).

Trois Symphonies a quatre ou a huit parties. Composées par J. C. Bach et Leduc l'aîné. [Paris: Leduc ? 1780.]

No. 2 is by Bach.

Allegro maestoso.

Andantino.

Allegro molto.

BM. Royal Music, 16 b. 17 (Strings, Flutes, Oboes, Horns).

VIII. CONCERTED SYMPHONIES

Sinfonie Concertante pour trois Violons, deux Alto, Basse, Violoncelle obligé, deux Hautbois et deux Cors de Chasse. Composée par J. C. Bach. Prix 3. 12. [Paris: Roullède de Chevardière.]

BER. Mus. 9466; BRUSS. No. 7231.

Simphonie Concertante a plusieurs instrument (*sic*) Composée par Cretien Bach. [Paris: Siéber ? 1770.]

BM. h. 423 (1) (Strings and Oboes; Violin and Violoncello concertante). Cf. *infra*, p. 289, No. 3.

Concert ou Symphonie a Deux Violons Obligés, Deux Violons Ripiens, Deux Flutes, deux Cors de Chasse, Taille et Basse. Composés par J. C. Bach, Maitre de Musique de Sa Majesté La Reine de la Grande Bretagne. [Amsterdam: Hummel.]

BER. Mus. 9464; EINS. 679. 7; STOCK. No. 327; UPS. i. tr. 44. 2.
Also as a Clavier Concerto (*infra*, pp. 290, 300).

In manuscript

BER. Mus. MS. Bach, P. 391.

Sei Sinfonia pour deux Clarinettes, deux Cors de Chasse et Basson. [London: Longman and Broderip.]

BM. Royal Music, 2 copies; BUCK.

BER. Hausbibl. No. 149 (Strings, Oboes, Horns; Violins and 'Cello concertante).   Cf. *infra* p. 290, No. 11.

BER. Hausbibl. No. 151 a (Strings, Flutes, Horns; Violin, Viola, Oboe, Violoncello obbligati).

BER. Mus. MS. Bach, P. 393 ('Concerto a Flauto traverso oblig. con più Stromenti ').   (Strings, Flute (concert), Horns.)

Allegro di molto.

BER. Hausbibl. No. 151 b (Violin 1 and 2 concertante; Strings, Flutes, Oboes, Horns. Cf. *infra* p. 290, No. 9.

Allegro moderato.

6

Tempo di Minuetto.

BER. Hausbibl. No. 148 (Strings, Horns, Oboe; Oboe and Violoncello concertante). Cf. *infra* p. 289, No. 2.

Allegro.

7

Larghetto.

Tempo di Minuetto.

MAIH. III. 4½ fol. 503 (Oboe concert., Strings and Horns. Probably composed for Johann Christian Fischer. Cf. Grove, 3rd ed., vol. ii, 251 b.

Allegro maestoso.

8

Larghetto.

Allegro.

BER. Hausbibl. No. 150 (Strings, Clarinets, Horns, Bassoon; Violoncello concertante).

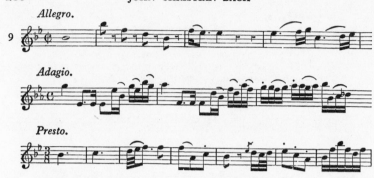

BER. Mus. MS. Bach St. 291; SCHW. No. 867 ('Concerto à Fagotto principale', with Strings and Oboes).

BER. Hausbibl. No. 151 c (Strings, Oboes, Horns; Violin 1 and 2 concertante).
BER. Mus. MS. Bach St. 290 and 603 ('Concerto à Fagotto concertato').

Minuetto 1° da Capo senza Ritornelli.

Minuetto 3°.

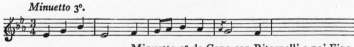

Minuetto 1° da Capo con Ritornelli e poi Fine.

BM. Royal Music 21 a. 8.; WIEN S. m. 2401 ('Concerto à più Stromenti obligati, osia Notturno dal Sig. Gio. Bach'). A version in F ma. in BM. Royal Music 21 a. 7 (*infra*, p. 290, No. 10).

The following Symphonies (inst. parts) are bound together in BM. Royal Music 21 a. 5–7. No. 1 is missing.

Allegro.

2

(See *supra*, p. 287.)

(Strings, Oboes, Horns, Bassoon.)

Andante di molto.

3

(See *supra*, p. 284.)

(Strings, Oboes, Horns.)

Allegro.   *Larghetto.*

4

Allegretto.

(Strings, Flutes, Oboes, Clarinets, Horns, Bassoons.)

Allegro.

5

Adagio sostenuto.

Rondo Allegretto.

(See *infra*, p. 300.)

(Pianoforte obbl., Strings, Flutes, Oboe, Clarinets, Horns.)

6 *Allegro.*

(See *supra* p. 284; *infra*, p. 300.)
(Pianoforte obbl., Strings, Flutes, Horns.)

7 *Allegro assai.*

Tempo di Minuetto.

(Strings, Flutes, Horns.)

8 *Andante.*   *Allegro.*

(Strings, Flute, Oboes, Bassoon, Horns.)

9 *Allegro.*

(See *supra*, p. 286).
(Strings, Oboes, Horns.)

10 *Andante.*

(See *supra*, *p.* 288, No. 11.)
(Strings, Oboe, Horns.)

11 *Andante.*

(See *supra*, p. 286.)
(Strings, Flutes, Oboes.)

12 *Allegro assai.*

Larghetto.

Minuetto.

(Strings, Oboes, Clarinets, Horns, Bassoon.)

IX. PIANOFORTE CONCERTOS

Six Concerts pour le Clavecin, deux Violons, &. un Violoncelle. Tres humblement dediés a Sa Majeste Charlotte Reine de la Grande Bretagne &c. &c. &c. Composés par Jean Bach. Oevre (*sic*) Premier [London, 1763]

Allegro assai.   *Andante.*

6

Allegro moderato.
    'God save the King'

'Sinfonia'.

BM. h. 32 b; Royal Music, 2 copies; HAMB.; SCHW.
Another edn. (London: Bremner): BM. g. 450 b (1); Royal Music,
16 b. 10; RCM. XXXVII. e. 32.
Another edn. (Amsterdam: Hummel): BER.; BRUSS. No. 5903;
BUCK; HAG (M).
Another edn. (Offenbach) BONN; EINS. Mka. 20.
Another edn. (Paris: Huberty): PAR. Vm.⁷ 18923 (Vn. II only);
PAR. Vm.⁷ 5963; PAR. (C).

In manuscript.

Nos. 1–6: DRES. 3374/O/4, 5, 7.
Nos. 1–4: GOT. mus. pag. 4.
No. 1: BER. St. L. 313/3; PAR. Vm.⁷ 5968.
Nos. 2: SCHW. No. 830.
Nos. 2, 3, 5: EINS. 679 (16, 17, 18).
(Nos. 2, 3, 5, 6): KON.
Nos. 2, 5, 6: BER. (uncatalogued).
Nos. 3, 4: BER. Mus. MS. Bach, 484–5–8.
Nos. 1–6 (accomod. à 2 Cemb.): DRES. 3374/O/6.

Sei Concerti per il Cembalo o Piano e Forte con due Violini e
Violoncello d'Accompagnamento.   Composti ed umilmente De-
dicati a Sua Maesta La Regina della Gran Bretagna &c., &c.,
&c. da Giovanni Cristiano Bach.   Op. VII. [London: Longman & Broderip, ? 1780.]

Allegro.

1

Menuetto.

Allegro con spirito.   *Tempo di Minuetto.*

2

BM. 9. 450 c.; Royal Music, 2 copies; BRUSS. No. 11595.
Another edn. (Paris: Chevardière): PAR. Vm.⁷ 5963, 2 and 3;
PAR. (C).
Another edn. (Amsterdam: Hummel): BER. Templin Bibl. Thul.
Sammlung; DRES. 3374/O/10; EINS. 679, 22; MUNCH.
Another edn. (London: Welcker, ?1770); BM. Royal Music, 16 b. 13;
SCHW.
Nos. 1–3 (Vienna: Torricella, ? 1785) as 'Trois Concertes pour le

Clavecin o Piano Forte. Composés par M. C. Bach. Dediées a
Madame la Comtesse de Fünfkirchen, Née Comtesse de Chorinsky':
BM. g. 450 d (3); also (dedicated to 'von Glocksberg'): DRES.
3374/O/11.
Nos. 3 and 6 (arranged for two pianofortes), Edn. Steingräber.
Nos. 107, 92.
No. 5 publ. in Edn. Peters 3873.

In manuscript

Nos. 1–6: DRES. 3374/O/12 ('accom. a due cembali'); HAG (M).
No. 1: BM. Add. MSS. 16155, fol. 100.
No. 2; BM. *ibid.* fol. 105.
Nos. 1–4: KON.
Nos. 1, 2, 3, 5, 6: BER. Mus. MS. Bach St. 604–608.

A Third Sett of Six Concertos for the Harpsichord or Piano Forte.
With Accompaniments for two Violins and a Bass, two Hautboys
and two French Horns ad Libitum. Humbly Dedicated to Mrs.
Pelham and Composed by John Christian Bach, Music Master to
Her Majesty the Queen of Great Britain. Opera XIII. Price 15s.
[London: Welcker. 1777.]

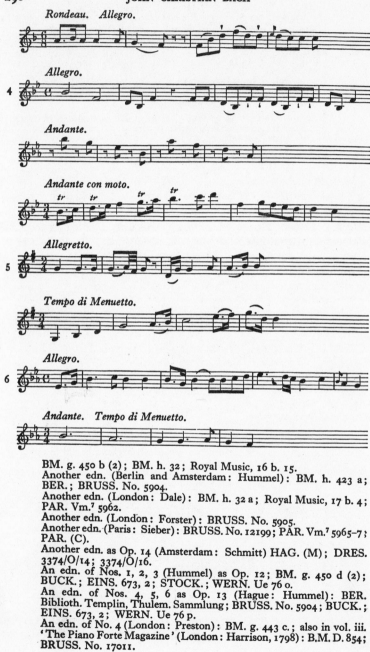

BM. g. 450 b (2); BM. h. 32; Royal Music, 16 b. 15.
Another edn. (Berlin and Amsterdam: Hummel): BM. h. 423 a;
BER.; BRUSS. No. 5904.
Another edn. (London: Dale): BM. h. 32 a; Royal Music, 17 b. 4;
PAR. Vm.⁷ 5962.
Another edn. (London: Forster): BRUSS. No. 5905.
Another edn. (Paris: Sieber): BRUSS. No. 12199; PAR. Vm.⁷ 5965–7;
PAR. (C).
Another edn. as Op. 14 (Amsterdam: Schmitt) HAG. (M); DRES.
3374/O/14; 3374/O/16.
An edn. of Nos. 1, 2, 3 (Hummel) as Op. 12; BM. g. 450 d (2);
BUCK.; EINS. 673, 2; STOCK.; WERN. Ue 76 o.
An edn. of Nos. 4, 5, 6 as Op. 13 (Hague: Hummel): BER.
Biblioth. Templin, Thulem. Sammlung; BRUSS. No. 5904; BUCK.;
EINS. 673, 2; WERN. Ue 76 p.
An edn. of No. 4 (London: Preston): BM. g. 443 c.; also in vol. iii.
'The Piano Forte Magazine' (London: Harrison, 1798): B.M. D. 854;
BRUSS. No. 17011.

An ed. of No. 4 (London: Weekes): 'Concerto for Pianoforte (in which is introduced the Scotch Air "The Yellow Haired Laddie"). Composed *circa* 1770 by John Christian Bach (Bach of London). Op. 13. Arranged by Haydn. First published in 1790. New Edition edited and revised by Edmund H. Turpin': BM. h. 1494, a. 2; an edn. by Walker: R.C.M. LXII. E. 12.

In manuscript

Nos. 1–3: DRES. 3374/O/15.
Nos. 2, 3, 4, 6: EINS. 679 (14, 15, 19, 21).
Nos. 4–6: DRES. 3374/O/17 ('accomodati a 2 Cembali').
No. 6: BER. Mus. MS. Bach St. 204.

Concerto per il Clavicembalo, due Violini, Viola e Basso, dal Sign. Giovani Cristiano Bach. [Riga: G. F. Hartknoch, 1770 ?]

BM. i. 55; EINS. 679, 20 a; HAG (M); BRUSS. No. 5906; LEIPZ. III. 9. 2; MUNCH; WEI. A. 106.

Concerto II. per il Clavicembalo, due Violini, Viola e Basso, dal Sign. Giovani Cristiano Bach. [Riga: G. F. Hartknoch, ? 1771.]

BM. i. 55; BER. (S). ZD. 1474; EINS. 679, 20 b; BRUSS. No. 5906; HAG (M); LEIPZ. III. 9. 3; MUNCH; WEI. A. 107.

JOHN CHRISTIAN BACH

In manuscript

Presto.

Allegro.

Poco Adagio con Sordini.

Allegro.

BER. P. 390 (Clav., 2 Vns., Va., Bass.).

('Concerto de Bach')

('Concerto de Bach')

('Concerto de Bach')

('Concerto de Bach')

Presto.

('De Bach')

Allegretto.

('De Bach')

PAR. Vm.⁷ 4877, fol. 20–2, 42, 43.

Allegro non tanto.

12

Adagio molto.

Allegro assai.

BER. Mus. MS. Bach St. 487 ('Concerto per il Cembalo obligato, 2 Violini, Viola e Basso ').

Un poco Allegro.

13

Adagio.

Allegro.

DRES. 3374/O/3.
Arrd. for 2 Pianofortes (Ed. H. Riemann) : Ed. Steingräber, 106.

Allegro.

14

BUCK. ('Concerto per il Piano-Forte, Oboe, &c.')

Allegro.

15

BER. Mus. MS. Bach P. 391 ('Concerto per il Cembalo Principale, due Violine, due Flauti, due Clarinetti, due Corni, Fagotto, due Viole e Basso '); STOCK.   Cf. *supra*, pp. 284, 289, 290.

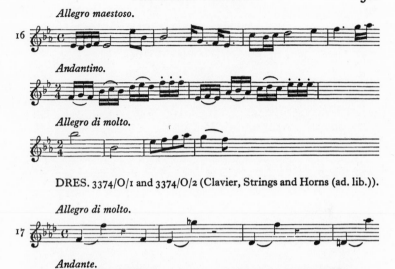

DRES. 3374/O/1 and 3374/O/2 (Clavier, Strings and Horns (ad. lib.)).

BER. Mus. MS. Bach St. 482 and 483 ('Concerto per il Cembalo conc. con due Violini, Viola è Basso . . . riveduto dal Sign. C. P. E. Bach').

INSTRUMENTAL MUSIC

(d) CHAMBER MUSIC

X. SEXTETS

Sestetto à Cembalo ò Piano Forte, Oboe, Violino, Violoncello e Due Corni. Del Signo. Giov: Christ; Bach. Opera III. Offenbach, presso Giovañi Andrē. No. 68.

(See Quartets, Luther's adaptations, No. 2.)

In manuscript.
BER. Bibl. Templin, Sammlung Thulem. 59 ; BER. (S) ZD. 1632 b.

XI. QUINTETS

Six Quintettos for a Flute, Hautboy, Violin, Tenor, and Bass. Composed by John Christian Bach, Music Master to Her Majesty the Queen of Great Britain, and most humbly dedicated to His most Serene Highness the Elector Palatin [London. Welcker.] [Op. XI. *c.* 1772–7.]

In manuscript

Deux Quintettes pour le Clavecin ou Piano Forte accompagné
(*sic*) d'un Violon, Flûte, Hautbois, Viola, et Violoncelle (on peut
les executer sans Instruments). Composée (*sic*) par Mr. J. C. Bach.
Oeuvre XXII.

(See Quartets, Luther's arrangements, Nos. 1 and 3.)

In manuscript.

No. 1 : BRUSS. No. 6376.

Quintetto per Due Violini o due Oboe, Alto Viola, Violoncello o
Sia Fagotto e Basso Del S^g. Jean Chretien Bach, Maitre de
Musique de Sa Majesté la Reine de la Grande Bretagne.   [Paris :
Bureau d'Abonnement Musical.]

STOCK.

In manuscript.

BER. Hausbibl. No. 152.
Schökel (p. 202) quotes the opening theme of the first movement from
Breitkopf's 1769 Catalogue.

XII. QUARTETS

Six Quartettos for a German Flute, Violin, Tenor, and Violoncello:
Composed by John Christian Bach, Music Master to her Majesty.
Dedicated to his Exellency S^r. William Young, Bar^t. Governor of
Dominico &c. &c. Opera VIII. Price 10s. 6d. [London: Welcker
? 1775.]

Rondeaux. Allegro.

Andante.

Tempo di Minuetto.

BM. g. 411 a (5); Royal Music, 16, f. 14; PAR. Vm.⁷ 6652.
Another edn. (Paris: Sieber): PAR. (C).
Another edn. (Amsterdam: Hummel): BER. Hausbibl. No. 154;
BITT.; STOCK.; UPS. i. tr. 114, 1.
Another edn. (La Haye: 'Gravé pour le Comte d'Antoine Stechwey.
Oeuvre IX'): BM. g. 417 a (2); MUNCH.; RAM.
Nos. 2, 5, 6 (Götz: Mannheim): EINS. 70, 13.
Nos. 1, 4, 5 in 'Fürs Haus' (Beyer), Nos. 119–21.
Nos. 1, 3, 5: Ed. A. Küster and M. Glöder, 1927.

In manuscript.

Nos. 1–6: DRES. 3374/Q/2; 3374/Q/3.
Nos. 3 and 6: BRUSS. No. 25,448.
Nos. 3, 4: DRES. 3374/Q/5 ('acc. a 2 Cembali').

Four Quartettos, two for Two Flutes, a Tenor and Violoncello,
one for Two Flutes, a Violin and Violoncello, and one for a Flute
and Hoboy, or Two Flutes, a Tenor and Violoncello. Composed
by the late John Christian Bach. Opera XIX. Pr. 8s. N.B. These
Original Quartettos were Composed for The Rt. Honble The Earl
of Abingdon, by whose permission they are now published [Lon-
don: Preston. ? 1785]

Allegro.

Allegretto.

Allegretto. Rondo.

BM. g. 435 1.
Another edn. (Frankfurt: W. D. Haueisen, ? 1790, as 'Oeuvre XVIII'):
BM. g. 411 a (1).
Another edn. (Berlin: Hummel, as Op. XX): BER (S) ZD. 1650.

In manuscript

No. 4: COP.

     * Bach's familiarity with the Soprano Aria in his father's Cantata 68 must be inferred.

Six Quartettos for a German Flute, Violin, Tenor, and Bass, or
Two Violins, a Tenor and Bass. By Messrs Bach, Abel, & Giardini. Price 10s. 6d. [London: William Napier. 1777.]

Three are by Bach:

BM. g. 435 (2); Royal Music, 26 c. 1.
Another edn. (Amsterdam: Hummel).
BER. Hausbibl. No. 155; STOCK.
Another edn. (Paris: Sieber): PAR (C).

In manuscript

Nos. 1–6: BM. Add. MS. 14337.

Four Sonatas originally composed as Quartetts for the Harpsichord, Violin, Flute, Hautboy, Tenor, and Violoncello, by the
late John Christian Bach, adapted for the Harpsichord or Piano
Forte, with a single Accompaniment for a Violin, by John Christian Luther. Dedicated by Permission to Her Majesty. [London:
? 1785.]

Rondo. Allegro.

BM. h. 60 (2).
No. 4: STOCK. ('Offenbach, presso Giovanni André, No. 66.')

In manuscript.

No. 1: WOLF. Vogel 16.
No. 2: BRUSS. No. 6376 (as a Quintet).
No. 3: as a Sextet (*supra*).

Three favorite Quartetts and one Quintett for the Harpsichord, Violin, Flute, Hautboy, Tenor, and Violoncello, by the late John Christian Bach Esq. Music Master to her Majesty, for whom they were originally compos'd. In order to render this capital Work as useful as possible these Quartetts are expressly adapted for the Harpsichord or Piano Forte, with a single Accompaniment for a Violin, by John Christian Luther. Dedicated by Permission to Her Majesty. [London ? 1785.]

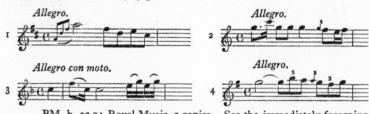

BM. h. 32 c: Royal Music, 2 copies. See the immediately foregoing edition.

In manuscript
No. 1 (Quintet): BRUSS. No. 6376.
No. 2 (Sextet): See *supra*.

Six Sonatas for two Violins and a Violoncello, with a Thorough Bass for the Harpsichord. Composed by Messrs Bach, Abel and Kammel. Price 10s. 6d. [London: Welcker. ? 1780]
No. 1 is by Bach:

Tempo di Minuetto.

BM. g. 415 11; and g. 420 e (6); Royal Music, 17 c. 3.
Another edn. (Berlin: Hummel): BER. Hausbibl. No. 159.
Another edn. (Frankfort: Haueisen): DRES. 7/Q./12.

In manuscript

Sinfonia ex D à 4 dell Sign. Back.

Allegro.

UPS.   (See MS. Symphonies and Overtures)

Sinfonia à 4.

Allegro assai.

UPS.   (See MS. Symphonies and Overtures)

XIII. TRIOS

Six Sonates, pour le Clavecin, accompagnées d'un Violon ou Flute Traversiére et d'un Violoncelle, dediées a Son Altesse Royale Augusta Princesse Hereditaire de Brunswick-Lunebourg &c., &c., &c. Composeès par Jean Chretien Bach, Maitre de Musique de S.M. la Reine d'Angleterre. Oeuvre II. A Londres. Printed for the Author and sold at his Lodgings in Meards Street, St. Ann's Soho [1763].

BM. g. 450; Royal Music, 16 b. 11.
Another edn. (London: Welcker): BM. Royal Music, 2 copies;
BRUSS. No. 12, 149.
Another edn. (Amsterdam: Hummel. Forkel and Cramer date it
1766): BUCK.
Another edn. (Paris: Huberty): LEIPZ. III. 9. 4; PAR(C). No. 8950;
WEI. A. 96. No. 3: in 'Collegium Musicium', Nos. 1737, 1738.

In manuscript

Nos. 1–6: DRES. 3374/Q/1.
Nos. 1 and 3: BER Mus. MS. Bach St. 611, 617.
No. 3: B.M. Add. MS. 16155, fol. 121.

Six Trio pour deux Violons et Alto Viola ou Basse obligé. Composés par Mr. Bach. Mis au jour par Mr. Huberty, de l'Academie Royale de Musique. Gravés par Me. Son Epouse. Oeuvre II [Op. 4] Prix 4ll. [? 1765]

BM. h. 2851 d(1); BER. P. 392 (as 'Oeuvre IV'); EINS. 67, 8;
PAR. (C) No. 8950.
Another edn. (London: Simpson): RAM.
Another edn. (Amsterdam: Markordt: Nos. 1–4 only): PAR. Vm.[7]
1209.
Another edn. (Amsterdam: Hummel): STOCK.
Another edn. (London: Hummel): BM. Royal Music, 16 b. 20.

In manuscript.

BAS. Sara 215, 242–6; BER. Hausbibl. Nos. 156–8; BER. Mus. MS.
Bach P. 705; MUNCH. Nos. 1342–7; STOCK.

Six Trios pour le Clavecin, ou le Piano Forté, accompagnéz d'un
Violon. Composés par J. C. Bach. Oeuvre 7ᵉ. [Vienna: Huberty]

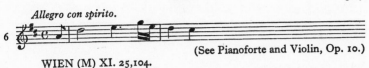

Allegro con spirito.

6

WIEN (M) XI. 25,104.

(See Pianoforte and Violin, Op. 10.)

Two Trios for two German Flutes, or Flute, Violin, and Violoncello, selected by T[heobald] Monzani. Pr. 3ˢ. N.B. These Original Trios were Composed for the Rigᵗ. Honᵇˡᵉ. Earl of Abingdon, by whose Permission they are now Published [London: Monzani. ? 1800].

No. 1 is by Bach.

Allegretto.

Adagio.

Allegro.

BM. g. 274 b (3).

In manuscript.

Allegrino.

Menuet.

MIL. 980/26 ('Del Sigʳᵉ Bach in Milano'. 2 Violins and Basso); STOCK.

Allegro assai.   *Larghetto.*

Presto.

MIL. 979/25 ('Del Sigʳᵉ Bach in Milano') 'Trio à due Flutte Trauersiere obligate'.

BAS. kr. iv. 19; MIL. 974/20 ('Del Sig^{re} Bach in Milano').

BAS. kr. iv. 18; MIL. 976/22 ('Del Sig^{re} Bach in Milano').

MIL. 978/24 ('Del Sig^{re} Bach in Milano', 2 Violins and Basso.)

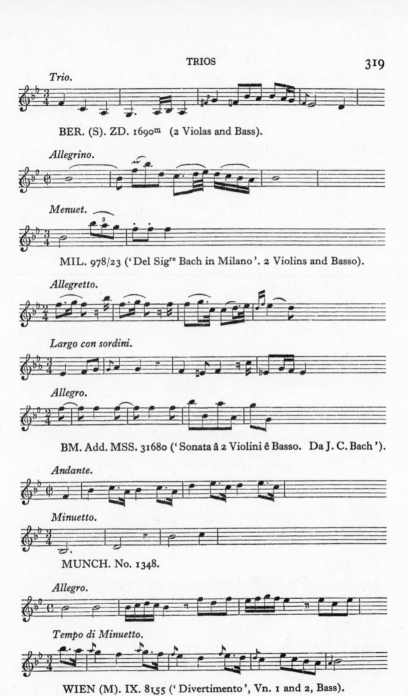

Trio.

BER. (S). ZD. 1690ᵐ   (2 Violas and Bass).

Allegrino.

Menuet.

MIL. 978/23 ('Del Sigʳᵉ Bach in Milano'. 2 Violins and Basso).

Allegretto.

Largo con sordini.

Allegro.

BM. Add. MSS. 31680 ('Sonata â 2 Violini ê Basso. Da J. C. Bach').

Andante.

Minuetto.

MUNCH. No. 1348.

Allegro.

Tempo di Minuetto.

WIEN (M). IX. 8ᵢ55 ('Divertimento', Vn. 1 and 2, Bass).

Allegro cantabile.

Larghetto.

Minuetto.

MUNCH. No. 1349.

Affetuoso.

Minuetto grazioso.

STOCK. (2 Violins and Basso. ' Del Sr. Gio. Bacch.')]

Allegro moderato.

Andante.

Allegro moderato.

MS. in possession of Herr Hugo Socznik, Danzig ('Trio ex Es♮. Violino Primo, Violino Secundo, e Basso, dell Sign. Bach ').

Allegro.

Adagio.

Vivace.

KARL. (' Sonata à 3 (Fl. tr., V. u. B.) Es dur, 3/4 ').

MUNCH. No. 4473 (Cembalo obbl. e Violini).

MIL. 974/21 ('Del Sig^re Bach in Milano'. 2 Violins and Basso).

INSTRUMENTAL MUSIC

(e) *VIOLIN MUSIC*

XIV. VIOLIN AND PIANOFORTE

Six Sonatas, for the Harpsichord or Piano Forte; with an Accompagnament for a Violin. Humbly dedicated to The Right Honble. Lady Mellbourne. And composed by John Cristian Bach, Music Master to Her Majesty. Opera X. [London: Welcker? 1775].

BM. f. 44.
Another edn. (London: A. & P. Thompson ? 1780): BM. e 230 b.
Another edn. (Paris: Mme. Berault): BER.
Another edn. (Vienna: Huberty): WIEN (M). XI. 25104 ('Six Trios
pour le Clavecin, ou le Piano Forté, accompagnéz (sic) d'un Violon.
Oeuvre 7ᵉ'). See p. 316 supra.
Another edn. (Paris: Leduc): PAR. Vm.⁷ 5339; WEI. A. 97.
Another edn. (Amsterdam: Hummel): DRES. 3374/R./2. MUNCH.
Another edn. (Vienna: Torricella): BRUSS. No. 14,969; HAG. (M).

In manuscript

Nos. 1, 3, 4, 5: EINS. 65, 96.
Nos. 1-6 GOT.; DRES. 3374/R./3.

Four Sonatas and two Duetts for the Piano Forte or Harpsichord
with Accompaniments, humbly dedicated to the Right Honᵇˡᵉ
the Countess of Abingdon and Composed by John Christian Bach,
Music Master to her Majesty & the Royal Family. Opera XV.
Pr. 10ˢ. 6ᵈ. [London: Welcker ? 1779]

See Pianoforte Sonatas, Op. 15.

BM. g. 443 (5); LEIPZ.
Another edn. (London: Joseph Dale): RCM.
Another edn. (Berlin: Hummel): DRES. 3374/J./12; EINS. Mka. 21; STOCK.
Another edn. (Paris: Sieber): BER. Hausbibl. No. 240; PAR. Vm.[7] 5338; STOCK.
Another edn. (Paris: Leduc): PAR. Vm.[7] 5340.

In manuscript
No. 3: BER. Mus. MS. Bach St. 298.
No. 5: EINS. 65, 49; LUN.

Six Sonatas for the Harpsichord or Piano-Forte, with an Accompaniment for a German-Flute or Violin. Dedicated to the Miss Greenlands and Composed by John Christian Bach, Music Master to Her Majesty and the Royal Family. Opera XVI. Price 10s. 6d. [London: Joseph Dale ? 1783]

Allegretto.

BM. e. 5. f (3).
Another edn. (Paris: Sieber): EINS. C. 318; PAR. Vm.⁷ 5341.
Another edn. (Amsterdam: Schmitt): BUCK.
Another edn. (Berlin: Hummel): BRUSS. No. 26,692; DRES.
3374/R./1; HAG (M); Par. Vm.⁷ 5342; WEI. A. 98 B.
Another edn. (London: Welcker): HAMB.
Nos. 1 and 2 in 'Nagels Musik-Archiv' (Hannover), No. 1.

In manuscript

Nos. 1, 3, 4, 5: EINS. 22, 1.
No. 1: SCHW. No. 821.
No. 2: WOLF.

Quatre Sonates et deux Duo pour le Clavecin ou Piano-Forte avec Accompagnement de Violon ou Flutte. Par Jean Chrestien Bach. Opera XVIII. Prix 10ˢ. 6ᵈ. [Paris: Chevardiere. ? 1780]

Allegro.

Allegro.

Rondeau. Allegretto.

Allegretto.

Allegretto. See Pianoforte Sonatas, Op. 18.

BM. g. 272 (9); BRUSS. No. 26,694; PAR. Vm.⁷ 5349; PAR (C).
Another edn. (London: Welcker): BM. i. 40 (1); PAR. Vm.⁷ 5343.
Another edn. (Berlin: Hummel): BER. Staatsbibl. Mus. 9473 (Nos.
5 and 6); BRUSS. No. 11,596; DRES.
Another edn. (London: Vogler): SCHW.
Another edn. (Paris: Bonin): PAR. (Ste. G.).
Another edn. (Paris: Leduc): PAR. Vm.⁷ 5340.
A transcription (by J. B. Cramer) of the Rondo of No. 4: BM. h.
1482. b (11).

In manuscript

No. 1: SCHW. No. 822.
Nos. 1-4: BER.
No. 4: EINS. 22, 1 (No. 3).
Nos. 5, 6: DRES. 3374/J./8.

Six Sonatas for the Piano Forte or Harpsichord with an Accom-
paniment for a German Flute or Violin. Compos'd by the late
Celebrated John Christian Bach. Op: 19. Price 10ˢ. 6ᵈ. [London:
James Freeman ? 1785]

Moderato.

Rondo.

BM. g. 450 a (2).
Breitkopf publishes Sonatas in A and D (ed. Fr. Piersig).

Three Sonatas for the Piano Forte or Harpsichord, with an Accompanyment for a Violin, Composed by J. C. Bach. Op. XX. Pr. 5ˢ. [London: Joseph Dale. ? 1790]

BM. h. 1480 c (2).
Another edn. (London: W. Campbell. ? 1783): BM. h. 3055 (1).
Another edn. (London: Goulding, d'Almaine Potter): RCM. No. 1433.
Another edn. (London: Harrison): BM. D. 854 ('Pianoforte Magazine', Vol. xiii. 1801).

Four Sonatas originally composed as Quartetts for the Harpsichord, Violin, Flute, Hautboy, Tenor, and Violoncello, by the late John Christian Bach, adapted for the Harpsichord or Piano Forte, with a single Accompaniment for a Violin, by John Christian Luther. Dedicated by Permission to Her Majesty. [? 1785]

See Quartets.

BM. h. 60 (2); h. 32. c.; BER. Bibl. Templin, Thulem. Sammlung. Breitkopf publishes two Sonatas, in A and D (ed. Fr. Piersig).

Musical Remains: or the Compositions of Handel, Bach, Abel, Giuliani, &c.; selected from original manuscripts never before published: and now adapted for the Harp, or Harpsichord, with accompaniments for the Flute, or Violin; Respectfully Dedicated to his Scholars, by Edward Jones, Harpist to the Prince of Wales. [London: ? 1796].

No. 6: Sonata 'For the Harp; with Accompaniments for a Violin and Violoncello, or may be Played on the Harpsichord as a Duet with the Harp. Composed by G. C. Bach, on purpose for the Editor to play'.

Allegro.

BM. g. 247 (1); Royal Music, 17 f. 9.

In manuscript

Sonata a Cembalo conc. e Violino 1771.

Adagio.

1

Allegro.

Presto.

BER. Mus. MS. Bach St. 492; also 297.

Sonata a Violino solo col Basso.

Allegretto.

2

Andante.

Later form.

Tempo di Minuetto.

BER. Bibl. Templin M. Th. 260.

Adagio.

Allegretto.

Allegro assai.

BER. Mus. MS. Bach St. 296 ('Sonata a Flauto traverso e Cemb. conc'.)

[Sette] Sonate per Cembalo con Violino del Sig^r. Gio. Bach.

Allegro.

I

Andante.

Minuetto.

Allegro assai.

2

Andante.

Minuetto.

Allegro assai.

3

JOHN CHRISTIAN BACH

Andante.

Minuetto più tosto Allegro.

MIL. 991/37.
No. 3: DRES. 1/T./58, 3 (as 'Sonata per il Cembalo col Flauto').

XV. VIOLIN DUETS

Six Duetts for two Violins. Composed by Sig[r]. Bach. Price 5[s].
(London : Longman, Lukey & Co. ? 1775)

Andante assai.

Andante assai.

Spiritoso.

Allegro.

Andante.   *Tempo di Minuetto.*

BM. g. 421 C (5).

In manuscript

Four Canzonette.

Andantino.

Andantino.

Allegro.

Andantino.

BM. Add. MSS. 34074-5.

III. Sonate per il Flauto e Violino. Del Signore Bach (? J. C. B.).

WIEN. S. m. 2902.

INSTRUMENTAL MUSIC

(f) *PIANOFORTE MUSIC*

XVI. SONATAS AND ARRANGEMENTS

Six Sonates pour le Clavecin ou le Piano Forte, dediées a Son Altesse Serenissime Monseigneur le Duc Ernest, Duc de Mecklenbourg &c., &c., Chevalier de l'Ordre de l'Aigle Blanc, et Major General des Armées de S. M. Britannique; Composées par Jean Cretien Bach, Maitre de Musique de S. M. La Reine d'Angleterre. Oeuvre V [? 1770]

BM. e. 230 (1); Royal Music, 15 h. 4; BRUSS. No. 14,426; PAR.
Vm.⁷ 5337.
Another edn. (London: Welcker. ? 1775): BM. e. 5 q (1); WEI.
A. 99.
Another edn. (Amsterdam: Hummel. 1768): BER. Hausbibl. No.
248; BRUSS. No. 26,691; DRES. 3374/J./12; MUNCH.; STOCK.
Another edn. (Paris: Huberty): PAR (C).
Nos. 2-6 in Edn. Peters 3831.
No. 4 in Edn. Bernouilli, No. 16.
No. 5 (Adagio) in Edn. Universal 745.
No. 6 in Edn. Steingräber 168.
No. 6 (Allegretto) in Edn. Universal 745.

In manuscript

No. 1 : BER. (uncatalogued); PAR. Vm.⁷ 5345 ; PAR. Vm.⁷ 1941.
No. 2 : BER.
No. 5 : EINS. 63, 62; MIL. 982/28; MUNST. B. 56.
No. 6 : EINS. 64, 3; LEIPZ. III. 9. 1.
Nos. 1–6 : STOCK.
Nos. 2, 3, 4 arranged as Pianoforte Concerti by Mozart: BER. (Autograph).

Four Sonatas and two Duetts for the Piano Forte or Harpsichord with Accompaniments, humbly dedicated to the Right Honᵇˡᵉ. the Countess of Abingdon and Composed by John Christian Bach, Music Master to her Majesty & the Royal Family. Opera XV. [London: Welcker. ?1779.]

See 'Pianoforte and Violin'.

'Due Cembali obligati.'

'For two performers on one Pianoforte or Harpsichord'.
BM. g. 443 (5); Royal Music, 16 b. 15.
No. 5 in Ed. Steingräbner, No. 2,260.
For other editions see Pianoforte and Violin, and 'Sonata à Quatre mains' (*infra*).

In manuscript

No. 5 : BER. Mus. MS. Bach 288 ; BRUSS. No. 5,909 ; EINS. 65, 49.
No. 6 : BER. Mus. MS. Bach 288 and 395.

Six Sonatas for the Harpsichord or Piano Forte. Compos'd by John Christian Bach, Music Master to her Majesty and the Royal Family. Opera XVII. Price 10s. 6d. [London : Welcker. ?1779.]

BM. e. 230 c.; EINS. 57, 13; HAG.
Another edn. (Berlin: Hummel; dedicated to Princess Julie of Hesse-
Philippsthal): BER.; BRUSS. No. 26,693; DRES. 3374/J./5; BUCK.
R.C.M.; WEI. A. 100.
Another edn., as Op. 6 (Huberty: Vienna): WIEN. VII. 14313.
Another edn., as 'Op. XII' (Paris: Sieber): PAR (C); WEI. A. 101.
Another edn. (Paris: Chevardière): PAR. Vm.⁷ 5963.
Another edn. (Giov. André Offenbach): DRES. 3374/J./1 ('con un
Viol. ad libitum, composto dal editore').
Nos. 2–6 in Edn. Peters, No. 3831.
No. 4 in Edn. Cotta, Neue Folge, No. 925.
No. 6 in 'Alte Klaviermusik' (Senff), Zweite Folge, Heft 4.

In manuscript

Nos. 1–6: DRES. 3374/J./6.

Quatre Sonates et deux Duo pour le Clavecin ou Piano-Forte avec
Accompagnement de Violon ou Flutte. Par Jean Chrestien Bach.
Opéra XVIII. Prix 10ˢ. 6ᵈ. [Paris: Chevardière ?1780]

See Pianoforte and Violin.

BM. g. 272 (9); BRUSS. No. 26,694; PAR. Vm.⁷ 5349; PAR (C).
For other edns. see Pianoforte and Violin.

In manuscript.

No. 5: BM. Add. MSS. 31680, f. 7; BER. Mus. MS. Bach 954;
Nos. 5 and 6: BUCK.

Sonata pour le Clavecin ou Forte Piano, qui Represente La Bataille de Rosbach. Composées (*sic*) par Mr. Bach. N.B. Dans
cette Sonata La Musique vous montre Le Comencement (*sic*)
d'une Bataille, Le feu des Cannons et Mousqueterie, L'Ataque de
La Cavalerie et les L'Amendations (*sic*) des Blessées (*sic*). Prix 2ˢ.
[London : Jackson and Smith ?1782]

Commencement de la Bataille.

Canonade.

BM. e. 230 (e).
This puerile composition is identical with a Sonata on the Battle of Bergen-op-Zoom, attributed to C. P. E. Bach in Wotquenne's *Verzeichnis* (No. 272). Both pieces were published after the death of their alleged authors, and both, undoubtedly, are spurious. Another edition, in which Graun (? C. H. or J. G.) is named as composer, is in the B.M.

Trois Sonates pour Clavecin. Op. 21 (*sic*) [Paris : Bonin]

Poco largo.

Allegro spiritoso.

[Allegro.]

PAR (C).

Quatre Sonates pour le Clavecin. Op. 16 (*sic*) [Paris : Baillieu]

Lesson 1.
Allegretto.

Lesson 2.
[*Allegretto.*]

Lesson 3.
Allegretto.

Lesson 4.
Allegretto.

PAR (C). See ' Four Progressive Lessons ' (*infra*, p. 350).

Sonata à Quatre mains sur un Clavecin. Composé par J. C. Bach [Amsterdam : Joseph Schmitt. ?1783]

Allegro.

Rondo. Allegretto.

BM. g. 418 (1); BER. Mus. MS. Bach P. 395. In ' Nagels Musik-Archiv ' (Hannover), No. 4. See Op. 15, *supra*.
In manuscript
BER. Mus. MS. Bach St. 288; BRUSS. No. 5908; PAR. Vm.⁷ 5344.

Six Favourite Opera Overtures set for the Harpsichord or Organ. Compos'd by Sigʳ. Bach [London : Walsh. ?1770]

Allegro con brio.

' Orione '.

'Zanaida'.

'Artaserse'.

'La Cascina'.

'Catone nell' Indie' and 'Astarto'.

See Symphonies and Overtures.

BM. e. 12 (2); BRUSS. No. 30,218.
No. 4 (first and last movements) in Edn. Bernouilli, No. 8.

Overture to 'Orfeo'.

BM. g. 271 b (10).

A favourite Ouverture. Composed for two Orchestras by J. C.
Bach, late Music Master to Her Majesty. Adapted for two per-
formers on one Piano-Forte or Harpsichord by C. F. Baumgarten.
Pr. 3/-. [London : Wm. Forster]

See Symphonies and Overtures.

PAR. Vm.⁷ 12,406.

Six Overtures composed and Addapted for the Harpsichord by
John Christian Bach [London : Welcker. ?1770]

See Symphonies and Overtures, Op. 3.

BM. g. 450 a (1); Royal Music, 17 e. 9.

The Celebrated Overture to Orione by John Christian Bach, adapted for Two Performers on the Harpsichord or Piano Forte, by [Charles] Thomas Carter [London: George Goulding. 1788]

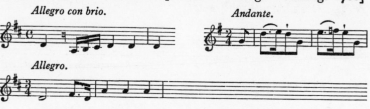

BM. G. 351 (as No. 12 of 'The Feast of Apollo').

Fuge für das Pianoforte oder die Orgel komponirt von Christian Bach über die Buchstaben seines Namens. [Leipzig: C. F. Peters.]

RCM. XXIX. A. 27 and B. 4; BER. Hausbibl. No. 198; BER (S); Berlin Hochschule f. M.; LEIPZ. III. 6. 10; STOCK. Another edn. (Paris: Sieber): BRUSS. Nos. 5,910 and 14,928.

God save the King, with Variations for the Piano Forte or German Flute, by J. C. Bach. Pr. 1ˢ/. [No title page]

BM. G. 807, No. 34 (? 1790); BONN; RCM., No. 812; STOCK.

Six Progressive Lessons for the Harpsichord or Piano Forte in different Keys. Composed by Mr. Bach, master to the celebrated Mr. Schroeter. The Expression & fingering are properly marked by Mr. Bach. Pr. 8/-. [London: William Forster. 1783].

Allegro Siciliano e scherzando.

Allegro di molto.

5

Adagio assai mesto e sostenuto.

Allegretto arioso ed amoroso.

Allegro di molto.

6

Adagio affettuoso e sostenuto.

Allegro moderato.

Each Lesson is styled 'Sonata'.
BM. g. 543 u (1).
The six (in MS. and dated 1753) are attributed to C. P. E. Bach in Wotquenne's *Verzeichnis*, p. 19.

In manuscript

No. 1: DAN. MS. 7040.

Four Progressive Lessons for the Harpsichord or Piano Forte, and Two Duetts, for two Performers on one Harpsichord or Piano Forte, composed by Mr. Bach. Pr. 10sh. 6d. [London: Longman & Broderip. ?1780]

Allegretto.   *Minuetto.*

1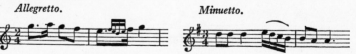

The melody of the Arioso is Bach's 'No, 'twas neither shape nor feature' (see p. 245).

Rondo.   Allegretto.

BM. h. 726 e (1); PAR (C).

The Feast of Apollo, containing Eleven Lessons, a Duet for Two
Performers on One Harpsichord or Piano Forte, and Twenty Two
Favorite Songs [London : George Goulding. 1788]

[*Allegro.*]

Tempo di Minuetto.

BM. G. 351 (2).   The Lesson is No. 7 in the volume, which contains
nothing else by Bach.

Symphonie, composée par J. Haydn, arrangée par Jean Chrétien
Bach, pour Clavecin ou Fortepiano. [Paris : Sieber]

Allegro.

SCHW.

In manuscript

Alla Polacca del Sig. J. C. Bach aus Clavier Stücke Rosina Elisabetha von Münch 1777

BER. Mus. MS. 30,327.

Variationen.
Un poco allegro.

DRES. 3374/J./10.

Rondeau. Menuetto favori di Fischer. Con 12 Variationi per il
Cembalo Solo.

DRES. 3374/J./11.
Mozart also treated the theme.

Six Sonates à quatre mains Sur un Clavecin ou Forte Piano
composées par J. C. Bach.

Minuetto.

Trio.

BRUSS. No. 5907.

Sonata composta dell Sigr. Bach

Allegretto.

Adagio.

Allegro.

BRUSS. No. 27,134.

Sonata 2da per il Cembalo di Bach

Allegro.

Tempo di minuetto.

PAR. Vm.^{7} 4864.

Sonata a Cembalo Solo del S. Gio Bach.   1768

Allegro.

Andante.

Allegro.

MIL. 989/35.

Allegro vivace.

1

Sonata per cembalo.   (65. 47)

2

Andante.

3

Menuetto.   (65. 50)

4

EINS. 65. 47; 65. 50; 66. 12; 66. 37 (? J. C. B.'s).   (66. 12)

XI Variationen über eine bekannte Ariette

Thema.
Moderato.

BER. P. 206.

Ballo Montezuma per il Clavicembalo. Del Sig. Ca. Bach

Atto I.
Allegro.

Six movements follow (Allegro, Maestoso, (?) Adagio, Adagio, Allegro, Laure).

Atto II.
Adagio.

Six movements follow (March, Adagio, Allegretto, Adagio, Chaconne, Adagio).

Atto III.
Allegro moderato.

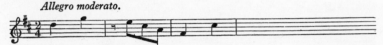

Seven movements follow (March, Adagio, Allegro, (?) Adagio, Adagio, Moderato, Vivace).

Atto V.
[*Tempo signature lacking.*]

Four movements follow (Allegro assai, Allegro, Adagio, Allegro). WIEN (M). XIV. 9508. Act 4 is missing. The identity of J. C. Bach and 'Ca[valier] Bach' is not established. Bitter (*Die Söhne Bachs*, ii. 349) attributes to J. C. Bach a letter, in French, signed 'A. H. Ch[evalier] B.'

Ballet Music. 'Amadis des Gaules'

Lentement.

Gavotte.

Andantino grazioso.

Allegretto.

Tambourin.

Gavotte.

Passacaille.

BER. Mus. MS. Bach 985; WEI. A. 103.

Raccolta di Preludia, Fantasie, Sonate, ammass. di G. H. Möring.
Parte I.

Allegro.

Andante.

Allegretto.

BER. Mus. MS. 30385.

INSTRUMENTAL MUSIC

(g) *MILITARY MUSIC*

XVII. MARCHES

Marcia. Del. Sig^r. Bach [London : Dale. ?1785]

BM. h. 62 (16) ('From 'Scipione').

In manuscript

Marche du Régiment de Prince Ernst

SCHW.

Marche du [Infanterie] Regiment de Braun.

SCHW.

Marche du [Husaren] Regiment de Wurmb.

SCHW.

2 Märsche, N^r. 1. vom ersten, Nr. 2. vom zweiten Bataillon Garde-regiment in Hannover.

BER. Hausbibl. M. M. 386 (2 Oboes, 2 Bassoons, 2 Horns, 2 Clarinets). Published (Leipzig: Breitkopf) as Nos. 75 and 76 'Armee-und Prä-sentirmärsche'.

Due Marce di Cavalleria e d'Infanteria le Prince Wallis de la Gran Bretagna d'un Regimento di Dragoni

BER. Hausbibl. M. M. 382 (2 Horns, 2 Clarinets, Bassoons).

Due Marce di Cavalleria e d'Infanteria della Maesta Regina della Gran Bretagna d'un Regimento di Dragoni

Marcia zu Fuss.

Marcia zu Pferde.

BER. Hausbibl. M. M. 381 (2 Horns, 2 Oboes, 2 Clarinets, Bassoon).

Six Marches.

BM. Royal Music 24 k. 15.   (The instrumentation is not indicated.)

Two Entradas for Horns.

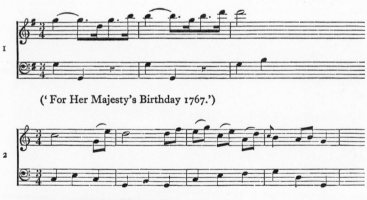

('For Her Majesty's Birthday 1767.')

('For Her Majesty's Birthday 1769.')
BM. Royal Music 24 i. 16.

INDEXES

I. PERSONS

Aaron, Piero, 30.
Abel, Carl Friedrich, 75 f., 78, 79, 83, 87, 92 f., 96, 103, 104, 109, 113, 115, 123, 124, 138, 139, 140, 141, 142, 143, 151, 161, 166, 167, 182.
Abingdon, Willoughby, Earl of, 96, 143, 172, 184, 187.
Abingdon, Countess of, 172.
Adamberger, Valentino, 153, 154, 156, 159, 161.
Adolph Friedrich, Duke of Mecklenburg-Strelitz, 60, 171.
Adriani, Signore, 99, 100, 106, 111.
Agricola, Johann Friedrich, 6, 7, 11.
Aguilar, Signora Girelli, 144, 145.
Albert, Frederick, 151, 166, 167.
Alessandri, Felice, 110, 111, 114, 115.
Allegranti, Signora, 168.
Altnikol, Johann Christoph, 3, 4.
Amalia, Princess, 5, 6.
Amicis, Anna Lucia de', 66, 67, 68, 69, 70, 71, 72.
Amicis, Domenico de', 66, 67, 70.
Amorevoli, Angelo, 147.
Amour, M., 106, 111.
Amour, Mlle, 106.
Anfossi, Pasquale, 148, 152, 154, 168.
Angelo, Domenico, 92, 94.
Angelo, Henry, 75, 92, 94, 103, 124.
Ansani, Giovanni, 163, 164.
Argyll, John, Duke of, 89, 90.
Arnaud, François, 132.
Arne, Michael, 63.
Arne, Thomas, 63, 91, 96, 97, 119.
Arnold, Samuel, 63, 97.
Ashe, Andrew, 158.
Asselin, M., 145.
Asselin, Mlle, 66, 68, 72, 86.
Astrua, Giovanna, 13.
Augusta, Princess, 77, 170, 183.

Baccelli, Mlle, 150, 156, 163, 164.
Bach, Anna Magdalena, 1, 4, 48.
Bach, Carl Philipp Emanuel, 1, 4 f., 71, 112, 125, 159, 189.
Bach, Catharina Dorothea, 2.
Bach, Elisabeth Juliane Friederica, 2, 4.
Bach, Gottfried Heinrich, 2, 4.
Bach, Johann Christoph Friedrich, 1 f., 128, 159.

Bach, Johann Elias, 2.
Bach, Johann Sebastian, 1 f., 8, 15, 76, 112, 125, 174, 188.
BACH, JOHN CHRISTIAN, his birth, 1; godparents, 2; early education, 3; his father's bequests, ib.; received at Berlin by his brother, 4; his Berlin associates, 5; first introduction to Opera, 6; early tuition in composition, 7; his first harpsichord concerts, 8; an early flute sonata, 10; L'Olimpe, a choral ode, ib.; his inclination to visit Italy, 11; circumstances of his departure, 12; first letter from Italy (1757), 14; relations with Chevalier Litta and Martini, ib.; visit to Naples, 15; with Martini at Bologna, 17; early compositions for the Church, 18; becomes a Roman Catholic, 20; consults Martini on problems of part-writing, 22; public rehearsal at Milan of his Messa, 23; performance in San Fedele, 25; much occupied in composition, ib.; desires to study Palestrina, 27; is writing music for the festival of St. John Nepomuk (1758), 28; his Magnificat, 29; his Messa performed in San Francesco, 31; first composition for the Milan Opera, 32; an Aria for Elisi much applauded (1759), 33; his Te Deum, 34; death of his mother (1760), 48; appointed organist of the Duomo, Milan, 49; a visit to Bologna abandoned (1761), 50; production of his Artaserse at Turin, 51; Catone in Utica produced at Naples, 52; qualities of his music, 53; Alessandro nell' Indie produced at Naples (1762), 54; complaints of neglect of his Duomo post, 57; sudden visit to Strelitz, 59; invitation to London, ib.; sets to music Lockman's Ode to Queen Charlotte, 60; he succeeds Cocchi at Opera, 65; his first pasticcios, 66; production of his Orione (1763), 67; publication of his harpsichord concertos (Op. I), 70; qualities of his playing, ib.; production of his

Zanaida, 72; termination of his engagement, 73; reports his intention to remain in England, 74; appointed Music Master to Queen Charlotte, *ib.*; joins Abel in Meard's Street, 75; their first concert (1764), 78; royal licence to print and publish his music, *ib.*; the Mozarts in London, 79; Bach's influence on Mozart, 80; re-engaged at the Opera (1765), 82; production of *Adriano in Siria*, 83; assists at Cremonini's 'benefit', 87; Bach and Abel move to King's Square Court, 92; relations with Angelo, *ib.*; relations with Gainsborough, 93; views regarding Dr. Dodd's execution, *ib.*; Dr. Johnson and Bach, 94; the 'Soho Concert' founded in association with Mrs. Cornelys, 95; the Bach-Abel Concerts transferred to Almack's, *ib.*; connexion with Vauxhall, 96; engaged at Covent Garden, 97; Cecilia Grassi in London, 103; Angelo's unfounded scandal, *ib.*; production of *Carattaco* (1767), 106; contributions to *Sifare*, 108; his alleged marriage to Grassi at this time, 109; the royal Danish visit (1768), 112; introduces the pianoforte as a solo instrument, 113; concerts at Almack's (1769), 115; his expansion of Gluck's *Orfeo ed Euridice* (1770), 117; Oratorios at the King's Theatre, 119; his *Gioas*, 120; Wendling's visit (1771), 123; Bach's *Endimione* (1772), *ib.*, 129; the Mannheim visit, 125 f.; Bach and Augusta Wendling, 127; produces his *Temistocle*, 128; *Amor Vincitore* (1774), 130; *Lucio Silla* (1776), *ib.*; the Paris visit (1778), 131; his *Amadis des Gaules* (1779), 133; association with Pasquale Ricci, 134; Bach moves to Queen Street, Soho (1772), 138; to Newman Street (1774), *ib.*; Bach-Abel Concerts transferred to Carlisle House, 139; the Hanover Square Rooms, 140; partnership with Gallini dissolved (1776), 143; Gainsborough's portrait promised to Martini, 151; Bach's establishment at Richmond, *ib.*; aloofness from the Opera, 155; produces *La Clemenza di Scipione* (1778), 156; revived (1805) by Mrs. Billington, 158; visited (1778) by his Bückeburg brother and nephew, 159; dispatches his portrait to Martini, 160; association with Tenducci (1779), 161; gives up his Richmond establishment, 162; engaged at the Opera (1781), 164; Macfarren's allegations of dissoluteness, 164; relations with the Prince of Wales, 165; the last Bach-Abel Concert, *ib.*; executes his Will, 166; death (1782), *ib.*; his disordered affairs, 167; the Queen's generosity, 168; Tenducci's commemorative concert, *ib.*; Bach's place in music, 169.

WORKS

(See also Thematic Index, p. 195)

Arias and Songs:
Con si bel nome, 33.
Confusa, smarrita, 54, 83.
Dal dolor cotanto oppressa, 157.
Ebben si vada, 147.
Frene le belle lacrime, 157.
Infelice in van m'affano, 157.
Io ti lascio, 147.
Misero pargoletto, 33, 161.
Nel partir, idolo mio, 157.
Non so d'onde viene, 55, 82.
Principe, non temer, 33.
Se il ciel mi divide, 55.
Se mai turbo, 56.
Tu parti, mio ben, 77.
Vauxhall Songs, 96.

Cantatas:
Amor Vincitore, 130, 162.
Aurora, 168.
Endimione, 78, 110, 123, 129, 181.
Ode on the Arrival of Queen Charlotte, 60.
L'Olimpe, 10.
Rinaldo ed Armida, 168.

Church Music:
Attendite mortales, 52.
Beatus vir, 33.
Confitebor, 47.
Credo, 28.
Dies irae, 18, 19, 20, 32, 33.
Dixit Dominus, 28.
Domine ad adiuvandum, 33, 50.
Gloria, 33.
Introito, 27.
Invitatorio, 18, 19.
Kyrie, 28.
Laudate pueri, 33, 50.
Magnificat, 27, 28, 29, 30.
Messa, 22 f., 31, 32.
Officio per gli morti, 18, 19, 24, 28.
Pater noster, 25, 26, 32.
Si nocte tenebrosa, 52.

BACH, JOHN CHRISTIAN: Works—
Church Music (cont.):
Tantum ergo, 22, 47.
Te Deum, 34 f., 50.

Instrumental Music:
Symphonies, 172 f., 181 f.
Overtures, 180 f.
Pianoforte Concertos, 8 f., 70, 182 f.
Chamber Music, 10, 28, 74, 78, 80,
152, 162, 183 f.
Violin Music, 28, 187.
Pianoforte Sonatas, etc., 113, 135,
188 f.
Military Music, 191.

Operas:
Adriano in Siria, 83, 155, 181.
Alessandro nell' Indie, 54, 181.
Amadis des Gaules, 133 f.
Artaserse, 51, 181.
Carattaco, 106 f., 109, 155, 181.
Catone in Utica, 33, 52 f., 152, 181.
La Clemenza di Scipione, 156 f.,
164, 181.
Lucio Silla, 130, 155, 181.
Orione, o sia Diana vendicata, 67 f.,
153, 155, 181.
Temistocle, 128, 155, 181.
The Fairy Favour, 108.
Zanaida, 72 f., 155, 181.

Oratorio:
Gioas, Re di Giuda, 120, 122, 155,
174.
Bach, Veit, 21.
Bach, Wilhelm Friedemann, 1, 3, 4, 6.
Bach, Wilhelm Friedrich Ernst, 159.
Backers, Americus, 113.
Badini, Signore, 149, 150.
Baini, Signora, 76, 77.
Balbi, Ignazio, 18, 27, 28.
Banister, John, 94.
Banti, M., 156.
Banti, Mlle, 156.
Barbieri, Signore, 33.
Baretti, Joseph, 17.
Barthélémon, François-Hippolyte, 81,
87, 102.
Barthélémon, Mrs., *see* Young, Polly.
Bartolozzi, Francesco, 92, 93, 103.
Bassanese, Signore, 114.
Bates, Joah, 63.
Battishill, Jonathan, 63.
Beard, John, 63, 96, 97.
Beckford, William, 89.
Beethoven, Ludwig van, 125, 169.
Bellamy, Richard, 120.
Benda, František, 6.
Bernacchi, Antonio, 103.
Bernasconi, Antonia, 160, 161, 162.

Bertoni, Ferdinando Giuseppe, 77,
160, 161, 162, 163, 164.
Bianchi, Francesco, 163, 164.
Bianchi, Signore, 116, 117, 118, 120.
Bibiena, Joseph Galli, 7.
Bickerstaff, Isaac, 97.
Bigari, Signore, 106, 118.
Billington, Elizabeth, 96, 104, 154,
158.
Binetti, Signora, 66, 68, 72.
Binetti, Signore, 66, 68, 72.
Bolingbroke, Henry, Earl of, 88.
Borde, Jean-Benjamin de la, 133.
Bose, Christiane Sibylla, 2.
Bose, Georg Heinrich, 2.
Boswell, James, 96.
Bottarelli, Giovan Gualberto, 66 f.,
99, 112, 117, 145, 146, 148.
Bremner, Robert, 79.
Brent, Charlotte, 96, 97.
Brickler, Miss, 113.
Britton, Thomas, 94.
Brogli, Anna, 52.
Brook, Mrs., 145.
Brown, Sir James, 92.
Bruscolini, Pasqualino, 7.
Bulgarelli, Marianna, 72.
Buntebart, Gabriel, 142, 167.
Burner, Margaret, 109.
Burney, Charles, 5, 7, 15, 54, 65, 66, 67,
68, 69, 70, 77, 81, 82, 83, 84, 85, 94, 97,
98, 99, 102, 103, 105, 108, 114, 121,
125, 126, 129, 144, 145, 146, 148,
149, 151, 152, 153, 155, 159, 160,
161, 163.
Buroni, Signora, 154.
Byrd, William, 63, 93.

Cafaro, Pasquale 109.
Caffarello, Gaetano (Majorano), 17.
Caldara, Antonio, 6.
Calori, Angiola, 86.
Calzabigi, Raniero, 117.
Campbell, Joseph, 92.
Campioni, Signore, 116.
Campolini, Signora, 111, 112.
Cannabich, Christian, 125, 126, 129,
130.
Cantelo, Anne, 138, 165, 167.
Capitani, Signora, 99.
Carara, Signora, 145.
Cardarelli, Signora, 150.
Carl Philipp, Elector Palatine, 125.
Carl Theodor, Elector Palatine, 125 f.,
171, 187.
Carlini, Agostino, 92.
Carlisle, Charles, Earl of, 88.
Carmignani, Giovanna, 65, 66, 67, 68,
70, 72, 74.

Carnaccia, Francesco, 50.
Carnoli, Pietro Paolo, 130.
Carpara, Signora, 123.
Cascani, Padre, 34.
Caselli, Michele Angelo, 49.
Canter, Mr., 114.
Cattaneo, Signore, 114.
Cervetto, James, 156, 157, 158.
Charlotte, Queen of Great Britain, 51, 59, 60, 70, 74, 80, 104, 166, 168, 170, 171.
Chollet, Signora, 122.
Christian II, King of Denmark, 112.
Chrysander, Friedrich, 19.
Ciampi, Legrenzio Vincenzo, 83.
Ciardini, Domenico, 65, 66, 68, 72.
Cibber, Susanna Maria, 116.
Cicognani, Giuseppe, 32.
Cimarosa, Domenico, 16.
Ciprandi, Ercole, 81, 82, 83, 84, 85, 98, 99, 102.
Cipriani, Giovanni Battista, 92, 93, 103, 139, 141.
Cirri, Signore, 87.
Clarke, Samuel, 141.
Clementi, Muzio, 5.
Cocchi, Gioacchino, 65, 98, 102, 123, 143.
Colman, George, 92.
Como, Signore, 122.
Consorti, Salvatore, 54.
Conti, Signore, 106.
Cooke, Benjamin, 63.
Coppola, Giuseppe, 153, 154, 156, 159, 161.
Coppola, Nicola, 52.
Coradini, Signora, 110, 111.
Cornacchini, Emanuele, 87.
Cornelys, Teresa, 89, 90, 94, 95, 139, 143, 146.
Corri, Domenico, 148.
Costa, Luigi, 54.
Courteille, Lucy, 92.
Cramer, Johann Baptist, 5.
Cramer, Wilhelm, 156, 157, 158, 182.
Crawford, Peter, 69, 73, 81, 97, 110, 116, 122, 123, 144, 164.
Cremonini, Clementina, 65, 68, 70, 72, 81, 82, 83, 84, 85, 87.
Crespi, Mlle, 145.
Crossdill, Mr., 115, 161, 162, 182.
Cumberland, William Augustus, Duke of, 90.

Danby, John, 166.
Danzi, Francesca, 153, 154, 156, 157, 159, 160, 162, 163, 164.
Danzi, Innocenz, 153.
Dassio, Carlo, 51, 74.

Danvers, Sir John, 140.
d'Auvigny, M., 145.
Davies, Cecilia, 146, 152.
Delaval, John, Lord, 92.
Delsire, M., 116, 118.
Demena, Marianna, 122.
Denner, Johann Christoph, 68.
D'Eon, Chevalier, 92.
Dibdin, Charles, 63, 97, 113.
Dillon, Henry Viscount, 140.
Dodd, Dr. William, 93.
Dorset, John Frederick, Duke of, 150.
Dubois, Lady Dorothy, 115.
Duport, Jean-Pierre, 120, 123.
Durante, Francesco, 16.
Elisi, Filippo, 33, 83, 98, 99, 100, 102, 144, 161.
Ernesti, Johann August, 2, 3.
Esterhazy, Nicolas Joseph, Prince, 154.
Evans, Mr., 150.

Farinella, Signora, 147, 148, 149.
Farinelli, Carlo Broschi, 82.
Farnese, Marianna, 152.
Fauconberg, Mary, Countess, 89.
Fauconberg, Thomas, Earl, 88.
Feo, Francesco, 16.
Fermier, Mr., 81.
Fierville, M., 144, 145, 150.
Fioroni, Giovanni Andrea, 48, 49, 50.
Fischer, Johann Christian, 93, 103, 113, 115, 161, 162, 165, 182.
Fischer, Ludwig, 32.
Fischietti, Domenico, 109, 114.
Fitzpatrick, Richard, 121.
Flavis, Catterina, 54.
Florio, Signore, 156, 157.
Fochetti, Signore, 146, 149, 152.
Foote, Samuel, 63.
Fourmantel, Catherine, 75.
Francesco III, Duke of Modena, 27
Francischin, Signore, 86.
Frederick, Sir John, 140.
Frederick II, King of Prussia, 4 f., 15 127.
Fünfkirchen, Countess of, 171.
Fuentes, Count de, 89.

Gabrieli-Bleckmann, Rosa, 127.
Gabrielli, Catterina, 52, 53, 146, 149, 150, 152.
Gabrielli, Francesca, 149, 150.
Gainsborough, Mary, 113.
Gainsborough, Thomas, 92, 93, 103, 104, 141, 151, 160.
Galeotti, Signore, 116, 118, 122.
Galli, Signora, 146, 147, 148, 149, 150.
Gallini, Giovanni Andrea, 65, 66, 68, 71, 72, 140 f.

Galuppi, Baldassare, 76, 98, 114, 146, 155, 163.
Gardel, Mlle, 116, 118.
Gardi, Signora, 146.
Garrick, David, 63, 92.
Gassmann, Florian Leopold, 146, 154.
Gazzaniga, Giuseppe, 150, 153.
Geminiani, Francesco, 94.
Geohegan, Ignatius, 92.
George III, King of Great Britain, 74, 78.
George, Prince of Wales, 108, 165.
Georgi, Dorothea Elisabeth, 4.
Georgi, Signora, 142, 161.
Gherardi, Signore, 82, 162, 163, 164.
Ghiretti, Giacinta, 98, 99, 102.
Giacomazzi, Signora, 112, 114, 115.
Giardini, Felice de', 65, 73, 76, 77, 81, 84, 93, 94, 98, 120, 152, 159, 161, 162, 164.
Gibetti, Signora, 103, 105, 108, 114.
Giordani, Tommaso, 117, 144, 146, 147, 149, 151, 154.
Giordani, Signora, 144.
Giorgetti, Silvio, 129.
Giustinelli, Giuseppe, 65, 66, 67, 68, 70, 72, 77, 118, 122.
Glenorchy, Willielma, Viscountess, 171.
Gluck, Christoph Willibald, Ritter von, 1, 125, 132 f., 143, 145, 160, 161.
Goldoni, Carlo, 67, 105.
Görner, Johann Gottlieb, 3.
Gordon, John, 97, 98, 102, 110.
Gordon, Rev. William, 98.
Gori, Signora, 114.
Gotti, Antonio, 51, 52.
Graf, Friedrich Heinrich, 48.
Grassi, Andrea, 52.
Grassi, Antonio, 53.
Grassi, Bernardo Pasquini, 53.
Grassi, Cecilia, 50, 102 f., 105, 108, 109, 110, 116, 117, 118, 119, 120, 122, 123, 128, 138, 144, 146, 164, 165, 166 f.
Grassi, Luigi, 53, 106 (?), 108.
Graun, Carl Heinrich, 6, 7, 12, 13.
Graun, Johann Gottlieb, 6.
Graziani, Signore, 79.
Greenland, Augur, 19, 166.
Greenland, Emma Jane, 19, 172, 188.
Grenier, Mlle, 144, 145.
Grenville, George, 82.
Grétry, André, 161.
Grey, Mr., 109.
Grimaldi, Nicolino, 110.
Grimm, Fr. Melchior, Baron von, 134.
Grocet, M., 122.

Guadagni, Gaetano, 51, 52, 116, 117, 118, 119, 120, 121, 122, 144.
Guadagni, Signora, 103, 105, 110, 111, 112, 114, 115, 116, 117.
Guarducci, Tommaso, 54, 55, 103, 105, 106, 108, 109, 110, 111, 112, 113.
Guglielmi, Achiapati, 117, 118, 120, 122.
Guglielmi, Pietro, 110, 111, 112, 114, 115, 116, 117, 143, 149.
Guglietti, Signore, 77.
Guidi, Signora, 116, 118, 122.

Hache, Mary, 92.
Handel, George Frederick, 52, 60, 63, 74, 75, 80, 116, 119, 120, 125, 146, 169.
Hare, James, 121.
Harrington, Mr., 158.
Harris, Gertrude, 81, 82, 139, 141, 142, 143.
Harris, James, 81, 82, 139, 141, 142, 143.
Harris, James, 81, 141.
Harrison, Mrs. Samuel, see Anne Cantelo.
Hasse, Johann Adolph, 6, 7, 53, 98.
Hawkins, Sir John, 63.
Haydn, Joseph, 1, 125, 154, 169, 173, 174, 175, 183.
Heinel, Anna, 123, 143, 145.
Hillsborough, Wills, Viscount, 140, 141.
Hobart, Hon. George, 143, 145.
Hooper, Thomas, 89.
How, Mrs., 92.
Hull, Thomas, 108.
Hüllmandel, Nikolaus Joseph, 123.
Hummel, Johann Nepomuk, 5.

Jacob, Benjamin, 142.
Jansen, Sir Stephen Theodore, 90.
Jermoli, Guglielmo, 153, 154, 155, 159, 161.
Jermoli, Signora, 153, 154, 155, 159, 161.
Johnson, Samuel, 94.
Jommelli, Niccolò, 16, 52, 53, 98, 109, 119, 120.
Jones, Susanna, 92.
Junker, Carl Ludwig, 127.

Kammel, Anton, 115.
Kauffmann, Angelica, 89.
Kent, James, 93.
King, Gregory, 88.
Kirnberger, Johann Philipp, 6.

Lafond, Mlle, 145.
Lampugnani, Giovanni Battista, 47.
Langley, Batty, 75.
Lauchery, Étienne, 129, 130.
Lawes, Henry, 93.
Lebrun, Ludwig August, 153, 156, 157, 182.
Lebrun, Mme, see Danzi, Francesca.
Leduc, Pierre, 134, 135.
Leicester, Margaret, Countess of, 140.
Leo, Leonardo, 16.
Lepy, M., 145.
Lindley, Robert, 158.
Linley, Elizabeth Ann, 138.
Litta, Chevalier Agostino, 14 f., 74, 75, 185.
Lockman, John, 60, 86.
Lodi, Stella, 146.
Lorenzini, Signora, 168.
Lovattini, Giovanni, 103, 105, 106, 108, 109, 111, 112, 114, 115, 116, 117, 122, 123, 148, 149.
Luciani, Signore, 112, 114, 115.
Lully, Jean-Baptiste, 132, 133.
Luther, John Christian, 184.

Maczura, Antonio, 99.
Maddan, Miss, 168.
Maggiore, Signora, 105, 111, 112.
Majo, Francesco di, 53.
Manzoletto, Signore, 161, 162, 163, 164, 168.
Manzuoli, Giovanni, 80, 81, 82, 83, 84, 85, 87.
Mara, Mme, 168.
Marchetti, Signora, 146, 161.
Marie-Antoinette, Queen of France, 132.
Martini, Giovanni Battista, 12, 14 f., 74, 75, 139, 151, 159, 160, 182.
Mattei, Colomba, 64 f., 73, 87.
Mattocks, Mr., 97.
Mattocks, Mrs., 120.
Mazziotti, Giuseppe Antonio, 76, 77.
Mazzoli, Teresa, 51.
Mecci, Francis, 166.
Melbourne, Viscountess, 171.
Merlin, Joseph, 89.
Messier, Antonio le, 52.
Metastasio (Pietro Trapassi), 72, 130, 146, 148, 149.
Mezzo, Pietro di, 51.
Micheli, Leopoldo, 81, 82, 83, 85, 99 (?), 103, 105, 106, 108, 109, 112, 114, 145, 146, 152, 154, 155, 159, 161, 162, 163, 164, 168.
Micheroux, Mme, 129.
Miller, John, 92.

Millico, Giuseppe, 143, 144, 145, 146, 152.
Mingotti, Regina, 65, 73, 76, 77, 98.
Mönch, M., 145.
Molteni, Benedetta Emilia, 11.
Monari, Fabris, 99, 100.
Monari, Signore, 99.
Monmouth, James, Duke of, 88.
Monticelli, Angelo Maria, 7.
Monzani, Theobald, 184.
Morigi, Andrea, 122.
Morigi, Pietro, 103, 105, 106, 108, 109, 111, 112, 114, 116, 117, 118, 120, 122, 144, 168.
Morley, Thomas, 63.
Moser, Signora, 106, 108, 111.
Moser, Signore, 112.
Mossop, Henry, 82.
Mount Edgcumbe, George, Earl of, 144, 147, 149, 150, 152, 153, 160, 163.
Mozart, Leopold, 80, 84, 87, 134.
Mozart, Wolfgang Amadeus, 1, 15, 52, 53, 54, 57, 66, 79 f., 87, 125, 127, 128, 130, 131, 144, 153, 160, 169, 173, 183.
Mucciolo, Vincenzo, 129.
Muzio, Antonio, 52, 54.

Nichelmann, Christoph, 6.
Nicolai, F., 151.
Nicolini, Carlo, 51, 52.
Nollekens, Joseph, 88.
North, Frederick, Lord, 82.
Novello, Vincent, 19.

Oglethorpe, James Edward, 89.
Onofrio, Signore, 149.
Onslow, Sir Arthur, 89.
Onslow, Sir Richard, 88.

Pacchierotti, Gasparo, 154, 160, 161, 162, 163.
Paisiello, Giovanni, 16, 152, 154, 155, 164.
Palestrina, Giovanni Pierluigi da, 27.
Pallavicini, Vincenzo, 114.
Palmer, Sir John, 90.
Papendiek, Mrs., 104, 105, 120, 124, 138, 151, 162, 165, 166, 167, 168.
Parigi, Maddalena, 50, 51.
Parsons, William, 151.
Pasini, Signore, 147, 148, 149.
Paxton, Stephen, 166.
Pelham, Mrs., 172.
Pepys, Samuel, 96.
Peretti, Signore, 150.
Perez, Davide, 77.

Pergolesi, Giovanni Battista, 16, 71, 120, 150.
Perti, Giacomo Antonio, 22.
Philidor, Anne, 94.
Piatti, Signora, 103, 105, 106, 108, 109, 112, 116, 117.
Piatti, Signore, 116, 117.
Piccinni, Niccola, 16, 105, 108, 109, 110, 111, 114, 116, 119, 131, 132 f., 145, 150, 153, 154, 155, 164.
Pigot, George, Lord, 89.
Pinto, Thomas, 96.
Pinto, Mrs. Thomas, see Brent, Charlotte.
Plymouth, Other Hickman, Earl of, 140.
Polko, Elise, 11, 50, 52.
Polone, Signora, 161.
Pompeati, Signora, see Cornelys, Teresa.
Ponce, Signora, 103, 106, 108.
Porpora, Niccolò, 16, 148.
Porter, Sir James, 141.
Pozzi, Anna, 152, 154, 161, 162.
Prudom, Signora, 152, 154, 155, 156, 159, 162, 163, 164.
Pugnani, Gaetano, 110, 113, 114, 115, 145.
Purcell, Henry, 63.

Quantz, Johann Joachim, 6.
Quercioli, Signora, 103, 105, 111, 112.
Quilici, Gaetano, 65, 66, 67, 68, 70, 72, 86.
Quinault, Philippe, 133, 134.

Raaf, Anton, 52, 54, 55, 82, 129, 130, 131.
Radicati, Signora, 106, 111, 116, 118, 122.
Rameau, Jean-Philippe, 132.
Ramsay, Allan, 93.
Randall, William, 180.
Rauzzini, Venanzio, 147, 148, 149, 150, 152, 155, 164, 167.
Rebecca, Biagio, 89.
Reynolds, Sir Joshua, 92.
Ricci, Pasquale, 134, 189.
Ricciardi, Signore, 114.
Rigerboos, Cornelis de, 91.
Rimbault, Edward F., 104.
Ripperda, Jan Willem, 89.
Ristorini, Catterina, 122, 144.
Ristorini, Giovanni, 122, 145.
Rivinus, Johann Florens, 2.
Rodolphe, Jean-Joseph, 120.
Romani, Signora, 122.
Roncaglia, Francesco, 129, 130, 153, 154, 156, 159, 160, 163, 164.

Rossi, Antonio, 153, 154, 155, 159, 161.
Rovedino, Carlo, 153, 154, 155, 161, 162.
Roxburghe, John, Duke of, 140.

Sacchini, Antonio Maria, 16, 98, 110, 144, 145, 146, 147, 148, 149, 150, 151, 152, 154, 155, 157, 159, 161, 162, 163, 164, 167.
Sachsen - Hildburghausen, Joseph Friedrich, Duke of, 171.
Salpietro, Signora, 168.
Sampieri, Signore, 162.
Santoli, Signora, 99, 106, 111.
Sarmetti, Signora, 114.
Sarselli, Peter, 128.
Sartori, Angiola, 76, 77.
Savoi, Gasparo, 98, 99, 101, 102, 103, 105, 106, 108, 109, 111, 112, 120, 122, 123, 144, 145, 149, 150, 152.
Scarlatti, Alessandro, 16.
Scarlatti, Domenico, 16.
Schaffrath, Christoph, 6.
Schaumburg-Lippe, Count Wilhelm von, 1.
Schindler, Marianne, 147, 148, 149.
Schiroli, Signore, 146.
Schmidt, Balthasar, 5.
Schneider, Johann, 3.
Schroeter, Johann Samuel, 124, 147, 155, 166.
Schubart, Christian Friedrich Daniel, 46, 125, 126, 127.
Schwertz, Baron von, 12.
Scotti, Teresa, 81, 82, 83, 84, 85, 100, 102.
Segantini, Livia, 65, 66, 68, 72.
Sestini, Vincenzio, 147, 148, 149, 150.
Sestini, Signora, 148, 149, 152, 161, 163, 164.
Sharp, Samuel, 16.
Shelburne, Mary, Countess of, 140.
Sheridan, Richard Brinsley, 138.
Sheridan, Thomas, 92, 93.
Shovel, Sir Cloudesley, 89.
Shudi, Burkat, 113.
Siéber, Jean-Georges, 134.
Simonet, M., 156, 164.
Simonin, M., 116, 118.
Simpson, Mr., 151.
Sirmen, Maddalena Lombardini, 123, 145.
Slingsby, Mr., 106, 109, 111, 116, 118, 144, 145, 164.
Smith, John Christopher, 120.
Smith, John Daniel, 138.
Smith, Robert, 74.
Sodi, Pietro, 77, 99, 100, 106, 111, 114.

Spagnoli, Clementina, 54, 98, 99, 100, 101.
Spiletta, Signora, 148, 149.
Spurni, Dorothea, 123, 127, 129, 130.
Stanley, Charles John, 120.
Stidman, Mr., 113.
Stillingfleet, Thomas, 92.
Storace, Anna Selina, 150.

Tacet, Mr., 113, 115.
Tantini, Signora, 164.
Tenducci, Ferdinando, 81, 82, 83, 84, 85, 86, 117, 120, 121, 122, 131, 144, 161, 168, 183.
Tibaldi, Pietro, 27, 32, 33, 34.
Todi, Luiza, 153, 154, 155, 159.
Toëschi, Carlo Giuseppe, 129.
Tooke, Horn, 92, 93.
Traetta, Tommaso, 16, 53, 114, 152, 153, 164.
Travers, John, 63.
Trebbi, Giuseppe, 149, 150, 152, 162, 163, 164.
Trombetta, Signore, 64.
Tyers, Jonathan, 96.
Tyrconnel, George, Earl of, 140.

Valentini, Michel Angelo, 32.
Valouys, M., 150, 156.
Valsecchi, Marianna, 65, 66, 67, 68, 70, 72.
Vento, Matthias, 77, 83, 84, 99, 100, 108, 143, 144, 147, 149, 150, 151, 152, 155.
Verazi, Mattia, 130.
Vernon, Joseph, 120.
Vestris, Gaetano A. B., 123, 163, 164.
Vestris (Allard), Marie Auguste, 163, 164.
Viganoni, Signore, 168.
Vincent, Thomas, 97, 101, 102, 110, 114.
Visconti, Giulia, 98, 99, 101.
Vismes, M. de, 134.
Vivaldi, Antonio, 8.
Vogler, Georg Joseph, 130, 131.

Wagenseil, Georg Christoph, 79.
Walpole, Horace, 83, 84.
Waterhouse, William, 139

Webbe, Samuel (?), 146.
Weichsell, Carl, 96.
Weichsell, Mrs. Carl, 96, 97.
Weichsell, Charles, 154, 158.
Welcker, Peter, 79, 96, 99, 113.
Wendling, Augusta, 127, 138.
Wendling, Dorothea, see Spurni.
Wendling, Elisabeth Auguste, 128, 129, 130.
Wendling, Franz Anton, 128.
Wendling, Johann Baptist, 123, 127, 182.
Wenham, Philip Viscount, 140.
Wesley, Samuel, 142, 180.
West, Benjamin, 141.
Westmorland, Susan, Countess of, 140.
Wharton, Maria Teresa, Duchess of, 90.
Wieland, Christoph Martin, 127.
Wilkes, John, 92, 93.
Woodfall, Henry, 86, 156.
Worgan, John, 63.
Wren, Sir Christopher, 88, 91.
Wright, William, 92.
Wynn, Sir Watkin Williams, 122.

Yarmouth, William, Earl of, 88.
Yates, Mrs., 145.
York, Edward Augustus, Duke of, 171.
Young, Polly, 81, 82, 83, 85, 97, 101, 102, 103, 106, 108, 109, 115, 120, 122, 163.
Young, Sir William, 171.

Zamparini, Anna, 116, 117.
Zamparini, Antonia, 116, 117.
Zamparini, Signora, 103, 105, 108, 109.
Zamparini, Signore, 105.
Zanca, Michele del, 122.
Zeller, Georg Bernhard, 60.
Zeno, Apostolo, 112.
Zingoni, Giovan Battista Leopold, 66, 67, 68, 70, 72.
Zoffany, John, 92, 162, 165, 168.
Zoffany, Mary, 162, 166.
Zonca, Giovanni Battista, 129, 130.
Zuchelli, M., 156.
Zuchelli, Mme, 156.
Zumpe, Johannes, 113, 183.

II. PLACES

Berlin, 4 f.
Bologna, 14 f., 159, 160.
Brunswick, 54, 110.
Bückeburg, 1, 128, 159.

Dresden, 4, 6, 7, 76.
Dublin, 117, 121.

Edinburgh, 121, 148.
Einsiedeln, 19.

Genoa, 112.

Halle, 4.
Hamburg, 1, 19, 112, 159.

Leipzig, 1, 6, 128.
London, 52, 58, 60 f.
  Academy of Ancient Music, 63, 104.
  Almack's, 95, 96, 109, 115, 122, 123, 124, 139, 142.
  Bateman's Buildings, 88.
  Richmond's Buildings, 93.
  Carlisle House, 90, 95, 139, 143, 175.
  Carlisle House (Old), 91.
  Catch Club, the, 64.
  Covent Garden Theatre, 62, 96, 108, 113, 119.
  Dean Street Concert Room, 76.
  Drury Lane Theatre, 63, 119.
  Fauconberg House, 89.
  Golden Square, 110, 123, 138.
  Hanover Square Rooms, 104, 140 f., 158, 165, 167, 168, 180.
  Hickford's Concert Room, 79, 87, 94.
  King's Square Court, 91, 110, 138.

  King's Theatre, 62, 64 f., 97 f., 105 f., 110 f., 114 f., 116 f., 120, 122 f., 143 f., 160, 162, 163 f., 168.
  Langford's Rooms, 104.
  Little Theatre, 63.
  Madrigal Society, 63.
  Monmouth House, 88.
  Newman Street, 110, 138.
  Pantheon, 142.
  Queen Street, 110, 123, 138.
  Ranelagh Gardens, 63, 80.
  Richmond, 151, 162.
  Sadler's Wells, 63.
  St. Pancras, 166.
  Society of Musicians of Great Britain, 64, 71.
  'Soho Concert', the, 95.
  Soho Square, 88.
  Sons of the Clergy Corporation, 64.
  Spring Gardens Concert Room, 78, 80.
  Thatched House Tavern, 64, 113.
  Vauxhall Gardens, 63, 96.

Mannheim, 125 f., 153.
Milan, 14 f., 103, 144.

Naples, 14 f., 52, 53, 54, 71, 109, 112, 134.

Parma, 7, 48, 53.
Paris, 94, 131 f.

Reggio, 48.

Schwetzingen, 125, 130.
Strelitz, 59.

Turin, 13, 48, 51, 111.

III. OPERAS

Adriano in Siria (Bach), 83, 155, 181.
Alceste (Gluck), 132, 160.
Alcina (Gazzaniga), 150, 153.
Alessandro nell' Indie (Bach), 54 f., 181.
Alessandro nell' Indie (Corri), 148.
Alessandro nell' Indie, 77, 162.
Amadis de Gaule (Borde), 133.
Amadis de Gaule (Lully), 133.
Amadis des Gaules (Bach), 133.
Amintas (Tenducci), 121.
Antigono (pasticcio), 146, 151.
Antigonus (pasticcio), 85.
Apollo ed Issea (Pugnani), 145.
Ariana e Teseo, 112.
Armida (Jommelli), 16.

Armida (pasticcio), 147.
Armide (Graun), 7, 133.
Artaserse (Bach), 51, 181.
Artaserse (Bertoni), 161.
Artaserse (Giordani), 144.
Artaserse (pasticcio), 101.
Artaxerxes (Arne), 63, 96.
Astarto, Re di Tiro (pasticcio), 66, 122, 152, 181.

Berenice (pasticcio), 83.
Britannico (Graun), 7.

Caio Mario (Piccinni), 150.

Carattaco (Bach), 106 f., 109, 155, 181.
Catone in Utica (Bach), 33, 52, 152, 181.
Chimena (Sacchini), 145.
Cleofide (Agricola), 7.
Cleonice (pasticcio), 76.
Cleopatra e Cesare (Graun), 6.
Comus (Arne), 63.
Coriolano (Graun), 7.
Cosroe, 122.
Creso (Sacchini), 154.

Demofoonte (Vento), 84.
Demofoonte (pasticcio), 161.
Didone abbandonata (Hasse), 7.
Didone abbandonata (Sacchini), 149.
Don Trustullo (Jommelli), 109.

Enea e Lavinia (Giardini), 77.
Enea e Lavinia (Sacchini), 161.
Erifile (Sacchini), 154.
Eumene (pasticcio), 98.
Euriso (Sacchini), 164.
Ezio (Graun), 7.
Ezio (Guglielmi), 117.
Ezio (pasticcio), 55, 82, 106, 108, 109.

Fetonte (Graun), 7.

Germondo (Traetta), 152.
Gli Amanti ridicoli (Galuppi), 114.
Gli Stravaganti (pasticcio), 105.
Gli Ucellatori, 122.

I Capricci del Sesso (Traetta), 153.
I Fratelli nemici (Graun), 7.
Ifigenia in Aulide (Guglielmi), 111.
Il Bacio (Vento), 150.
Il Barone di Torre Forte (Piccinni), 164.
Il Cid (Sacchini), 145.
Il Duca d'Atene (Bertoni), 162.
Il Filosofo di Campagna, 112.
Il Geloso in Cimento (Anfossi), 152.
Il Marchese Villano (pasticcio), 155.
Il Matrimonio alla moda (pasticcio), 66.
Il Mercato di Malmantile (Galuppi and Fischietti), 114.
Il Padre ed il Figlio rivali (Giordani), 116.
Il Puntiglio amoroso (pasticcio), 146.
Il Ratto della Sposa (Guglielmi), 112.
Il Re alla Caccia (Alessandri), 114.
Il Re Pastore (Giardini), 84, 159.
Il Signor Dottore (Fischietti), 109.
Il Solimano (pasticcio), 85.
Il Trionfo d'Amore, 145.
Il Tutore e la Pupilla (pasticcio), 66, 71, 181.

Iphigénie en Aulide (Gluck), 132.
Iphigénie en Tauride (Gluck), 133
Iphigénie en Tauride (Piccinni), 133.
I Viaggiatori felici (Anfossi), 168.
I Viaggiatori ridicoli (Guglielmi), 112, 114, 149.

L'Amore Artigiano (Gassmann), 154.
L'Amore Soldato (Sacchini), 159.
L'Arcifanfano (pasticcio), 163.
L'Avaro deluso (Sacchini), 161.
La buona Figliuola (Piccinni), 105, 111, 112, 145.
La buona Figliuola maritata (Piccinni), 108, 109, 111.
La Calamità de' Cuori (pasticcio), 67, 71, 181.
La Cascina (pasticcio), 67, 181.
La Cecchina (Piccinni), 105.
La Clemenza di Scipione (Bach), 156 f., 164, 181.
La Clemenza di Tito (Cocchi), 98.
La Conquista del Messico (Vento), 108, 109.
La Contadina bizarra (Piccinni), 116.
La Contadina in Corte (Sacchini), 162.
La Contessina (Gassmann), 146.
La Difesa d'Amore (pasticcio), 149.
La Donna di Spirito (pasticcio), 149.
La finta Sposa (pasticcio), 70.
La Fraschetana (Paisiello), 152, 164.
La Governante (Bertoni), 161.
La Marchesa Giardiniera (Anfossi), 148.
La Moglie fedele (Alessandri), 111.
La Schiava (Piccinni), 110 f., 112, 153.
La Serva Padrona (Pergolesi), 71, 150.
La Sposa fedele (pasticcio), 149.
La vera Costanza (Anfossi), 154.
La Vestale (Vento), 150.
Le Ali d'Amore (Rauzzini), 150.
Le Contadine bizarre (Piccinni), 116.
Le Donne vendicate (Piccinni), 114.
Le due Contesse (Paisiello), 154.
L'Eroe cinese (Galuppi), 101.
Le Serve Rivali (Traetta), 114, 164.
Leucippo (Vento), 77.
Le Vicende della Sorte (pasticcio), 122.
L'Innamorata del Cisibeo, 109.
L'Isola d'Amore (Sacchini), 150.
L'Olimpiade (Arne), 85.
L'Olimpiade (pasticcio), 116, 119, 147, 161.
L'Ommaggio (pastoral), 164.
Lo Speziale (Fischietti and Pallavicini), 114.
Lucio Silla (Bach), 130, 155, 181.
Lucio Vero (Sacchini), 146.

Merope (Graun), 7, 13.
Mitridate (Graun), 7.
Mitridate (Mozart), 160.
Mitridate (Sacchini), 164.
Montezuma (Graun), 7, 12.
Montezuma (Sacchini), 148.

Nanetta e Lubino (Pugnani), 114.
Nitteti (Sacchini), 146.

Orfeo (Bertoni), 163.
Orfeo (Graun), 7.
Orfeo ed Euridice (Gluck), 117, 122, 133, 143, 145.
Orione (Bach), 67, 153, 155, 181.

Pelopida (Barthélemon), 102.
Perseo (Sacchini), 146.
Piramo e Tisbe (Rauzzini), 148, 164.

Quinto Fabio (Bertoni), 162.

Ricimero (pasticcio), 163.
Rinaldo (Sacchini), 163, 164.
Rinaldo ed Armida (Bach), 168.
Roland (Piccinni), 133.

Semiramide (Graun), 7.
Senocrita (Picinni-Perez), 77.
Sesostri (Guglielmi), 112.
Sifare (pasticcio), 108, 111.
Silla (Graun), 7.
Siroe (pasticcio), 77.
Sofonisba (Vento), 99, 100, 144.

Tamerlane (Handel), 68.
Tamerlano (Sacchini), 145.
Telemaco (Traetta), 153.
Temistocle (Bach), 128, 155, 181.
The Beggar's Opera, 96, 113.
The Fairy Favour (Bach), 108.
The Flitch of Bacon, 147.
The Maid of the Mill, 97.
The Royal Shepherd, 121.
Tigrane (pasticcio), 110, 145.
Trakebarne, Gran Mogul (pasticcio), 105.

Vittorina (Piccinni), 154.

Zanaida (Bach), 72, 155, 181.
Zemira ed Azore (Grétry), 161.
Zenobia (Piccinni), 16.

SET AT THE UNIVERSITY PRESS, OXFORD
AND REPRINTED LITHOGRAPHICALLY BY
JARROLD AND SONS LTD, NORWICH